The Years of Bloom

To Laura

The Years of Bloom

James Joyce in Trieste 1904–1920

JOHN McCOURT

THE UNIVERSITY OF WISCONSIN PRESS

First published in North America 2000 by
THE UNIVERSITY OF WISCONSIN PRESS
2537 Daniels Street, Madison, Wisconsin 53718–6772

Originally published by The Lilliput Press, Dublin, Ireland

Library of Congress Cataloging-in-Publication
Data is available from the Library of Congress.

ISBN 0–299–16980–4

Set in Adobe Garamond with Monotype Centaur display heads
Printed in Great Britain by MPG Books, Bodmin, Cornwall

Contents

Illustrations

Acknowledgments

In Dublin my first thanks must go to the staff of the Department of Anglo-Irish Literature at University College Dublin and especially to the late Augustine (Gus) Martin, whose friendship and scholarship were crucial to me as I embarked on this project. Following his death I was fortunate to have Anthony Roche take over as supervisor of the Ph.D. thesis from which *The Years of Bloom* originates, and I am most grateful to him for his efficient and penetrating criticism and his friendship and support. I would also like to acknowledge the encouragement of Declan Kiberd, Gus Martin's successor to the chair of Anglo-Irish Literature and Drama. Among the many others who helped me I must mention my mother, Moira McCourt, Father Bruce Bradley S.J., Ken and Lucy Monaghan, John Wyse Jackson (London), Colm Tóibín, Danis Rose and John O'Hanlon. At Lilliput Press, I was very fortunate to have been able to count on the support of Antony Farrell and the enthusiasm and editorial expertise of Brendan Barrington. I am deeply indebted to them both. I would also like to thank the staffs of the National Library in Dublin and of the University College Dublin library.

In Trieste I would like particularly to thank Renzo S. Crivelli, head of the Department of Anglo-Germanic Literature at the University of Trieste, for his support; the late Nonna Bianca (Spizzer Bonatelli), a relation of Amalia Popper's, who so often treated me to afternoon tea and was such a fund of information; the late Frida De Tuoni, who was also great afternoon company and who generously allowed me access to her late husband's archives; Teresita

Zajotti, Nicolò Vidacovich's niece, who allowed me access to her late uncle's library; Stefano Crise, for allowing me access to his late father's papers; the historians Anna Millo, Anna Vinci, and in particular Tullia Catalan, who patiently introduced me to the Jewish world of Trieste in Joyce's time; Guido Miglia, who set me right on Pola; PierLuigi Sabatti and Stella Rasmann, who often pointed me in the right directions; Raffaella Sgubin, who cast a careful eye over my occasional forays into Slovene; Signora Zennaro, who allowed me access to her extensive Svevo archive (which has since been transferred to the Biblioteca Civica); the late Anna Bonacci, who was Joyce's last surviving Triestine pupil; Marino de Szombathely; Nick Carter, for his friendship and encouragement and for his insightful reading of the early drafts of this work; and Roberta Gefter Wondrich and Monica Randaccio. The local knowledge offered by my friends, the members of La Bottega Joyce and especially Piero Sardos Albertini, Laura Collini, Giorgina Laghi, Rossella Spangaro, Bertha and Jole Stuparich, Simona Tartarelli, and Ilse Tassinari, was also greatly appreciated. I would also like to thank Federica Vetta, Benvenuto Fantin, Pietro Covre, Roberto Curci, Wilfred Schnabl, Zora Koren Skerk, and Mirella Schott Sbisà.

Most of my early research was done at the Biblioteca Civica di Trieste, where Anna Rosa Rugliano's staff in general and Renzo Arcon and Irene Battino in particular were of great assistance. I also wish to acknowledge the help received at Trieste's Museo Comunale Teatrale C. Schimdl, the Museo Comunale di Storia ed Arte, and at the Archivio di Stato di Trieste. I am also grateful to have been granted access to the archives of the Jewish community.

Elsewhere in Italy I must first acknowledge the great encouragement given to me by Giorgio Melchiori, who was an exacting reader of my original thesis and a source of numerous worthwhile leads and suggestions; Rosa Maria Bollettieri Bosinelli, who generously allowed me access to her unpublished thesis on Joyce and Trieste; as well as Franca Ruggieri, Nick Ceramella, and Anna Maria de Angelis. I also wish to acknowledge Baronessa Allard-Schott (Belgium), Adolfo Frigyessy (Milan), and Letizia Popper Lehmann (Jerusalem).

In the United States I would like to thank Sidney Huttner and Lori Curtis in the McFarland Library at the University of Tulsa, Mark Dimunation at Cornell University, and Shelley Cox at the University of Southern Illinois. Carol Kealiher and Corinna del Greco Lobner in Tulsa were also extremely supportive. Neil R. Davison of the University of Oregon is deserving of thanks for his insightful reading of Part Five.

Parts of this book were published in slightly different forms in the *James Joyce Quarterly*, the *James Joyce Studies Annual*, *Joyce Studies in Italy*, *Prospero*, and in *Bronze by Gold: The Music of Joyce*. I would like to thank the respective editors of these volumes – Bob Spoo, Tom Staley, Franca Ruggieri, Renzo S. Crivelli, and Sebastian Knowles – for permission to reprint material.

Invitations to lecture on the subject of Joyce and Trieste provided me with vital opportunities to refine my ideas and were gratefully accepted from Fritz Senn and the friends of the Zürich James Joyce Foundation (I also owe a special debt to Fritz for his patience, wisdom and encouragement over many years); Gráinne Gilroy of the Italian Cultural Institute in Dublin; Tina Mahkota and Meta Grosman of the University of Ljubljana; Kevin Barry of University College Galway; Jorg Rademacher and Karl Heinz Pötter in Münster; and Hans Walter Gabler and Claus Melchior in Munich. In this spirit I am happy to thank all the lecturers and students at the first three editions of the Trieste Joyce School, who gave me endless encouragement and challenged my developing views of Joyce and Trieste. I would also like to thank Franz Stanzel of the University of Graz, to whom I served for a year as research assistant on his Joyce and Austria project.

None of this would have served any useful purpose were it not for Laura Pelaschiar. She, in so many ways, is the joint architect of this work. Apart from contributing generously with first-hand knowledge of Trieste, the Triestines, and the dialect of *Triestino*, she has had to put up with my absorption in this book, to reread (and often rewrite) draft after draft. Quite simply, it would not have happened without her.

J.M.
Trieste, February 2000

Abbreviations

CW   Joyce, James, *The Critical Writings*. Edited by Ellsworth Mason and Richard Ellmann (Ithaca, New York: Cornell University Press, 1989).

D   Joyce, James, *Dubliners*. With an introduction and notes by Terence Brown (London: Penguin Books, 1992).

FW   Joyce, James, *Finnegans Wake* (London: Faber and Faber, 1989).

GJ   Joyce, James, *Giacomo Joyce*. With an introduction and notes by Richard Ellmann (London: Faber and Faber, 1984).

JJII   Ellmann, Richard, *James Joyce*, revised edition (Oxford: Oxford University Press, 1982).

LI   Joyce, James, *Letters of James Joyce*, Vol. I. Edited by Sturart Gilbert (New York: Viking Press, 1957).

LII   Joyce, James, *Letters of James Joyce*, Vol. II. Edited by Richard Ellmann (New York: Viking Press, 1966).

LIII   Joyce, James, *Letters of James Joyce*, Vol. III. Edited by Richard Ellmann (New York: Viking Press, 1966).

P   Joyce, James, *A Portrait of the Artist as a Young Man*. Corrected by Chester Anderson and edited by Richard Ellmann (London: Paladin, 1987).

SH   Joyce, James, *Stephen Hero*. Edited with an introduction by Stuart Gilbert (London: Faber and Faber, 1966).

SL   Joyce, James, *Selected Letters of James Joyce*. Edited by Richard Ellmann (London: Faber and Faber, 1975).

U   Joyce, James, *Ulysses*. The Corrected Text. Edited by Hans Walter Gabler et al. (New York: Random House, 1984).

All translations of original Italian materials are by the author unless otherwise stated.

The Years of Bloom

Introduction

"The cosmopolitan atmosphere of the Trieste of the early twentieth century did not inspire him at all. [...] No, Trieste did not give Jim anything."[1] So said Stanislaus Joyce, expressing what was to become a widely held view of Joyce's Triestine sojourn. This book sets out to re-evaluate the role of Trieste in Joyce's artistic formation by charting a course through what for most Joyce readers is still the undiscovered terrain of the Adriatic port in the first two decades of the twentieth century.

It was in Trieste that Joyce wrote most of the stories of *Dubliners*, all of *A Portrait of the Artist as a Young Man* and *Exiles*, and significant sections of *Ulysses*. While locating all of these works in Dublin, Joyce was also absorbing the social, political, literary, linguistic and religious atmospheres of "tarry easty" (*FW*, 228.23–4) – the land of the east. This influence is overtly reflected in the only prose work he set outside his native city, his short, intense Triestine prose poem *Giacomo Joyce*; is more surreptitiously present as a continental perspective in the Irish world and worldview of *Ulysses*; and is heard as a distinct voice in the linguistic meanderings of *Finnegans Wake*.

To date, the principal font of information about Joyce's Triestine sojourn has been Richard Ellmann's comprehensive and stylish *James Joyce*, first published in 1959, which, while remaining an indispensable map of Joyce's life, is not, as no book could ever possibly be, the last word on as complex and multi-layered a creative personality as Joyce's. With regard to the Trieste years, it brilliantly and movingly describes Joyce's day-to-day life there and his growth as a writer, but rarely seeks to connect this artistic development to the rich cosmopolitan texture of turn-of-the-century Trieste.

While it seems unlikely that any single work will ever challenge Ellmann's immense version of Joyce's life, several more recent biographical studies, including Bruce Bradley's *James Joyce's Schooldays* (1982), *Joyce in Rome: The Genesis of Ulysses*, edited by Giorgio Melchiori (1984), Brenda Maddox's *Nora* (1988), Morris Beja's *James Joyce: A Literary Life* (1992), Peter Costello's *James Joyce: The Years of Growth, 1882–1915* (1992), John Wyse Jackson and Peter Costello's *John Stanislaus Joyce: The Voluminous Life and Genius of James Joyce's Father* (1998), Peter Hartshorn's *James Joyce in Trieste* and Renzo S. Crivelli's *James Joyce's Triestine Itineraries* (both 1997), have all profitably set about the task of rewriting and re-evaluating certain periods of Joyce's life, while at the same time exploring new contexts for and influences on his writing.

In this spirit, *The Years of Bloom*, while fully acknowledging the continued centrality of Dublin in Joyce's creative consciousness, reassesses the impact of the Triestine years, from his arrival in 1904, aged just twenty-two (significantly Stephen's age in *Ulysses*), until his final reluctant departure in 1920, aged thirty-eight (Bloom's age). He was not one to suffer fools or foolish places gladly and clearly there were things about Trieste that kept him there: the Eastern atmosphere, the mix of peoples from "all the ends of Europe" (*U*, 18.1588–9), the linguistic mishmash, and the multifarious activity of a bustling port city, or, to put it in the local dialect of *Triestino*, "El gran mismas dela gente per le strade" (the great coming and going of people in the streets).[2]

On the political front, the imperial Austrian city with its indefatigable Italian irredentist spirit challenged and sharpened Joyce's ideas about socialism and nationalism, while in a literary key, with its contrapuntal echoes of Vienna and Florence, it provided many shaping influences, from the Futurists to the *Vociani* (not to mention Italo Svevo and other local writers with whom he was friendly), to the more mainstream Italian and international theatrical and operatic offerings Joyce attended assiduously. In religious terms, it was liberating to be in Trieste, where so many different faiths worshipped side by side and in harmony, a place where the power of the Catholic Church was kept in check by strong Jewish and Greek communities, many of whose members knew Joyce well and furnished him with primary information for *Ulysses*. As *Giacomo Joyce* shows, the women of Trieste (whom he was meeting on a daily basis in his private lessons) also left a crucial mark on Joyce, forcing him – because of their sophistication, education, beauty and sexual ease – to reconsider his rather reductive early visions of the feminine and to replace them with the fuller versions of womankind we find in the later fiction.

Trieste was the ideal location for Joyce to "blend a fidelity to his local origins with a counter-fidelity to the culture of the continent",[3] because it provided him with foreign echoes of Dublin while at the same time offering distinctive material of its own to be moulded to fit the world of his Hibernian metropolis. For much of the Oriental, Jewish and Greek elements of *Ulysses*, for much of the multilingual chaos of "Circe" and *Finnegans Wake*, Trieste was his principal source, his "città immediata" (*FW*, 228.23).

The influence of Trieste as a crossroads of competing cultures can be seen most clearly in the characters of Leopold and Molly Bloom. While Stephen Dedalus was largely formed by the time Joyce left Ireland, Leopold and Molly are in great part products of his exile in Trieste. Bloom – a Jew with Hungarian roots – does not fit into provincial Dublin, while Molly is as much a Mediterranean Jewess as she is Irish; and the elements that attract them to one another are precisely the non-Irish ones which Joyce found among "the cummulium of scents in an italian warehouse" (*FW*, 498.30) – Trieste.

The Blooms, therefore, are the literary embodiment and proof of how much Joyce received (and was open to accept) from the divided city of Trieste, caught between its links with *Mitteleuropa* and its aspirations towards Italy. They are testimony to the forces of attraction that made him linger for ten long years in the Adriatic city despite his endless troubles there.

ONE

Heading east

No one who has any self-respect stays in Ireland. (*CW*, 171)

1 *Ten days in Trieste*

In the early afternoon of 20 October 1904, a young "gentleman, Irish, mighty odd",[1] and his even younger female companion stepped wearily off the train that had just arrived at Trieste's busy Stazione Centrale. The couple, as yet unmarried, were James Joyce and Nora Barnacle, aged twenty-two and twenty respectively. They had met just four months earlier in Dublin and had united to defy convention and leave their country, their religion and their families in order to embark on a new life together on the continent. Unlike so many Irish emigrants, they were not following a familiar path to England or America but were destined for a singular adventure in the heart of Europe.

Financed by Lady Gregory (five pounds), a disapproving George Russell (ten shillings), John Stanislaus Joyce (he later claimed to have contributed seven pounds), and various other benefactors, they had departed on 8 October for Holyhead on the ferry from Dublin's North Wall. Joyce was seen off by his father, his sister Poppie, his brother Stanislaus and his aunt Josephine Murray, while Nora boarded separately and alone: Joyce did not want his father to meet her or know anything about her, and she herself had chosen to keep her own family in Galway in the dark about her flight.

Leaving Dublin, they had little idea of the odyssey that awaited them. From Holyhead they travelled through London and Paris before reaching Zürich, where, according to Joyce's letter of 11 October to Stanislaus, they consummated their de facto marriage: "Finalement, elle n'est pas encore vierge; elle est touchée" (*SL*, 40). Unfortunately, bad news awaited Joyce at the Zürich Berlitz School, where the position that had been promised was not available. As a result he and Nora had little choice but to follow the advice of the school director and undertake a further journey to a possible job at the Berlitz School in Trieste. Now penniless, they set off once again, but further misadventure befell them even before they reached the Adriatic:

> The train rushed southward and after an interminable period halted in the station of what appeared to be a great city, surely the end of a strange new journey. The young couple dismounted from their compartment and made their way out of the station and into the streets. A puzzled inquiry brought them the disturbing information that they were in Laibach, some seven hours from Trieste. The train they had deserted was already hooting its way through the darkness, for it was night, and there would be no more traffic for the south and Trieste until the dawn came. The two travellers crept into a near-by garden and remained there until the morning. There was an Observatory here and they watched and counted the stars, that great wheel of light that glowed above the mysterious city, and agreed that they were bright and glorious. The rich odour of autumnal earth suspired about them and they were not unhappy at all.[2]

After their night in Laibach (Ljubljana), they boarded the first train for Trieste. On arriving there, Joyce, as he had done in Paris, left Nora in the park in front of the station and walked into the town centre in order to make arrangements for the night. She probably did not know it, but she was sitting in the shadow of the imposing statue of the Emperor Franz Joseph's beautiful long-haired wife, the Empress Elisabetta, or "Sissi" as she was fondly known, who had been assassinated on 10 September 1898 and whose statue commemorated five hundred years of Austrian rule in the city.[3]

When he reached the Piazza Grande, the rather regal central square that looks imperiously out to sea, Joyce became involved in a dispute involving a few deserting English sailors.[4] Their drunken and disorderly behaviour had aroused the attention of a local policeman, who had approached and was in the process of arresting them when Joyce, perhaps keen to show off his Italian, intervened on their behalf. Unfortunately he only succeeded in having himself arrested along with the others. Stanislaus Joyce paints a typically colourful and indignant description of the misfortunes suffered by his brother on his first day in Trieste: "he was accosted in the Piazza Grande by three drunken English sailors. The sailors were arrested and the *guardia* asked Jim would he go with them as interpreter because he spoke Italian so well. Jim consented like a mug."[5] When they reached the police station, the Casa Castagna on via San Nicolò, Joyce found himself being put in a cell along with the others and insisted that the British Consul be called. When "that worthy", His Britannic Majesty's Consul for Dalmatia, Carniola and the Austrian Littoral, a career diplomat called Harry L. Churchill, finally turned up, Joyce informed him that he was "a Bachelor of Arts of the Royal University of Ireland" who had just arrived in Trieste to take up a position as a teacher in the Berlitz school. "The Consul of great, free England, after all had been explained to him, instead of resenting the unwarranted arrest in the public thoroughfares of an English subject (for it amounted to that) and his being run in with rowdy sailors, hoped Jim hadn't committed a felony in England."[6]

As soon as he was released Joyce hurried back to a worried Nora, whom he had left alone and penniless with their paltry luggage in a strange park in a foreign city where few people would have understood a word she said. The only thing that might have cheered her was the pleasant weather: the temperature was a balmy twenty degrees by lunchtime. Together they set off and found accommodation in the Hotel "Central" (Haberleitner), where they spent a few nights before moving to a room on the Piazza Ponterosso, one of the finest squares in Trieste, overlooking the canal and the fruit and vegetable markets. The square was later evoked by Joyce in *Giacomo Joyce*: "The sellers offer on their altars the first fruits: greenflecked lemons, jewelled cherries, shameful peaches with torn leaves" (*GJ*, 8).

Soon Joyce went to the Berlitz School on via San Nicolò to enquire about the possibility of employment there, but once again disappointment awaited him. During an interview with the local sub-director, Giuseppe Bertelli, he was told that there was no position available for him in Trieste. But all was not lost. The owner of the Trieste Berlitz, Almidano Artifoni, was in the process of opening a new school in the Istrian coastal city of Pola and might be able to offer him a position there. Joyce did not really know what to do. How much farther would he have to travel to find work? To keep the wolf from the door while he waited for Artifoni to return from Pola, he found two students for private lessons and somehow managed to borrow enough money to survive. Despite the appalling uncertainty of these days, Joyce continued to write, with a stoic determination which would rarely leave him, working especially on his autobiographical novel *Stephen Hero*. In so doing he was starting his life on the continent with Nora as he intended to continue it. His writing, no matter what the turmoil around him, would always remain his first priority.

After a couple of days Almidano Artifoni arrived back from Pola and, having met Joyce, offered him a position in the school there, at least in part because, as Joyce commented in a letter to Stanislaus, "By good luck he is a socialist like myself" (*LII,* 68). Perhaps more crucially, Artifoni was a shrewd businessman who had instantly recognized that the young Irishman with his Bachelor of Arts degree would be a good acquisition for the school. In order to prepare the way for Joyce, Artifoni set off again for Pola, where he placed an advertisement (the new school's twelfth since September) in the city's principal newspaper, *Il Giornaletto di Pola.*[7] This announced the arrival of the new teacher of English and encouraged those students for whom there had not been places available before to come now and enrol. Joyce was most impressed and enclosed a copy of what he called the "magnificent notice" in his first letter to Stanislaus from Pola, dated 31 October. He later conferred a rare tribute on Artifoni by using his extraordinary name – extraordinary because both the unusual 'Almidano' and the almost unique 'Artifoni' both have four stressed syllables – for Stephen's Italian teacher in *A Portrait of the Artist as a Young Man* and in *Ulysses.*

Having arrived in Trieste as James Joyce and Nora Barnacle just ten days earlier, the couple departed on Sunday 30 October 1904 for Pola, now calling themselves Mr and Mrs Joyce, as Artifoni had suggested they do in order to avoid unnecessary scandal or bureaucratic difficulties. They set off from the Molo San Carlo on the morning boat, the speedy "Graf Wurmbrand", and after a four-hour trip over sixty nautical miles down the beautiful Istrian coast, they arrived in Pola, the town which was to be their home for the next four months.

2 *A writer in Siberia*

After nearly three weeks travelling and living out of a suitcase, James and Nora arrived in Pola scruffy and exhausted and were glad to see Artifoni waiting for them as they disembarked. He led them from the port towards the centre of town, past the bunting which the civic authorities had put up to celebrate the unveiling of a new statue of the Empress Elisabetta. This event had taken place just a couple of hours before their arrival, in the presence of the highest-ranking dignitaries from both Pola and Trieste, led by the Archduke Stefano and the recently installed Viennese governor, Prince Konrad Hohen-lohe-Schillingsfürst (whom Joyce would later come to know in Trieste, where he would teach his wife and children). But all was quiet now as the new arrivals walked together through the fruit and vegetable market towards the heart of the city, which they would have seen at its best, brightened as it was by the gentle autumn evening sun.

Thus began their unhappy sojourn in Pola, the first leg of their thirty-seven-year "voluntary exile" (*LII*, 82) in Europe. Joyce was not impressed by the city at all. Soon he was describing it as a "a back-of-God speed place ... a long boring place wedged into the Adriatic peopled by ignorant Slavs who wear little red caps and colossal breeches" (*LI*, 57). Yet, contrary to the dismal impression which Joyce gives of it in his letters and Ellmann reinforces in his biography, Pola was a reasonably cosmopolitan place. It had a population of 45,205 people, 25,984 of whom were male, a fact which reflects the military role of the town. Official figures show that the majority of the population was Italian (24,056), but that there were also many Serbs and Croatians (10,388), Germans (4,654), and Slovenes (1,543).[8] The city housed a complex ethnic mixture which included Bohemians and Dalmatians, they of the "little red caps", whom the locals referred to as *Pomodori* (tomatoes). It also boasted a proud history which had seen it being ruled by the Romans, and successively by the Byzantines, the Venetians, and briefly by the French under Napoleon, until it became part of the Austrian Empire in 1815. But it retained its Italian character and justified Dante's description of its being "the end of Italy";[9] and it was a part of the Istrian lands which the irredentists would attempt to redeem and rejoin to Italy.

It was under the Austrians that Pola began to develop and prosper. In 1863 it was chosen as the chief military port and arsenal of the Austrian navy because of its deep, natural harbour, and as a result the city began to enjoy a long period of growth which continued until the outbreak of the First World War. Most of the houses in turn-of-the-century Pola had been built in the latter decades of the nineteenth century to accommodate the workers who were arriving from all over the Austrian dominions seeking employment in the new industrial works and in the navy. The new arrivals made their homes in the districts springing up around the old historic city centre, which remained firmly in the hands of the Italian middle classes.

For the most part, however, it would appear that whatever vibrancy and variety the city had, it made a less than favourable impression on Joyce. Perhaps he compared it negatively with the metropolises he had recently visited, London and Paris, and the two that had held out false promises of gainful employment, Zürich and Trieste. Joyce was a city man and with these four cities, each of which had an indisputable prestige and importance, Pola could not compete.

It was in the town's Venetian centre that the couple found what was to be their home for a little over two months, "a furnished room and kitchen, surrounded by pots, pans and kettles", in a newly-built Hapsburg house on the second floor of number 2 via Giulia, just round the corner from the Berlitz School (*LII*, 68). The flat was adequate for the first couple of weeks of November when the weather was still mild enough to allow the mosquitoes, or *musati* as they were called in the local dialect, to torment Joyce, who frantically tried to frighten them away with a candle. This hopeless gambit succeeded only in attracting more, as he wrote to his father: "The weather is good summer here but I am pestered with mosquitoes all night" (*LII*, 69). However, the clement weather did not hold and, as a particularly harsh winter set in, the flat, with no heater or cooker, was cold, damp and unhealthy. *Il Giornaletto di Pola* published articles every day about the severity of the weather, including one headed "Freddo Siberiano" – Siberian Cold – which compared the weather in Pola with that in Manchuria and went into detail about frozen and burst water pipes.[10] The temperature remained eight or nine degrees below zero for more than a week. Small wonder Joyce referred to his new home as "a naval Siberia".

Climatic problems notwithstanding, turn-of-the-century Pola was a civil and reasonably prosperous place with a certain amount of style. From their apartment James and Nora were able to appreciate the city at its best and would perhaps have been amused to peer out at the elegantly dressed wives of the naval officers who descended from the plush villas on the Monte Paradiso and paraded their fashionable new clothes, procured on shopping trips to Graz, Vienna or Trieste. This local display of style had its effect on Joyce who, mortified at his own shabbiness, grew a moustache, bought a new brown suit and a loose scarlet tie, got Nora to curl his hair "with a tongs – it is now properly en brosse", and declared in a letter to Stanislaus: "I look a very pretty man" (*LII*, 76). Despite his new-found sartorial elegance, he struggled to make friends and settle down, and had to rely almost completely on the school staff for company. Along with Nora, who began to study French in the hope of returning to live in Paris, he had major difficulties communicating with the locals as his Italian at this time was archaic and overly literary, and many of the *Polesi* simply would not have understood him. The Italian spoken, which to Joyce's untrained ears was corrupt, was in fact the Istro-Veneto dialect, which was often mixed with Istro-Croato. Not untypically, rather than face up to his own limitations, Joyce often blamed the city for his troubles, as in a letter to his aunt Josephine: "I am trying to move on to Italy as soon as possible as I hate this Catholic country with its hundred races and thousand languages" (*LI*, 57). Soon his resistance towards this linguistic confusion began to break down and within a few weeks he was already beginning to adopt a more colloquial Italian. By December he wrote of Nora to Stanislaus: "She calls me simple-minded Jim. Complementi, Signor!" (*LII*, 75). The use of "Signor" rather than the standard Italian "Signore" shows Joyce beginning to appropriate the Venetian dialect of Pola, one that was very similar to the *Triestino* he would later come to master in Trieste. Early on in Pola, however, many of his problems arose from his genuine inability to understand and make himself understood. His scholarly Italian was, as his friend Alessandro Francini Bruni put it, "a strange species [...] It is better to say archaic than strange, a crippled Italian full of ulcers. [...] At any rate, it was a dead language, which joined the babble of living languages coming out of that pit of poor devils at the school."[11] That same babble would later become one of the major inspirations of *Finnegans Wake*.

Given these difficulties it is hardly surprising that a rather homesick Joyce wrote to his father as early as February 1905 suggesting that Stanislaus might come out to join him. He was clearly missing home, the company of his brother and his former university companions, and he was suffering from what he termed his "worse than solitude of the intellect" (*LII*, 80). Perhaps because he was a young, untrained and inexperienced teacher overwhelmed by the relentless daily grind of the Berlitz School or because he found it a struggle to understand and meet the demands of his equally lonely and even more bored partner, who was condemned to spend her day in an icy, poorly furnished home, Joyce does not appear to have taken advantage of the more pleasant aspects of Pola. He never mentions the impressive Roman ruins, the arena, the Roman theatre, the Temple of Augustus, the fourth-century city walls, the Arco dei Sergei, the beautiful beaches, the surrounding Homeric villages, such as Cernico, or the famous *castellieri* (hill forts) which were dotted all the way down the Istrian peninsula. Only rarely did he use a day off to go on an excursion. Once he took Nora for a picnic in the little woods near Pola called Bosco Siano and in February of 1905 the couple went with a group of teachers from the Berlitz on a steamer to visit the island of Brioni,[12] but even its resplendent natural beauty was lost on Joyce, who commented only on the local goat cheese, "Pecorino".

From one who later would liken Rome to "a man who lives by exhibiting to travellers his grandmother's corpse" (*LII*, 165), his reticence about the attractions of Pola and environs should not come as too much of a surprise. Joyce was not interested in stunning scenery or in architecturally magnificent cities, but in people and their cultures. His letters are devoid of physical descriptions of the European places he travelled through and lived in. Broad panoramic description is also largely absent from his books. *Ulysses*, for instance, provides an extraordinary physical impression of Dublin, but does so without using much actual description, through a careful gathering of opinions, associations, colours and odours, and a relentless accumulation of small, significant details.

Although it cannot have been easy for Joyce to break into Pola's provincial intellectual environment, there were events taking place which would undoubtedly have roused his curiosity. The socialists, for example, of the Circoli degli Studi Sociali (the social studies circle) provided a chink of light to a larger world through the lectures they organized at the Teatro Ciscutti, which was just a couple of doors down from Joyce's flat on via Giulia. Later in Trieste and Rome, Joyce would take an active interest in socialist debate, so it is possible that he attended these lectures in Pola, which were given by the very speakers he would follow in Rome – Arturo Labriola (1873–1959), the famous socialist editor of *L'Avanguardia*, and Enrico Ferri (1856–1929), lawyer, university lecturer, public speaker and politician, and, from 1900 to 1906, editor of *L'Avanti!*, the socialist party's newspaper. A secondary, but not insignificant, reason why Joyce would have attended was that the talks were given in standard Italian which he understood and would have been happy to listen to.

At the beginning of December, Labriola delivered a series of lectures on Saint Francis of Assisi (attacking the might, cynicism and pomp of the official Church) and on the theme of trade unionism and parliamentary action in the socialist movement. His thesis, that politicians and parliaments could not change the social order, that the workers had to join together to bring about change through means such as international strikes, was essentially that which Joyce summarized in a letter to Stanislaus from Rome in 1906 when writing about another of Labriola's lectures given at the Socialist Congress there.[13] On 16 January Enrico Ferri extolled "the marvels of the nineteenth century", speaking about the Napoleonic era, the invention of electricity, steam power, and the results of industrial development in general.[14]

Joyce also had many opportunities to enjoy the cultural events staged in the Teatro Ciscutti, most of which were determinedly pro-Italian. Though he missed the opera season by a couple of days, his interest in immersing himself in contemporary European literature might have led him to attend some of the many readings of the works of Carducci and Pascoli, and of course his beloved Dante. He may also have chosen to reacquaint himself with Gabriele D'Annunzio's plays, having earlier travelled to London to see Eleonora Duse in *La Gioconda* and *La Città Morta*. During his stay in Pola these two plays were produced along with *Francesca da Rimini* and *La Figlia di Jorio*, so it was not by chance that he wrote to Stanislaus on 28 December asking him to "look up every English review for the past year and see if there is an article on D'Annunzio's 'Figlia di Jorio'. If there is not I would prepare an article" (*LII*, 76).

There were also regular lectures held in the Biblioteca Civica (the city library) on various aspects of Italian life, literature and culture. All in all, between theatrical productions, readings and lectures, Joyce had many opportunities to experience Italian culture at first hand while in Pola; the reports in *Il Giornaletto* of these happenings were so full of rhetorical enthusiasm that it is hard to believe he did not follow their lead, taking at least occasional advantage of what was available.

Joyce's interest in things Jewish might also have been stirred during those months. The Dreyfus affair formed a central part of "La Soirée all'Arco Romano" held on 17 December. Professor Antonio Charles gave a series of recitations which included "L'Hirondelle de prisonnier ou l'affaire Dreyfus" (The Prisoner's Little Swallow or the Dreyfus Affair), a poem that "was written in 1898 when nobody thought Dreyfus would return to Europe". The last two lines would certainly have been recognized by Joyce as Dante's words written over the gates to the Inferno:

> In ogni luogo, in ogni ora
> Echeggio la mia triste dimora
> Se voi venite dalla Francia
> Lasciate ogni speranza
> Voi ch'entrate.[15]

> (In every place, at every time
> my sad sojourn echoes
> If you come from France
> Abandon all hope
> ye who enter here.)

The political atmosphere in Pola was low-key (the council elections passed relatively quietly in January 1905), but the tensions within the community were fanned by the city's two newspapers – *Il Giornaletto di Pola* and *Nasa Sloga* – which represented pro-Italian and pro-Croatian sentiments respectively. Occasionally reverberations of outside events were felt and tensions grew in the city. The most dramatic example of this came with the riots that took place at the Italian Faculty of Law at the University of Innsbruck in November 1904. One of the constant demands of the Italian irredentists living in the Austrian dominions was for an Italian University in Trieste, which in itself was not the final end, but a first symbolic step towards the reunification of Trieste and the other Italian territories of Austria with Italy. This was always refused, but as a sop the Austrian authorities had finally agreed to set up an Italian faculty of law in Innsbruck. Although this decision deeply upset both the Italians, who felt hard done by, and the Austrians, who resented the concession, the imperial authorities pressed ahead. The inauguration of this new faculty in Innsbruck, which was held on 4 November, had disastrous consequences. *Il Giornaletto di Pola* did not miss the opportunity to report the events in full:

> A battle broke out when a huge crowd of German students attacked the Italians attending the faculty. Two people were killed, fifty-two wounded and two hundred and seventy-two were arrested. The Italian faculty was devastated, shops and hotels ransacked.[16]

These terrible events proved a godsend for the irredentists in all the Italian cities of the empire, who took to the streets to vent their anger. Even in sleepy Pola, as Joyce reported to Stanislaus, "There was a little disturbance here after the Innsbrück riots" (*LII*, 69). A performance of *Aidelberga Mia* in the Teatro Ciscutti on 5 November was interrupted when the actors, dressed as German students, sang the student song "Gaudeamus igitur". The report in *Il Giornaletto* of 6 November reads as follows: "As soon as they appeared, the audience began to whistle, some people shouted: 'Out with the barbarians of Innsbruck! We want an Italian university in Trieste! Enough! Get off the stage! Bring down the curtains!'" The protest spilled onto the streets. On 13 November two thousand people turned up at a meeting in the same theatre to condemn the events at Innsbruck and renew their demand for a university in Trieste.

Joyce occasionally went to the dances that were held in the Croatian National Hall and is reported to have enjoyed watching the navy officers dancing and to have sometimes sung with them.[17] He also paid his first visits to the "cinema", Il Bioscopio Elettrico, where eleven different programmes, ranging from comedy to scenes from the Russo-Japanese war, were presented between November 1904 and January 1905. Much appreciated among the films were *Ali Baba ed i 40 Ladri* and *La lampada magica di Aladino*. In a letter to Stanislaus, Joyce specifically mentioned going to the cinema and seeing "a series of pictures about betrayed Gretchen", and described how "Lothario throws her into the river and rushes off, followed by rabble" to Nora's comment "O, policeman, catch him" (*LII*, 75). He may also have enjoyed the various concerts featuring works by composers as diverse as Strauss, Suppé, Lehar, Schubert, Wagner and Donizetti, as well as William Vincent Wallace, which were put on by La Banda Cittadina and the Marine orchestra.

What was the nature of Joyce's relationship with Nora in this period? Alone and often with time on their hands, they certainly had ample opportunity to get to know one another more deeply. That Joyce had become genuinely protective of his partner is evident from his letter to Stanislaus:

> You are harsh with Nora because she has an untrained mind. […] Her disposition, as I see it, is much nobler than my own, her love also is greater than mine for her. I admire her and I love her and I trust her – I cannot tell how much. I trust her. So enough. (*LII*, 79–80)

In her book *Nora*, Brenda Maddox says that "Nora was delighted with her new life",[18] but this is surely to overstate the case. Nora, like James, was happy with certain aspects of their new life together – their freedom, her role as "La Signora Joyce", their new status as "Mr and Mrs Joyce" (she signed herself "Nora Joyce" in a letter of 28 December to Stanislaus), their enjoyment of a regular sex life. "She wonders", James wrote to Stanislaus on 19 November 1904, "how you can live at home and often asks me to help you to go abroad." In the same letter Joyce takes an almost juvenile delight in parading his sexual thrills to his brother, stuck at home in Dublin: "I really can't write. Nora is trying on a pair of drawers at the wardrobe" (*LII*, 71).

But she spent practically all of her time at home alone and had more than her share of low moments. Like any young couple, they had their misunderstandings and rows, and even if Nora told Joyce he had a "saint's face" she soon came to realize that he did not have a saint's demeanour. Their "lovers' quarrels", as Nora called them, were regular, and on more than one occasion she told Joyce he was childish (*LII*, 75). One such quarrel took place in the

Caffè Miramar in December 1904. Sitting alone, Joyce wrote a desperate note
to Nora, who was at another table:

> Dear Nora for God's sake do not let us be any way unhappy tonight. If there is
> anything wrong please tell me. I am beginning to tremble already and if you do
> not soon look at me as you used I shall have to run up and down the café. (*LII*,
> 74)

Yet despite these disagreements they seem to have experienced a joy in getting
to know each other, in sharing their own and their families' histories, and in
enjoying a frank and active sexual life. Joyce was keen that he should keep
nothing secret from his partner, and he expected the same of her. He also
reported many of Nora's intimate secrets to Stanislaus:

> Nora's father is a baker. They are seven in family. Papa had a shop but drank all
> the buns and loaves like a man. [...] She told me something of her youth, and
> admits the gentle art of self-satisfaction. She has had many love-affairs, one
> when quite young with a boy who died. (*LII*, 72)

Later, he would recycle much of this material in his writing. This element of
betrayal in Joyce's behaviour, in his doubling as husband who celebrated her
and artist who, at least partially, mocked her, would persist, and perhaps it
was just as well that she would never read his work too carefully.

In Pola James and Nora enjoyed a lifestyle well beyond their means, and
once they had established this habit they would (or could) never break it. In
his letter of 3 December 1904, Joyce described the rhythms of his new life in
copious detail to Stanislaus:

> We get out of bed at nine and Nora makes chocolate. At midday we have lunch
> which we (or rather she) buys, cooks (soup, meat, potatoes and something else)
> in a locanda opposite. At four o'clock we have chocolate and at eight o'clock
> dinner which Nora cooks. The[n] [we go] to the Caffé Miramar w[here we
> read] the 'Figaro' of Paris and we [come] back about midnight. (*LII*, 73)

The Caffè Miramar, which was advertised as "Il più elegante caffè della
città", was situated on the waterfront overlooking the port and Pola's famous
iron bridge. It was thronged with the middle classes: lawyers, officers, medical people, who came to chat and drink coffee, to play billiards, and were
served by both German- and Italian-speaking staff. Joyce and Nora went there
in the evenings after dining out cheaply in the *locanda* opposite their apartment, the Osteria da Piero, a down-to-earth place frequented by workers who
ate fried fish, drank wine, and sang drinking songs in the local dialect.

Stocked with a selection of international newspapers, the Caffè Miramar allowed the couple to stay up to date with what was going on in the world. Nora enjoyed *The Daily Mail* while Joyce read the English, French and Italian papers, and *Il Giornaletto di Pola*, which carried local and international news, parliamentary reports from Rome and Vienna, updates from Trieste (the administrative centre of the Austrian territories in Istria), as well as features on the theatre.

News of a more urgent and personal nature arrived shortly before Christmas when they discovered that Nora was pregnant. The couple were plunged into crisis. They were almost completely alone in this outpost at the far end of Europe, they had no experience of child-rearing, and to make matters worse, Joyce's position at the school seemed to be less than totally secure. Joyce complained of having little money or liberty and said in a letter of 28 December 1904 to Stanislaus: "My new relation has made me a somewhat grave person and I have got out of the way of dissertations. I drink little or nothing, smoke vastly, sing rarely" (*LII*, 75). Three days later he wrote telling his aunt Josephine that "The money here is all irregular for some weeks" and suggesting that they would have to move house: "It is possible that I shall leave this address next week as the house is unhealthy and I want as much health as possible for Nora" (*LI*, 57).

A move to a new apartment in number 7 via Medolino, where they went to live with Joyce's immediate superior in the school, Alessandro Francini Bruni, his wife Clotilde and their little son Daniele, eased things for James and Nora a little if only because this apartment was bigger and warmer and had a kitchen. On the down side it was farther from the centre of the city and situated in what was essentially a working-class district. (This was to be one of Joyce's few spells in an area which did not have middle-class pretensions.) Despite serious linguistic difficulties, Nora developed a close friendship with Clotilde and was reassured that she would have at least one other woman to turn to for help and advice following the birth of her child. Francini Bruni and Joyce also got on well together. Francini Bruni was born in 1878 in Siena and brought up in Florence, where he attended Catholic schools and then graduated in literature from the University. Like Joyce he had recently eloped, and he had arrived to take up his post in Pola just three weeks before his Irish colleague. Soon the two men were discussing literature and planning a joint translation of Moore's *Celibates*,[19] the title of which must have been a source of ironic amusement for this unmarried father and his new friend, an unmarried father-to-be. Francini Bruni and Joyce exchanged lessons, though it would appear that Joyce managed to have many more Italian lessons than he gave English.[20]

The greater part of Joyce's day was spent at the Berlitz School, which was situated in the Casa Scracin on Clivo Santo Stefano, near the Porta Aurata – the Roman Arch. The Berlitz was still finding its feet when Joyce arrived, and Almidano Artifoni had invested heavily in setting it up, being careful to find a suitable premises "of four or five well decorated rooms with tall ceilings in the city centre".[21] He strenuously publicized the school and on 1 October had placed a half-page advertisement in *Il Giornaletto* which specified that separate classes would be held for men and women, and for "signori ufficiali" (military officers) and "signori borghese" (civilians). By the time the school opened on 17 October, it had sixty-two pupils on its rolls. Probably in return for the advertising income it was earning from the school, *Il Giornaletto* printed an extremely complimentary "short par" (*U*, 7.989) telling of how a sister Berlitz school had won a prize in the World Exposition in St Louis. Two weeks later Artifoni had placed a large notice announcing the arrival of the new English teacher, "James Joyce B.A.". In the advertisement of 6 November, Joyce's Bachelor of Arts degree was somewhat flatteringly translated as "dottore in filosofia". By 8 February, more than thirty advertisements later, the school had some 180 students on its books.

Joyce took his place on a small, not particularly distinguished staff, including Amalija Globocnik from Ljubljana, who taught Croatian, Francini Bruni and Giuseppe Bertelli, both of whom came from Tuscany and taught Italian, Bibulich, the German teacher from Graz, Soldat and Née, French teachers from Paris, and finally Joyce's fellow English teacher, H.J. Eyers. Joyce became friendly with Globocnik, whom he normally referred to as "Fraulein" and described as "a melancholy little Androgyne and very sentimental with me" (*LII*, 75). Apart from feeling sorry for the Joyces, in her spare time she gave private lessons to Commander Miklós Horthy, the future admiral and later regent of Hungary. Joyce also spent time with Eyers, who was a good pianist but "a rather dull-witted young man with no manners and insipid as cork".[22] His closest friends remained the Francini Brunis.

Earning regularly for the first time, Joyce appears to have been reasonably happy. On 19 November he wrote telling Stanislaus, "I am fairly fixed here £2 a week for sixteen hours weekly" (*LII*, 70). This did not block occasional moments of melodramatic despair, in which he looked upon his life in Pola as though it were a sentence he was condemned to serve. One such expression of hopelessness came in his letter of 7 February to his brother: "My life is far less even than formerly in spite of its regularity. I reach prostrating depths of impersonality (multiply 9 by 17 – the no of weeks)"; but in the same letter he could still admit, "I reach levels of great satisfaction" (*LII*, 81).

His job, which he described to aunt Josephine as "all kinds of drudgery" (*LI*, 57), involved teaching the English language to the officers and technicians who had not been accommodated in Eyers's classes. The school hoped to attract a wider range of new students and claimed in its advertisements to cater for "doctors, engineers, medical people, lawyers, officials and professional people in general from businessmen to shopkeepers, and students from secondary and high schools".[23] As Herbert Gorman rightly pointed out, "The lot of a Berlitz School teacher is an arduous one",[24] and to survive it, Joyce had to acquaint himself quietly with the school's teaching method. Faced with several groups of beginners or near beginners, and being without an adequate command of their mother tongues or the dialects they spoke, Joyce was careful to follow Berlitz's methods faithfully, at least at the beginning. The textbook through which he led his students was M.D. Berlitz's *First Book* – an orderly, repetitive ninety-one-page volume which aimed to teach through the exclusive use of English. Joyce had no choice but to do this because it was what the newspaper advertisements promised: "Starting immediately from the first lesson, the student will not hear spoken anything other than the language he must study, and a teacher of the Berlitz School of Languages will never use the student's mother tongue to make himself understood."[25]

In order to teach English grammar, syntax, phonetics, and pronunciation, Joyce was forced to analyze patterns that he had always taken for granted, so as to render them understandable to students. In thus distancing himself from his own language, Joyce was in fact deepening his appreciation of it, and this process cannot but have helped him as a writer. The Berlitz method might well be traced in *Ulysses*, in particular in the impersonal catachetic technique of "Ithaca" (although Joyce's religious education at Belvedere was a more obvious and important source here). The novel contains linguistic echoes of the types of drills Joyce used in the Berlitz, repetitions of verb forms, tenses, and vocabulary.[26] Examples of this from "Ithaca" might include: "What did Bloom see on the range?" and "What did Bloom do at the range?" (*U*, 17.157–60) or "Alone, what did Bloom hear?" and "Alone, what did Bloom feel?" (*U*, 17.1242). Another classic method used by language teachers which Joyce employed was to have students describe in as much detail as possible pictures, each other, or the room they were in. Joyce repeats this technique in "Ithaca", when he poses questions such as "Describe the alterations effected in the disposition of the articles of furniture" (*U*, 17.1279–80) and then supplies endlessly detailed answers.

Joyce managed to squeeze a considerable amount of writing into the breaks between teaching in this period. He continued to work on *Stephen Hero* and wrote several of the short stories that would make up *Dubliners*, all of which he sent to Stanislaus, and one of which, "After the Race", was published in *The Irish Homestead* in Dublin on 17 December 1904. He also published two songs – "What counsel hath the hooded moon" and "Thou leanest to the shell of night" – in *The Venture*, an annual of art and literature in London. Finally, he had his ninety-six-line broadside "The Holy Office" printed in Pola. It was to be the last thing he published until March 1907.

All in all, despite bouts of loneliness and occasional moments of despair, things went reasonably well for Joyce in Pola. For the first time in his life he was earning regular money and managing to write. Meanwhile, as this article from *Il Giornaletto* of 18 February shows, the school was thriving:

> It's wonderful to see, and it is a tribute to the city – that of the 210 seats of *The Berlitz School of Languages*, spread around almost all the world, no other has ever achieved such immediate and conspicuous results. 160 is the remarkable number of students of the Berlitz, and how many have departed, called elsewhere by interests and duties to the state? They have left with that natural bitterness of those who must renounce spiritual gain.

Why then after just five months in Pola did he write to Stanislaus on 28 February 1905 telling him to address his next letter "to the Trieste school, Via S. Nicolo, 32, as I am transferred there. I leave Pola on Sunday morning for Trieste" (*LII*, 84)?

Joyce certainly would have been happy to get to Trieste and might even have requested a transfer there. He would have heard the people of Pola speaking of it as a mythic city, the great emporium of the Hapsburg Empire, a naval capital with an Italian heart. Perhaps, sensing his unease in their small, provincial town, they advised him to make for Trieste. But why would a school which was consistently attracting new students suddenly transfer one of only two English-language teachers? Francini Bruni suggests that Joyce was sent to Trieste because his superiors thought his teaching abilities could be better exploited by the school there:

> They thought, if Joyce is so useful in luring insects for the finch, he might do the same or even better for us in Trieste. And so as soon as they had him in their

hands, they seized him, packed him up like a salami, and sent him to Trieste by express freight.[27]

Over three decades later, in a 1954 interview with Ellmann, Francini Bruni offered a different explanation of Joyce's departure from Pola, recalling that the Austrian authorities had discovered an espionage ring in the city and, as a result, expelled all foreign residents (*JJ*, 194). The Triestine Joyce critic Stelio Crise has given some credence to this possibility as well. There is, however, no evidence that Joyce was suspected of anything or that any general expulsion order was issued. The expulsion theory also fails to explain why the Austrian authorities would "expel" anyone from Pola to Trieste, a bigger and far more politically sensitive city of the empire. For one month after Joyce's departure, Francini Bruni continued to offer his services in the local paper as a private language teacher, something he would hardly have done (or been allowed to do) if he or his fellow teachers were under pressure from the Austrian authorities. Moreover, it is most improbable that a British subject like Joyce would be forced to leave before his Italian colleagues, unless Joyce was seen as being too friendly with the naval officers, who were in a state-of-war alert.

Interestingly, Giuseppe Bertelli might have been in danger of expulsion at this time. According to Crise, "Bertelli was kept under constant watch by the Austrian police, both because he was an Italian citizen and because of his political beliefs. Bertelli had been the editor of *Il Lavoratore,* the newspaper of the socialist party in Trieste, and he spoke at numerous meetings held by the socialists."[28] As early as 22 January 1904, the police in Trieste were keeping Bertelli under surveillance and writing to their counterparts in Florence for information about him. On 30 December 1904 a police spy in Trieste reported that on the previous night an editorial board of the socialist paper *Il Lavoratore* had been formed at a meeting of the socialist party and that Giuseppe Bertelli, already known as a "diligent socialist agitator", had taken part. In early 1905 "L'evidenz Bureau della Marina da guerra austriaca di Pola" asked the police in Trieste for information on "Signor Bertelli, director of the Berlitz school of Pola", and underlined that the request for this information had be kept absolutely confidential.[29] But if there was any expulsion in 1905, Bertelli survived it; he didn't leave the empire until 1906, when he went to America having embezzled funds from the Berlitz school in Trieste.

According to the later records of the Austrian authorities in Trieste, Joyce was seen as a quiet person without any criminal record, certainly not as an agitator. Given his own written testimony of his dull life in Pola, and given the fact that Nora was not particularly happy there, it is likely that he either requested a transfer or gratefully accepted one when it was offered to him. While Pola was an out-of-the-way place which Joyce wanted nobody to know he was in, Trieste was an important city, big enough for him to develop his ambition in. He could look on a distinguished list of people who had spent lengthy periods of time there before him – Napoleon, Nelson, Casanova, Stendhal, Verdi, not to mention Charles Lever and Richard Burton, who had both served as British Consul there.

Joyce read Lever's *Lord Kilgobbin* while in Trieste and later sprinkled several allusions to this and Lever's other novels in *Finnegans Wake*. When he writes of Shem, who "quit to hail a hurry laracor and catch the Paname-Turricum and regain that absendee tarry easty" (*FW*, 228.22–4), Joyce invokes Lever's novel *Harry Lorrequer* and alludes to the Irish novelist's own six-year stay in the Adriatic city.[30] In Richard Burton, banished to Trieste as a punishment for his independent political views, Joyce found a most illustrious role model with whom he had much in common. At the wildest estimates, Burton is purported to have known forty languages and dialects, Joyce, eighteen. Both men were fascinated by "the East" and shared an uncommon interest in matters of sexuality. Burton used his enforced exile (he was never recalled from Trieste) to complete and publish books – *The Kama Sutra; A Plain and Literal Translation of the Arabian Nights' Entertainment; The Perfumed Garden of the Sheikh Nefzaoui, a manual of Arabian Erotology* – that would thoroughly scandalize late Victorian British society. Joyce too would send home books that would so scandalize the Irish reading (and non-reading) public that they would accuse him of being the Antichrist.

But first, Trieste awaited him.

TWO

A portrait of "tarry easty"

1 *His "italian warehouse" (FW, 498.30)*

> He liked to remember his happy days and spoke preferably of Trieste. His
> thoughts lingered on this topic with delight. There for a few short years he had
> enjoyed some moments of respite; fate had spared him some time. This pretty,
> good-natured Austrian city, half-Slavic and half-Italian (Edmund Gosse termed
> this "life in Germany"), with the gaiety of the Midi, the medley of languages,
> the animation of a harbour, and an already exotic, oriental flavour (as Veronese's
> Venice), had given him an extreme pleasure: there were no classical monu-
> ments, no Roman mementos as in Split or Ancona. But there was the rock of
> Ithaca, and on the sea, the sail of Ulysses.[1]

> Having taken a wife, the costs of keeping a family throw a man further into
> misery, the wife soon withers under the strain of having to look after the chil-
> dren, the kitchen, to pay the costs of her profession. The husband can no
> longer put up with the dark, small, cold and unhealthy house, full of the shouts
> of the children and the complaints of the wife. The pub nearby gives him the
> oblivion of drunkenness, he becomes nasty and is destined for a bad end. And
> with him the family …[2]

Thus wrote Louis Gillet and Giuseppe Bertelli respectively; the former, an
important French critic and intimate friend of Joyce in Paris, the latter his
loathed superior at the Berlitz school in both Pola and Trieste. The extract
taken from Bertelli's socialist pamphlet, *Chi siamo e che cosa vogliamo* (Who

we are and what we want), gives a rather dire prognosis, yet when applied to Joyce's early years in Trieste it is a somewhat apt summary of a period that was characterized by a permanent shortage of money, by tensions between the couple and by Joyce's frequent escapes to drown his sorrows in the *osterie* of the old city. These aspects of the couple's life are all too well known, having been documented in detail in Joyce's own letters and Ellmann's *James Joyce*.

In marked contrast, Gillet suggests that the city of Trieste was a place that at least sporadically offered Joyce consolations and pleasures and that exercised an influence on him as a writer. Herbert Gorman's biography, which was written under Joyce's watchful eye and cannot but have originated in Joyce's own memories of the place, lends weight to this belief and paints a brief but illuminating and affectionate portrait of Joyce's "city of the many kindnesses":

> ... he dove into the variegated life of Trieste with the pleasure of a dolphin diving in familiar waters. Every aspect of the city seemed to please him, the picturesque life along the quays, the diverse ways of the Città Vecchia with their wine-shops and cheap restaurants, the oxcarts rumbling through the streets, the constant processions when red blankets hung out of windows and candles glimmered behind them, the Albanians in native costumes and the brilliantly shawled women – for none of them wore hats – leaving the theatres, the countless barrels of coffee outside the shops and their rich odour impregnating the air, the giant watermelons piled in the squares and the lights flaring on their crimson succulence until two or three o'clock in the morning, the Sunday loiterers playing bowls or *mora*, the carnival masks crowding the streets on Shrove Tuesday, the nutria caps and fur coats and coloured collars and silk shawls passing on all sides, the side-whiskered image of the emperor Franz Joseph in white tunic adorning every tobacco shop, the huge powdered beadle at the Opera who bawled for carriages and the three opera seasons themselves – the Christmas and Carnival season at the Teatro Comunale and the summer seasons in the open-air theatre and the autumn season at the Politeama, the excited jabber of burghers and sellers in the markets for there were no set prices, the smell of fish and the sight of sea spiders cooked in their shells, the innumerable taverns bearing Christian names and, above all, the Triestines, charitable, witty, irreligious, sceptical, fond of cakes and the black wine of Istria and the fortified vin rosé – the Opollo from Lissa. Even the 'bora', that dreadful wind that blew so fiercely through the town that ropes had to be stretched across the streets to aid pedestrians, fascinated him as one of the irresistible phenomena of nature.[3]

If Joyce's experience of Trieste was not as enjoyable as Gorman suggests, it certainly was not as dull as Ellmann's version sometimes makes it seem.

While Ellmann is correct in noting that Joyce saw "certain resemblances to Dublin" in Trieste (*JJ*, 196) – both were cities on the sea, surrounded by hills; both were under foreign rule; and both were full of spirit, music, theatre, humour – there was far more to Joyce's relationship with Trieste than this. Not for nothing did Joyce's friend Philippe Soupault define "the Trieste period" as being "without doubt the most important of all his life".[4] Ellmann's account of the Trieste years does not take sufficient account of the complicated nature of the writer's personal and artistic relationship with the city, which he both fondly and ironically referred to as *la nostra bella Trieste* (our beautiful Trieste) and which he left six times – three times for Dublin, once each for Pola, Rome, and Zürich – only to return, of his own volition, on each occasion. Joyce's tartly dismissive descriptions of Rome and of another Italian port city, Ancona – "Filthy hole: like rotten cabbage" (*LII*, 114) – serve to remind us that he was not backward about criticizing even the most admired and famous cities. He was, however, also susceptible to the pleasures, qualities and particularities of places he felt at home in, and Trieste was one of these.

Upon arrival, Joyce was impressed by the city. From his apartment on Piazza Ponterosso he noticed the tall merchant ships that were berthed along the canal, symbols of Trieste's vital role as "the Hamburg of the Mediterranean".[5] The wonderful view he had is evoked by the Triestine writer Silvio Rutteri, who mourned the decline of Trieste as a port following the Great War:

> Now the turn-bridges are gone, having been replaced by permanent constructions, and with them everything that was picturesque is gone, especially the sails and masts, offered by the city's only waterway, which reflected the Churches of San Spiridione and that of Sant'Antonio, on the steps of which once sat our nice and lively girls, darning socks and cutting cloaks, waiting to be called to their work as coffee and rubber cleaners. No more then, on the canal, the arrivals of the sailing ships coming from the Italian coasts and from the Orient, carriers of the flourishing trade and the merchandise which was unloaded from them: perfumes, fruit, olive oil, wine from Samo, wood, salt. No longer even the din or the hunt of the young girls looking for muscatel raisins, dried figs, pistachio nuts, hazelnuts, locusts. All that movement, that orgy of colours, that mixture of smells, that confusion of languages and dialects, in which everyone, despite the difficulties, understood one another, is gone forever. All too quickly forgotten are the small sailing boats carrying the mountains of watermelons, which, during the hot humid summers were eaten in slices on the spot or bought whole, and taken home carefully, almost religiously, to be cut up to feed and wash(!) an entire family.[6]

It did not take the future author of *Ulysses* – the epic of an eternal wanderer – long to understand the city's maritime spirit and vocation, which was so evocatively symbolized in the Canale Grande at Ponterosso:

> Have you ever reflected what an important sea the Mediterranean is? In the canal here the boats are lined along the quays. [...] Perhaps the Baltic will replace the Mediterranean but till now importance seems to have been in the direct ratio of nearness to the Mediterranean. (*LII*, 90)

As Joyce's almost exact contemporary, the Triestine writer Scipio Slataper, pointed out, Trieste was a city whose fate was tied to the sea, and its power was now at a peak:

> The history of Trieste is in its ports. We were a little harbour for fishermen pirates and we knew how to see to it that we were looked after by Rome, by Austria, and we knew how to resist and fight until Venice began to lose its power. Now the Adriatic is ours.[7]

But it was not always thus. Although it dated back to pre-Roman times, the city (under the control of the Duke of Austria from 1382 on) traditionally occupied a marginal place in history, playing second fiddle to its near neighbours, Venice and Aquileia. In 1719, following the Peace of Passovitz – a commercial treaty with the Ottoman empire which made the Adriatic the central canal of trade – the Emperor Carlo VI established a free port in Trieste, thus laying the basis for its development as Austria's gateway to the Mediterranean, its only merchant seaport.

Throughout the eighteenth century, the role of the port, given its superb location close to Ljubljana and within easy reach of Vienna and the dukedoms of Mantua and Milan, gradually increased until it became the vital link for the traffic of goods between Austria-Hungary, the Mediterranean and the East. A stock exchange was opened, several important commercial and insurance companies were established, and by the end of the century the population had risen to 30,000 and a quarter of the total commercial output of the Austrian empire was passing through the city. A few brief interruptions of the city's progress came in 1797, 1805–6, and 1809–13, when it was occupied by French troops under Napoleon. The French problem was brought to a definitive conclusion in 1813, when the Austrians retook control. From this moment on, although Trieste retained some autonomy, all of the major decisions affecting it were taken in Vienna.

The establishment of new shipping lines caused a relentless rise in the city's importance in the economic system of Austria-Hungary. With the arrival of a merchant class drawn from distant parts, Trieste began to assume a highly cosmopolitan middle-European identity. The newcomers from all the ends of Europe settled in the impressive new houses being built in the orderly new districts – the Borgo Teresiano and the later Borgo Giuseppino – largely constructed on top of the old salt-works, while the poorer elements of the population continued to be concentrated in the *città vecchia*. Although there were occasional tensions between the two dominating loyalties – German and Italian – for the most part the citizens of Trieste managed to live in harmony. The Triestines were prospering under Austria and even if many resented the increasingly stubborn attempts to Germanize their city – the use of German for the street-names, the local administration, the schools – they were happy to make use of their relative autonomy to develop its commercial role as a liberal centre embracing differing traditions. In 1858 a new railway was completed that linked Trieste with Vienna, Budapest, Prague, Berlin and northern Germany. By now Trieste was the world's seventh busiest port, the second in the Mediterranean after Marseilles, and it played an instrumental role in the planning, financing, and construction of the Suez canal. At the same time the link with Vienna continued to strengthen as rich Triestine merchants and entrepreneurs were awarded Imperial titles. In 1856 the Archduke Ferdinand Maximilian ordered work to begin on what was to be his new summer residence, the splendid castle at Miramare.

But as Trieste grew, becoming the third urban centre in the empire after Vienna and Prague, something in the political atmosphere was quietly changing: the seeds of nationalism were beginning to take root. In the latter decades of the nineteenth century, Trieste's predominantly Italian identity, constantly boosted by a stream of new arrivals, was beginning to be challenged by a growing community of Slavs, many of whom had been encouraged to settle there by the Austrian administration, anxious to employ their *divide et impera* policy and to counter the city's growing irredentist spirit. Both the Italians and the Slavs resented being part of the empire (the former seeing Trieste as part of Italy, the latter yearning for it to become part of a large Slav nation), yet both were partially accommodated, at least for the moment, in the notion of *Municipalismo* (an autonomous Trieste) and later neutralized by the Austrian-Italian alliance and larger European politics which cemented the city's place in Austria.

Trieste remained Austria's key to the Adriatic and continued to expand right up to the outbreak of the First World War. New factories were being opened, Triestine insurance companies were continuing to consolidate their positions as market leaders in Austria and Italy, the coffee and sugar markets were assuming a global importance, and the tonnage of merchandise passing through the port increased by over 250 per cent between 1890 and 1913.

But there was more to Trieste than business. Indeed, given its predominantly middle-class population which deeply valued education, it was a place where new intellectual ideas were warmly embraced and where competing loyalties ensured a lively, even a combative cultural environment.

A DYNAMIC CITY characterized by commercial solidity but also notable for its intellectual curiosity and openness was what awaited James and Nora on their arrival back from Pola at the beginning of March 1905. They travelled, by train this time, arriving at the Stazione Sant'Andrea and found themselves in a city that Isabel Burton, wife and biographer of the great explorer Captain Sir Richard Burton, British Consul in Trieste from 1872 until his death in 1890, had described with the following words:

> Trieste is beautiful; I know of no more fascinating panorama than that of the Carnian Alps from the rive [quays] of Trieste. In summer they are hid by the exhalations of the Aquilejan lowlands, but in winter, when they raise their giant heads, hoar with snow, and extend their lower garments of light azure over the plain, whose foreground is the deep blue Adriatic dotted with its lateen sails, they give an inconceivable majesty to the north-western horizon. All round our bay the hills are covered with woodland and verdure, and are overtopped on one side by the bit of wild Karst which looks like stony Syria.[8]

James and Nora were just in time to enjoy the lively Carnival celebrations, which culminated in lively, entertaining parades in the centre, and especially along Corso Italia, the city's most impressive and fashionable shopping street. Judging from Stanislaus's diary accounts of subsequent Carnival celebrations, which they enjoyed with friends from the windows of the via Santa Caterina apartment in 1907, James and Nora probably took the trouble to watch the colourful masked pageant as it wound its way up the Corso.

2 *Settling down*

They found a place to live in the heart of the city, a little room without cooking facilities, which overlooked Piazza Ponterosso and was just around the corner from the Berlitz school at number 32 via San Nicolò. Joyce immediately began working, and notwithstanding all the interest Trieste may have aroused in him, the hard grind of his life as a poorly-paid English teacher took its toll and he rapidly came to realize that things were going to be no easier than they had been in Pola. He wrote as much in a letter to Stanislaus, declaring his current situation to be "a bloody awful position for me to be in. Some day I shall clout my pupils about the head, I fear, and stalk out" (*LII*, 87). Such rash action, he knew, would have been most unwise as "the slightest disapproval" on the part of his "genteel pupils" would be sufficient to obtain his dismissal (*LII*, 94). But it was heavy going, and it certainly got worse when the "torrid heat" of summer set in and he was still obliged to struggle through eight lessons per day "during which I must keep continually on the alert and interested" (*LII*, 98). Advertisements for the school, such as the following, which appeared in *Il Piccolo* on 15 December 1905, provide a clear idea of what was expected of the teaching staff: "The Berlitz School – ten qualified teachers available to teach their mother-tongue languages in classes or private lessons, or in the students' homes, at any hour." Joyce was somewhat impressed by the fact that his students were "noblemen and signori and editors and rich people", and might well have gone along with Francini Bruni, who suggested that the students constituted the only satisfaction in the school: "You wouldn't believe me if I told you how awful things were. But we met very interesting people. This at least kept us in good spirits. I have to admit that we used to laugh."[9]

Joyce continued the process he had initiated in Pola of drilling himself mechanically with what he knew so well instinctively – the forms and structures of English grammar – in order to convey them to his students by means of "examples and ocular demonstration".[10] Perhaps bored by this dull but effective rote-learning method, Joyce asked Stanislaus: "Would you be surprised if I wrote a very good English grammar some day?" (*LII*, 86). But he never lost faith in the Berlitz method. In order to teach himself Danish in 1906 he ordered "a Danish Berlitz book from Berlin" and continued to use the Berlitz books for his English lessons right up to the time of his departure from Trieste in 1915. At the same time, his lessons with his more advanced students became informal conversations, at first in English, then more animatedly in Italian, in which he laid down the law on a variety of subjects, from Irish to Italian literature, from the state of the English parliament to a subject that haunted him – his own financial problems.

Joyce regularly borrowed money and demanded advances on his salary, which was paid grudgingly by Giuseppe Bertelli. As befitted a man one step from the top of an organization he would never control, Bertelli was eager to be seen to extract the maximum effort from his staff of ten teachers and to entice the greatest possible number of students to attend at whatever time of the day or night they wished, as Francini Bruni's colourful testimony shows:

> To get more money he packed students into holes that were as slimy as cesspools and smelled like manure piles. He would have put them in the toilets. When in a friendly way I made him see that this did not consort with the school's reputation and that it was unsanitary besides, Beppino said, drawing out his favorite learned reference:
> "Shut up, you baboon. Socrates used to teach in the middle of the street."[11]

It is interesting to note that the same Bertelli was the opinionated author of the aforementioned *Chi siamo e che cosa vogliamo*, a sixty-page socialist manifesto published at the turn of the century, which posed several questions including the following:

> Well then, you work from morning to night, how is it that you don't have a penny? And how is it that all those people who have a lot of money, or who are making a lot of money, generally work very little and sometimes do nothing at all? Either it's not true that you make money by working, or else your work is not paid as it should be.[12]

Joyce and the other teachers might well have asked themselves the same questions. Their salary was low and they were not allowed to supplement it by giving private lessons. Lest he should get any notions of walking out, Joyce's degree certificate was kept locked away at the school and he was warned that he would be immediately sacked if he tried to give private lessons on his own account, so it would have been difficult for him to follow Signor Bertelli's advice:

> You need to free yourself from misery, you need to shake off the yoke of the owner monopolizer, you need to achieve an ever better existence, you need to reach for the dignity of a man who is truly free, not only free in name.[13]

In the summer of 1906 Bertelli would enact a strange interpretation of his own advice and abscond to America with the greater part of the school's funds. For the moment, however, he did his all to keep his teachers on their toes and caused enormous resentment among them by changing their timetables on a weekly basis with little or no notice. He was also clever enough to spot that Joyce was a popular and effective teacher – in the words of the Triestine journalist and writer Silvio Benco, "a marvel at teaching English"[14] – and took the unusual step of naming "Dr. Joyce" as the teacher of

English courses in the school advertisements that were placed in *Il Piccolo*. No other teacher was thus singled out.

This favouritism unfortunately did not extend itself to Joyce's pay packet. He was paid 190 crowns a month, at a time when the average monthly income ranged from 150 to 400 crowns, and therefore he was at the lower end of the pay scale. To compound this, the population of Trieste rose from 176,000 in 1900 to 239,000 in 1910, creating a serious shortage of affordable housing. That said, with careful management Joyce and Nora could have lived in reasonable comfort. Instead he spent his money unwisely and embarked on a series of intrepid projects, each of which was designed to ease his financial difficulties and allow him freedom to devote himself to his literary pursuits. He instructed Stanislaus to investigate an inheritance that had supposedly been left to Nora; he attempted to work as an agent in Trieste for an Irish clothes company, Foxford Tweeds; and he entered a puzzle contest. None of these enterprises yielded the desired results.

In a city like Trieste which offered endless possibilities for spending money, it was not surprising that he found it extremely hard to make ends meet. He outlined his difficulties to Stanislaus as follows: "Trieste is not very cheap and the difficulties of an English teacher living with a woman on a salary fit for a navvy or a stoker and expected to keep up a 'gentlemanly' appearance and to ease his intellectual heart by occasional visits to a theatre or a bookshop are very great" (*LII*, 94). Joyce did not manage to maintain the sartorial elegance expected of a teacher, and noted with resentment the insensitive comments of one of his colleagues to this effect:

> The other English teacher here said to me last night as he looked at my suit 'I often notice that eccentric people have very little taste: they wear anything. I give you a tip. If you have no taste you go in for grey. Stick to grey. Doesn't matter what kind – always looks gentlemanly.' (*LII*, 87)

Trieste was a centre of fashion, a world of *la bella figura*, but Joyce and Nora had neither the money nor the style to fit in. The few clothes they had were far too heavy for the spring and summer weather, and Joyce, who would later advise Stanislaus to come to Trieste "very well dressed" (*LII*, 112), was embarrassed not only by his own shabby attire, but even more so by the heavily pregnant Nora, who did not possess suitable maternity clothing.

> The Trieste people are great 'stylists' in dress, often starving themselves in order to be able to flaunt good dresses on the pier and she with her distorted body (Eheu! peccatum?) and her short four crown skirt and hair done over the ears is always nudged at and sniggered at. (*LII*, 94)

Joyce was nevertheless well able to dismiss what the respectable middle- and upper-class Triestines might have thought. When he should have been paying bills or buying clothes or kitchenware, he took his own counsel and bought as many books as his pocket would allow and treated himself and Nora to nights out in the city's theatres.

Trieste was the envy of many a city for its superb theatres, so much so that Joyce could have attended something different every night, had funds permitted. During the spring of 1905, the operatic highlights included Donizetti's *Lucia di Lammermoor*, Verdi's *La Traviata*, Bellini's *La Sonnambula*, Offenbach's *The Tales of Hoffmann*, Mascagni's *L'Amico Fritz* and Massenet's *Manon Lescaut*. An eclectic selection of plays was also presented by authors as varied as Roberto Bracco, Ermanno Sudermann, Marco Praga, August Strindberg and Henrik Ibsen. Joyce went to a wide range of theatrical productions and regularly watched the opera from the *loggione* (upper gallery) of the Teatro Verdi, where he sat among an odorous cross-section of humanity and kept an eye on his rich pupils down below in the best seats. Later in *Giacomo Joyce*, he left a D'Annunzian impression of the scene:

> Loggione. The sodden walls ooze a steamy damp. A symphony of smells fuses the mass of huddled human forms: sour reek of armpits, nozzled oranges, melting breast ointments, mastick water, the breath of suppers of sulphurous garlic, foul phosphorescent farts, opoponax, the frank sweat of marriageable and married womankind, the soapy stink of men ... (*GJ*, 12)

The Teatro Verdi, the most impressive of Trieste's theatres, was flanked by the comfortable and elegant La Sala della Filarmonica Drammatica, which was used for lectures, commemorations and plays. The city's biggest theatre, Il Teatro Politeama Rossetti, opened in 1778 and was used for plays, operas and public meetings and lectures. Il Teatro Goldoni, so named in 1902, was built in 1852 as the Teatro Armonia and was home to a host of visiting dramatic companies. Il Teatro Fenice in via Stadion was the stage of plays, opera, operetta and variety shows, while La Sala del Casino Schiller on Piazza Grande specialized in choral and orchestral concerts. Trieste also had a 2000-seat open-air theatre, the Anfiteatro Minerva, where a rich season of opera was mounted in summer. It opened for the first time on 8 June 1905 with Apolloni's opera *L'Ebreo,* which was followed by Petrella's *La Contessa d'Amalfi* and Verdi's *I due Foscari.*

Trieste attracted international singers (Caruso sang in *L'Elisir d'Amore* in 1901 and in *Rigoletto* in 1902 in the Teatro Politeama Rossetti) and was far more than what Brenda Maddox terms "a convenient stopover on the route between Milan and Vienna".[15] Isabel Burton vividly described the atmosphere and quality of the opera in Trieste as being second only to what was available in Milan's La Scala:

> I always think of a *prima donna* at Trieste, with regard to the public. We import our operas from Milan two years before they appear in London. We have an excellent Opera house [...] and the Triestines are so severe and so critical that artistes become extremely nervous; they know if they can pass Trieste they can sing anywhere. One evening, a very plain, but first rate, *prima donna* appeared on the stage. She had not yet opened her mouth; they all began to hiss and hoot. She advanced with great resolution to the footlights, and said: "*Cari Triestini*, I know I am frightful, but I did not come to be looked at, I came to sing. Hear me before you hiss." There was a dead silence. She opened her mouth, and before she had finished the first few bars, the applause was deafening and prolonged. She remained a favourite ever after.[16]

The more refined merchant families that settled in Trieste brought with them a passion for education and self-improvement along with the literature, art and music of a cultivated middle-European bourgeois class. Music was perhaps the most comprehensively middle-European aspect of their culture and before long they and their descendants had made Trieste into a small version of the Vienna of the eighteenth and nineteenth centuries, a city eagerly visited by figures such as Toscanini, Martucci and Nikisch, all of whom conducted there between 1905 and 1910. Gustav Mahler took the baton there in 1905 and 1907 and was most impressed by the city and its orchestra:

> The orchestra plays well. [...] The people are terribly nice. [...] The orchestra is really quite good, excellently prepared and full of zeal and of fire. I'm hoping for a good performance. All the seats have been sold.[17]

He would have also found a well-prepared and carefully critical audience: typically, the children of the upper middle classes were not brought to the concerts or the opera if they had not read the libretto, and, when they were older, learned the scores. Many of them studied at the city's conservatory, the Tartini (as Joyce would do a couple of years later), and others learned at least one instrument from a private teacher.[18] In addition to opera and symphonic concerts, there was a taste for skilled dilettantism and for entertainment at home and in music salons.

3 *Coping with "married life"*

If in moving from Pola to Trieste Joyce hoped that life would get easier and
that the bigger city would bring an improvement in Nora's health and raise
her low spirits, he was mistaken. As the summer wore on and her pregnancy
progressed, she became more depressed, so much so that Joyce wrote to
Stanislaus asking him to seek Aunt Josephine's advice.

> I must tell you some more things about Nora. I am afraid that she is not of a
> very robust constitution. In fact she is not in good health. But more than this
> I am afraid that she is one of those plants which cannot be safely transplanted.
> She is continually crying. [...] She is really very helpless and unable to cope
> with any kind of difficulties. (*LII*, 95)

Nora's exhaustion was entirely understandable: she was almost always alone
and suffered hugely in the impossibly hot summer of 1905, which elicited
countless articles in the local press:

> A Tropical Sunday yesterday. The blazing midday sun was such that it seemed
> that the earth was burning under the feet of the miserable mortals. The ther-
> mometer, in its inexorable climb, reached 30 degrees centigrade before midday,
> went beyond that in the afternoon and only fell slightly in the late evening.
> The citizens had nothing other than the heat to talk about, nothing to worry
> about aside from protecting themselves from it. The swimming baths were
> swarming with people; the walks, deserted in the hottest hours, welcomed a big
> sweating and tormented crowd, and rivers of beer flowed.[19]

Despite the torrid heat, Joyce strove to continue working on his short stories: "Many of the frigidities of *The Boarding-House* and *Counterparts* were
written while the sweat streamed down my face on to the handkerchief
which protected my collar" (*SL*, 69). They must both have longed for the
autumn and the arrival of the Bora, a strong, cold north-easterly wind.

Indeed when autumn did finally arrive, Joyce wrote gladly to Stanislaus:
"The damned monotonous summer was over and the rain and soft air made
me think of the beautiful (I am serious) climate of Ireland. I hate a damn silly
sun that makes men into butter. I sat down miles away from everybody on a
bench surrounded by tall trees. The bora (the Trieste Wind) was ro-aring
through the tops of the trees" (*LII*, 109). Later the violent wind would make
its onomatopaeic appearance in *Finnegans Wake* as "the Boraborayellers, blo-

hablasting tegolhuts up to tetties and ruching sleets off the coppeehouses, playing ragnowrock rignewreck, with an irritant, penetrant, siphonopterous spuk" (*FW*, 416–17). Anybody who has heard the Bora blow through the city's streets would recognize its powerful voice in these lines, which masterfully recreate the rise and fall of its irregular rhythm, its unpredictable gusts, the many notes and tones of its multiple voices. To give authenticity and local colour to his *Finnegans Wake* description of the Bora, Joyce employs many words which are either in Italian or in the Triestine dialect. McHugh's *Annotations* suggests that "tegolhuts" comes from the Dutch "tegel", but it could just as easily come from "tegole" – the Italian for slates. Another Italian word for the slates or roofs is "tetti", which becomes "tetties" in Joyce's quote. "Coppeehouses" suggests Trieste's coffeehouses (the city was one of Europe's main coffee-importing ports) and the Triestine "copi", which also means roof tiles or slates. The dictionary of the Triestine dialect gives several examples of the use of this word, for instance: "La Bora fa svolar un mucio de copi" (the Bora makes a bundle of slates fly away) and "èser fora dei copi" (to be off your head – crazy).[20]

Cold winds were not, however, Nora's immediate problem. Indeed, it is difficult not to pity her, especially as she is described by Joyce in a letter to Stanislaus, heavily pregnant, lying "all day on the bed powerless with fatigue" (*LII*, 94) in a small stuffy apartment and worrying about Joyce's drinking, her own physical condition and how they would provide for the child when it was born. But, as the same letter shows, her mood drove Joyce to exasperation. "Nora", he wrote, "is almost always complaining. She can eat very few of the sloppy Italian dishes and whatever she eats gives her a pain in the chest. She drinks beer but the least thing is enough to make her sick." Apart from Joyce she was utterly alone; she depended on him entirely, and yet she still did not have the security that only marriage could bring. As Brenda Maddox comments, Joyce at this time "was still pleased with himself for having had the courage to reject the institution of marriage".[21]

One of Joyce's ways of coping with his relationship with Nora was to redraw it in his fiction. It is not without significance that *Dubliners*, saturated as it is with an atmosphere of betrayal, presents a series of unhappy couples and a damning evocation of the institution of marriage as it was lived in Ireland. Many of the stories can be seen as commentaries on Joyce's troubled vision of the life ahead with his partner. Later, in 1906, he made his own dissatisfaction clear to Stanislaus when he wrote from Rome:

> A woman's love is always maternal and egoistic. A man, on the contrary, side by side with his extraordinary cerebral sexualism and bodily fervour (from which women are normally free) possesses a fund of genuine affection for the 'beloved' or 'once beloved' object. I am no friend of tyranny, as you know, but if many husbands are brutal the atmosphere in which they live (vide Counterparts) is brutal and few wives and homes can satisfy the desire for happiness. In fact, it is useless to talk about this any further. I am going to lunch. (*LII*, 192)

There is not a happy marriage to be found in *Dubliners*. "Counterparts", for instance, sees the dissatisfactions of incompatible parents, the one addicted to drink, the other to the Church, being visited upon their unfortunate son. "A Mother" is dominated by the grasping, scheming "Miss Devlin [who] had become Mrs Kearney out of spite" (*D*, 136) while Mrs Sinico in "A Painful Case" wants to betray her husband with Mr Duffy. In "The Dead", Gabriel is devastated at finding out that Gretta is crying, not for him, but for Michael Furey, her long lost love. In "Grace", while Mr Kernan takes refuge in drink he lets himself and his marriage be dominated by his wife: "After three weeks she had found a wife's life irksome and, later on, when she was beginning to find it unbearable, she had become a mother." In "The Boarding House" we meet Mrs Mooney who, having escaped from a failed marriage to a drunken, useless husband, connives with her daughter Polly to force one of their lodgers, Mr Doran, into what is bound to be another unfortunate marriage. Indeed when Mr Doran (or Bob Doran as he becomes) reappears in *Ulysses* he has declined into the role of an unfortunate drunk, who is more scorned than pitied as he lurches about in the corner of Barney Kiernan's and various other public houses. His fate earns a nasty, cynical comment from the narrator of the "Cyclops" episode.

> — The finest man, says he, snivelling, the finest purest character.
> The tear is bloody near your eye. Talking through his bloody hat. Fitter for him to go home to the little sleepwalking bitch he married, Mooney, the bumbailiff's daughter ... (*U*, 12.396–9)

But in "The Boarding House" Mr Doran is still in the throes of coming to terms with his fate. The portrait of his torments as he prepares to bow to the inevitable is in many ways a reflection of the struggle going on in Joyce's own mind when he was writing the story and living in Signora Canarutto's Trieste boarding house:

> He could not make up his mind whether to like her or despise her for what she had done. Of course, he had done it too. His instinct urged him to remain free, not to marry. Once you are married you are done for, it said. (*D*, 66)

And so it was for Joyce who, despite his earnest justifications to Stanislaus as to why he had not married, was happy to allow himself the illusion that he was not completely tied down, not yet a prisoner for life. "Why", he asked, "should I have brought Nora to a priest or a lawyer to make her swear away her life to me?" (*LII*, 89). As early as June he had spotted a useful precedent for escape, in his old hero Ibsen: "Do you know that Ibsen's married life ended by his leaving his wife?" (*LII*, 91). He did not seem to realize that Nora, in running away with him, had long since sworn away (however hastily or casually) her life with him. While she was matter-of-factly taking in washing to help make ends meet just a couple of weeks after Giorgio's birth, Joyce was still trying to decide whether *he* could swear away his life with her, and this uncertainty cannot but have fed the misery, insecurity and depression which followed the initial thrill of their adventure together and drove her repeatedly to threaten to pack up and leave him.

The pressure to marry weighed heavily on Joyce. While he may have hoped to escape it by leaving Dublin, now in Trieste his employers and some of his students frowned upon him for openly living with his pregnant part- ner whom he had not yet had the decency to marry. Indeed Joyce reported to Stanislaus: "The director when he saw Nora said he thought I must be stark mad. The sub-director is also appalled" (*LII*, 93). Joyce also encoun- tered problems with his landlords for the same reasons:

> … as soon as she began to be any way noticeable we were turned out of our lodgings. This happened three times until I conceived the daring plan of liv- ing in the house next the school and astonishing the landlady by the glamour of that wonderful establishment. This ruse has succeeded so far but we are still in imminent danger of being put out. (*LII*, 93)

Luckily they were not put out of their second-floor flat in number 30 via San Nicolò, where they had been living since April. In fact it seems that they got along rather well with their Jewish landlady, Signora Moisè Canarutto,[22] who had something of a soft spot for them. She was also directly involved in Giorgio's birth. On the afternoon of 27 July 1905, Joyce, instead of going for a swim, decided to call home to see Nora. When he got there he found that she was in pain:

> I had no notion it was for birth but when it continued for a long time I went to the landlady and told her. She sent for her midwife and then there was proper confusion if you like. The room was all pulled about. Nora had hardly anything made not expecting the event till the end of August. However, our landlady is a Jewess and gave us everything we wanted. I told her to get every-

thing that was wanted and gave her all the money I could lay hands on. Then I went for Dr Sinigaglia who is one of my pupils. He came at once and returned in time to help Nora to give birth to the child. He says I must have miscalculated the time as it is a perfectly normal child. The people here made me go in to dinner with them and at about nine in came the old aunt Jewess smiling and nodding "Xe un bel maschio, Signore". So then I knew an heir was born. (*LII*, 100–1)

As he had promised, Joyce refused to have Giorgio baptized, but he did eventually go to register the birth on 28 July 1906, a year and day after the event. The birth certificate, signed by Joyce, the midwife Giuseppina Scaber, and Joyce's teaching colleagues Joseph Guye and Paul Scholz, as witnesses, shows that Joyce pretended he and Nora were married in order to declare Giorgio legitimate. Peculiarly, the entry under "mother" is "Joyce Nora in Barnacle" (Barnacle Nora née Joyce) when of course it should have been "Barnacle Nora in Joyce" (Joyce Nora née Barnacle). Presumably this error was committed by the "commissario distrettuale" Dr Carlo Susina, who registered the birth, and not by Joyce himself.

The new father was quicker in sending word of the news to Dublin. He immediately wired a telegram: "Son born Jim" (*LII*, 100), but his family's reaction was cool, which upset Nora. Joyce himself found Giorgio amusing:

> The child has got no name yet, though he will be two months old on Thursday next. He is very fat and very quiet. I don't know who he's like. He's rather like that pudgy person of two years old who frowns at the camera in my first photograph but he has the 'companion's' eyes. (*LII*, 107)

With Giorgio's birth came new worries. Joyce was all too aware that their already precarious financial situation would become even more delicate now, and he clearly found his newly assumed responsibilities daunting. He later recalled a moment when he held his newborn son and thought: "You were quite happy, happier than I."[23] Soon his anxiety began to grow into frustration, a frustration that is accurately reflected in "A Little Cloud", the story he was writing around this time, in which Little Chandler, a man whose literary aspirations, like Joyce's, have been thwarted, tries to read from Byron but is interrupted by the crying of his child:

> It was useless. He couldn't read. He couldn't do anything. The wailing of the child pierced the drum of his ear. It was useless, useless! He was a prisoner for life. (*D*, 79)

"A Little Cloud" can indeed be read as a reflection of the crisis in which Joyce and Nora found themselves around the time of Giorgio's birth and in the latter half of 1905, and therefore it is highly significant that Little Chandler finds himself attracted by the idea of "rich Jewesses. Those dark Oriental eyes, he thought, how full they are of passion, of voluptuous longing!" (*D*, 78). He compares these passionate eyes with those he sees in the photograph of his wife, wonders why "there was no passion in them, no rapture", and asks himself "Why had he married the eyes in the photograph?" (*D*, 78).

4 *Visions of the East*

In his linking of "rich Jewesses" and "dark Oriental eyes" Joyce was drawing on a common Western European vision and revealing that he saw Jewishness as being at least partially synonymous with "Oriental-ness". Explicitly in *Giacomo Joyce* (as will be seen in Part Five), but also in *Ulysses*, Joyce would merge Western European commonplaces about the Orient with traits drawn from Triestine acquaintances and friends such as Annie Schleimer, Amalia Popper and Ettore Schmitz. For Trieste was in two crucial ways an Oriental workshop for Joyce. Firstly, it genuinely contained aspects of Eastern countries, in its population, its culture and its architecture; and secondly, it actively partook in the creation and maintenance of standard Western stereotypical visions of the East.

Long before he set foot in Trieste, Joyce was deeply indebted to that brand of Irish Orientalism "that looked to the East for the highest sources of national identity and the very origins of the Irish language, alphabet, and people"[24] and to a wide range of writers of "pseudo-Oriental European works" such as Lord Byron, Thomas Moore, James Clarence Mangan and Sir Richard Burton, all of whom participated in "Europe's collective day-dream of the Orient".[25] And yet, while it is true that the Orient was for him "less a place than a *topos*, a set of references, a congeries of characteristics",[26] it is equally true that his Orientalism was not simply the product of his reading, not simply an intertextual event. Rather it derived, at least in part, from his encounters with aspects of the Orient as they presented themselves in Trieste, where he encountered people born or descended from countries traditionally described as "Oriental" who proudly maintained their links with their original cultures, sometimes by preserving their language, customs and dress, by establishing business links with their ancestral homes, and by styling their houses with Oriental touches that underlined their sense of identity.

For this reason, Joyce's arrival in Trieste, a commercial and cultural cross-roads between Western Europe and the East, brought him into contact with concrete and living examples of many of the Oriental elements celebrated, romanticized and demonized in the fiction, fantasy and art of *fin-de-siècle* Europe and allowed him to put flesh on his generalized ideas about the Orient. Trieste pertained to what Edward Said has defined as "the familiar (Europe, the West, 'us')"; but it also incorporated within its population groups, its history, its architecture, its culture, its very *anima*, consistent elements of what Said called "the strange (the Orient, the East, 'them')".[27] Applying the term "Oriental" to Trieste makes sense in so far as the city was "exotic" to Joyce, and in so far as it had a rare capacity to absorb and preserve "the other", to allow space for ethnic and linguistic diversity. In Joyce's view, the "Orient" would have essentially comprised everything east and south of Trieste, which itself was commonly referred to as *la porta d'oriente* – the gateway to the East – and more specifically for the purposes of *Ulysses*, included Hungary, the Near East (especially Palestine), and also southern European countries such as Spain and Greece. Joyce's compass might have ranged widely, but his Orient was no more extensive than that of many of his literary precursors, as R. Brandon Kershner writes:

> Just where this Orient was to be found was debatable. The *Arabian Nights* themselves covered a great deal of ill-defined territory, including China; Edward William Lane thought the collection Egyptian in origin, Burton thought it Persian. The Near East, including the Biblical lands, was seen as Oriental, although, depending upon the writer's preference, either a Biblical or an Oriental intonation might be given to this geography. Byron's tales, reflecting his travels, steered the European imagination toward Turkey, Albania, and Greece under Turkish occupation. And since the Moslem element in most literary evocations of the Orient predominated, the entirety of the Ottoman Empire, including Moorish Spain, came to be seen as eastern. This of course, validates Molly's claim to be considered the Oriental prize of Dublin, at least by her husband. [...] in [its] broadest perspective, the Oriental and the exotic became virtually synonymous.[28]

Though he never visited any of the key "Oriental" countries that figure in *Ulysses* – Hungary, Palestine, Spain – Joyce drew on elements from all of their cultures not simply to provide *Ulysses* with a touch of the exotic but to create truly hybrid characters – Leopold and Molly Bloom. Precisely because it was a bridge that allowed Joyce to come face to face with real people who challenged, contradicted and confirmed so many of the stereotypes about the Orient with which he had been brought up, Trieste furnished him with important elements of both Bloom's and Molly's pasts and of their relationship.

Trieste exuded an Eastern atmosphere which was sometimes authentically faithful to the diverse origins of its mixed population and at other times as false and stereotyped as that to be found in any other major European city. Thus a colourful variety of sellers of spices, fruits, carpets and other goods from the countries of the East, many of whom were clad in native dress, such as a Turkish Jew called "Michelin de le Forchete" (Little Michael of the Forks), a seller of trinkets, could exist side by side with fashionable young ladies who happily paraded about in the trendy *jupe-culotte*, or Oriental-style trousers, which had been created in 1911 by a Parisian tailor, Paul Poiret, to widespread indignation and criticism in other European cities.[29] On Piazza Ponterosso and Piazza della Legna the air was scented with the spices being sold in the markets and under the awnings, while many of the city's buildings (for example the 1850 Serb Palazzo Gopcevich, whose outer murals recount the epic battle between the Serbs and the Ottomans in 1389; the Palazzo Romano, with its famous "camera Ottomana"; or the Casa Bartoli, a sensitive combination of Art Nouveau and architectural methods borrowed from Japan), and places of worship (the Serb Orthodox Church, for example, was built in the traditional "Byzantine Oriental" style with five cupolas in the shape of a Greek Cross), contributed to creating an exotic atmosphere. Many other buildings revealed an eclectic mix of Oriental-style decoration on their façades and several bars were decked out in furnishings and decorations evoking the East. In addition to favourite haunts of Joyce such as the Caffè Bizantino, and the Caffè degli Specchi on Piazza Grande, which proudly advertised as a "Caffè Orientale", and which, like many other coffee-houses, served coffee imported directly from Arabia, Trieste could boast of its "Club Egiziano" and, in a classic example of how the Orient was appropriated by the West to signify sensual pleasure, its Villa Orientale – the most luxurious brothel in town.[30] Many medical cures were also advertised as coming from the Orient, such as that for the "Pillole Orientali" (Oriental pills) which produced "a splendid bust in just two months".[31]

The growing role of the city's port was the single most important factor in placing Trieste among those cities at the forefront of Western Europe's fascination with the East:

> With this Pharaonic work (of opening routes to Venice, Istria, Dalmatia, Greece, Corfu, the Black Sea, Egypt, Constantinople, Syria, Trebizond, Marseilles, Barcelona) in which so many of our people took part at all levels from

financiers to expert sailors, Trieste found itself in regular and immediate contact with the Indies and the far East. [...] Now Trieste visited the far East as
though it were a second home and from there brought to Europe everything
Europe was capable of absorbing. The continuous contact with that far-off
world gave the city a close pioneering knowledge of the facts, people and the
things of the East and this caused a subsequent assimilation and re-elaboration
of the city's tastes and styles: it did not only bring about the formation of collections and the creation of exotic corners in the houses, but also pushed local
artists, sometimes even amateurs, to produce a new type of art. They often decorated their studios in an Oriental style.[32]

Later Joyce used these "Oriental" aspects of this city where diverse cultures collided, its climate ("that damn silly sun that turns men into butter"),
its awned streets, its colourfully costumed sellers, in Bloom's vague Dublin
daydreams juxtaposing the mysterious East and Italy:

> Wander through awned streets. Turbaned faces going by. Dark caves of carpet
> shops, big man, Turko the terrible, seated crosslegged, smoking a coiled pipe.
> Cries of sellers in the streets. Drink water scented with fennel, sherbet. Dan-
> der along all day. (*U,* 4.88–91)

When Bloom stops at "the Belfast and Oriental Tea Company" (*U,* 5.18) he
goes into a sensual reverie which significantly links the exotic, erotic, spice-
laden, East with Italy through the evocation of *dolce far niente*:

> The far east. Lovely spot it must be: the garden of the world, big lazy leaves to
> float about on, cactuses, flowery meads, snaky lianas they call them. Wonder
> is it like that. Those Cinghalese[33] lobbing about in the sun in *dolce far niente*,
> not doing a hand's turn all day. Sleep six months out of twelve. Too hot to
> quarrel. Influence of the climate. Lethargy. Flowers of idleness. (*U,* 5.29–34)

The Mediterranean-Oriental mix in Trieste also informed Joyce's creation of
Molly, whom Bloom praises as follows: "That's where Molly can knock spots
of them. It's the blood of the south. Moorish" (*U,* 13. 968–9). What Bloom
finds attractive about Molly often mirrors what Joyce appreciated in the
mysterious Jewish girl with dark Oriental eyes he celebrates in *Giacomo Joyce.*
Both are "washed in the blood of the sun" (*U,* 16.889–90). As Bryan
Cheyette has observed, "Bloom is initially attracted to Molly precisely
because of her perceived Jewishness":[34]

> ... the first night ever we met when I was living in Rehoboth terrace we stood
> staring at one another for about 10 minutes as if we met somewhere I suppose
> on account of my being jewess looking after my mother ... (*U,* 18.1182–5)[35]

Like the mystery girl of *Giacomo Joyce*, Molly Bloom would have a Jewish mother (Lunita Laredo)[36] and would be physically very much in keeping with a certain female type to be found in Trieste, where, as one traveller put it, "The women have a southern graciousness and charm united with a statuesque beauty of the East."[37] Stanislaus Joyce comments in his diary about a student of his who embodies many of these features, and even refers to her as "the odalisque":

> She is very Turkish in appearance, wearing her black hair in a plait and loose over her forehead, and when she smiles at you she closes up her eyes, completing the Oriental illusion. I call her the odalisque – It is intended as a compliment but to one who knows Turkey and odalisques it may not sound one. Her manner is direct and demure, the pretty obedience of a well-reared convent girl, the composed freedom from embarrassment of a girl who has been educated in many lands. Her *aia* always comes with her and waits for her during the lessons, sitting silently in the corridor. She talked about her Papa. She has lived all her life in the Levant, in French and American convents, and in Constantinople. She speaks Turkish, Arabic and Greek.[38]

It is significant that Leopold Bloom makes little distinction between Spain and Italy – both for him represent the South, and in this regard it is useful to note that the Anglican community of Trieste was officially part of the Diocese of Gibraltar, Molly's birthplace. Never having visited Gibraltar or lived in any port south of Trieste, Joyce read up on the Spanish elements in Molly's background while drawing on his adopted city in order to convey something of the Mediterranean aspects Bloom so approves of in his wife:

> My wife is, so to speak, Spanish, half that is. Point of fact she could actually claim Spanish nationality if she wanted, having been born in (technically) Spain, i.e. Gibraltar. She has the Spanish type. Quite dark, regular brunette, black. I for one certainly believe climate accounts for character. That's why I asked you if you wrote your poetry in Italian (*U*, 16.876–81).

Bloom points out to Stephen "The splendid proportions of hips, bosom. You simply don't knock against those kind of women here" (*U*, 16.892–3) and later links his wife with Kitty O'Shea, whom he believes also has Spanish roots and thus the "passionate abandon of the south" (*U*, 16.1409–10). We also come to know that Molly has her mother's eyes, wears Peau d'Espagne (Spanish skin), a perfume which was advertised regularly in the *Wiener Mode* magazines on sale in Trieste in Joyce's time,[39] speaks Spanish, understands Italian, and remembers Gibraltar and especially the multi-ethnic nature of its markets in "Penelope": "the auctions in the morning the Greeks and the jews and the Arabs and the devil knows who else from all the ends of Europe" (*U*, 18.1587–9)[40] – a description that fits Trieste perfectly and echoes that of George Eliot, who describes Trieste in *Daniel Deronda* as a place "where the garments of men from all nations shone like jewels."[41]

Like Molly, Bloom too is more than just a native Dubliner. In "Nausicaa" he recalls Molly's answer to his question "Why me? Because you were so foreign from the others" (*U*, 13.1209–10), and Gerty MacDowell notices him as "that foreign gentleman" (*U*, 13.1302). While he is "a citizen of the British Empire" and "an Irishman", he is also a foreigner, one who is different. His breakfast of inner organs was a standard feature of the diet of *Mitteleuropa* and a speciality in Trieste, while his chosen repast of "a few olives too if they had them. Italian I prefer. Good glass of burgundy take away that. Lubricate. A nice salad, cool as a cucumber" (*U*, 8.758–9) and his actual snack of burgundy, olives and gorgonzola cheese certainly owe more to the typically Mediterranean diet of Trieste than they do to Dublin, even if they were available there for the sophisticated palate. He is, as Kershner has written, "a European but [also] an Oriental both because he is a Jew and because he is Irish".[42] This equating of Oriental and Irish was fairly common long before Joyce put pen to paper; it is to be found in Thomas Moore's *Lalla Rookh*, in William Collins's *Persian Eclogues*, and in Mangan's poetry, as celebrated by Joyce: "East and West meet in that personality (we know how); images interweave there like soft, luminous scarves and words ring like brilliant mail, and whether the song is of Ireland or of Istambol it has the same refrain, a prayer that peace may come again ..." (*CW*, 78).

The narrator of "Oxen of the Sun" describes Bloom as an Oriental, "at his best an exotic tree which, when rooted in its native orient, throve and flourished and was abundant in balm but, transplanted to a clime more temperate, its roots have lost their quondam vigour" (*U*, 14.937–40). In "Circe" he "hitches his belt sailor fashion and with a shrug of oriental obeisance salutes the court, pointing one thumb heavenward" (*U*, 15.959–61). His Jewishness is signalled by a physical description in "Ithaca": "height 5 ft 9 1/2 inches, full build, olive complexion, may have since grown a beard, when last seen was wearing a black suit" (*U*, 17.2002–4). Bloom is also ironically depicted by Joyce as a child of Israel wandering in the wilderness of Dublin, longing for the sustenance of fruit, thinking of his family roots in Palestine, and of the passage from there to the Mediterranean, a passage which mirrored that of many settlers in Trieste.

These Mediterranean and Jewish elements merge in Bloom's surprisingly visible, almost sinful, evocations of exotic fruits and in his erotic longings for his wife. Suzette Henke has pointed out that "in *Ulysses*, food and love are conflated".[43] More specifically, sexual attraction is linked to fruit, as in "Circe", for example, when Bella Cohen is described: "Her olive face is heavy, slightly sweated and fullnosed with orangetainted nostrils" (*U*, 15.2747–8). Later, as Bloom witnesses Boylan and Molly together, he offers him "orangeflower" and Mina Kennedy comments that "it must be like the scent of geraniums and lovely peaches!" (*U*, 15.3799–800). Throughout the text, whenever Bloom's thoughts are invaded by erotic images of Molly, "the oriental prize of Dublin", his visions are accompanied by, connected with, or even brought on by images of fruit from the Mediterranean and the East, the very goods Joyce saw in the markets of Trieste and has Molly see in the markets of Gibraltar – chiefly oranges, olives and melons.

> Orangegroves and immense melonfields north of Jaffa. You pay eighty marks and they plant a dunam of land for you with olives, oranges, almonds or citrons. Olives cheaper: oranges need artificial irrigation. [...] Silverpowdered olivetrees. Quiet long days: pruning, ripening. Olives are packed in jars, eh? I have a few left from Andrews. Molly spitting them out. Knows the taste of them now. Oranges in tissue paper packed in crates. Citrons too. Wonder is poor Citron still in Saint Kevin's parade. And Mastiansky with the old cither. Pleasant evenings we had then. Molly in Citron's basketchair. Nice to hold, cool waxen fruit, hold in the hand, lift it to the nostrils and smell the perfume. Like that, heavy, sweet, wild perfume. ... Coming all that way: Spain, Gibraltar, Mediterranean, the Levant. Crates lined up on the quayside at Jaffa, chap ticking them off in a book, navvies handling them barefoot in soiled dungarees ... (*U*, 4.194–213).

When Bloom is buying Molly's oils in "Lotus-Eaters" he remembers that the orangeflower water "certainly did make her skin so delicate white like wax", and this leads him to ask for "white wax", which "Brings out the darkness of her eyes" (*U*, 5.492–4). In "Laestrygonians", the similarities between the ripe, exotic, perfumed Mediterranean fruits and Molly are made so explicit that the two become almost indistinguishable from each other. Bloom tries to distract himself from his cravings for his wife, but cannot help thinking about her betraying him with Boylan, who is jingling his way to number 7 Eccles Street. Again images of Molly merge with images of fruit:

> Useless to go back. Had to be. Tell me all.
> High voices. Sunwarm silk. Jingling harnesses. All for a woman, home and

houses, silkwebs, silver, rich fruits spicy from Jaffa. Agendath Netaim. Wealth
of the world.

A warm human plumpness settled down on his brain. His brain yielded.
Perfume of embraces all him assailed. With hungered flesh obscurely, he
mutely craved to adore. (*U*, 8.633–9)

Finally, in "Ithaca", Bloom contemplates Molly in a sexually excited
silence and equates her with the image of a melon, a fruit full of significance.[44] When writing this Joyce may have had in mind the idiomatic Italian use of the melon as a symbol of marriage: "Il matrimonio è un melone
chiuso" (marriage is a closed melon), even if he also regularly associated the
melon (in classic Western style) with prostitutes and Oriental women. Joyce
would also have been well aware that the melon was also the official symbol
of the city of Trieste and could not but have noticed the several monuments
featuring melons to be found dotted around the city. Corinna del Greco
Lobner explains the melon's significance for Trieste as follows:

> Triestine humor is often irreverent, but only because it feels comfortable with
> the subject of its mockery. Such is the case with San Giusto, the Triestini *mulo*,
> "boy," who preferred martyrdom to apostasy. It seems he was condemned to
> drown, a mistaken punishment for Triestines, who are the best swimmers on the
> Adriatic, as the soldiers of the emperor Diocletian (A.D. 245–313) soon found
> out. To retain their credibility as executioners, Diocletian's soldiers had no
> choice but to tie a *scojo*, "stone," around the neck of the young man. The *scojo*,
> stylized by centuries of devout painters, resembled less and less the original. Tri-
> estines decided it looked like a melon. Joyce, who [...] celebrated his feast days
> even if he could afford only "a cheap small pudding" (*Letters* I, 86), must have
> appreciated this bit of homespun poetry:
>
> A Roma i g'ha San Pietro a Venezia i g'ha el leon, per noi ghe xe San Giusto
> col vecchio suo melon.
>
> (In Rome there is Saint Peter, in Venice there is the lion, for us there is
> Saint Justin with his old melon.)[45]

All the more reason therefore for Joyce to pay underhand homage to Trieste
and its noble melon by making it such a vital symbol in *Ulysses*:

> Then?
> He kissed the plump mellow yellow smellow melons of her rump, on each
> plump melonous hemisphere, in their mellow yellow furrow, with obscure pro-
> longed provocative melonsmellonous osculation. (*U*, 17.2240–3)

5 Trieste and Triestino: into the cultural melting pot

Joyce was so overwhelmed by his difficulties with Nora and his unsatisfactory situation at the school that he wrote telling Stanislaus in July 1905 that "there is no hope of advancement and a continual fear of collapse" (*LII*, 94). The only practical solution he could conceive of was to have Stanislaus come out from Dublin. Joyce sent his younger brother a barrage of increasingly insistent letters urging him to travel to Trieste without delay. In truth, even if he did not like the idea of abandoning his young sisters to the mercies of his father, Stanislaus was already keen to get out of Ireland. Not even a year earlier he had noted in his diary how he loved "listening to barrel-organs, not piano organs. They have such quaint old airs and they grind them so slowly. They remind me of the south of France, of oranges, of Spain, that I want to live in."[46] It did not take him long therefore to decide that he would prefer the adventure of taking up his brother's invitation to come to work as a language teacher in the Berlitz school in Trieste to a dull life as a poorly paid clerk in Dublin.

While making it clear to Stanislaus that he was doing him a favour, James also advised him to "learn a little Italian – enough to spare yourself disadvantages at first", and to "come very well dressed as this is a 'highly respectable' position I offer you" (*LII*, 113). Initially Joyce made the city sound inviting: "You might do no more than winter here if you have other plans in Ireland: and a few months of the best season (opera and carnival) in Trieste might not be too disagreeable to you" (*LII*, 113). But the reality Stanislaus came to share was a lot harsher. From the moment he stepped off the train in Trieste in late October 1905 until the outbreak of the First World War, Joyce took advantage of Stanislaus's fraternal devotion. No sooner had Stannie arrived in the city than his brother was asking him if he had any money, and before long it was clear to him that Jim intended to exploit his sober sense of responsibility, leaving him to shoulder, almost exclusively, the burden of keeping the family. For the next few years, Joyce's careless spending on books, theatre, drink and dining-out would be largely facilitated by Stanislaus, who paid for the essentials – rent, food and clothes – although Joyce himself did continue to give private lessons, to do translations of commercial letters and to wheedle loans both from his students and from various lending institutions. Not for nothing would Stanislaus later write that

Joyce had "an attitude towards money that to me, with my middle-class ideas on the subject, was like a hairshirt during our life together".[47] For the moment, however, Stanislaus was more shocked at the poor state of relations between Joyce and Nora, Joyce's restlessness, Nora's exhaustion and bad temper and the bitter atmosphere that permeated their apartment.

From the outset Stanislaus was also struck by the mixture of peoples and religions which made Trieste into a small European "salad",[48] as he called it affectionately in his diary. Joyce himself had reacted in the same manner immediately after his arrival in the Adriatic port, manifesting his fascination with the variety of religious communities that existed side by side. In *Finnegans Wake* Joyce refers to "Jimmy the chapelgoer" (*FW*, 587.35–6), and he certainly did much to merit this title during his stay in Trieste. He was struck in particular by the splendid neo-Byzantine Serb Orthodox Church of San Spiridione, which was built at a slight remove from the banks of the Canale di Ponterosso in 1858 so as not to upset the Catholic faithful pouring out of the Church of Sant' Antonio Taumaturgo, located at the end of the canal, and by the equally impressive 1787 Greek temple, the Church of the Most Holy Trinity and San Nicolò, the "Ciesa dei greghi" as the Triestines called it,[49] where he liked to attend the religious rites.[50] He also attended the Holy Week ceremonies in the Catholic churches. Later he would explore some of the other ethnic and religious groups that had been thriving in Trieste since the Edict of Tolerance of 1781, which had allowed Greeks and Jews freedom of worship and freedom to establish their business ventures. At the beginning of the century, in addition to large Catholic, Jewish, Greek and Serb Orthodox communities, the city boasted sizeable groups of Armenian Mechitarists, Swiss and Valdesian Protestants, Lutherans, Anglicans and Methodists. The religious and ethnic communities that settled in Trieste maintained their native traditions:

> These people, who came from every part of the world, did not only bring to Trieste the adventurous side of their characters, the art of commerce, the willingness to become wealthy. They also brought their songs, their soul, their culture and a great desire to conserve it.[51]

The link with the home countries was essential for these exiles:

> All the groups that lived in Trieste looked elsewhere to a far-off country, identifiable only through an imaginary projection. The Italians, or at least the most passionate standard-bearers among them, looked, like the irredentists, to Italy, or at least saw Italy as a reference point, feeling that they lived in a world apart;

the Germans and the Austro-Germans looked beyond the Alps, while the Slovenes waited for the awakening of their land, or later, that of the Slavs in the Empire.[52]

Despite these close links with their home nations and the continued use of their native languages, especially in their homes, members of these ethnic groups all became Triestines and learned, like the Joyces, the local *lingua franca*, the dialect of *Triestino*, the linguistic glue that bound the city together. It united elements of many other Italian dialects as well as Armenian, English,[53] Spanish, Turkish, Sicilian, Maltese, German, Hungarian, Slovenian, Croatian, Czech and Greek. How liberating it must have been for Joyce to come to a city where the native tongue had been allowed to flourish, mutate, multiply, and assimilate so many words from other cultures, and where so many imported languages were allowed to coexist. As his students were largely drawn from the middle-classes and the élite, many of them would have attended school in German, spoken Italian or Triestine with their friends and taken private lessons in English and French.[54] Constantin von Economo, a noted medic and brother of one of Joyce's students, Leo, "spoke Greek with his father, German with his mother, French with his little sister Sophie and his brother Demetrio, *Triestino* (that is Italian) with his brother Leo".[55] Joyce's boss in the Berlitz school, Almidano Artifoni, also contributed to the linguistic variety of Trieste when, in 1902, he founded a newspaper entitled *Il Poliglotta*, which published articles written in Italian, English, German, French and Spanish.

This linguistic wealth occasionally became mayhem, but a mayhem which other writers before Joyce had used for satirical, comical and political ends. The pro-Italian satirical weekly *La Coda del Diavolo* liked to use a variety of languages impishly mixed together in a playful linguistic pot-pourri that anticipated the language of *Finnegans Wake*. It published articles and letters written in Italianized Slav and Triestinized German and in "friulana infrancesata" (frenchified Friulan).[56] Joyce later put a reference to *La Coda del Diavolo* in *Finnegans Wake*, where he wrote: "Rota rota ran the pagoda *con dio in capo ed il diavolo in coda*. Many a diva devoucha saw her Dauber Dan at the priesty pagoda Rota ran" (*FW*, 466.19–21). "Devoucha" suggests the nearby Slovene town of Divaca (pronounced "Divacia"), "Rota" recalls the noted Triestine musician Giuseppe Rota, while "Dauber Dan" comes from the Slovene "Dober dan", meaning "Good Day", and also carries a hint of the martyred Triestine patriot Guglielmo Oberdan. As Giovanni Bruggeri wrote:

Trieste began to take a grip of him, but he was even more taken by its men, their customs, their talk. The cordiality of the waiters in the Hotel Haberleitner, for example; the mangling of his surname into Zois in the pronunciation of his student Alois Skrivanich or Jesurum as he was; his barber Criscuolo di Apollosa's offer "Would you like a high shading, Professor?" or Count Sordina, who, despite his Greek origins, wrote him a letter in highly refined Italian; and many others as well as these. Joyce was surprised by the abundance of Italian, Greek, German, Slav, and Jewish names brought by those men; and astonished because all of them spoke *Triestino* even if it was with thousands of different inflections. It is easy to understand that discovering this excited him, stimulated him intellectually, above all as a glotologist, one who knew and studied languages.[57]

It is not difficult to imagine that Joyce, who in *Ulysses* is so sensitive to the linguistic codes that exclude Bloom from belonging, would have noted the differences in the varieties of *Triestino* being spoken: he would have heard the different accents on each word from the mouths of the different nationalities, all trying, like Bloom, to fit in. He would also have experienced in a new way Stephen Dedalus's description of the linguistic differences between himself and the Dean of Studies in *A Portrait of the Artist as a Young Man*:

> The language in which we are speaking is his before it is mine. How different are the words home, Christ, ale, master, on his lips and on mine! I cannot speak or write these words without unrest of spirit. His language, so familiar and so foreign, will always be for me an acquired speech. I have not made or accepted its words. (*P*, 194)

In the Triestine environment this statement could have been made by an Italian who resented the Austrian imposition of the German language, or the use of *Austriacans*, the Austrian version of the Triestine dialect used by the Austrian upper classes in the city; or it could have been uttered by a Slovene whose use of *Triestino* would have been very different from that of an Italian.

But *Triestino* was essentially an inclusive force which, in each of its varieties, embraced different civilizations and became a living encyclopaedia of the cultures, nations and languages that had been assimilated in the city. Later, when writing his encyclopaedia of Irish culture in *Finnegans Wake*, Joyce would create his own international portmanteau language, rooted in English but brimming with different traditions, in which few individual words could be safely reduced to one single, authoritative meaning. In this respect the language of *Finnegans Wake* is like an exaggerated, exploded version of *Triestino*, "one of the richest, one of the most 'composite' [languages] in the world that Joyce listened to with passionate attention",[58] which itself was used and misused, understood, half-understood, sometimes misunderstood by all.[59]

Joyce quickly learned *Triestino* and, as his roughly one hundred letters in Italian and Triestine to Stanislaus, Lucia, Giorgio, Francini Bruni, Giuseppe Bertelli, Ettore and Livia Schmitz, and others show, never confused it with standard Italian, which the Triestines (or the "terriestini", as Joyce called them in a letter to Livia Schmitz in 1939 [*LIII*, 439]), referred to as *regnicolo*. He also spoke better *Triestino* than he did Italian,[60] and Silvio Benco noted how "the Triestine dialect" remained "the family's customary language" long after the Joyces had settled in Paris, where they continued to speak "our dialect, taking pleasure in preserving the harshness of the local accent".[61] That the dialect was spoken in the family can also be seen in a letter written in Italian to Lucia in the thirties, where Joyce tells the punch-line of a funny story in *Triestino*:

> One of my pupils in Trieste was very heavy, stupid, bald, slow and fat. But one day he told me this little story a propos of the "education" of a sister of his who must have been like him. This little girl was learning how to knit at school but could get nothing into her head. The teacher tried to show her how to do it. Like this, like this. Now do you see? Pass the needle under, then pull it through and so on. At last she asked if the girl had an older sister. The girl replied she had. Then, said the teacher, show her your work and tomorrow bring in everything done properly. Do you understand? Yes, Miss.
>
> The next day the girl came to school but the work was worse than before. How is this? said the teacher, don't you have an older sister at home? Yes, Miss. And didn't I tell you to ask her to show you? Yes, Miss. And what did your sister say? She said that you and the knitting both should go to hell. (*LIII*, 378)

The last line in *Triestino* reads: "La ga dito che vadi in malora lei e la calza."[62] Joyce uses the word "malora" again in *Ulysses* as part of the name of one of the visiting delegation present at Robert Emmet's execution in "Cyclops": "Señor Hidalgo Caballero Don Pecadillo y Palabras y Paternoster de la Malora de la Malaria" (*U*, 12.562–4). While this is obviously Spanish, the "de la Malora" is certainly *Triestino*. The "ga dito" ("ha detto" in standard Italian) is also to be found in *Finnegans Wake*, where Joyce gives his own very peculiar version of *Triestino* as supposedly spoken in a sermon by a Slovene priest: "*Senior ga dito: Faciasi Omo! E omo fu fò. Ho! Ho! Senior ga dito: Faciasi Hidamo! Hidamo se ga facessà. Ha! Ha!*" (*FW*, 212.34–6). In English it reads approximately as follows: "The Lord said: Let man be made! And man was made. Ho! Ho! The Lord said: Let Adam be made. And Adam was made. Ha! Ha!"

Another aspect of the Triestine dialect which Joyce appears to have particularly relished was its rich collection of words to do with sex. The "Circe" chapter of *Ulysses*, with its graphic descriptions of Boylan and Molly and of Bloom and Bella/Bello, represents the sexual climax of the book and owes much to Trieste. Just fifty lines into the episode, the Virago says "more power the Cavan girl" (*U*, 15.53). If we add an "a" to Cavan we get Cavana – the name of Trieste's old city and the place where its nighttown was situated. With the exception of Irish, the range of languages spoken during this episode – French, Spanish, Esperanto, Latin, German, Yiddish and Italian – are more representative of a Triestine reality than any Dublin one.[63] Towards the end of "Circe", Don Emile Patrizio Franz Rupert Pope Hennessy says "Werf those eykes to footboden, big grand porcos of johnyellows todos covered of gravy!" (*U*, 15.4508–9), and this is traditionally glossed as a polyglot mixture of "garbled German and Spanish".[64] Polyglot it is, but it is also, above all else, precisely the sort of mixture of languages Joyce would have heard late at night in the old city, where the Slovene members of the Austrian police struggled to use their little bit of German to keep the drunken Italians in order. The "porcos" derives from the Italian "porco" (pig), a word commonly used in curses and more particularly the Triestine "*El xe un gran porco*" – he is a (sexually) dirty man.

Again in *Finnegans Wake*, Joyce alludes to sexual issues in this passage brimming with Triestine echoes:

> Not to wandly be woking around jerumsalemdo at small hours about the murketplots, smelling okey boney, this little figgy and arraky belloky this little pink into porker but, porkodirto, to let the gentlemen pedestarolies out of Monabella culculpuration live his own left leave, cullebuone, by perperusual of the petpubblicities without inwoking his also's between (*sic*) the arraky bone and (*suc*) the okey bellock (*FW*, 368.9–15).

The "jerusalemdo" suggests of course Jerusalem, and by extension a place inhabited by Jews, a Jewish quarter. By the time Joyce came to Trieste, the old ghetto, abandoned by most of its original Jewish population but still commonly referred to (as it still is today) as the ghetto, was part of the seamier old city which housed the brothels. It was also close to the fruit markets (the "murketplots"). In the passage quoted above, Joyce clearly links the sale and "tasting" of fruit to the sale of women through a series of images and sexual innuendoes which a speaker of *Triestino* would easily spot. The "little figgy", apart from the obvious reference to the sweetest fruit of all, suggests the Triestine word "figa", deriving from the Latin "fica" or the Greek "pheke", both meaning vagina.[65] The "Okey boney" hides the *Triestino* "O che boni" (Oh how good they are) while the "arraky belloky" and the "arraky bone" perfectly reproduce the sound of the Triestine "Ara, che bello che" (Look how nice it [is]), and "Ara che bone" (Look how nice they [female] are). The "ara" is a Triestine word that does not exist in Italian, but that is also written with a double "r" by Joyce, who thus very subtly reproduces the sound an enthusiastic Triestine would make while admiring/tasting/enjoying something (or someone) he likes, or being admired, tasted, enjoyed by that same something or someone. The sexual innuendoes become more explicit as the passage progresses and the reader encounters "the little pink", which suggests the English slang for the little finger, while the "pedastarolies" points to pederasts, and the "Monabella" is perfect Triestine for "beautiful vagina" ("mona" being a Triestine version of "figa"); the "Cullebuone" suggests both the Italian "con le buone" (by fair means) and the Triestine "cul", meaning "arse", giving "nice arses", a meaning also hinted at in the "culculpuration".

The evident pleasure Joyce derived from this playing around with coarse Triestine expressions does not, of course, prove that he frequented any of the brothels in what a student of Stanislaus's described as "the most immoral city in Europe, worse than Berlin and Moscow".[66] At the same time, Stanislaus reports him as saying to Francini Bruni that "woman is an aperture. We make no difference between a whore and a wife except that a whore we have for five minutes and a wife for all our life."[67] Men of all backgrounds, married and single, visited Trieste's *Case di Tolleranza*, the carefully state-regulated brothels that are evoked in *Giacomo Joyce* in the description of the "kind gentlewomen wooing from their balconies with sucking mouths, the pox-fouled wenches and young wives that, gaily yielding to their ravishers, clip and clip again" (*GJ*, 9). Typical was Il Metro Cubo (The Cubic Metre), so called because of its cramped conditions. La Chiave d'Oro (The Golden Key), one of the few brothels not in the old city, was located behind a locksmiths owned by a certain Gottardo Artico on via del Solitario, just a few metres from where Joyce would live on via della Barriera Vecchia in 1910. The enormous key (the "chiave") at the front of his shop inspired much ironic comment, especially in the light of the Triestine word "ciavar", meaning "to screw". Joyce, who was well aware of this, included a phrase in

Finnegans Wake which is immediately linked to what is termed "the vice out of bridewell" (*FW*, 172.2–3), and which sounds exactly like what a Triestine prostitute might say when trying to chat up a client ("Ciao Ciavi?" – Hi, do you want to screw?) Soliciting was prohibited by law in Trieste, but even Stanislaus recalls an occasion on which he refused an explicit proposition made to him by "donne mascherate", that is, prostitutes with covered faces. The brothels were obliged to block all doors and windows and, as a result, were referred to as "case chiuse".[68]

The matter-of-fact manner with which Trieste dealt with sex as just another commodity on the market must have left an impression on Joyce, even if he never went near a brothel. In his diary Stanislaus mentions several times that he himself did *not* visit brothels, for instance when he speaks of "my prejudice against availing myself of whores, because they are the scapegoat class of humanity" or when he quotes a fellow teacher called Sholz who thought him very cute because he had saved a great deal of money during the winter "neither drinking nor whoring".[69] It would appear that Stannie was an exception among the young men of his generation in Trieste. There is also a passage in *Finnegans Wake* which suggests that "dear sweet Stainusless" certainly did not go whoring: "You are pure. You are in your puerity. You have not brought stinking members into the house of Amanti. Elleb Inam, Titep Notep, we name them to the Hall of Honour" (*FW*, 237.25–7). Stanislaus, therefore, has not been to the lover's house – "the house of Amanti" – and he has not met the prostitutes, Elleb Inam (belle mani, Italian for beautiful hands) or "Titep Notep" (petit peton, French for little feet,[70] but also Triestine for large breasts). These four words spelled backwards could be the names of prostitutes, especially as French names were *à la mode* for prostitutes in Trieste at this time.

6 *The Greeks – in the original*

Trieste as a multilingual, multi-ethnic, multicultural and multi-religious reality was for Joyce, from the very beginning, a rich field to observe. The first target of his attentions was the Greek community. As early as May 1905 he wrote to Stanislaus about one of his teaching colleagues jibing him about his strange interests: "He says I will die a Catholic because I am always moping in and out of the Greek churches" (*LII*, 89). But Joyce, as always, was observing in order to serve his creative needs.

The Greek presence in Trieste dates from the early eighteenth century and was strengthened by a second wave of settlers who arrived during the Greek War of Independence from 1821 to 1829.[71] They became an integral part of the city's economy, establishing themselves as merchants specializing in the trade of grain and tobacco with the Ottoman Empire, Albania, and southern Italy. Theirs was a powerful community with its own Greek-language newspaper *Nèa Imèra* ("New Day"), which from 1855 to 1912 was the principal organ of information for exiled Greeks in the Mediterranean area. In the mid-eighteenth century, the Oriental or Greek wing of the Orthodox Church split from the Serb wing and built the Chiesa della Santissima Trinità e San Nicolò, which became famous for its many artistic icons from Palestine, Asia Minor and Persia. As Trieste was a crossroads of so much trade with the East, hundreds of icons were donated to the community, many of which could not be accommodated in the Greek church and eventually found their way into the Catholic Cathedral of San Giusto and other Catholic churches.

Joyce had direct contact with a variety of members of the Greek community. Many years later he wrote to Harriet Shaw Weaver:

> I spoke or used to speak a modern Greek not too badly (I speak four or five languages fluently enough) and have spent a great deal of time with Greeks of all kinds from noblemen down to onionsellers, chiefly the latter. I am superstitious about them. They bring me luck. (*LI*, 167)

One of the onion sellers was a greengrocer named Nicolò Santos,[72] whose wife, who avoided going out in the sun in order to preserve her complexion, Joyce later used as a model for Molly Bloom. The nobles were Baron Ambrogio di Stefano Ralli and Count Francesco Sordina, who ardently admired Joyce's teaching abilities and later took their places among Joyce's more devoted private students and supporters.[73] Right from the start Sordina worked to better Joyce's situation in the Berlitz school:

> The director has offered to give me some furniture. He is very friendly with me because one of my pupils – Count Sordina has praised me very highly and brought several real live ladies and gentlemen of his acquaintance to the school. (*LII*, 123)

Ralli, a staunch pro-Austrian, lived on the very exclusive Piazza Scorcola, and when Joyce met him was about to inherit a fortune from his wealthy but ailing father, who died in 1907. In the early years of the century, the Ralli family were part of a small network of exceedingly rich pro-Austrian Greeks, the cream of Trieste's social élite, who were among those in control of the city's most important financial and insurance companies. The Rallis held an enormous share in the powerful Riunione Adriatica di Sicurtà (RAS), which was second only to Assicurazioni Generali – one of Europe's biggest insurers. They also played an important role in Assicurazioni Generali along with another of Joyce's Greek students, Baron Economo,[74] who married another Ralli, Eugenia, in 1905. But their influence went far beyond Trieste: through a series of careful marriages, the Rallis unified an empire that spread from Trieste beyond Austria, beyond the Mediterranean to England, France, and east to Turkey, Persia, Rumania, Russia and the East Indies.

Count Sordina's family originally came from Corfu but were long settled in Trieste, where they were major shareholders of the RAS and in Assicurazioni Generali. Sordina, later president of the local tramway company, was a pillar of Triestine high society. He served as one of the administrators of the modern art gallery, as a director of the Teatro Verdi, and was a member of the city's oldest and most prestigious gentleman's club, the Casino Vecchio. In 1890, along with Leo Economo, Augusto Cavallar and Otto von Lichtensteiger, father of Nelly von Lichtensteiger, Stanislaus Joyce's future wife, Sordina founded the Hippodrome at Montebello, where fashionable and popular horse-racing events were regularly held and occasionally attended by Joyce and Nora. Sordina was also president of the fencing club and the city's finest swordsman – "the only great champion in Trieste".[75] At any rate, Joyce appears to have been anything but overwhelmed by his student's high social place, and allows him just one dismissive comment in his Trieste notebook: "His books are dogeared."[76]

Aside from his friendships with various Greeks, the Greek world of Trieste and the rites of the Orthodox Church influenced Joyce and spurred him into adapting elements of his short story "The Sisters". He says as much in a letter to Stanislaus, in which he mentions how he started thinking about the story when he was at a Greek mass:

> While I was attending the Greek mass here last Sunday it seemed to me that my story *The Sisters* was rather remarkable. The Greek mass is strange. The altar is not visible but at times the priest opens the gates and shows himself. He opens and shuts them about six times. For the Gospel he comes out of a side gate and comes down into the chapel and reads out of a book. For the elevation he does the same.[77] (*LII*, 86)

Nothing in Joyce's writing, even in his letters, is accidental or simply occasional so this juxtaposition of "The Sisters" and the Greek rite demands

closer examination. In May–June 1906 Joyce added the following passage
when substantially rewriting the original version of the story which had been
published in *The Irish Homestead* on 13 August 1904:

> As I walked along in the sun I remembered old Cotter's words and tried to
> remember what had happened afterwards in the dream. I remembered that I had
> noticed long velvet curtains and a swinging lamp of antique fashion. I felt that
> I had been very far away, in some land where the customs were strange – in Per-
> sia, I thought. ... But I could not remember the end of the dream. (*D*, 5–6)

The additions are significant. Both the image of the curtains, which are suggestive of the doors of the iconostasis in the Greek Church, and the rather
exotic image of Persia, of a place "where the customs were strange", have
their roots in Trieste and more specifically in the Greek masses he attended
there.[78] In the later version of the story, the liturgy and liturgical imagery,
which owe as much to the Greek as to the Latin rite, are given a more central role: in the Greek rite, the priest is separated from the congregation by
means of the *iconostasis*, while Fr Flynn in "The Sisters" is hidden from the
street by the shutters and from his sisters by a wall, and both are seen to function as types of domesticated *iconostasis*. In the second version of the story
the guests are served with sherry, while in the final version they are also
offered cream crackers. In this way the story mirrors the Orthodox ceremony
of communion in which the brethren receive both bread and wine from a
chalice. Joyce mocked this ceremony in his letter to Stanislaus and trans-
formed it in "The Sisters", where the cream crackers and sherry come to represent the blood and wine.

   The changes Joyce put into this story along with his regular visits to the
Greek church show his ongoing interest in Christianity, and not merely as a
system from which to draw metaphors. Umberto Eco writes that Joyce
"abandons the faith but not religious obsession. The presence of an orthodox past reemerges constantly in all his works under the form of a personal
mythology and with a blasphemous fury that reveals the affective perma-
nence."[79] Stanislaus reveals that there was still a trace of rather idiosyncratic
faith behind Joyce's religious interest as late as 1907. According to what Stannie recorded, Joyce stated his belief that every man was religious and had in
his heart some faith in a deity. He did not exclude himself from this gener-
alization.[80] Stanislaus's anti-clericalism is well known and he certainly would
not have ascribed religious belief to his brother without having firm grounds
on which to base it. He also noted that James sometimes visited Catholic

churches, and, on one such occasion, the feast of the Madonna della Salute, accompanied Francini Bruni to hear mass in the Jesuit church.[81]

But even if he darkened the door of Catholic churches once in a while, Joyce's more sustained attention at this time was for the Greeks. Later he would draw on the impressions he was picking up in the Orthodox church and recycle them in *Ulysses*, where he mixed the doctrines of "The Roman Pontiffs and the Orthodox Churches" (*FW*, 307.17–18). The fact that he experienced the Greek mass for the first time in the Church of the Holy Trinity cannot have been lost on Joyce, especially as he would later make the Trinitarian theme so crucial to his artistic theory and would closely examine the doctrine of the Trinity in both *A Portrait of the Artist as a Young Man* and *Ulysses*.[82] Inside this church, at once familiar and unfamiliar, Joyce witnessed a rite that mirrored the Catholic mass and which, in its foreignness and difference, made him question the rites he had followed from birth, in a manner similar to that of the boy-narrator of "The Sisters":

> His questions showed me how complex and mysterious were certain institutions of the Church which I had always regarded as the simplest acts. The duties of the priest towards the Eucharist and towards the secrecy of the confessional seemed so grave to me that I wondered how anybody had ever found in himself the courage to undertake them. (*D*, 5)

Joyce's visits to the Orthodox churches showed him just how complex and mysterious were the Catholic rites he had always taken for granted. The difference he perceived in the Greek rite of St John Chrysostomos made him think anew about the more familiar Catholic equivalents, which in turn became strange to him.

Another result of this process of estrangement may have been to bring Joyce to look on the Greek Orthodox mass as something of a mockery of the Latin one, a mockery he would later find useful when writing the opening of "Telemachus": "He peered sideways up and gave a long slow whistle of call, then paused awhile in rapt attention, his even white teeth glistening here and there with gold points. Chrysostomos. Two strong shrill whistles answered through the calm" (*U*, 1.26–7). In this episode the golden-mouthed Greek Chrysostomos, in the guise of the false priest Buck Mulligan, is the celebrant. Photius, a later Patriarch of Constantinople, who initiated the schism which eventually led to the separation of the Greek and Roman Churches in 1054, is also identified with Mulligan, when Joyce writes of "Photius and the brood of mockers of whom Mulligan was one" (*U*,

1.656–7). The communion of that mass is, significantly, not only the Catholic bread, but also the Orthodox wine, with a stress on the wine:

> For this, O dearly beloved, is the genuine christine: body and soul and blood and ouns. Slow music, please. Shut your eyes, gents. One moment. A little trouble about those white corpuscles. Silence, all. (*U*, 1.21–3)

In "Scylla and Charybdis" Mulligan reappears in his priest-like role and is again identified with Photius by Stephen. And this is followed by another parody of an important Catholic rite – the Creed:

> He Who Himself begot middler the Holy Ghost and Himself sent Himself, Agenbuyer, between Himself and others, Who, put upon by His fiends, stripped and whipped, was nailed like bat to barndoor, starved on crosstree, Who let Him bury, stood up, harrowed hell, fared into heaven and there these nineteen hundred years sitteth on the right hand of His Own Self but yet shall come in the latter day to doom the quick and dead when all the quick shall be dead already. (*U*, 9.493–9)

Joyce also drew on his own experience as an outsider, a spectator and observer at the Greek liturgies in Trieste, when writing about Leopold Bloom attending the Catholic mass in St Andrews Church in Westland Row in "Lotus Eaters" and later Paddy Dignam's funeral in "Hades". Joyce's own letter describing the Greek rite and Bloom's description of the Catholic mass contain a similar mixture of unreliable description coupled with sometimes erroneous deduction and comment. In his letter, Joyce notes that "the Greek Mass is strange", while Bloom feels something very similar: ("Queer the whole atmosphere") and later thinks it would be "More interesting if you understood what it was all about" (*U*, 5.392 and 423–4). Particularly similar are Joyce's and Bloom's descriptions of communion. In Joyce's letter of April 1905 it is as follows:

> At the end when he has blessed the people he shuts the gates: a boy comes running down the side of the chapel with a large tray full of little lumps of bread. The priest comes after him and distributes the lumps to scrambling believers. Damn droll! The Greek priest has been taking a great eyeful out of me: two haruspieces. (*LII*, 86)

The "little lumps of bread" which Joyce took to be communion were in fact *antidoron* (blessed bread), as the Greeks received communion very irregularly. In *Ulysses*, as Bloom watches the priest distribute communion, he does not know the name of the ciborium, which he calls the "thing":

A batch knelt at the altarrails. The priest went along by them, murmuring, holding the thing in his hands. He stopped at each, took out a communion, shook a drop or two (are they in water?) off it and put it neatly into her mouth. (*U*, 5.343–6)

7 *His Bacchic indulgence*

If Joyce occasionally spent his days visiting churches in search of spiritual inspiration he more often spent his nights wandering from bar to bar looking for liquid consolation. After work, if he did not drink at home, which he often did, particularly in the summer of 1905, he headed out to one of Trieste's many bars. It was in this period, according to Francini Bruni, that "he reached the summit of his Bacchic indulgence. A litre of Opollo wine and later a flask of Tuscan had a place of honor on his work table."[83] Joyce liked to go to the *cità vecia* (the old city, in *Triestino*) and although he already had plenty of experience to draw on from Dublin, it seems likely that the environment he found there cannot but have helped him to create *Ulysses,* and in particular the latter part of "Oxen of the Sun" as well as "Circe" with its loud confusion of drunken navvies, prostitutes, policemen, loiterers and hangers-on. He revelled in this confusion and felt no pressure to adhere to the quiet and orderly world which was so deeply important to the middle classes and to his brother Stanislaus, who with Francini Bruni now tried to rein him in. Joyce ignored their reproofs and oscillated between spending drunken nights with sailors and workers in Cavana – the centre of the old city – and sitting in the poorer seats at the theatre, from where he enviously eyed his rich pupils in the best seats. He would never properly belong to either group, as his education set him apart from the workers and his obvious poverty, his constant borrowing, and his threadbare clothes underlined the social gap between him and the prosperous families he taught.

According to Francini Bruni, "Joyce drank absinthe, whisky, little wine; drank sligovic, a liquor like whisky, made with prune alcohol."[84] Stanislaus wrote of Joyce's excessive habits in the 1905–6 period: "Jim went out at night until one or two o'clock, ranging from one smoky pothouse or low bar to another, and then came falling in about the place, or I went out to look for him."[85] Joyce would have been delighted with the choice of bars in Trieste. Indeed, what Bloom says of Dublin – "Good puzzle would be cross Dublin without passing a pub" (*U*, 4.129–30) – was equally true of Trieste, which boasted over six hundred different *osterie, birrerie* and *trattorie*.[86] They were often staffed by former sailors, many of whom spoke German, Hungarian, French and English. Joyce's budget usually allowed for visits to the more modest drinking houses in the c*ità vecia*, which were known as *bettole* (dives) or *petesserie*, rough places where one went to drink "Petess" (the cheapest brew), named from the French *pète-sec*, meaning "strong man". Joyce often chose to dine in the open air outside what Stannie describes as "a workman's Trattoria", where they would eat badly with Stanislaus fretting all the while that he might be spotted in this down-market dive by some of his snobbish students.

One of Joyce's regular haunts was L'Osteria alla città di Parenzo on via del Ponte, which sold his favourite white Opollo wine and remained open until two in the morning. Another spot he liked was Il Ristorante Bonavia, which served both Italian and German food and was one of the first places in Trieste to have electric lighting. He also went regularly to the Trattoria Viola for both lunch and dinner and occasionally to the more expensive Ristorante Berger, in Stannie's words "a middling good restaurant in the centre of the city".[87] Other haunts included Ai tre pompieri, Ai due Dalmati and Ai due Leoni; this last advertised regularly in the socialist newspaper *Il Lavoratore* and was quite a fine restaurant with a pleasant summer garden and an exceptionally large selection of wines and beers. He may also have visited the Osteria al Bon Citadin (the good citizen's) on via Crocifisso, and he certainly imbibed at Andemo de Toni, Andemo de Nini, and Andemo de Pepi,[88] a bar more formally known as l'Osteria de Pepi Sofita, which has been vividly described as follows:

> At the back were the wine casks, then the counter to drink at, some wooden tables to sit at and in the middle a picture of the emperor Franz Joseph. [...] During the day it was full of porters from the council and in the evening there were many arty types – members of the theatre chorus, painters and poets.[89]

One positive feature of Joyce's experience in Trieste's bars was that he enjoyed good relations with the bar keepers, who were considerably more generous in allowing him credit than their Dublin counterparts had been. He was particularly friendly with a Sicilian who kept a bar on via Belvedere:

> During his many reconnoitres around Trieste he had discovered among the various bartenders and tipplers a certain Sicilian tavern owner whom he nicknamed "Storky." He wanted me to meet him. His place was in via Belvedere. He was a chubby little barrel, rosy as a doll's face, with two little elf's eyes in

which all the alertness and craftiness of his race shone. He was all eyes when it came to checking on the crew camped among the vats. His nickname fit him perfectly because he had a strange way of carrying his neck to one side and of standing balanced on one foot when he was listening to someone, just like a stork.

"It takes one to know one, Joyce," I told him. "Storky is a character but, admit it, you are one, too." And Joyce would laugh, his chin protruding like an old shrew's. He laughed because, although already drunk and glassy-eyed, he enjoyed stuffing poor Storky's head with extraordinary stories about the Emerald Isle. He would go on and on with a loquacity well oiled by wine. Storky, who was the only sober one among that unsteady herd, became stupefied. Without understanding a particle of what Joyce was saying, he would smile and say, "What things you know."[90]

At the end of a night's drinking, Francini Bruni and later Stanislaus sometimes had to go and drag a drunken Joyce home. Luckily for them and for Nora, Joyce "was never at any time in his life a belligerent drunk but rather a floppy, public one. As he weighed so little, he was often carried home by friends and put to bed. The next day when he awoke, he was complaining – his eyes hurt and so on – but he was not, by all accounts, surly."[91]

Very occasionally, he went drinking early in the day and was unable to get through his lessons, as one student remembered:

> One day while teaching he slumped to the ground without a word. The family, from the respectable middle class, urgently sent for a doctor in panic. He diagnosed alcoholic poisoning, possibly complicated by malnutrition.[92]

Some nights he did not go straight home from the bars but, much to Francini Bruni's chagrin, joined in with the revellers who spilled out onto the streets and continued singing. Among the favourite choruses was "La Vergine degli Angeli" from Verdi's opera *La forza del Destino*. The choice of songs was not always so highbrow, however, and songs in Triestine dialect were very popular:

> I had to accept the situation and smell Joyce's alcoholic breath, while in chorus with the other drunkards he roared a high-pitched out-of-tune,
> Ancora un litro de quel bon...[93]

As the following article from *Il Piccolo* in May 1905 shows, Francini Bruni was not the only one to register his disapproval:

> Many citizens have complained to us that they are not able to sleep on Saturday, Sunday or very often on Monday nights. On every street where there are

a couple of *Osterie* (and what street in Trieste does not have them?), at a certain hour of the night there is always someone who has the vocation to try to
be Tamagno: sometimes two or three feel the desire, and when the noise is at
its worst, it is not rare that some Bellincioni or some Patti joins in. The programme does not vary much, and usually ends with the piece it started out
with, that is the noble song dedicated to Antonio Freno; nor are the musical
effects very varied, all of them are out of tune. Nonetheless this monotony is
not even capable of inducing sleep, and if these "divi" of the little streets would
stay quiet a moment, they would probably hear their listeners hissing in their
beds like vipers. It would be better if the police asked these errant swans to
respect the night peace, which at least two nights a week is violated in Trieste
as in no other city on this earth.[94]

In certain *osterie* popular with the socialists the singing took on political
overtones, and the Austrian police kept a close eye on what was happening.
A police report referred to these bars as

> the usual hangouts of anarchists and socialists, who cursed God, incited hos-
> tility towards those from different classes of civilized society and mocked the
> doctrines and beliefs of a religion legally recognized by the state, supplying
> clear evidence of crimes under article 122 and offences listed in articles 302 and
> 303 of the Penal Code of the Empire.[95]

Through visiting these *osterie*, Joyce absorbed much of Trieste's socialist
political culture.

8 *Socialistic tendencies*

There were many avenues to socialism open to Joyce in this growing city
with its sizeable modern proletariat of, by 1910, some 30,000 industrial
workers.[96] Trieste was a place where grinding poverty, serious unemployment
and chronic housing shortages existed side by side with ostentatious wealth
(it had more millionaires per capita than any other city in the Austro-Hungarian Empire). To be labelled a socialist in turn-of-the-century Trieste could
have meant a variety of things – being a card-carrying member of the 3000-
strong Socialist Party, attending the lectures organized by the Socialist study
circle, buying the right books, reading *L'Avanti!* and *Il Lavoratore*,[97] or simply drinking, as Joyce did, in the right bars.

The first place Joyce came into direct contact with socialists was at the
Berlitz school, where Artifoni[98] had placed a large life-sized picture of
"Benoit Malon, a famous French writer, socialist, and economist", in the

entrance hall.[99] The school had close contacts with the free socialist newspaper *Il Diritto*, which was published by *la Società di protezione fra impiegati civili* (the society for the protection of clerks).[100] *Il Diritto*, known for its fiery editorials, argued against party politics and urged the masses of workers to rise and overthrow the meagre group of idlers who exploited them. The Berlitz school advertised regularly in this paper and offered readers a 30 per cent discount on English courses, so Joyce would have taught many of the society's members, perhaps discussed socialist ideas with them and listened to their first-hand accounts of the paltry lot of poorly paid minor clerks, mere cogs in a great bureaucratic machine, the kind of people who make up one of the key social groups represented in *Dubliners*. They may even have given him the idea for the hopeless situation in which Farrington, the copy clerk, finds himself in "Counterparts".

Trieste's socialists had organized a successful general strike in 1902 and now were waiting for the day when the workers would unite to overthrow the bourgeoisie. For Joyce's superior, Comrade Bertelli, there was an almost Viconian inevitability that the tides of time would turn in their favour:

> And as the Eastern civilization had to cede its position to the Greeks and die in the mud of its corruption, so the Greek civilization, after a glorious reign which still astounds us, fell in its turn to the Romans, but that same Roman civilization fell when its mission was accomplished, as did the feudal civilization, and so too will the bourgeois fall. Not because men want it to be so, but because it is inevitable, because everything evolves, because everything finishes by yielding its place to something new which makes itself known. No power can stop this immense wheel from turning.[101]

A sustained campaign of propaganda aimed at rousing the proletariat helped keep the immense wheel turning. The highlight of the year was May Day, a strictly observed holiday:

> The first of May – By now it is a major celebration of the modern age: a celebration similar to what Christmas and Easter used to be. All the shops were strictly kept closed. [...] The whole city was swarming with people. [...] There was a considerable number of workers at the assembly organized by the socialist party in piazza di Foraggi. Mr Pittoni spoke first, illustrating the human idea behind the May Day celebrations. [...] Finally Mr Cicotti exorted people to protest in favour of Maxim Gorky and the Russian intellectuals who were being persecuted. All the speakers were applauded.[102]

Gorky was a particular favourite. In May 1905 his *L'Albergo dei Poveri* was presented to shouts of "Viva Gorky" and his *Nei Bassi Profundi* was also well

received; indeed, "as soon as the curtain went up the public burst into fre-
netic applause shouting, 'Long live Gorky! Long live the Russian Revolution!
We want Gorky free!'"[103]

The very active interest in Trieste in the Russian writers is mirrored in
Joyce's own reading at this time and in what he says in his letter of September 1905 to Stanislaus: "I think many admire [Turgenev] because he is 'gentlemanly' just as they admire Gorky because he is 'ungentlemanly'. Talking
of Gorky what do you think of him? He has a great name with Italians" (*LII*,
106). Joyce's own favourite remained Tolstoy, whom he termed "a magnificent writer".

The most powerful and constant means of spreading socialist thought in
Trieste was through public lectures organized by the *Circolo di studi sociali*.
In common with the evening school run by the Society for the Protection of
Clerks (where both Artifoni and Joyce would later teach), the aim of these
lectures was to bring about emancipation through education. Yet some peo-
ple complained that the lectures were too difficult for the proletariat, who
were more interested in the bread-and-butter issues of wages and conditions.
As one critic noted:

> Yes, the lectures were many and very nice, but they served only to entertain a
> hundred or so intellectuals. People did not take part en masse because they did
> not understand a damn thing about any of the admirable subjects being
> addressed by the valiant lecturers.[104]

These meetings seem to have been characterized by a problem which was the
exact opposite of the one encountered by Mr Duffy in "A Painful Case",
when he attending meetings of "an Irish Socialist party" where "the workmen's discussions, he said, were too timorous; the interest they took in the
question of wages was inordinate. He felt that they were hard-featured real-
ists and that they resented an exactitude which was the product of a leisure
not within their reach. No social revolution, he told her, would be likely to
strike Dublin for some centuries" (*D*, 107).

Regular large-scale public lectures were also held in these years and given
by figures of the stature of Arturo Labriola, Enrico Ferri, Angelica Bala-
banoff, and Guglielmo Ferrero, who also wrote articles for *Il Piccolo della
Sera*. From Rome in August 1906 Joyce instructed Stanislaus: "If there is anything interesting (Ferrero etc) in the *Piccolo della Sera*, you might send it"
(*LII*, 152); he had already become well acquainted with Ferrero's work while
in Trieste.

Ferrero's influence on Joyce was immediate, and the Irish writer was pleased to admit that he had taken the idea for "Two Gallants" from him, as Susan Humphreys has pointed out:

> By saying that Ferrero gave him the idea for "Two Gallants," the young and unknown Joyce did two things: first, he identified his beliefs with ideas of a famous and daring contemporary; second, he underlined the social purpose of the story. In both cases he may have overemphasized the debt, but at this point in his life he still considered himself a socialist and saw literature as a political act in the plainest sense.[105]

There is some disagreement today among critics as to which of Ferrero's books inspired Joyce. Susan Humphreys and Giorgio Melchiori are among those who claim that the likely source of influence was Ferrero's *Il Militarismo*, which contained a passionate attack on militarism, expressed the hope that twentieth century would see the end of soldiering and war, and asserted that "the habit of arms and the perils of war can be combined with great moral cowardice".[106] According to Melchiori, *Il Militarismo* not only suggested "Two Gallants" but also provided Joyce "with arguments against the shocked British printer who was refusing to print the story".[107] In May 1906 Joyce wrote to Grant Richards, stating, of this printer, that the "idea of gallantry has grown up in him (probably) during the reading of the novels of the elder Dumas and during the performance of romantic plays which presented him cavaliers and ladies in full dress. But I am sure he is willing to modify his fantastic view. I would strongly recommend to him the chapters wherein Ferrero examines the moral code of the soldier and (incidentally) of the gallant. But it would be useless for I am sure that in his heart of hearts he is a militarist" (*LII*, 133). Stanislaus Joyce wrote that "The idea for 'Two Gallants' came from the mention of the relations between Porthos and the wife of a tradesman in *The Three Musketeers*, which my brother found in Ferrero's *Europa Giovane*". While no direct reference to this is to be found in *L'Europa Giovane*, there is one in the third chapter of *Il Militarismo*, entitled "Le civiltà militari", devoted to "Officers and women in the seventeenth century". Melchiori reports that "The section opens with a reference to the 'Memoirs of Seigneur D'Artagnan, Lieutenant-Captain of the First Company of the Royal Musketeers' and quotes directly from it: 'The famous hero of Dumas' novel is not a fiction but a historical character who, even if he did not accomplish the extraordinary actions devised by the novelist, was a man who ate, drank and wore clothes.'"[108] According to Melchiori:

Ferrero then insists on the sociological relevance of these memoirs, even if they are considered spurious, in describing the life of the small country gentry whose younger sons "were drawn by poverty or ambition to Paris, serving as lower officers in the king's army." As an example of the degraded moral standards of this society, Ferrero relates that, considering the mercantile class as their inferiors, "these officers, being short of money to pay for the dissolute lives they were leading, tried, nearly all of them, to become the lovers of rich middle-class ladies, getting money out of them as a recompense for the honour conferred upon those ladies by condescending to make them their mistresses" (*Il Miltarismo*, 129–30).[109]

While Joyce's story is not, of course, about "officers" or "rich midle-class ladies" it does adopt the dynamics and motives described above and transfers them successfully to a couple of Dublin layabouts and a slavey. As Humphreys writes:

> Joyce's story subjects all senses of the word "gallant" to irony, including its connotations of military bravery, nobility of conduct, glamorous appearance, and chivalrous treatment of women. To this he adds political implications; it is, as he said, "an Irish landscape," and he is setting up the same sort of social-political-sexual connections that Ferrero makes in all his early books. The gallants, living by a soldier's base code of honor, milk and corrupt the servant girl. According to Ferrero's theories, Corley and Lenehan, a brute and a leech, are primitive or uncivilized men, and they sponge and destroy as though looting a conquered city. "Two Gallants" is a political statement in Ferrero's terms; it indicates a primitive condition of society which must be reformed if old Europe is to compete with *l'Europa giovane*.[110]

L'Europa Giovane also played an important role in Joyce's creative consciousness in these years. Robert Spoo sees this book as having influenced the later stories of *Dubliners*, and finds in it a source for one of Joyce's more mysterious titles, "A Little Cloud", which he added to the story in early 1906, after he had read Ferrero's book.[111] Spoo quotes Ferrero as follows: "What are the greatest conceptions of the human spirit before the infinite reality of life? A little cloud [una piccola nuvoletta] against the unbounded expanse of the sky; a breath disperses it and no human eye will see it more."[112] In *L'Europa Giovane* Ferrero defined young Europe as northern, Germanic Europe, which he saw as being modern, progressive, industrialized and open to the influence of socialism, culturally distant from Southern or Latin Europe. One critic has said that "Two Gallants" "can be viewed as a fictional footnote to Ferrero's book, and Joyce's intention appears to have been to assign to Ireland both

Germanic and Latin attributes, as far as his psychological depiction of her is concerned".[113] In this regard, it is not without note that Trieste, a cultural crossroads between two great cultural traditions, was the perfect ground on which to test Ferrero's ideas about the differences between old and young Europe. Giulio Caprin saw the city's problems in these very terms, writing of "this Italian city in Austria which suffered as a result of the fatal incompatibility between its Italian spirit and the Austrian system, between Latinism and Germanism".[114]

Try though they did the socialists could not ignore these tensions and they were increasingly being forced to come to terms with irredentism. Many began to believe that the aim of getting Trieste out of the Austrian Empire would have to be achieved before the emancipation of the masses could be realized. The party leader Valentino Pittoni tried to appease this element when he addressed the Socialist Congress in Trieste on 21 May 1905:

> We live politically in Austria, but in the field of culture and socialist thought we live at the sides of our companions in Italy. [...] Our Italianness pulsates with a feeling of socialist solidarity, the national spirit unites in the international spirit and saturates it with a socialist spirit.[115]

With irredentism an increasingly important factor, the Triestine socialists continued to campaign against their three traditional enemies: the rich local aristocracy; the Catholic Church, which they saw as being in the pocket of the Austrians and on the side of the Slovene nationalists;[116] and the middle-class irredentists, whose movement they saw as being "the most cretinous of stupidities [...] the spanner in the works of socialism",[117] and "the microbe of national hatred which obstructs the organization of the proletariat".[118]

The socialists' objections to irredentism made sound economic sense: they feared that "Trieste, cut off from the nexus of the empire, would stand to lose a major part of its commercial importance".[118] They suggested a different type of irredentism – not an exasperated nationalism but an attempt at achieving a federation of free nations:

> Real Irredentism would be the socialist one, which is summed up in Janrès formula for Alsace–Lorraine: "That peoples, freed from the yoke of politics and economics, be free to choose on their own the groupings they wished to belong to."[120]

However, the Triestine socialists were not above a little compromise or even connivance, particularly after the arrival in October 1904 of "*Il Principe*

Rosso" (the Red Prince), Lieutenant Governor Konrad von Hohenlohe-Schillingsfürst, who worked behind the scenes with them and, in return for being guaranteed a muted opposition to his 1906 bill to limit the automony of Trieste, helped them win an historic victory over the Liberal Nationalists in the parliamentary elections of 1907. This victory was also facilitated by the introduction of universal suffrage, which the socialists had long campaigned for. Now that more people had the vote, they were happy to use it to remove Felice Venezian's Liberal Nationalist party, whose total lack of a social policy contributed significantly to its undoing in this election. The socialists brilliantly exploited Venezian's careless comment that "We will give our superfluous wealth to the poor" by publishing a "poster caricaturing Venezian sitting at a banquet and eating the flesh off a chicken while tossing the bones to a poor woman carrying a child".[121]

Long before he went to Rome, these events in Trieste afforded Joyce the opportunity to become familiar with opinions that were similar to and probably informed his own, and that allowed him to add flesh to his 1905 claim to Stanislaus that he was "a socialistic artist" (*LII*, 89). When from Rome Joyce asked his brother if he had seen that there was "a split in the socialistic camp here between Ferri and your friend Labriola?" (*LII*, 152), it was evident that they had both become familiar with these two important Italian socialist leaders while in Trieste. Labriola lectured there on Napoleon III in January 1906 while Ferri, who spoke many times in Trieste in 1905 and 1906, later described holding a lecture in the Politeama Rossetti on Garibaldi as one of his greatest satisfactions as a public speaker.

There are valid reasons for qualifying the traditional view that Joyce's interest in socialism matured when he was in Rome. It is true that his involvement reached its climax and anticlimax there, but the plot had been brewing from his last years in Dublin and really took shape in Trieste. Already in Rome his reports of the Socialist Congress were somewhat critical, although he still warmed to certain of the more important themes under discussion:

> I am following with interest the struggle between the various socialist parties here at the Congress. Labriola spoke yesterday, the paper says, with extraordinarily rapid eloquence for two hours and a half. He reminds me somewhat of Griffith. He attacked the intellectuals and the parliamentary socialists. He belongs or is leader of the sindacalists. They are trades-unionists or rather trade-unionists with a definite anti-social programme. Their weapons are unions and strikes. They decline to interfere in politics or religion or legal

questions. They do not desire the conquest of public powers which, they say, only serve in the end to support the middle-class government. They assert that they are the true socialists because they wish the future social order to proceed equally from the overthrow of the entire present social organisation and from the automatic emergence of the proletariat in trades-unions and guilds and the like. Their objection to parliamentarianism seems to me well-founded but if, as all classes of socialists agree, a general European war, an international war, has become an impossibility I do not see how a general international strike or even a general national strike is a possibility. (*LII*, 173–4)

Six months later, in March 1907, Joyce's doubts about socialist ideas had grown to such an extent that he wrote to Stanislaus that "The interest I took in socialism and the rest has left me. [...] I have no wish to codify myself as an anarchist or socialist or reactionary" (*LII*, 217). Back in Trieste, just three weeks later, he dismayed his socialist friends by writing his first article for the irredentist *Il Piccolo della Sera* on Fenianism.

The fact remains, however, that for almost three years Joyce called himself a socialist, even if, as Stanislaus and many other critics have attested, he attached "himself to no school of socialism".[122] Beyond his sympathies for various mainstream Italian socialist thinkers, Joyce's socialist views may have owed more to Trieste than has previously been recognized. Like the Triestine socialists he believed in economic liberation, in avoiding the clash of nationalisms, in pacifism; like them he was dubious about what results parliamentary action could bring and favoured union agitation. But as time passed he came to witness, with some distaste, the fudging of central issues at the Socialist Congress in Rome and the awkwardness with which the Triestine socialists attempted to manoeuvre around the inexorable rise of nationalism. By the time he came to write *Ulysses,* he had long abandoned the absolutism of his pronouncements on socialism of this early period. Socialist discourse by then had become for him just another limited set of beliefs to draw on. And yet, the characters of all of his works are working-class or lower-middle-class people, often poor and struggling to come to terms with the issues that dominated socialist talk in Trieste – a betterment of their lot, the problem of nationalism, the issue of marriage, and the heavy-handed influence of the Catholic Church (in his diary, Stanislaus noted his brother's belief that "there was no thinking proleteriat" in Ireland, a fact which he blamed on the stifling power of the priests).[123]

More than any other character, Leopold Bloom is a product of what Joyce heard in Trieste in these years. Bloom's ideas, more than just a political code, were in reality a mode of living and of being. Central to them was the belief in freedom and the rejection of nationality, of persecution, of "perpetuating national hatred among nations" (*U*, 12.1417–18), all concepts which owed much to what Joyce would have heard in Trieste about the "microbe of national hatred" which so offended the socialists there.

> — But do you know what a nation means? says John Wyse.
> — Yes, says Bloom.
> — What is it? says John Wyse.
> — A nation? says Bloom. A nation is the same people living in the same place (*U*, 12.1419–23).

Bloom's answer is exactly that which a Triestine socialist would have given. Members of many diverse nationalities lived within the city and the socialists hoped to contain them all through openness, economic progress and *Municipalismo* – the long-established idea that the municipality of Trieste was capable of embracing different peoples and traditions. This idea was rejected by the irredentists, who looked on their socialist counterparts as traitors (later in *Ulysses* Bloom's fidelity to Ireland would be called into question in similiar fashion by the Citizen). The socialists' aspiration "that peoples, freed from the yoke of politics and economics, would choose, on their own, their own groupings" is very close to Bloom's but it was mocked by the irrendentists in Trieste just as it is mocked by the nationalists in Barney Kiernan's:

> By God, then, says Ned, laughing, if that's so I'm a nation for I'm living in the same place for the past five years. (*U*, 12.1424–5)

Finally, some of the utopian social-democratic ideals expressed by the socialists – who, according to Stanislaus, took refuge in "philosophical politics and talk about equality and brotherly love"[124] and felt that everybody was entitled to a dignified standard of living, that different races should be able to live in common, that the products of industrial progress should be open to all, that war must never be allowed to happen again, that the role of the Church must be separated from that of the state – are also attributed to Bloom:

> I stand for the reform of municipal morals and the plain ten commandments. New worlds for old. Union of all, jew, moslem and gentile. Three acres and a cow for all children of nature. Saloon motor hearses. Compulsory manual labour for all. All parks open to the public day and night. Electric dishscrubbers. Tuberculosis, lunacy, war and mendicancy must now cease. General

amnesty, weekly carnival with masked licence, bonuses for all, esperanto[125] the universal language with universal brotherhood. No more patriotism of bar-spongers and dropsical impostors. Free money, free rent, free love and a free lay church in a free lay state. (*U*, 15.1685–93)

9 *Waiting for a breakthrough*

Bloom, however, was a long way off and for now *Dubliners* remained fore-most in Joyce's mind. He continued to work well on his stories, noting that he was able to "write much better now than when I was in Dublin" (*LII*, 92). Gorman reports that he later "recalled with some nostalgia calm evenings when he had strolled along the Triestine streets and thought over the phrases in his stories".[126] In September 1905, refreshed by the arrival of the Bora, he had taken advantage of the fact that Stanislaus was still in Dublin by send-ing him a list of details to check out for the stories before he came to Trieste. Joyce was confident that *Dubliners* would be published and that this event would save them all. "If *Dubliners* is published next spring I hope to be able to help you to get out of your swamp" (*LII*, 105), he wrote to Stanislaus, but he obviously had his own swamp in mind as well. When his brother was preparing to come to Trieste, Joyce warned him not to carry any of the man-uscripts, stressing that "They are our only hope for the future" (*LII*, 121).

And so he worked through the autumn and early winter, refining and putting the stories in order until he had brought the collection to a satisfac-tory close. He sent the whole lot off to Grant Richards in November. Christ-mas came and went but he had still received no reply. He sent a reminder and an additional story – "Two Gallants" – in January, and Richards finally replied in February; his reaction was so positive that Joyce did not think twice about sending off yet another extra story, "A Little Cloud". He even suggested to Richards that if the book "had any sale in England you might perhaps be able to arrange an edition for America where there are some fif-teen millions of my countrymen" (*LII*, 131). In response to Richards's idea that he write an autobiographical novel, Joyce informed him that he had already embarked on such a project and had written 914 pages.

In this hopeful atmosphere, which made his teaching and his difficulties with Nora more bearable, Joyce began to take singing lessons. He talked a lot about music at this time and his main interest was in tenors. According to Stanislaus, Jim thought most sopranos "simply screeched" and listened to

baritones with displeasure. In order to improve his own "voce tenorile" he
went to Francesco Riccardo Sinico (1869–1949), who praised his voice but
told him he would need two years to train it properly. Predictably, neither
Joyce nor Stanislaus had enough money to enable him to persevere, but for
as long as the lessons lasted he was lucky to be taught by the heir to an illustrious musical dynasty that had been teaching music in Trieste for three generations.[127] Indeed Sinico, the most distinguished singing teacher of his time
in Trieste, the principal music teacher in the Scuola Popolare and choirmaster of the Greek and Serb Orthodox church choirs as well as of the second
Jewish synagogue, made such an impression on the writer that he took the
unusual step of using his name for Captain and Emily Sinico in "A Painful
Case".

Joyce also took the time now to enjoy some of the theatre on offer during the autumn and winter. Among the highlights of the opera season were
Massenet's *Werther*, which Joyce and Nora attended. In 1909, Joyce wrote
twice of this to Nora: "Do you remember that Sunday evening coming back
from *Werther* when the echo of the sad deathlike music was still playing in
our memories ..." (*LII*, 256); and later: "I have just wired you the beautiful
motive from the last act of the opera you like so much *Werther*: 'Nel lieto dì
pensa a me'" (*LII*, 281). Other highlights included Rossini's *Il Barbiere di
Siviglia*, Bellini's *La Sonnambula*, Donizetti's *l'Elisir d'amore* and *Navarese*,
Thomas's *Mignon*, Leoncavallo's *I Pagliacci* and, at Christmas, Wagner's
Siegfried. A number of interesting plays were staged, particularly in the
Teatro Goldoni and the Teatro Verdi, including Gorky's *L'Albergo dei Poveri*,
Tolstoy's *Resurrection*, a work he liked, and Gerhardt Hauptmann's *Rosa
Bernd*, a copy of which he bought the following October in Rome and
warmly praised. Joyce was an old fan of Hauptmann, having translated his
Before Sunrise and *Michael Kramer* while he was still at university in Dublin.
He may also have attended the season of D'Annunzio's plays which included
La Gioconda, La Fiaccola sotto il Moggio and *La Figlia di Jorio*.

The wealth of entertainment that Trieste offered is well illustrated by taking a look at just a couple of the productions on offer in the first week of
December 1905. On 5 December Eleonora Duse,[128] performing in *La Moglie
di Claudio*, clashed with Gustav Mahler, who came to conduct the Orches-
trale Triestina in a concert that comprised works by Mozart and Beethoven
and his own Fifth Symphony. This concert was the brainchild of an acquaintance of Joyce's, a certain Enrico Schott,[129] who had formed *Il Comitato per i
concerti sinfonici* along with other patrons of the arts in the city. On the next

night there was a production of Suppé's operetta *In cerca di felicità* in the
Fenice, and "La Duse" appeared in Renan's *L'abbadessa di Jouarre* and *La
Locandiera*. Given that Joyce regularly mentions Renan in his letters and
judged him to be "a good writer" (*LII,* 57), he would have had good reasons
for attending. Other highlights of the same week were Ibsen's *Rosmersholm,*
Shaw's *Eroi* and the *feérie* (fairy play) *Ali-Babà.*[130]

But Joyce could not distract himself indefinitely. In February 1906, partly
to ease their financial problems, partly to provide Nora with some company
during the long day at home with Giorgio, they followed Francini Bruni's
suggestion that they share a flat together, and later in the same month they
all (including Stanislaus and Francini Bruni's wife Clotilde and son Daniele)
went to live in number 1 via Giovanni Boccaccio. This did not prove to be a
very successful move; in fact Francini Bruni later termed it "the most tor-
mented period of our communal life".[131] He and Joyce were a volatile combination, and Nora did not get on well with her husband's friend, although
she did learn some Italian from Clotilde.

There was one positive element in their cohabitation with their Italian
friends, however: Joyce was afforded ample opportunity to improve his Italian, resuming the lessons in Italian language and literature which he had
begun with Francini Bruni in the early days in Pola. Evidence for this is to
be found in the large notebook with the title "Italiano" written in Joyce's
hand and containing three sections, as follows: pages 2 to 69, which contain
an eclectic variety of passages in Italian and a series of useful Italian exercises
in idioms and commonplace phrases; page 135, devoted to French language
exercises; and pages 244 to 274, containing German vocabulary. The remaining pages are blank.[132] The Scholes catalogue states that the notebook was
"begun in 1904",[133] and it is clear that substantial parts were written as late
as 1910.[134] According to Joyce's annotations, the Italian passages are taken
from the following works: Luigi Barzini's *La Metà del Mondo,* Raffaello For-
naciari's *Letteratura Italiana,* Gabrielle D'Annunzio's *Il Trionfo della Morte,*
Libero Merlino's *I Principi dell'Anarchia,* Torquato Tasso's *Aminta,* Giacomo
Leopardi's *Pensieri,* A.C. Firmani's *Tacito e le sue opere,* Paolo Giacometti's *La
Morte Civile,* Brunetto Latini's *Il Libro delle Bestie,*[135] and Francesco Bricolo's
I Drammi dell'Irlanda (in reality this book was written by Lucien Thomin
and translated by Bricolo). These passages were either copied out by Joyce or
perhaps taken down by him as dictations during his lessons with Francini
Bruni. Each page contains several carefully noted corrections which are
partly in Joyce's hand and partly written by somebody else, presumably

Francini. Apart from improving Joyce's use of Italian language, these exercises enriched his knowledge of Italian and classical thought. They reveal his enduring fascination with the Italian language and his eagerness to become acclimatized with the colour of its dialects – mainly Tuscan and Triestine. The notebook is also telling evidence that Joyce was not simply gifted at languages but was also ready to put in the hours of study necessary to improve his knowledge.

Whatever satisfaction Joyce may have drawn from these studies, his anxiety for news about the publication of *Dubliners* grew as the months passed without any decision being reached. Everything depended on it being accepted by Grant Richards as another publisher he had approached, William Heinemann, had already rejected it. In February Richards wrote ominously to say that he could not print *Chamber Music* unless Joyce contributed to the costs. But the even worse news arrived on 23 April, when Richards wrote again to tell Joyce that the printer was not willing to set *Dubliners* unless Joyce made several changes, particularly to "Two Gallants" and "Counterparts". Stunned and disappointed, Joyce decided not to accept Richards's decision.

Thus he began a battle that would cost him dearly and that would take until 1915 to resolve. He became so deeply discouraged by this wrangle with his publisher that he began to think seriously about leaving Trieste. He felt that he had reached a series of dead ends there. By now it was clear that living with Francini Bruni was never going to be a solution to their financial difficulties, and worse still the school was no longer in a position to secure Joyce's, Stanislaus's or even Francini Bruni's positions, so even the drudgery of a life spent teaching for paltry financial rewards, which always left him struggling to make ends meet, was no longer guaranteed.[136] What was more, that life could only be justified if it provided a means to a substantial literary breakthrough; now, given the stalemate over the publishing of *Dubliners*, that breakthrough seemed more distant than ever. On top of this, tensions at home with Nora had never really abated and were not being made any easier by Stanislaus's presence. In desperation, Joyce continued to drown his sorrows and Nora to draft letters to her mother in which she threatened to leave him. The more he drank, the more she despaired and the more Stanislaus attempted to rein him in, succeeding only in becoming part of and, at worst, the scapegoat for all their problems.

Such was the state of affairs which convinced Joyce that he would have to try something new. In early May he applied for a job in the Nast-Kolb &

Schumacher Bank in Rome, enclosing with his application letters of recommendation from Roberto Prezioso, Timothy Harrington, Lord Mayor of Dublin, and William Greenham, a Trieste businessman of English descent for whom he regularly translated commercial letters. Shortly afterwards he received word that he had been accepted for a two-month trial. In June he wrote to Grant Richards telling him that he would "leave this delightful city at the end of next month and go to Rome where I have obtained a position as correspondent in a bank" (*LII*, 140).

Joyce's principal motivation seems to have lain in his belief that in the bank he would earn almost double his current salary for fewer hours of work and would therefore be able to devote more time to his writing. It was a serious miscalculation. On 30 July 1906 he and Nora took the train from Trieste to Fiume and a night boat from there to Ancona before travelling on to begin their difficult adventure in the Eternal City. Joyce left behind the few bits of furniture he had begun to purchase by instalment but was careful to take with him an advance of thirty shillings on Stannie's salary from the school. He left Stanislaus behind in Trieste, not for the last time, to deal with a string of bills and an angry crew of unpaid creditors.

THREE

Was ist eine Nation?[1]

What is your nation if I may ask? says the citizen. (*U*, 12.1430)

1 *Roman interlude*

Little or nothing went right for Joyce in Rome. He worked too hard, accommodation was a constant problem and he did not like the Romans. He spent his days copying out letters in the bank before hurrying off to meet Nora and Giorgio for dinner. In whatever little time was left he tried to distract and amuse himself by reading the anti-clerical writings in *L'Asino* and by following the pronouncements of Enrico Ferri and Arturo Labriola in *L'Avanti!*. Although he took a considerable interest in matters religious, his sojourn in Rome served only to alienate him further from the Catholic Church, whose wealth and opulence he now saw at first hand.

In August he wrote to Stanislaus making it clear that he missed Trieste more than he ever could have expected:

> The first thing I look for in a city is the café. Rome has one café and that one is not as good as any of the best in Trieste. This is a damn bore for me. (*LII*, 146)

Perhaps it was a case of faraway hills being greener, but in his letters he gave the impression of being genuinely curious about what was happening in Trieste. He wrote asking Stanislaus if there was any news about Giuseppe Bertelli, the sub-director of the Berlitz who had absconded to America with most of the school funds, and he manifested his amused interest in the Triestine dialect several times. In a letter of 13 November 1906, for example, he wrote that Gissing's books reminded him of *pastefazoi* (*Triestino* for a heavy soup of pasta and beans); and writing about the Vatican Council of 1870, he mentioned the two bishops who had questioned the dogma of Papal infallibility, MacHale of Tuam and an unnamed bishop "of Capuzzo" (*LII*, 189–94), who was, in fact bishop of Caiazzo, but Joyce wanted to play on the Triestine word *capuzo* meaning cabbage.

While in Rome Joyce kept in constant contact with Stanislaus for a number of reasons. The first and most pressing was that he had left a lot of unfinished business – mostly in the form of unpaid bills – behind him in Trieste. His instructions to Stanislaus were despatched in regular instalments and were extremely detailed:

> You may pay the baker. His bill should be five or six crowns. Send its amt to me if it appears to you excessive. But if not pay him in two instalments. Tell the tailors my address is Edinburgh or Glasgow. You can give my address and compliments to the doctors. You enclose one (not two) postcards: from the daughter. About paying F. rent. Let him speak first. Then you might say: I cannot pay my brother's debts but I will pay for 1 month's occupancy of my room at the full rent. Don't do this, however, before asking time to write to me. Before entering Canarutto's cousin's, go to Can. and ask him has the furniture been sold. Explain to him that he promised to sell it for a good price and remind him that I paid him 120 crowns and that it would be unfair to refund me none of it. (*LII*, 146–7)

It must have been quite a struggle for Stanislaus to carry out his brother's orders, especially as his Italian was still approximate. In a diary entry of 16 January 1907 Stanislaus noted as much, writing: "I was not able to bargain about a pair of boots yesterday and I make a poor show when I speak all in Italian." He blamed this fact on his not having time to go to the caffè, not having friends, and on talking and thinking in English all day. Joyce was not particularly concerned about his brother's difficulties, just as he was not terribly worried about having left debts with most of the people who had helped him in Trieste – the shopkeepers who had allowed him generous tabs, Francini Bruni who had taken him into his house, or Signor Canarutto whose wife had helped look after Nora during her pregnancy. As if to rub salt into Stanislaus's wounds, he scolded him for not eating properly and sent him long reports on his acquisitions in Rome along with detailed descriptions of how well they were eating there, before imploring him to ask Artifoni for yet another advance on his salary:

> Got your letter today. You really are a mumchance – living on bread and ham. Listen. Go at once to Artifoni and tell him it is a matter of urgent necessity for you to get a week's pay in advance – and you'll get it. Keep 10 crowns yourself and telegraph 20 to me. Go to Effore or to Fantini or to Canarutto – eat anyway. Tell A you can't give lessons without food, that you are a year in his service and have never asked for any advance and that you gave back the 30 crowns he gave me. (*LII*, 155)

Yet if life was difficult for Stanislaus, it was doubly so for Joyce and Nora, and Joyce was not backward about keeping his brother up to date with his miseries. Foremost among them was the fact that he had still to make a literary breakthrough while various mediocre contemporaries were achieving fame in Dublin:

> They are all in the public eye and favour: even Dr O.S. Jesus Gogarty. And here am I (whom their writings and lives nauseate to the point of vomiting) writing away letters for ten hours a day like the blue devil on the offchance of pleasing three bad-tempered bankers and inducing them to let me retain my position while (as a luxury) I am allowed to haggle for two years with the same publisher, trying to induce him to publish a book for which he has an intense admiration. Orco Dio![2] (*LII*, 154)

It was becoming clear that by moving to Rome Joyce had merely transferred his problems to a city where he and Nora received less understanding, support and friendship than they had had in Trieste. Nora was totally out of sorts, with no one to turn to and nowhere to go with Giorgio, while Joyce's job in the bank was proving utterly unsuitable. Before long he was commenting to Stanislaus that "Even the atmosphere of the BS [Berlitz School] was better than this" (*LII*, 157). At the same time his superiors at the bank were quite relaxed about allowing "Signor Joyce" time to write innumerable letters of his own during office hours.[3] Things seemed to improve slightly in September, when he organized a private lesson or two to supplement his income, and was moved from the correspondence to the reception room, where he at least got to meet clients. But by the end of the month it was clear that he was poorer than he had ever been in Trieste, and again he appealed to his brother:

> My funds are now 8d. If nothing comes I shall have to ask my pupil to lend me a lira as I am hungry. I have had no breakfast and read no papers for five days past but I could not spin out the money longer. (*LII*, 162)

Stanislaus dutifully sent money in regular despatches, but it was never enough. Soon Joyce was suggesting that he come and join him in Rome and work in the Berlitz school there. But by now Stanislaus, angry and tired of placating his brother's Triestine creditors and subsidizing the Roman misadventure, had begun to threaten to go back to Dublin. He felt that with planning Joyce could have made ends meet in Rome, and cannot but have been frustrated by the fact that Joyce and Nora always ate out there. Perhaps for this reason, Joyce announced that from November onwards Nora would arrange to cook at home and he began to express his embarrassment about always asking Stanislaus for money. He was continually on the lookout for new ways to augment his income and in late November he got a job in "an Ecole de Langues (which is an offshoot at low prices of the B.S.)" (*LII*, 195), which meant that after working until seven in the bank he taught nightly from 7.15 to 10.15.

Joyce did not even have the satisfaction of seeing progress with regard to the publication of *Dubliners*. He continued to write to Grant Richards but to little avail. At the end of September, Richards wrote saying he was not willing to publish the collection but that he would consider publishing the "autobiographical novel and then do the stories later" (*JJ*, 231). Joyce immediately sensed he was getting the brush-off and was angry with Richards for breaking what he considered to be an agreement. He took advice from a solicitor who told him to appeal directly to Richards himself, which he did. Thus, more epistolary negotiations took place during October and Joyce eventually agreed to the "suppression of *Two Gallants* (and of *A Little Cloud*)" and to the "deletion of [a] passage in *Counterparts*" and the "deletion of word 'bloody' in *Grace*" (*LII*, 184). But it was all in vain. On 26 October, Richards confirmed his original unwillingness to publish the book, returned the manuscript to Joyce and told him that the decision was in both their interests (*LII*, 185).

Correspondence with Arthur Symons brought the more encouraging news that Elkin Mathews was willing to consider *Chamber Music* for publication. Joyce was not particularly keen about this project, however, because he knew well that *Dubliners* was infinitely more important than what he described as his "poor and trivial" poems (*LII*, 182). In October, in a "P.P.S." to a letter written in late September to Stanislaus, he mentioned almost casually: "I have a new story for Dubliners in my head. It deals with Mr Hunter" (*LII*, 168). Yet he was too busy to do more than think about possible new stories and invent titles, and by February reported that "*Ulysses* never got any forrader than the title. I have other titles, e.g. *The Last Supper, The Dead, The Street, Vengeance, At Bay*: all of which stories I could write if circumstances were favourable" (*LII*, 209).

Because of the demands of his new job and his lack of enthusiasm for Rome, he took only occasional days off to see the city or take a trip to the nearby countryside with Nora, who was desperately lonely and worn out from looking after Giorgio all day long. In early December Joyce and his family were turned out of their lodgings and Joyce's subsequent exasperation at not being able to find a place to live is reflected in his description of the city as "the stupidest old whore of a town ever I was in" (*LII*, 198). He described the chief pastime and favourite joke of the Romans as "the breaking of wind rereward", objected to their "mechanical obscenity" (*LII*, 198), wrote of how he hated "to think that Italians ever did anything in the way of art" and described himself as being "damnably sick of Italy, Italian and Italians, outrageously, illogically sick" (*LII*, 201). He even went so far as to praise his fellow countrymen: "I think the Irish are the most civilised people in Europe, be Jesus Christ I do: anyway they are the least burocratic [*sic*]" (*LII*, 202). His Roman Christmas brought little or no cheer and appears to have provoked some nostalgia for Dublin. He and Nora faced a festive season without having the necessary means to enjoy it – "we shall dine on paste" (*LII*, 204) he announced to Stannie – and the genuine lack they suffered probably contributed to the sumptuousness of the post-Christmas dinner Joyce later described in such lavish detail in "The Dead".

From this point on, Joyce began to write more openly about how much he was missing Trieste, perhaps already with an eye to a return. His life no longer had the variety it had had in Trieste and Joyce did not have the time to enjoy any of the stimulation offered by Rome. He would have enjoyed, for instance, attending the union of rites being celebrated in Saint Sylvester's Church but his rigid work routine ruled this out: "I might as well be in Cabra for all I see of anything Coptic, Greek, Chaldean &c" (*LII*, 206).

Things with Nora do not appear to have improved much during their Roman stay, and indeed it is hard to imagine how they could have. In most respects they continued as before, Joyce away at work all day and the couple dining out every night. In a letter of 6 February Joyce reported: "The news here is that we leave our present quarters on the 15th and go to live in the Corso, where Nora found a room. I expect she will be satisfied for a week or so." But the real news, which Joyce seems almost to make light of, was that Nora was pregnant, "as Reynolds's Newspaper would say, *enceinte*" (*LII*, 209).

This discovery brought further pressure to bear on Joyce, who was becoming ever more aware of the folly of his flight to Rome, which he now defined as "a *coglioneria*" – a balls-up (*LII*, 215). (Joyce was appropriating the vulgar language used by his bank colleagues: "When I enter the bank in the morning I wait for someone to announce something about either his *cazzo* [dick], *culo* [arse] or *coglioni* [balls]" [*LII*, 218].) As Gorman wrote:

> Trieste, the city he had left in disgust, began to draw him like an irresistible magnet. He was known there. He remembered that here he would meet people who shared his temperament to some degree. He would be able to talk all he pleased about Dublin with Stanislaus.[4]

His return to Trieste, therefore, was not simply his response to a rejection of the Italian capital; he felt drawn to the Adriatic city, and a letter to Stanislaus in February suggests the nostalgia he felt: "Anyway I am a fish out of water. I would like to go back to Trieste because I remember some nights walking along the streets in the summer and thinking over some of the phrases in my stories" (*LII*, 215). He also knew he would be able to depend on Stanislaus's support, which would be increasingly necessary given Nora's new pregnancy. On Valentine's Day 1907 he wrote the following telegram to his brother: "given notice returning Trieste send forty urgent monte brianza [*sic*] wire if Artifoni accepts" (*LII*, 214–15). Stanislaus was less than pleased by this hasty announcement and opposed Joyce's plan to move back to Trieste, pointing out that Artifoni did not have a position available for him. But Joyce had decided: his life in Rome made little sense, he was working from dawn till dark and still never seemed to have enough money to get by on, and, more worrying still, he was losing faith in his abilities ("the verses are not worth talking about: and I begin to think neither are the stories" [*LII*, 220]):

> I gave notice here on Thursday. If I will be permitted I will resume teaching at the school. Artif. promised me I could go back when I liked. I have 9, 10 hrs a day work: a little more pay in a much dearer city. Since I came here I have not put pen to paper. I would write fully but am hourly awaiting your news. A little more of this life and J.F.B.'s prophecy[5] would be fulfilled. I have no 'carriera' before me in commerce. Not because I can't make one, but because I won't. (*LII*, 214)

On Stanislaus's insistence, Joyce gave some thought to going to a city other than Trieste, but it was clear that his heart was set on returning there. On 6 March a series of unfortunate events brought his purgatory to an end. Having just received his monthly salary from the bank he went drinking. As he made his way home, late in the night, he was attacked by two men who robbed him of everything he had. By the time he got back to Nora, his mind was made up. He wired Stanislaus and, with Nora and Giorgio, began the journey home to Trieste the very next day.

Despite all his troubles in Rome, Joyce would long reap the benefits of his time there. The sojourn, for all its misery, had allowed him to gather, among other things, crucial elements for "The Dead", *Exiles*, and *Ulysses*, elements which he would begin to put to use as soon as he got back to Trieste.

2 *Schmitz / Svevo*

The circumstances of the Joyces' return to Trieste could hardly have been less auspicious. Stanislaus was shocked to see them emerging from the train looking filthy and "almost as thin and poverty-stricken as Italian immigrants"; Jim, "in a manky shapeless capecoat", was pale, unshaven, even thinner then when he left and looked as if he had been drinking, while Nora was "more bedraggled than ever" with a fat and rosy-cheeked Georgie in her arms.[6] Once again Joyce was penniless and jobless; when Stanislaus pointed this out, his response was "Well, then, I have you" (*JJ*, 255). Indeed for the following seven years he would lean heavily and often unfairly on his younger brother, who, over the coming weeks, listened with surprise as Joyce, perhaps anxious to hide the extent to which his Roman adventure had been a failure, now told him that he had been conceded more freedom than the other employees at the bank because he was "inglese", that he had been able to "stand dinners, go to the theatre and buy books" and that Nora and Georgie had gone to the cinema on an almost nightly basis.[7]

Stannie found his brother little changed after his months in Rome, noted how he had lost none of his bad habits but continued to "eat little, smoke filthy Virginian cigars, drink stray ottavos of wine, without, however, becoming really drunk, and snip absinthes".[8] At the same time, he did not stint in helping Jim and his family get back on their feet in the early weeks following their return. Indeed he even gave them the room he had sub-let in Francini Bruni's flat on via San Nicolò and moved to another, "a dirty looking little closet quite filled by bed, sofa and a table, and the bed small and low" in the run-down via Beccherie, which he described in the diary as "the whores' quarter".[9] Soon, however, James, a heavily pregnant Nora and Georgie managed to find their own new lodgings in number 45 via Nuova (a street that runs parallel to via San Nicolò) and a rather relieved Stannie was able to go back to his old place with Francini Bruni on 15 March.[10] Although it does not appear to have been a very salubrious dwelling, the Joyces remained in the via Nuova flat until September 1907 – long enough for Georgio to pick up bad language from the four-year-old girl who lived next door who, in turn, had learnt it from what Stanislaus refers to as a "Slav bitch". Joyce never used this address on his letters but preferred to write c/o his brother or c/o Francini Bruni, presumably because of the temporary and unsettled nature of his domicile there.

Shortly after returning from Rome Joyce had his first encounter with Ettore Schmitz, a Triestine who shared his passion for writing and literature. At the outset, it probably seemed to Joyce that this would be just another lesson in commercial English, because his new student was a well-heeled Triestine businessman who needed to brush up his English. Schmitz already had a reasonable command of the language, having taken lessons from 1900 to 1903 with an Englishman named Phillip Cautley, but now he needed to resume his study as he had been asked to spend two or three months each year looking after the interests of a new factory to manufacture anti-corrosive paint for the keels of ships, which his wife's family were opening in Charlton, England. Soon, however, Joyce would come to realize that there was more to Schmitz than initially met the eye.

He was Italian by language and politics, Austrian by citizenship, Austro-German by ancestry and education, Jewish by religion – in short a not untypical personification of the Triestine hybridity. This is reflected in his pseudonym, Italo Svevo, which combines the ultra-Italian "Italo" (whose initial letter pays homage to the lone vowel in his family name) with the invented surname "Svevo", which is the Italian adjective for the Swabian provinces of Germany.

Theirs was a most propitious encounter – the beginning of a personal and creative relationship that would endure until Schmitz's death in 1928. Their relationship – and it was not a straightforward friendship, because of the age difference (Schmitz was forty-six in 1907), the social gulf between them,[11] and the reservations of Schmitz's wife's family about this peculiar young Irishman who was distracting Ettore from his "real work" of running the family's varnish factory – was hugely important for both men.

Despite their very different backgrounds, Schmitz and Joyce had a surprising amount in common. For example, both were born into enormous families: Schmitz's mother had sixteen children, eight of whom lived; Joyce's fifteen, of whom ten had survived. Each time a new Schmitz was born, the father Francesco was said to have exclaimed: "Today my capital has been increased by a million!"[12] John Stanislaus Joyce's reactions towards each new addition to his large family, with the exception of James, were never so benign.

Both Schmitz and Joyce would be truly close to one brother alone, who would be capable of recognizing their talents and encouraging them in their artistic endeavours. In Schmitz's case the brother was Elio, who lived in Ettore's shadow and recorded his every move in a diary which supplies us with much of our knowledge of Schmitz's early life. Elio wrote of "confining himself to the humble task of being his bookkeeper and historian". As Livia Veneziani Svevo recorded in her memoir of her husband: "Elio was his brother's first biographer, the first to read his mind, to have faith in him, to examine him and stimulate him, to follow every literary effort he made. In his short life he was closer than anyone else to Ettore. 'No historian admired Napoleon as much as I admired Ettore,' Elio wrote in his diary ..."[13]

Stanislaus's admiration for Joyce's talents was similar although always tempered by his exasperation with James's excesses and possibly made more human by his frustration at knowing himself to be a less interesting human being than his brother was. Stannie summarized his fate in his diary when he was about eighteen – "It is terrible to have a cleverer elder brother, I get small credit for originality"[14] – and he never completely managed to free himself of the burden of being Joyce's closest sibling, the "one brother alone", as Joyce put it in a letter to Nora in August 1904, who was "capable of understanding" him (*LII*, 48).

At six and a half, Joyce had been dispatched to boarding school at Clongowes Wood College; Schmitz, too, was sent away at a young age, to a private college for the sons of Jewish businessmen in Wurzburg, Austria. His family hoped this education would thoroughly prepare him in languages and business studies. "Manly men are not made from boys brought up at home,"[15] his father believed, without realizing how close his opinion was to the philosophy often ascribed to the Jesuits who took on Joyce in Clongowes: "You give us the boy and we'll give you back the man." From a young age, Schmitz's principal interest was in literature. During his teens he read widely and escaped the boredom of his studies by whiling away his evenings reading, among others, Shakespeare and Turgenev. At the age of seventeen he returned to Trieste and began to study in the Scuola di Commercio "Revoltella" (where he would later, like Joyce, teach for a time), but he still found the time to pursue his love of literature and to write.

Just as Joyce's family suffered from a huge downturn in their financial fortunes, so too did Schmitz's, with the result that young Ettore was forced to cut short his studies and to take up a position, which would otherwise have been considered below him, as a correspondence clerk in Trieste's Banca Union. He liked this occupation about as much as Joyce enjoyed his banking experience in Rome.

Both men had difficult relationships with the nationalist politics of their respective cities. Schmitz, despite being a member of the Lega Nazionale and the Ginnastica Triestina and contributing articles and reviews to the rather high-brow irredentist daily *L'Indipendente*, always remained somewhat at a remove from the rather crude nationalist attitudes that dominated so many of the cultural and political activities in Trieste. He was still largely unknown when Joyce met him in 1907, in part because his books were seen as not sufficiently Italian in style or subject matter. His first novel, *Una Vita*, a psychological study of a Jewish bank clerk, which he had published in 1892, was almost completely ignored by the critics; and his second, a brooding, melancholic novel called *Senilità*, first published in serial form in *L'Indipendente* in 1898 and in book form shortly afterwards, suffered a similar fate. Schmitz was so totally discouraged that he simply stopped writing and took solace in other, happier aspects of his life.

In 1895 he married Livia Veneziani, the daughter of the ultra-irredentist entrepreneur Gioacchino Veneziani, and found himself being warmly welcomed into a new family, a new home and prosperous family business. Ettore and Livia's was a happy marriage, and the birth of their daughter Letizia was greeted with great joy. It was also the occasion of Ettore's conversion to Catholicism, a move to which he had agreed in order to please his wife. After his marriage he was given an important role in the family's ships' varnish company and thus liberated from the dreary routine of eighteen years spent in the correspondence department of the Banca Union. He and Livia went to live on a floor of the family villa in Servola, a village just a couple of miles to the east of Trieste, and it was here, some eight or nine years later, that Joyce went for their private lessons, sometimes travelling the long distance between his flat and the Villa Veneziani by tram, other times going on foot, often accompanied on the long walk by Stanislaus.

The Irishman and his Triestine student immediately got along well together. Schmitz's wife recalled that "lessons were conducted in a manner that was unusual. Grammar was not mentioned, they talked about literature and raised nearly a hundred different topics."[16] Schmitz was impressed by his teacher and his bohemian way of life, a lifestyle he himself had perhaps flirted with but never dared to adopt. Joyce also reminded him of his friend

Umberto Veruda, an influential and daring local artist who had revolution-
ized nineteenth-century painting in Trieste before dying at the tender age of
thirty-seven. If Veruda was, as Silvio Benco says, "the first person to understand [Schmitz] completely and courageously, with the gifted artist's breadth
and sureness of outlook",[17] then Joyce was the second. According to John
Gatt-Rutter, Schmitz's biographer, "the stimulus which Joyce gave to Svevo,
especially in terms of encouragement, is immeasurable".[18] Schmitz fully
acknowledged this and used to say that Joyce had worked the resurrection of
Lazarus on him.[19]

In their early lessons Joyce and Schmitz talked about Irish and English literature and within a short time the teacher was bringing the pupil his own
work to read – *Chamber Music* and the stories of *Dubliners*. Soon afterwards
Joyce read Schmitz's early novels and was so delighted with them that he pronounced that "there are passages in *Senilità* that even Anatole France could
not have improved" (*JJ*, 282). The Triestine novelist was so overjoyed by
Joyce's admiration that he started writing again. Joyce also set about telling
the Triestines what an excellent novelist they had in Italo Svevo, but to little
or no avail:

> He was simply laughed at and given the eternal refrain that Svevo could not
> write good Italian. 'There is no unanimity so perfect as the unanimity of silence,'
> Svevo told Joyce sadly, and Joyce found he could not disturb this silence. Nicolò
> Vidacovich, president of the Società di Minerva, more honestly told him that
> Svevo's writing was too negative and unpatriotic to be acceptable in Trieste. The
> silence about Svevo in Trieste was politically motivated and conspiratorial.[20]

The early Triestine readers of Svevo felt he wrote poor, rough Italian, and
allowed this opinion to overshadow the real strengths of his novels. As Brian
Moloney has commented, "Schmitz's books were undoubtedly out of tune
and written at the wrong time, but only in the sense that they were extremely
modern European novels."[21] Joyce, however, immediately knew he was on to
something special, and, for the moment, Schmitz was only too pleased to
have finally found an understanding reader. In 1909 he returned Joyce's
favour by encouraging the Irish writer to resume work on *A Portrait of the
Artist as a Young Man*, which he had abandoned in April 1908. Having read
the first three chapters Schmitz sent his teacher such a glowing and insightful critique that Joyce was roused from his inertia and started writing again.

But Schmitz would soon come to play an even bigger role as one of the
most important prototypes for Leopold Bloom, as Stanislaus Joyce notes:

> In an odd and rather amusing way [...] Svevo did have some part in *Ulysses*.
> My brother [...] needed various details to complete the picture of the central
> figure, the Jew, Leopold Bloom. It was Italo Svevo that supplied him with
> much of the information he needed.[22]

Joyce bombarded Schmitz, who had read Hebrew as a child and been
brought up to observe the Sabbath and Jewish holidays, with questions
about the Jews, so much so that one day, during a lesson with Stanislaus,
Schmitz asked: "Tell me some secrets about Irishmen. You know your
brother has been asking me so many questions about Jews that I want to get
even with him" (*JJ*, 374).

But the Italian writer did not simply provide Joyce with information. In
many crucial ways he incarnated many of Bloom's vital features. The difference in age between Joyce and Schmitz is almost the same as that between
Stephen and Bloom, and both Bloom and Schmitz have Hungarian roots
(Schmitz's grandfather was from Hungary), are born Jews but convert and
marry Catholics, think as much about the identities adopted by their parents
(Irish and Italian) as about their being Jewish, and both have a daughter but
suffer from not having a son. John Gatt-Rutter points to other pertinent links:

> It must have crossed both Svevo's mind and Joyce's that the name of the wan-
> dering hero Ulysses would have suited Schmitz much better than that of Hec-
> tor, seeing that much of his time was spent travelling away from home through
> many lands, often leaving his wife behind. ... In Svevo's lecture on Joyce in
> 1927 he seems almost to see himself in Bloom, 'the assiduous reader of news-
> papers' ... He also quotes Bloom reading about 'a planter's company. To pur-
> chase vast sandy tracts from Turkish government and plant with eucalyptus
> trees. Excellent for shade, fuel and construction. Orange-groves and immense
> melonfields north of Jaffa.' And so on. So Ettore had fantasized in 1900 about
> resinous pine plantations in France. I think, therefore, that in Leopold Bloom
> we have in large part a moral portrait of Ettore Schmitz.[23]

There are a few other small but significant connections between Schmitz
and Bloom. Why does Bloom eat gorgonzola cheese? Perhaps Schmitz's son-
in-law Antonio Fonda Savio, writing about him many years later, unwittingly provided the answer:

> He [Schmitz] had his own light-hearted and almost paradoxical way of
> explaining a concept. "The man of our times", he said for example, "is still a
> savage when he is born, even more, he is a little animal. He is fed with natural
> and simple foods, then with difficulty he gets used to the more complicated
> ones which civilization offers. He becomes more sophisticated slowly and

becomes completely civilized only when the day arrives in which he can fully enjoy … gorgonzola."[24]

This is something only Bloom manages in *Ulysses*, when he relishes "the feety savour of green cheese" (*U*, 8.819). The expression "feety savour" corresponds to the much used Triestine expression "spuzza de pie" or the Italian "puzza dei piedi", which roughly translate as "stink of the feet".

Another link can be identified in the fact that when Schmitz was a child, he and his brothers and sisters kept a newspaper, full of "sensational" family news, such as the following, which Joyce just may have been shown later:

> A dog has been lost (fattish) answering to the name of Ettore. As he is rather lazy and likes sleeping in the sun, it will be easy to find him near the aqueduct. If he is found asleep, please do not wake him. Ettore, Ettore, a plump little dog.[25]

This is echoed in *Ulysses*, where Bloom described in an advertisement for a "missing gent" in a manner which recalls that of the Schmitz family paper (also because, like Bloom, Schmitz had "almond eyes" and "an olive complexion"):

> What public advertisement would divulge the occultation of the departed?
>
> £5 reward, lost, stolen or strayed from his residence 7 Eccles street, missing gent about 40, answering to the name of Bloom, Leopold (Poldy), height 5 ft 9 1/2 inches, full build, olive complexion, may have since grown a beard, when last seen was wearing a black suit. Above sum will be paid for information leading to his discovery. (*U*, 17.2000–5)

Schmitz's wife Livia, meanwhile, was an inspiration for the Anna Livia Plurabelle character of *Finnegans Wake*. Joyce himself drew attention to this in a letter to Schmitz on 20 February 1924, just after he had published the Anna Livia segment of *Work in Progress*: "A propos of names: I have given the name of Signora Schmitz to the protagonist of the book I am writing. Ask her, however, not to take up arms, either of steel or fire, since the person involved is the Pyrrha of Ireland (or rather of Dublin) whose hair is the river beside which (the name is Anna Liffey) the seventh city of Christendom springs up, the other six being Basovizza, Clapham Junction, Rena Vecia, Limehouse, S.Odorico in the Vale of Tears and San Giacomo in Monte di Pietà." Livia was less than pleased at finding herself thus fictionalized through the mouths of two low-class washerwomen. More than Schmitz she attached importance to class, and more than once she ignored Nora on the street even though they had known one another from the time Nora had, in desperation, taken in washing and ironing for her.[26]

Perhaps Joyce was making a point. In any case, he tried to soothe Livia by writing light-heartedly to "Hector", as he called her husband, on 21 November 1925: "Reassure your wife with regard to the character Anna Livia. I have taken only her hair, and that merely as a loan, to adorn the little river of my city, the Anna Liffey, which would be the longest river in the world if it were not for the canal that comes from afar to join the celebrated divo, Anthony the worker of Miracles, and then, having changed its mind, returns whence it came." He was referring to Trieste's beautiful but short Canal Grande, which lapped the steps of the Church of Sant'Antonio Taumaturgo. Perhaps this palliative was accepted by Schmitz, even though he knew all too well that Joyce rarely repaid his loans and that the borrowing of Livia's hair and name was permanent and would later be enshrined within the pages of *Finnegans Wake*. Indeed, as Joyce wrote to Livia on the occasion of that book's publication, that was just the case: "Dear Signora: I have at least finished my book. For three lustra I have been combing and recombing the hair of Anna Livia" (*LIII*, 435).[27]

3 *"old Auster and Hungrig"*

> Austria is a Babel-like state, a real Noah's ark, in which we Italians are the least satisfied and the most beaten down of the animals. [...] And what is the logic and what are the desired results of this? Race hatred, with the usual interminable, deadly and inhumane internal struggle which are the real causes of the ever more deplorable regression of this state.[28]

Shortly after his return from Rome, Joyce was pleased to receive invitations, partially engineered by Francini Bruni, to write for *Il Piccolo della Sera* and lecture at the Università Popolare. These helped him to get established again and allowed his attention to be drawn back to the cultural, socio-political and historical issues of Ireland.

The first invitation came from his student Roberto Prezioso, acting editor of *Il Piccolo della Sera* and political editor of *Il Piccolo*, who, according to Ellmann, asked him "to do a series of articles on the evils of empire as found in Ireland. The Piccolo's readers could be depended upon to see the parallel with the evils of empire as found in Trieste" (*JJ*, 255). Stanislaus Joyce explains that Joyce had a lengthy conversation with Prezioso and discussed with him "the ignorance that existed about Ireland on the continent". To make his point Joyce showed the Italian editor that evening's issue of *Il Pic-*

colo della Sera drawing his attention to how John O'Leary's name "had been mutilated as almost to be unrecognisable".[29] At the end of their conversation Prezioso asked him if he would be willing to write a piece himself on Fenianism and Joyce was pleased to accept: a leading article in *Il Piccolo della Sera* would guarantee him front-page exposure in the midst of an important election campaign being fought on issues of irredentism and socialism. Had not two of his favourite Italians, Arturo Labriola and Guglielmo Ferrero, also written leading articles for *Il Piccolo della Sera*? Joyce's evident pride in these journalistic activities, and his realization that he would not have had similar opportunities in Dublin, can be seen in his later comment to Stanislaus: "I may not be the Jesus Christ I once fondly imagined myself, but I think I must have a talent for journalism. I could scarcely have written for the papers my articles have appeared in, if I hadn't artistic talent but in Dublin I could do nothing."[30]

He would not be the first to write from Trieste on issues of empire and independence, nor the first to comment, albeit allusively, on the parellels between Ireland's relationship with Britain, Trieste's relationship with Austro-Hungary, and Hungary's relative autonomy within Austro-Hungarian empire. As early as 1886, Sir Richard Burton had used the example of Trieste to lend weight to his opinion that the British government should concede a measure of home rule to Ireland. In a letter written from Trieste in 1886 to the editor of *The Morning Post*, Burton had pointed out:

> Every province of Austro-Hungary enjoys the greatest amount of 'Home Rule' by means of its own Landstag or Diet. The little volumes, each in the local dialect, containing the rules and regulations for legislative procedure are broadcast over the country; and I would especially recommend those which concern the Diet of Istria and – a thing apart – the Diet of Trieste City to the many who are now waxing rabid with alarm at the idea of an Irish Parliament in the old house on College Green.[31]

Joyce himself had drawn on the Hungarian analogy with Ireland in *Stephen Hero*, where he makes Stephen doubtful of its validity:

> A glowing example was to be found for Ireland in the case of Hungary, an example, as these patriots imagined, of a long-suffering minority, entitled by every right of race and justice to a separate freedom, finally emancipating itself. (*SH*, 60)

Isabel Burton also linked the Hungarians closely with the Irish, although she did so in a far less positive manner than her husband had earlier done.

Hungary is, as regards civilisation, simply the most backward country in Europe. [...] The cities, like historic Gran on the Danube, have attempts at public buildings and streets: in the country towns and villages the thorough-fares are left to Nature; the houses and huts, the rookeries and doggeries are planted higgledy-piggledy, wherever the tenants please; and they are filthier than any shanty in Galway or Cork. [...] The peasantry [...] speak a tongue of Turkish affinity, all their sympathies are with their blood-kinsmen the Turks, and they have toiled to deserve the savage title of 'white Turks,' lately conferred upon them by Europe. [...] All Englishmen who have lived long amongst Hungarians remark the similarity of the Magyar and the southern Irish Catholic. Both are imaginative and poetical, rather in talk than in books; nei-ther race ever yet composed poetry of the highest class. [...] As regards politics and finance, Buda-Pest is simply a modern and eastern copy of Dublin. The Hungarian magnate still lives like the Squireen and Buckeen of the late Mr. Charles Lever's 'earliest style;' he keeps open house, he is plundered by all hands, and no Galway landowner of the last generation was less fitted by nature and nurture to manage his own affairs. Hence he is drowned in debt. [...] And where, we may ask, is the power that can muzzle these Eastern ban-dogs? who shall take away the shillelaghs of these Oriental Paddies?[32]

In linking the Irish, the Hungarians and the "savage" Turks in the image of the Oriental Paddy, Mrs Burton was conforming to an all-too-typical English habit, and adopting a common Western European attitude towards rebellious people in colonies everywhere from Ireland to India. Joyce used Ireland's similarities with other suppressed nations to do precisely the oppo-site. Many of Bloom's redeeming features, those aspects of his personality which distinguish him from the other characters in *Ulysses*, exist not because he is some kind of pure Irishman, but precisely because he is a "mixed mid-dling" whose background and interests link him indelibly with Hungary, Israel and the East. In creating Bloom, Joyce turned on its head the negative idea of the "Oriental Paddy" by drawing on what he saw in Trieste, where Jewishness and "Oriental-ness" were seen as positive qualities and under-stood as terms covering multifaceted cultural and religious realities.

In Trieste, Joyce came to know several Hungarians, including Nidia Frigyessy Castelbolognese, president of Il Circolo dei Magiari, whose father was born near Budapest, and Teodoro Mayer,[33] founder and owner of *Il Pic-colo* and *Il Piccolo della Sera*, the city newspapers that led the irredentist struggle. Joyce is said to have laughed at the idea of Mayer, a Hungarian Jew, leading the Italian nationalists, but he kept him in mind and later adopted him as one of his models for Leopold Bloom.

There are several striking parallels between Bloom and Mayer, even if one is a mediocre put-upon Dubliner and the other a successful Triestine entre- preneur and irredentist leader. At various times during the day in *Ulysses*, "We see the canvasser at work" (*U*, 7.120) trying to sell advertising space, an activity which recalls Mayer's second paper, *L'Inevitabile*, a purely commer- cial entry into "the gentle art of advertising", in which advertisements were intermingled with the sort of occasional trivia that passes through Bloom's head: anecdotes, poetry, short stories, and sketches of popular authors. Again like Bloom, who delights in the discovery in his drawer of "valuable adhesive or impressed postage stamps" (*U*, 17.1678), Mayer also had a passion for stamps which led him to launch his first journalistic project, *Il Corriere dei Francoboli*, a four-page journal dedicated to stamp-collecting, in 1875.

Mayer's third and certainly most important journalistic enterprise – *Il Piccolo* – may also have been a source of inspiration for Joyce in his creation of Bloom. The Hungarian Triestine had founded *Il Piccolo* (so called because it was just a single two-sided page) in 1881 to offer an affordable and easy-to- read irredentist voice in the city. Its openly pro-Italian, anti-Austrian and anti-Slav stances caused it to have constant battles with the Austrian author- ities, who tried every means at their disposal to put it out of business, yet only succeeded in helping it become the effective leader of the irredentist cause not only in Trieste but also in Venezia Giulia and in the Italian cities in Dalmatia. In the early years of this century it was at the height of its pow- ers, with a circulation of over 100,000. Despite, or perhaps because of, his success, Mayer was attacked by his Slav political opponents in Trieste on the grounds that he was Jewish (though he had long since abjured his religion and become a Mason), and he was criticized on similar lines by some extreme irredentists who accused his newspaper of adopting too moderate a political line. On a more modest scale, the Hungarian Bloom, a former Jew with supposed links with the Masons, is suspected by agents in Dublin Cas- tle of being involved in nationalist politics, yet his credentials with regard to the cause are scorned by ultra-nationalists like the Citizen:

> — A wolf in sheep's clothing, says the citizen. That's what he is. Virag from Hungary! Ahasuerus I call him. Cursed by God. [...] Saint Patrick would want to land again at Ballykinlar and convert us, says the citizen, after allowing things like that to contaminate our shores. (*U*, 12.1666–72)

While Joyce was of course already impressed by Griffith's espousal of a Hungarian policy in his pamphlet *The Revolution of Hungary*, it could still be argued that the root of what the Citizen sees as contamination was Trieste, that the suggestion in *Ulysses* that Bloom provided Griffith with the ideas for his Hungarian programme at least partially derived from the Adriatic port, where the successful politics practised by the Hungarians with regard to their country's autonomy within the Empire was well known and widely respected.

The Hungarian-Irish parallel is restated time and time again in *Ulysses*, where Joyce uses several words of Hungarian and repeatedly reinforces Bloom's Hungarian connections[34] and ancestry: "Rudolph Virag, now resident at no 52 Clanbrassil street, Dublin, formerly of Szombathely in the Kingdom of Hungary" (*U*, 17.1869–72). He would have known of the Hungarian town of Szombathely from the list of markets and fairs given in *La Guida di Trieste*,[35] and may also have wished to remember Marino de Szombathely, who was working on an Italian translation of the *Odyssey* in the same period that Joyce was writing *Ulysses*, and with whom he shared many acquaintances. Born in Trieste in 1890, de Szombathely studied in Trieste and Rome; his first collection of sonnets was dedicated to the irredentist leader Felice Venezian in 1912. He taught Italian (he knew *La Divina Commedia* by heart) and classics. He began publishing his translation of the *Odyssey* in 1918 with the aid of Silvio Benco and was known to have chosen it over the *Iliad* for reasons that resonate with Joyce's own: "The *Iliad* resounds with the roars of weapons and battles; the *Odyssey* is dominated by a continuous aspiration towards peace, and by the intimate joys of family."[36]

If Hungary, with its patron Saint Leopold and its contemporary political parallels with Ireland, was a formative influence on Joyce in his creation of Bloom, can a similar importance be attached to Austria – whose patron, after all, is Saint Stephen – or, more broadly, to the Austro-Hungarian Empire? The answer is probably no. Joyce had Stephen Dedalus well formed in his mind before he set foot in the empire. With the passing of years Joyce's affection for "old Auster and Hungrig" (*FW*, 464.27–8) grew, and he would later remember his time spent in its dominions with fondness, writing: "I cannot begin to give you the flavour of the old Austrian Empire. It was a ramshackle affair but it was charming, gay and I experienced more kindnesses in Trieste than ever before or since in my life ... Times past cannot return but I wish they were back." To Mary Colum he confirmed this, saying: "They called the Austrian Empire a ramshackle empire ... I wish to God there were more such empires."[37] The references to the empire in *Ulysses* show that Joyce, from a relatively early date, was doubtful that it would survive. In "Aeolus", Crawford,

McHugh and Stephen speak about the Wild Geese and the fact that the Austrian Emperor Franz Joseph was saved by the heroics of an Irish general:

> Habsburg. An Irishman saved his life on the ramparts of Vienna. Don't you forget! Maximilian Karl O'Donnell, graf von Tirconnell in Ireland. Sent his heir over to make the king an Austrian fieldmarshal now. Going to be trouble there one day. Wild geese. O yes, every time. Don't you forget that!
> — The moot point is did he forget it, J.J. O'Molloy said quietly, turning a horseshoe paperweight. Saving princes is a thankyou job.
> Professor MacHugh turned on him.
> — And if not? he said.
> — I'll tell you how it was, Myles Crawford began. A Hungarian it was one day ... (*U*, 7.540–50)

The professor sees the irony in this and notes: "We were always loyal to lost causes." It is interesting that Joyce thus gives his character such foresight, allowing him, as early as 1904, to foresee the end of the Austrian Empire, when such an end was far from inevitable (even if the possibility of a war between Italy and Austria was increasingly likely).

Joyce may have read about the fact that the Austrian Emperor was saved by an Irishman in the Triestine socialist writer Angelo Vivante's book *Irredentismo Adriatico*, which was published in Trieste in 1912 and recounted the story of O'Donnell, or "O'Connell" as Vivante calls him, noting with pride that he had been made a Freeman of Trieste in 1856:

> The ten-year council spent 60,000 florins on the visit of the royal couple in 1856 and named as a Freeman of the City the Sovereign's aide-de-camp, the Irishman O'Connell. He it was who sucked the King's wound clean after he was stabbed in the neck with a dagger which they feared was poisoned by the Hungarian soldier Libeny.[38]

By the time Joyce was writing *Ulysses*, he was also fully aware of the negative side of the Austrian authorities, having been arrested on his arrival in Trieste and having later seen Stanislaus interned for the duration of the First World War. In "Ithaca" there is a clear image of the brutal aspects of Austrian rule when Bloom thinks of Milly, and her blondness reminds him that she "had blond ancestry, remote, a violation, Herr Hauptmann Hainau, Austrian army, proximate, a hallucination, lieutenant Mulvey, British navy" (*U*, 17.868–70). The reference to Hainau is significant here: Hauptmann Julius von Haynau (1786–1853)[39] was a notoriously violent Austrian general, a hate-figure for the irredentists, the personification of all that was evil in the Austrian Empire. Joyce would have had to look no further than Attilio Tamaro's history, in which the author, having accused the Austrians of barbarous atrocities, complained that: "Murder and rape are common enough in the history of most invasions. But that the Austrian troops should burn their victims alive soaked in turpentine or bury them alive in quicklime, or that children should be crucified, was not altogether to have been expected." He then laid the blame on General Haynau and Field Marshal Radetzky, before quoting Haynau's description of his own actions:

> I employed the extreme arguments of war, giving orders that no more prisoners should be taken, that all combatants found with arms in their hands should be slaughtered, and that all houses from which resistance was offered should be burned and razed to the ground.[40]

As Franz Stanzel has pointed out, "Joyce made the meekest of characters in modern literature (Bloom) descend through the paternal line from one of the most ruthless military bullies of the nineteenth century, who, by the way, imposed a fine of 2,300,000 fl. (guilders) on the Jewish population of Hungary for their active support of the rebellion against Habsburg in 1848–9; and … this most non-Jewish of characters was the son of a Jewish mother. The double-edged irony of such a conjunction of personal fates would certainly not have been beyond Joyce."[41]

4 *The nightmare of history*

> Trieste is waking rawly: raw sunlight over its huddled browntiled roofs, testudoform; a multitude of prostrate bugs await a national deliverance. (*GJ*, 8)

In agreeing to write for Mayer's *Il Piccolo della Sera* Joyce had to come to terms with the complicated political reality of Triestine irredentism. And who better to guide him than Attilio Tamaro,[42] one of his better-known students, who, in his capacity as secretary of the openly irredentist Università Popolare[43] had invited him to give three public lectures at the University on matters Irish.

The foremost historian of that Trieste which was awaiting "a national deliverance", Tamaro worked tirelessly to counter the Austrian aim of keeping the city cosmopolitan and to prove beyond doubt the Italian nature of the city. Along with his fellow propagandists he offered a falsified history of the city, justified as being a means to achieving unification with Italy.[44] Like the Irish nationalists, the Triestine irredentists turned a blind eye to the complexities of the past in order to present a mythical vision of it which they hoped to re-create in the future. In this sense Trieste contributed to Joyce's sense of history by providing another teleological and visionary master-narrative. In Trieste, as in Ireland, history was an obsession:

> Another typically recurring position was a historiographical hyper-awareness
> [...] Triestine intellectuals [...] because of the thinness of the history at their
> shoulders, being too closely linked to it and having too much faith in it, often
> show themselves to be lacking in elegance and freedom with regard to their past.
> Nietzsche's famous pages on contemporary man being overcome, overwhelmed
> by historical memory and by a historicity which stops him from freeing himself
> from the past, apply well to this city and to this intellectual group without a history. The fact that history is, in the case of Trieste, so poor and short, makes the
> reflection on that same past, the compulsion to wear the masks of the past, to
> use the Nietzschean terminology, all the more intense and obsessive.[45]

Joyce would never accept this use of history, whether it was written by Tamaro or Pearse, whose version of patriotism, as enunciated in 1914, was close to what the irredentists sought from their supporters in Trieste.

> For patriotism is at once a faith and a service [...] a faith which is of the same
> nature as religious faith and one of the eternal witnesses in the heart of man to
> the truth that we are of divine kindred [...] So that patriotism needs service as
> the condition of its authenticity, and it is not sufficient to say 'I believe' unless
> one can say also 'I serve'.[46]

Joyce gave up taking lessons in Irish with Pearse because of the latter's chauvinism and because of his "continual mockery of the English language",[47] and what he rejected in Ireland he was hardly going to embrace in Trieste. In fact, in his newspaper articles, while giving conditional support to the Irish nationalist cause, Joyce was far keener to assert his independence from nationalists of all shades, from Pearse to Yeats, even if that meant exposing the limits of a broad movement that, in theory, he wanted to engage with and at least partially endorse. He had earlier condemned Gogarty for not doing likewise and had asked: "Am I the only honest person who has come out of Ireland in our time?" (*LII*, 171). Just as for many Italians in Trieste the desire to belong to Italy was not necessarily accompanied by anti-Austrianism, for Joyce the aspirations of Irish nationalism did not have to involve pointless anti-Englishness. In his articles, Joyce sought to assert the often obscured foundations of his country's complex identity; later he would go further and try to re-create it.

For Tamaro things were simpler: his aim was the destruction of all things that challenged his crusade to bring Trieste back into Italy. His work towards this aspiration provided Joyce with useful material, as it paralleled so many similar enterprises back in Ireland; in the rhetoric of Tamaro's contribution to *Italy's Great War and Her National Aspirations*, he may have found inspiration for the "Cyclops" episode of *Ulysses*. Tamaro's basic thesis was that "None of the numerous peoples of which the Austro-Hungarian Empire is composed has been harassed and martyrized more than the Italians. The aim was to destroy them."[48] Giulio Caprin, another prominent Triestine irredentist intellectual, expressed Austria's motives similarly in his *Trieste e l'Italia*,[49] which Joyce kept in his Trieste library: "To destroy Trieste's Italianness without, naturally, destroying Trieste: to do it in a such a way that the city's nationalism would die, but that the city would live, prosper and flower as a city of the Empire for the Empire, that the Italian would die and be reborn Austrian."[50]

Tamaro's earlier and more important book, *L'Adriatico – Golfo d'Italia. L'italianità di Trieste*, described Trieste's fate in almost biblical terms, stating that "the dedication to Austria in 1382" was "the original sin of Triestine history".[51] Tamaro read the history of his city in terms of a continuing struggle against the Austrians to put right this fatal error, this monstrous betrayal by the city fathers.[52] In the lecture he delivered for Tamaro, "Ireland, Island of Saints and Sages", Joyce considered Ireland's past in a similar light: at the origin of both problems lay the sullied hand of a betrayer. As Emer Nolan has written, Joyce "insists that the Anglo-Norman invasion (the originary 'English' occupation of Ireland, in nationalist mythography) was instigated by an Irish King, and that the Act of Union was legislated by an Irish parliament".[53] Joyce concludes this section of his essay by stating that "when a victorious country tyrannizes over another, it cannot logically be considered wrong for that other to rebel" (*CW*, 163).

According to Tamaro, the development of Trieste as an emporium and the subsequent arrival of foreigners threatened the very identity of the city, especially in the nineteenth century. So while intellectuals such as Scipio Slataper and Angelo Vivante extolled the open cosmopolitan virtues of Trieste, Tamaro firmly condemned the arrival of the "scheming and lawless Germans, Illyrians, Greeks and Jews" whose presence threatened to deform "the civil and national character of the city",[54] and he accused Austria of having "deliberately dumped Slavs on Italian soil with a view to denationalizing it".[55] Although Tamaro's version of facts is certainly biased and xenophobic, it is true that the Austrian authorities *did* encourage Slavs to move to Trieste to counter the growing Italian sentiment, and in Joyce's years the government ignored the claims of the *Regnicoli* (native Italians living in Trieste) while favouring the Slavs. By the beginning of the twentieth century, the Slavs had gained considerable economic clout and were every bit as politically active and entrenched as the irredentists. Not surprisingly, Tamaro summarily dismissed their civilization:

> It remains to be noted that the Slavs who immigrated into Julian Venetia have not succeeded in forming even an elementary civilization of their own. [...] they have no civilization as they have no history. On the other hand the Italians of the Julian Region may pride themselves on a most noble history, both as regards their splendid municipal record and their contribution of soldiers, statesmen, artists and scientists to the greatness of Venice and Italy. [...] There is only one type of civilization in Julian Venetia, namely the Italian, which holds exclusive and glorious sway.[56]

There is a resounding echo of these sentiments in the Citizen's anti-British outburst in the "Cyclops":

> — Their syphilisation, you mean, says the citizen. To hell with them! The curse of a goodfornothing God light sideways on the bloody thicklugged sons of whores' gets! No music and no art and no literature worthy of the name. Any civilisation they have they stole from us. Tonguetied sons of bastards' ghosts. (*U*, 12.1997–1203)

Tamaro had equally harsh words for the Austrians, whom he considered barbarous oppressors. He lauded the Triestines who had taken up arms against them, sanctified those who had rebelled and been martyred for the cause, and celebrated with particular ardour Guglielmo Oberdan, a Triestine equivalent of Robert Emmet, who was responsible for plotting to assassinate Franz Joseph on his visit to the city in 1878. When his plot was discovered by the police Oberdan was arrested, court-martialled, and, after admitting his intention of blowing up the Emperor, sentenced to death by hanging. His mother, Victor Hugo and Giosuè Carducci appealed in vain to the Emperor for clemency and his execution provided unprecedented ammunition for the irredentists, who drew strength from his last words – "Long live Italy! Long live free Trieste! Out with the foreigners!"

But while there were many parallels between the nationalist movements of Ireland and Trieste, one great difference remained: since 1800 Ireland's economic fortunes had been in a steady decline, while Trieste's had constantly improved. As Stanislaus noted in his diary on 22 April 1907, "They don't count of course that now Venice is under Italian government and is poor, and that Trieste was under Italian government and was poor, but Trieste is under Austrian government and is rich." One of the biggest problems for the irredentists was to counter the politics of empire which had so successfully augmented the economic power of the city. In order to do this, they claimed with increasing insistence that Trieste's economic miracle had been made possible by the city's geographical location and the excellence of its merchants, while the *Austriacanti* (pro-Austrian Triestines) and more neutral observers argued that the city's development depended on its position within the Austro-Hungarian Empire. By the time Joyce had settled in the city, this tug-of-war between the two factions was reaching its climax.

The arrival in 1904 of the Prince Hohenlohe-Schillingsfürst as governor coincided with a heightening of tensions, and it was clear from the outset that he was going to have a tough job in bringing disobedient Trieste to heel, even if he was enthusiastically supported by the *Austriacanti* and their numerous pro-Austrian societies and clubs, including La Lega Monarchica, L'Unione Dinastica Cittadina, and La Società Triestina Austria. This last aimed to bring about "the union and solidarity of people of honourable behaviour and patriotic sentiment in order to keep alive and manifest the sentiments of Austrian citizens publicly, by participating in the feast days and propitious national events as well as those which refer to the most high Royal Family and the Imperial House".[57] It must have been intriguing for Joyce, who taught Hohenlohe's family and many other rich *Austriacanti*, but was also on friendly terms with their sworn enemies, to watch this battle of competing loyalties unfold.

A most intelligent servant of the empire, Hohenlohe was, in Tamaro's words, "a man with a brutal, uncommon intellect, who believed in the future of Austria and was utterly determined not to be defeated".[58] It seemed for a couple of years at least that he might just be successful. In 1906, to the fury of the irredentists, he deprived the Trieste Municipality of its so-called *attribuzioni delegate* (the various "Home Rule" powers or functions of state which Richard Burton had lauded in 1886). This decree, which greatly diminished the autonomy of the Municipality, was issued without prior notice and permitted the government to found a new office (the Council of the Lieutenancy) which, according to the irredentists, was promptly filled with Slav clerks. Tamaro thundered against the governor's actions, condemning "the notorious decrees of Hohenlohe against the Italianism of Trieste, the brutal contempt for Italian national sentiment, the deliberate and systematic destruction of the Italian race within the confines of the Empire", and declaring that the "calvary of Italianism in the unredeemed lands is known to all the civilized world".[59]

In order to counter the popularity of the irredentists, Hohenlohe formed an alliance with the socialists and thus helped them win an historic victory in the Council elections of 1907. He also kept the irredentist leaders under an increasingly vigilant eye, which Tamaro described as "a state of oppression which in turn fed and reinforced Irredentism".[60]

> The press was treated worse than any other: indeed it was the most powerful enemy of the government whose reaction was justified, but the fight carried out by the press was superb. These were the years of the rich *Piccolo* (edited with witty and subtle diplomatic art by Roberto Prezioso), of the poor *Indipendente*, which represented, on their own, the aim of the vast majority of the people. Being incapable of understanding the simple truth of the national phenomenon, the Austrian government blamed the newspapers for the hostility of the citizens, and so it happened that in a report of the Austrian government in Trieste, it was said that between Trieste and Austria there was only one obstacle: *Il Piccolo*. The more the government denied the freedom of the press the more the public held the press dear.[61]

Tamaro explains Hohenlohe's thinking clearly:

> Prince Hohenlohe, while he realized the impossibility of forming a pro-government party in Trieste of the old style, understood clearly that only socialism could cement the political armoury with which Trieste would always be chained to the Austrian state. So it was natural that he would support the socialists in every way.[62]

But even if his alliance with the socialists brought a certain success, it also had the effect of uniting his enemies and in bringing all the strands of irredentism together. Many moderates began to side politically with the irredentists as the question of an Italian university in the city re-emerged.

The parallels between the Irish and the Triestine struggles for the right to control their own educational systems and by extension to choose their own forms of government are again very striking. This similarity was exploited by the Triestine nationalists in 1909, when a long article, on the Irish University question, entitled "L'Università di Dublino", was published on the front page of *L'Adriatico*. In the codes so well known to the readers of such papers, the parallel with Trieste emerged clearly:

For a long time Ireland sought its own university, but its voice was always stifled. Even Gladstone was not able to deliver this. The problem was serious, worrying for every Irish Catholic patriot. One of the world's richest and most brilliant universities, Trinity College, was established in Dublin, but that same institution, founded by Elizabeth to spread Protestantism in Ireland, was so steeped in the Protestant spirit and so prejudiced that the Catholic hierarchy believed it necessary to ban its followers from attending it and so the Irish were deprived of any type of higher education. [...] Protestant fanaticism blocked every effort to found a university for the Catholics of Ireland. [...] The Senate of the National University chose Monsignor Walsh, Archbishop of Dublin, to be its first chancellor. The choice could not have been better. A man of enormous culture, the speaker of very many modern languages, he was well suited to the high position he was called to take up. Now, even Ireland has its Catholic university, which it needed so badly. Generous and strong, the intellect of the Irish never matched their generosity and energy. Now, they see new horizons opening up before them. The Liberal ministry did not agree on Home Rule and it could not, but now the Catholics have a University of Dublin which can give Irish Catholicism a new splendour, a fresh energy.[63]

The writer knew that the Austrians could never grant Trieste "Home Rule", but, as in Ireland's case, a university could be a good first step towards giving the city "a fresh energy" to fight for it.

Irredentists rarely missed an opportunity to challenge the Austrian authorities by organizing mass public demonstrations, pouring onto the streets waving their Italian tricolours and exalting "the holy aim of defending these lands, this sky, these Italian seas".[64] Protests and propaganda came in June 1909, when municipal elections coincided with the fiftieth anniversary of the unification of Italy. Huge celebrations were organized, capped with a performance in the Politeama Rossetti of D'Annunzio's *La Nave*, a work that "highlighted the rebirth of Italian nationalism and imperialism in a newly aggressive and politically organized form".[65] The nationalists triumphed in the elections, which were fought as a battle to preserve the independence of the Municipality against the bullying might of the Austrian Empire under Franz Joseph.

As was the case in Ireland, the struggle for freedom and the development of a national identity was fought on many fronts and with varying levels of intensity. Just as Ireland had its literary revival led by Yeats, Synge and Lady Gregory, Trieste had a similar if less complex and accomplished movement led by men like Attilio Hortis, Riccardo Pitteri, and, most importantly, by D'Annunzio's most notable disciple in the city, Silvio Benco, whose highly successful novels *La Fiamma Fredda* (The Chill Flame) and *Il Castello dei Desideri* (The Castle of Desires) were praised by Marinetti as being second only to the works of D'Annunzio himself.

Joyce's *entrée* into this literary scene was provided by his friend Nicolò Vidacovich, a highly educated multilingual translator and essayist.[66] He had impeccable irredentist credentials, having trained to be a lawyer in the offices of Felice Venezian, while his grandmother was the first woman to have been expelled from Austria for her irredentist activities. In his circle Italian literature was almost blindly celebrated, mostly because it was not Austrian. Among an array of irredentist publications, a short-lived but important literary magazine, *Il Palvese* (the Pavis or Shield-bearer), was published on a weekly basis throughout 1907 from the Libreria Maylander on via San Nicolò. Joyce would have found himself mentioned there shortly after he gave his first lecture in the Università Popolare: "Professor James Joice [*sic*] spoke about the Island of Saints and Scholars (Ireland) and brought this rare and interesting subject to life."[67] The irredentist aims of *Il Palvese* were couched in suitably high-flown terms, as in this extract from the front page of the first issue:

> *Il Palvese* gathers around itself all those who represent – within and beyond the borders – the thoughts and the art of the Italians who are subject to Austria. A symbol of joy, it will celebrate the human spirit in its perpetual rise towards a superior form of life. A symbol of protection, it will defend whatever is the country's heritage.[68]

It celebrated a small number of Italy's great writers, principally Dante, D'Annunzio and Carducci (a writer whose "vain pompous bombast" Joyce disliked heartily[69]), and exercised a form of patriotic cultural terrorism which was similar to that of the various Irish-Ireland movements. Joyce seems to have reacted to this type of material by dismissing not only the motivation behind it but also much of the literature that it sought to sponsor. He made an exception only for Dante:

> I love Dante almost as much as I love the Bible. He is my spiritual nourishment. The rest is ballast. I don't like Italian literature because in the degenerated mentality of Italian writers only these four basic themes predominate: begging orphans and hungry people (when will Italians stop being hungry?), battlefields, animals and patriotism. Italians have a strange way of showing their patriotism. They want to impose with their fists their intellectual superiority over other people.[70]

While most of the contributors to *Il Palvese* were firmly in the camp of "patriotic ambition", there were some important exceptions. Both the poet Umberto Saba, using the name Umberto da Montereale, and Scipio Slataper, writing as Publio Scipioni, made their publishing debuts for *Il Palvese*. In February 1907, Vidacovich, who shared Joyce's fascination with Ibsen and was an acknowledged authority on Scandinavian literature in general, published his translation of *Siesta*, a short novel by the Danish writer A.L. Kielland, and in April he reviewed *Memorie giovanili di Giorgio Brandes*.[71]

While *Il Palvese* was read by an intellectual élite there were also a number of more populist irredentist cultural outlets. First and foremost there was the Teatro Verdi, which was flanked by a host of other highly active irredentist sporting and cultural associations, such as the Dante Alighieri, the Circolo Sportivo Juventus, the Società di Minerva, the Circolo Mandolinistico – so many that Gabriel's question with regard to Miss Ivors in "The Dead" might well have been asked of the Triestine irredentists: "Had she really any life of her own behind all her propagandism?" (*D*, 192). For many of Trieste's leaders, their irredentism was not simply a political stance but a philosophy that thoroughly dictated how they lived. For each of these pro-Italian associations there were smaller Slovene and German equivalents.[72]

One of the most important irredentist associations was the liberal nationalist La Giovine Trieste (Young Trieste), of which Vidacovich was president. It had close links with the Lega Nazionale, an important cultural-political organization for the defence of the Italian language, whose aims were strikingly similar to those of Ireland's Gaelic League.[73] La Società Ginnastica Triestina, which by 1910 boasted over 3,000 members, was involved in the mission to foster "Italian" sports such as "swimming, swordsmanship, outdoor sports and rowing", and its aims and methods had much in common with those of the Gaelic Athletic Association.

Most of the irredentist organizations were part of a network under the control of Felice Venezian, the uncontested leader, who, along with Teodoro Mayer, maintained vital links with Ernesto Nathan, mayor of Rome, future Italian Prime Minister and Grand Master of the Masonic lodge "Grande Oriente d'Italia", of which all three were members. Joyce knew Mayer and both he and Stanislaus taught several of Venezian's family, including his cousin and fellow Mason and irredentist Sansone Venezian, to whom he also later sold Irish tweed.[74]

Il Piccolo and, to a lesser extent, its evening edition, *Il Piccolo della Sera*, were the public faces, the opinion leaders of this political world. That said, the fact that Joyce wrote a series of signed leaders in *Il Piccolo della Sera* about

Ireland's situation should not be given more importance than it deserves. Stanislaus's comment about Joyce's writing for the Dublin *Daily Express* provides a salutary reminder of Joyce's independence.

> Through Lady Gregory's influence Jim obtained a promise from E.V. Longworth of the *Daily Express* of books to review for the paper's literary page. [...] The *Daily Express* was conservative and pro-English, but my brother gave no thought to the politics of the newspaper, because knowing himself he knew that he would never alter a comma in what he wanted to say either to suit the editor's views or flatter his patroness.[75]

There is no reason to suggest that Joyce had become any more flexible by the time he came to write for the Triestine evening paper. His early articles are complex and wide-ranging, and while sections can be read as damning condemnations of British rule in Ireland, and by extension of Austrian rule in Trieste, they are just as often highly critical of Ireland.

It should be stressed that *Il Piccolo della Sera* had a less openly political agenda then *Il Piccolo*; it published less local news, seeking instead to keep its readers up to date with events in Italy. It carried many reports on international politics, fashion, culture, and gossip from a variety of European newspapers, took cartoons for its daily *nota satirica* from a wide selection of publications including *Pasquino* (Italy), *Volschebuyl Fonar* (Russia), *Borszem Janko* (Hungary), *Taiyo* (Japan), *Kladderadatsch* (Germany), *Punch*, *Freelance* (England), *Rire* (France), *Gedeon*, *Campana de Gracia* (Spain), and published novels in serial form at the bottom of its front page. Its London correspondent, Fabian, gave a lot of space to the Irish question and provided in-depth coverage of the passage of the Irish Home Rule Bill in 1907. On 17 April 1907 he devoted a long article to the colonial conference being held in London and to the growth and management of the British Empire. The writer portrayed Britain's colonial ambitions and methods, which he saw as being locked into a process of degeneration:

> From 1887 till today, England has waged fourteen wars and colonial expeditions and has added four million square miles to its dominions, expanding the empire by almost one third. The enthusiasm for an era of peaceful commerce was followed by a desire for a period of decisive expansion; the tender care for the spiritual salvation of the blacks of Africa was followed by the fear of coming off worse in the partition of Africa; Tennyson's sentimental lyrics were followed by the barrack verses of Rudyard Kipling![76]

On 11 May 1907, in an article entitled "A Half Measure for Ireland",

Fabian wrote: "One by one the liberal government keeps the promises made to the electorate. Yesterday it was Ireland's turn. But of all the bills presented so far, this last one is perhaps the least satisfying from the liberal point of view."[77] He strongly criticized the bill, which he felt conceded too little to Ireland: "The history of the British government in Ireland has been, for the last hundred years, a history of famine, misery, insurrection and depopulation. But even if it had been good rather than bad and if it had brought about material progress for Ireland, the nationalists would continue to be equally dissatisfied, because they believe that not even a good government is better than an autonomous government."[78]

In an opinion piece published on 28 May 1907, the British authorities were chided about "the Irish question which has come back to haunt them (when was it ever dealt with in depth?)",[79] and another article on the same day described the tense situation in Ireland and pointed out that Irish indignation at the Home Rule Bill had caused the British to withdraw it. As the summer wore on, the political crisis in Ireland worsened and *Il Piccolo della Sera* did not neglect to keep its readers up to date. In accepting the invitation to write for this newspaper, Joyce was also accepting the risk of being seen to conform to a particular political stance; indeed his socialist friends were said to be dismayed that he accepted this opportunity. Yet *Il Piccolo della Sera*'s agenda was also partly his own; if by criticizing another foreign empire and the Catholic Church he was also lending a hand to the newspaper's cause, what harm? In a letter to Stanislaus from Rome in partial support of Arthur Griffith's programme, Joyce wrote:

> A great deal of his programme perhaps is absurd but at least it tries to inaugurate some commercial life for Ireland and to tell you the truth once or twice in Trieste I felt myself humiliated when I heard the little Galatti girl sneering at my impoverished country. (*LII*, 167)

In most of the wired reports in the local papers, Joyce would have read of Ireland as a place of poverty, famine and insurrection, a country, as he put it in "Ireland, Island of Saints and Sages", destined to be "the everlasting caricature of the serious world" (*CW*, 167). He tried to counter these stereotypes by engaging in activities that might broadly be defined as constructive nationalism. That is, he sought to introduce the Triestines to the art, literature and mystery of Ireland and to educate them about the tragedy of its politics.

Long before he published a word in *Il Piccolo della Sera*, he was already engaged in these activities with his private students, as Nicolò Vidacovich recalled in a letter written to Nino Frank in 1929:

> Your recent letter pleased me very much, taking me back to the good times, in which James Joyce, not yet illustrious, gave me English lessons and introduced me to the Irish Revival and to Yeats and Synge etc.[80]

Vidacovich's library contains testimony to this in the shape of first editions of *On Baile's Strand* (1907),[81] *Poems* (1908), *The King's Threshold* (1911), *The Land of Heart's Desire* (1912), and *The Countess Cathleen* (1912). Stanislaus Joyce reports in a diary entry dated 21 March 1908 that Joyce bought *The Tables of the Law* by Yeats, and galloped through it immediately over dinner – evidence of Joyce's fervent interest in (if not necessarily enthusiasm for) the new writing being produced in Ireland by Yeats and his followers.

Joyce chose "the turbid drama of Fenianism" (*CW*, 188) as the topic for his first article in *Il Piccolo della Sera*, using the death, just five days earlier, of John O'Leary as the focus for his comments.[82] Francini Bruni probably helped correct the Italian in this and subsequent articles. Indeed in 1909, when Joyce, temporarily in Dublin, sent his fifth article for *Il Piccolo della Sera* to Stanislaus, he warned him to "go over it with F [Francini Bruni]" (*LII*, 240) before forwarding it to the newspaper. Silvio Benco, a senior journalist, was asked by the paper to take a look at Joyce's first articles, but found little or nothing to correct after he had gone through them with their author:

> He wanted the revision to take place under his own eyes; I do not think it was from distrust so much as from a desire to learn. In fact, there was very little to change in the articles. The Italian was a bit hard and cautious, but lacked neither precision nor expressiveness. [...] My collaboration did not last long. The day we argued about a word and he was right, with his dictionary in his hand, it became clear to me that his manuscripts no longer needed my corrections.[83]

The Fenianism article appeared on 22 March 1907, having been "senselessly changed in some points"[84] by the newspaper's editorial staff, to both Joyce's and Francini Bruni's fury. Compared with the articles that follow it, this is a cautious piece which essentially points to two Irish struggles: the first, that "of the Irish nation against the English government"; the second, "no less bitter, between the moderate patriots and the so-called party of physical force". Citing history as his witness, Joyce notes that any concessions from the English are "granted unwillingly" or "at the point of a bayonet", yet he is critical of the advocates of physical force who "preach the dogma of separatism" but know "that in view of England's power armed revolt has now become an impossible dream" (*CW*, 188–9). Although he criticizes a doomed "foolish uprising" like Robert Emmet's, he does not condemn violence *per se*.

He supports the Fenianism of '67 because it was an efficient country-wide organization that had a realistic chance of success; the tragedy of it was that an informer betrayed the cause. Joyce terms subsequent violent actions (even if similarly motivated) as "crimes" although he admits that they usually managed to provoke some kind of legislative provision for Ireland. The reception of such progress was marred by the squabbling of the constitutional nationalists and the Fenians, both of whom habitually tried to claim credit.

Although by now Joyce's interest in socialism was on the wane, he still depicts these political happenings almost as a sideshow to the tragedy of poverty, starvation and death that was being enacted in Ireland on a daily basis. He takes issue with nationalists of various shades, whom he sees as having little interest in building the nation, improving the lot of the people. "As a backdrop to this sad comedy is the spectacle of a population which diminishes year by year with mathematical regularity, of the uninterrupted emigration to the United States or Europe of Irishmen for whom the economic and intellectual conditions of their native land are unbearable". Joyce counts himself among the emigrants and condemns Ireland for this and for fulfilling "what has hitherto been considered an impossible task – serving God and Mammon, letting herself be milked by England and yet increasing Peter's pence" (*CW*, 190).

What is the answer? Joyce does not suggest one, but he does say that "it is impossible for a desperate and bloody doctrine like Fenianism to continue its existence" (*CW*, 191), while also asserting his profound scepticism as to whether the Irish representatives in Westminister will deliver any substantial results. Having dismissed these two possibilities, he outlines Sinn Féin's programme and concludes that "this last phase of Fenianism is perhaps the most formidable".

In a low-key and matter-of-fact tone, totally in contrast to the rhetorical style that would have been adopted by the Triestine cultural nationalists or by their Irish counterparts such as D.P. Moran and company, Joyce's second essay, "Home Rule Comes of Age", is a more substantial piece which surveys a century of Anglo-Irish relations and the awful disappointments offered by history. He was more pleased with this second article and managed to resist *Il Piccolo della Sera*'s attempts to shorten it, claiming that it was the best-informed article in the continental press on the issue that had been the "hinge of English politics for twenty years".[85]

No matter how great Joyce's fascination with the Irish situation, this piece shows that he neither had faith in nor wished to serve the Irish cause. So what is offered is an entry into the "nightmare" of Irish history, and the reader – like the Irish themselves – is ultimately left dissatisfied by an analysis that is as inconclusive as the history it attempts to narrate. Joyce the journalist/artist consciously sticks his pen into the spokes of history, into the standard temporal trajectory of most nationalist narratives, and provides a snapshot of the situation in his native land, presenting a clear if harsh image of the Irish and taking advantage of the fact that he can provide an insider's view yet not be judged for it by the insiders themselves. It is just the type of anecdotal, involved and personalized reportage that readers would not have found in the international dispatches or in Fabian's more neutral pieces. While the article is critical of British rule in Ireland and especially of the manoeuvrings of the devious Liberal government, the harshest attack of all is kept for the Irish religious and political leaders themselves.

The piece begins by evoking the promise of an historic moment – 1886 – when Gladstone introduced his Home Rule Bill, and then proceeds to explain the devastating shock felt in the aftermath of this moment of hope, a betrayal that reached its lowest point in "the moral assassination of Parnell" (*CW*, 193) and was then prolonged for a further twenty-one years of procrastination over the same Bill. Joyce expresses his outrage at the deceit of the English Liberals whose 1907 legislation, he maintains, is no better than that offered by "the imperialist Chamberlain" (*CW*, 194), and will probably not, in any case, be passed by the Lords. He then turns his ire on the Catholic Church – "the priests and the priests' pawns" of *A Portrait of the Artist as a Young Man*, who "broke Parnell's heart and hounded him into the grave" (*P*, 133) – the excesses of which he had recently had occasion to witness at close quarters in Rome. But, more than anything else, Joyce, who had already written about this "degradation of politics to merely pathetic gesturing or ineffectual manoeuvering" in "Ivy Day in the Committee Room"[86] (composed in 1905 in Trieste), sees the Irish as their own worst enemies, divided against themselves and serving two masters, God and Mammon. Worse again are their political leaders, who talk and agitate but manage to do little more than line their own pockets.

Joyce's third piece, "Ireland at the Bar", published on 16 September 1907, was his strongest yet on what he termed the "snarled" Irish question. The article begins by describing the trial of a poor old man, Myles Joyce, for the Maamtrasna murders. Despite the fact that he was a native Irish-speaker with absolutely no knowledge of English, Joyce's trial was carried out in English. Although he was patently innocent, he did not have the language to defend himself and was condemned to be hanged. Joyce recreates and embellishes the scenes carefully:

> The magistrate said:
> 'Ask the accused if he saw the lady that night.' The question was referred to him in Irish, and the old man broke out into an involved explanation, gesticulating, appealing to the other accused and to heaven. Then he quieted down, worn out by his effort and the interpreter turned to the magistrate and said:
> 'He says no, "your worship".' [...]
> When the questioning was over, the guilt of the poor old man was declared proved, and he was remanded to a superior court which condemned him to the noose. On the day the sentence was executed, the square in front of the prison was jammed full of kneeling people shouting prayers in Irish for the repose of Myles Joyce's soul. The story was told that the executioner, unable to make the victim understand him, kicked at the miserable man's head in anger to shove it into the noose. (*CW*, 197–8)

Joyce meant for his readers to see the story as a metaphor for the relationship between England and Ireland. If any guilt is to be attributed in this scene, it is to English justice, or rather the lack of it. England has utterly failed (and never really tried) to understand Ireland properly, yet it continues to condemn it brutally.

> The figure of this dumbfounded old man, a remnant of a civilisation not ours, deaf and dumb before his judge, is a symbol of the Irish nation at the bar of public opinion. (*CW*, 198)

Joseph Valente sums up Joyce's methods succinctly:

> "Ireland at the Bar" works an analogy between the plight of a Gaelic tribal patriarch, Myles Joyce, on trial in a British court of law and the place of Ireland itself making its case for nationhood in the court of European public opinion. The emphasis on justice in this essay is particularly significant because, unlike other rhetorical dominants he might have selected, it allows Joyce to explore not only the patent abuses of English law in the Myles Joyce trial, but also the hidden complicities of the Irish themselves in the affair.[87]

In Joyce's view, public opinion in Europe is largely controlled by English journalists, and Ireland cannot make her voice heard in the world except through their biased filter, which ensures that the country is as poorly represented as Myles Joyce was by his interpreter. Joyce complains that there is no mention of Ireland "except when uprisings break out, like those which made the telegraph hop these last few days" (*CW*, 198).

His belief was that the injustice of the British government in Ireland was compounded by its press's biased reporting of its effects and of matters Irish in general. Joyce would have seen several articles in *Il Piccolo della Sera* in August that would have backed up this thesis. A look at just one proves his point; on 6 August 1907, *Il Piccolo della Sera* published a leader by the usually well informed and pro-Irish Fabian, entitled "Ireland in Ferment – the Police Strike". It makes no attempt to go behind the problems it describes, portraying only the reaction to a series of highly complex causes and injustices:

> In Ireland we have a situation in which the comic and the serious elements are easily confused. Everything is like this in Ireland, where, as a local proverb says, people know how to spice even their misery with humour. Above all we have a serious re-emergence of agrarian violence in the west. The moonlighters go about at night under the light of the moon committing all sorts of acts of vandalism in the pastures, hunting and driving the beasts off in all directions. For two or three months, that is since the Dublin Convention decided not to support the Irish Council Bill and so declared war against the Government, all of the region west of the Shannon has been in a genuine state of war. The members of the Land League organize groups which, armed with shotguns, sticks and knives, either go about intimidating anyone who rents the pastures; or go around the country knocking down sheds, setting fire to hay barns, cutting down trees and letting the stock loose. Because of this, the landlords cannot find anyone who will rent the pastures because nobody is willing to risk their sheep and cows.[88]

Reading pieces like this, Joyce has ample reason to write, "Skimming over the dispatches from London [...] the public conceives of the Irish as Highwaymen with distorted faces, roaming the night with the object of taking the hide of every Unionist" (*CW*, 198). He also laments the fact that Britain "proceeds with a wealth of good judgement in quickly disposing of more complex questions of colonial politics" and wonders "why St. George's Channel makes an abyss deeper than the ocean between Ireland and her proud dominator" (*CW*, 198), an observation which suggests that Joyce did not equate Ireland with the other colonies and was not set against the idea of colonization *per se*. In this article, Joyce aims "to make a modest correction of facts", to counter what he terms in his "Notes on Ireland"[89] the "Celtofobia of French and Italian papers". He is consciously setting out to counter this and to oppose the British gloss on Irish affairs as it often appeared in the short dispatches from London. He points to some of the causes of nationalism, to bread-and-butter issues like poverty and starvation, writing: "Twenty-eight years ago, seeing themselves reduced to misery by the brutalities of the large landholders, they refused to pay their land rents and obtained from Gladstone remedies and reforms. Today, seeing pastures full of well fed cattle while an eighth of the population lacks means of subsistence, they drive the cattle from the farms" (*CW*, 198). He also seeks to contradict the stereotype of the Irish as a violent race by stating, rather dogmatically, that "there is less crime in Ireland than in any other country in Europe" (*CW*, 200).

Joyce did not write another article on Ireland for *Il Piccolo della Sera* until 1909. Are we to conclude from this that the first three did not deliver what the paper had been looking for? Even if Ireland was of limited interest, the paper continued to publish wire reports and leading articles by Fabian on the subject. Would the Triestine irredentists have approved of what Joyce wrote or could his articles have been read as much as a criticism as an endorsement of their agenda and methods? Certainly his subject in his article on Fenianism – "the struggle of the Irish Nation against the British Government" – would, by extension, have been read as that of the Triestine "nation" against the Austrian government. Ellmann contends that Joyce's criticism of the Irish diminished the propaganda value of the articles, and Stelio Crise comments that "Dr Prezioso's disappointment must have been great when he realized Joyce's restless Irish mind did not sympathize with the Sinn Féiners nor with the patriotic Triestine members of the Liberal Nationalist party."[90] But this is to simplify and misread Joyce's intentions. By virtue of the very even-handedness of his writing, the new-found Irish journalist would have won a lot more sympathy from his discerning and predominantly moderate Triestine readership. Furthermore, he did make various comments that would have been appreciated by the Liberal Nationalists as they faced into an election in which their authority was being challenged. In focusing on and criticizing the endless divisions within the Irish nationalist movement and its failure to present a united front, he was putting the Triestine irredentists, who for the most part were united into a genuine mass movement, into a good light. Joyce's condemnation of hopeless acts of physical force could also have been read as an admonition to the more fanatical irredentist element in Trieste, while his criticism of the Catholic Church would have been appreciated by the anti-clerical irredentists, who resented the Church's openly pro-Slav stance and felt that it played too political a role in the Austro-Hungarian Empire, which they mockingly referred to as "Il Santo Impero Romano" and "L'Impero Vaticanesco".[91] Finally, the criticisms that Joyce made about the Irish parliamentary party lining their own pockets while the country lived in poverty could not be applied to their Triestine counterparts, who had used irredentism (perhaps cynically, but successfully nonetheless) as a bargaining plank from which to wrest as much for Trieste from Austria as possible.

But it is hard to imagine that Joyce set out to please the irredentists or the Liberal Nationalist party, for which he probably had little time, at least as little as he had for the establishment politicians of the Irish Party. Indeed Joyce's lectures and articles do very well what he congratulated Mangan on doing, refusing, that is, "to prostitute himself to the rabble or to make himself the loudspeaker of politicians". He kept to his own agenda, which was firstly a personal one and secondly a national one. His lectures and articles show his hurt sense of national pride, dented at the hands of some of his well-off students. Secondly, they reveal, in a more general sense, his constructive reaction to what Arthur Griffith was trying to do, as Dominic Manganiello writes: "Not only did he keep abreast of the Irish political scene, but Joyce staunchly defended Griffith's line of argument on key issues."[92] Both the aim and the content of the articles indeed confirm just how close many of Joyce's positions were to those expressed by Griffith in the *United Irishman* and *Sinn Féin*, which he received regularly from Dublin. He clearly felt that Ireland was at a crossroads when he wrote to Stanislaus saying "Either Sinn Féin or Imperialism will conquer the present Ireland" (*LII*, 187), and while he had reservations about the former's Irish-language policy, he had little hesitation in taking sides.

When, in April 1907, Stanislaus accused him of being hypocritical in his choosing "to be 'a Sinn Feiner'", and at the same time having his books published in England, he replied by saying that he "had always refused to become a member of any league" but that he "believed that if the Sinn Fein policy were followed out it would save the country".[93] There were enough favourable elements in Griffith's policies to allow him to tentatively support Sinn Féin, which he called "the highest form of political warfare he had heard of".[94] He appreciated the fact that Griffith was "an unassuming person", who "didn't indulge in any flights" and "liked his policy because there seemed to be an element of practical commonsense in it".[95] Griffith was contemptuous of the Irish Party in Westminster, attacked (at least sporadically) the Vatican and wanted to set up an Irish consular service abroad to give voice to Irish feelings, thoughts and aspirations, to explain Ireland to the world. This is precisely what Joyce attempted to do in Trieste. As has already been shown, in his articles he was also setting out to counter the anti-Irish propaganda that made its way into the Italian papers from London, as this extract from "Ireland, Island of Saints and Sages" demonstrates:

The English now disparage the Irish because they are Catholic, poor, and ignorant; however, it will not be so easy to justify such disparagement to some people. Ireland is poor because English laws have ruined the country's industries,
especially the wool industry, because the neglect of the English government in
the years of the potato famine allowed the best of the population to die from
hunger, and because under the present administration, while Ireland is losing
its population and crimes are almost non-existent, the judges receive the salary
of a king, and governing officials and those in public service receive huge sums
for doing little or nothing. (*CW*, 167)

Many years later, as Emer Nolan has pointed out,[96] he would put echoes
of these opinions into much of the Citizen's discourse in *Ulysses*, a fact which
should caution against any simple identification of Joyce with Bloom and
induce the reader to understand his at least partial sympathy with some of
the contents of the Citizen's claims. Regardless of how much of the rewriting of his own ideas in the "Cyclops" is parody, Joyce too was concerned with
the opportunities offered by an increase in Irish trade and commerce as a
means to improve the economic conditions of his country:

There's no-one as blind as the fellow that won't see, if you know what that
means. Where are our missing twenty millions of Irish should be here today
instead of four, our lost tribes? And our potteries and textiles, the finest in the
whole world? And our wool that was sold in Rome in the time of Juvenal and
our flax and our damask from the looms of Antrim and our Limerick lace, our
tanneries and our white flint glass down there by Ballybough and our
Huguenot poplin that we have since Jacquard de Lyon and our woven silk and
our Foxford tweeds and ivory raised point from the Carmelite convent in New
Ross, nothing like it in the whole wide world ... (*U*, 12.1240–8)

The author of this passage had himself sought to do his bit to further the
cause of Irish industry abroad. Stanislaus noted in his diary that his brother
wondered "why no Irish firm had the enterprise to send out men to push bog
oak ornaments and duleek china on the continent, and here especially Limerick lace",[97] and described how Joyce set about becoming a commission
agent for Irish goods in the summer of 1908, writing letters to several suppliers of Irish homespun and tweed. Twenty-two invoices and six letters from
the Dublin Woollen Co. to Joyce survive and serve as ample proof of his success as a salesman.[98] Joyce was less successful in his attempts to interest one
of Trieste's biggest clothes shops in these products: despite sending one hundred samples to Ignazio Steiner's on Corso Italia in 1909, he does not appear
to have even received the courtesy of a reply.

In his multi-faceted roles of unofficial Irish consul and part-time Irish sales representative, Joyce was being patriotic on his own terms while arguably fulfilling another aspect of Griffith's programme. A letter from his brother Charles Joyce to Stanislaus some years later explains Joyce's attitude clearly and gives a sense of the importance he placed upon these activities:

> Dixon then said it was a pity that Jim did not use his 'undoubted' talent for a better purpose than writing a book like *Dubliners*. 'Why did he not use his talents for the betterment of his country and of his people?' Jim replied that he was probably the only Irishman who wrote leading articles for the Italian press and that all his articles in 'Il Piccolo' were about Ireland and the Irish people. He said that he was the first to introduce Irish tweeds into Austria although that business was not in the least in his own line.[99]

Joyce's lecture at the Università Popolare can be read as an extension of this constructive nationalism. Such was the importance and prestige attached to the event that the directors of the Berlitz, hoping to bask in their illustrious English teacher's reflected glory, decided to close the school early to allow students to attend. Originally Joyce was to give three lectures on the history of Ireland, Mangan, and the Celtic Renaissance and to be paid 25 crowns for each one, but later he was asked to give two instead of three and offered a reduced fee of 20 crowns per lecture, on the grounds that the University had very limited financial resources. Joyce asserted that he could do nothing complete in two lectures and, although he had been working extensively on the Mangan paper, which he based on his earlier Dublin lecture, chose to deliver just one long essay entitled "Ireland, Island of Saints and Sages".[100] The University accepted this proposal and Joyce gave his lecture on 27 April 1907. Oddly enough, in the history of the Università Popolare, it is not listed under literature or history but under "Geografia e Astronomia".[101]

For the occasion, Joyce borrowed a decent suit from Artifoni and Stannie's overcoat and was delighted to find a big crowd of people awaiting him in the Sala della Borsa. Most of his students and friends were in the audience although Stannie had seen to it that Nora, who did not possess clothes worthy of such an occasion, spent the evening out of sight at the cinema with Giorgio. Even if he judged the lecture "too long and somewhat braggart" and found Jim's reading it from start to finish a little boring, Stannie acknowledged that "it was listened to with attention and greeted at the end with loud applause", and did not object afterwards when Jim decided to reward himself with an absinthe in his coffee and a quarto of wine.[102]

Joyce's talk provides a rich survey of Ireland, its history and culture, and proof, if proof were needed, of the absolute centrality of Ireland in his mind, of his deep involvement in the politics and culture of the country. He sets out by explaining why the Irish referred to their country as the island of saints and sages. In pointed contrast to the Revival view, he emphasizes the role played by early Irish Catholicism in forming the Irish, and by extension the European mind, and dwells on the ancient times "when the island was a true focus of sanctity and intellect, spreading throughout the continent a culture and a vitalizing energy" (*CW*, 154). He then stresses that Ireland's links over these centuries were not with Britain but with Europe, lauds Irishmen like Columbanus for carrying their learning abroad, and notes how highly they were appreciated for their actions. He gives a vivid picture of ancient Ireland as a centre of learning, "an immense seminary, where scholars gathered from the different countries of Europe, so great was its renown for mastery of spiritual matters", and speaks of the age of the Irish language and of "a civilisation that had decayed and almost disappeared before the first Greek historian took his pen in hand" (*CW*, 156).

All of this, of course, had a personal relevance for the exiled Irish writer, who was consciously seeking Irish precedents for his own enterprise and revelled in finding mythic footsteps to follow, in discovering role models and putting them to use in his life and, more grandly, in his works. He found himself in the heart of Europe spreading his own learning among the native Triestines, who comprised as wide a mixture of European cultures as he was likely to find anywhere.

Having given ample attention to this golden age of Irish culture, Joyce enters the darker period of the Irish past, commenting that "anyone who reads the history of the three centuries that precede the coming of the English must have a strong stomach, because the internecine strife, and the conflicts with the Danes and the Norwegians, the black foreigners and the white foreigners, as they were called, follow each other so continuously and ferociously that they make this entire era a veritable slaughterhouse" (*CW*, 159). Eventually all these invaders were assimilated, and even in these troubled times "Ireland had the honour of producing three great heresiarchs: John Duns Scotus, Macarius and Vergilius Solivagus" (*CW*, 160).

These Irish scholars, who became figures of European importance, were significant for Joyce who, more than any Irish writer before him, was embarking on a literary adventure that was utterly European. When he came to write *Ulysses* and *Finnegans Wake*, he would consciously and effectively reconnect Ireland with Europe and attempt to circumvent the narrow English–Irish stalemate, even if that stranglehold would prove hard to break, as Stephen Dedalus reflects in *Ulysses*, where Buck Mulligan urges him to "touch" Haines the "oxy chap downstairs" for a guinea (*U*, 1.154–5).

The English invasion effectively saw Ireland being cut off from Europe and caused the rise of "a new Celtic race [...] compounded of the old Celtic stock and the Scandinavian, Anglo-Irish, and Norman races", all of whom "made common cause against the English aggression, with the Protestant inhabitants (who had become *Hibernis Hiberniores*, more Irish than the Irish themselves)" (*CW*, 161). Joyce presents this amalgam of peoples as "the Irish Race" and remembers how an Irish member of parliament chided a fellow Irish colleague "for being a descendant of a Cromwellian settler. His rebuke provoked a general laugh in the press, for, to tell the truth, to exclude from the present nation all who are descended from foreign families would be impossible and to deny the name of patriot to all those who are not of Irish stock would be to deny it to almost all the heroes of the modern movement" (*CW*, 161–2).[103] Indeed, Joyce goes further in an appeal for a tolerance that was as necessary in Trieste as it was in Ireland, by pointing out that Irish civilization "is a vast fabric, in which the most diverse elements are mingled" (*CW*, 165).

Joyce notes that "Ireland prides itself on being faithful body and soul to its national tradition" but criticizes it for being equally faithful "to the Holy See" (*CW*, 162). His native country essentially sold itself out to the Church and to the English, as "the English came to Ireland at the repeated requests of a native King" (*CW*, 162). Joyce admits that "a moral separation already exists between the two countries" (*CW*, 163), and although he deplores those who "heap insults on England for her misdeeds", he provides his strongest condemnation yet of British policy and does not stint in describing those same misdeeds. In the process he links England with Austria by pointing out that "her principal preoccupation was to keep the country divided" (*CW*, 166) – in a manner reminiscent of Austria-Hungary's *divide et impera* policy. Having made this connection, his audience would have been pleased to hear him state that:

> She was as cruel as she was cunning. Her weapons were, and still are, the battering-ram, the club, and the rope; and if Parnell was a thorn in the English side, it was primarily because when he was a boy in Wicklow he heard stories of the English ferocity from his nurse. A story that he himself told was about a peasant who had broken the penal laws and was seized at the order of a colonel, stripped, bound to a cart, and whipped by the troops. By the colonel's orders, the whip-

ping was administered on his abdomen in such a way that the miserable man died in atrocious pain, his intestines falling out onto the roadway. (*CW*, 166)

If this is the lot of the Irish in Ireland, Joyce sees the fate of those who leave in a more positive light, noting that "when the Irishman is found outside of Ireland in another environment, he very often becomes a respected man" (*CW*, 171). Thus the Irish continue to emigrate from their homeland whose "economic and intellectual conditions ... do not permit the development of individuality" (*CW*, 172), and as a result the country reaps no benefits from its sons, who, when they settle abroad, achieve greatness in all sorts of fields – in foreign armies, as writers and translators.

Unable to endorse the Irish renaissance, Joyce remains pessimistic: "I, at least, will never see that curtain go up, because I will have already gone home on the last train" (*CW*, 174). His negative opinion was driven, according to Stanislaus, by his belief that "no intellectual or artistic revival is possible until an economic one has already completed because people haven't the time or the stomach to think".[104] Joyce therefore views the Irish literary revival as a false start and is wry about the role of the Anglo-Irish in the attempt to resurrect a language and a culture they had spent hundreds of years trying to wipe out. Particularly in his undelivered lecture on James Clarence Mangan, Joyce reveals a position clearly at odds with Yeats, as Platt observes in a slight overstatement of Joyce's position:

> For Yeats the nineteenth century marked the resurgence of a national culture; for Joyce it saw the final destruction of a native Irish culture. Yeats saw himself as the inheritor of traditions rediscovered in the nineteenth century; for Joyce there were no real traditions to be had from that period of Ireland's history, except that this century had produced Mangan.[105]

In the written version of this second lecture, having briefly surveyed Ireland's literature and stressed its European dimensions, Joyce focused on the still relatively obscure Mangan ("the most significant poet of the modern Celtic world and one of the most inspired singers that ever used the lyric form in any country"), and on the European elements in his poetry: "He knew well the Italian, Spanish, French and German languages and literatures, as well as those of England and Ireland, and it appears that he had some knowledge of oriental languages, probably some Sanskrit and Arabic" (*CW*, 175, 178). Joyce's public view was confirmed in private to Stanislaus, whom he told that "Mangan was beyond the shadow of doubt the national poet of Ireland".[106]

Joyce does not hesitate in blaming his fellow-countrymen for Mangan's lowly status, writing: "Mangan will be accepted by the Irish as their national poet on the day when the conflict will be decided between my native land and the foreign powers – Anglo-Saxon and Roman Catholic, and a new civilization will arise ..." (*CW*, 179). In the meantime Joyce attempts to celebrate the diverse elements in Mangan's poetry, and especially his recording of injustice and tribulation: "No other poems are full, as those of Mangan, of misfortune nobly suffered, of vastation of soul so irreparable" (*CW*, 184). Ireland has betrayed men like Mangan. "Love of grief, despair, high-sounding threats – these are the great traditions of the race of James Clarence Mangan, and in that impoverished figure, thin and weakened, an hysterical nationalism receives its final justification" (*CW*, 186).

Joyce's piece in many ways is a summary of his state of mind with regard to his native land in 1907. He shows a central concern with the issue of justice on both a personal and a national level and seems to endorse the idea of a moderate constructive nationalism as the route towards a national deliverance, which cannot come simply as a reaction to a foreign power or because of a hatred of it but through an achieved understanding of one's own race and its complex roots. What is also important to stress is that he was seeking to place Irish nationalism in a European context. In Trieste he would witness the inexorable rise of an increasingly intolerant form of nationalism, which his lectures were already warning against as his pages of *Ulysses* would later do. Seven more years would pass before he began that work, but already he was carefully combing the Irish historical and cultural landscape as well as that of Trieste, and would soon begin to draw upon the two for his new creative enterprises.

5 *Two of the hardest years*

After a spring of promise, the summer of 1907 brought the birth of Lucia and a crescendo of discontent in the Joyce household. Joyce had run out of articles to write for the local press and any faint hopes he may have nurtured of contributing to newspapers other than *Il Piccolo della Sera* came to nothing when *Il Corriere della Sera* of Milan turned down his proposal to travel to Dublin and cover the Dublin Exposition for them, and both *La Stampa* of Turin and *Il Mattino* of Naples declined his offer to cover Irish affairs on the grounds that they already had correspondents working for them in this field.

Joyce's only steady means of support remained his meagre part-time salary from the Berlitz school. Predictably, the demand for the usual private English lessons which served to supplement his income also dipped as the summer wore on, and this is probably why in July Joyce wrote applying for a position in the South Africa Colonisation Society. In his diary, Stanislaus gives the impression that his brother thought seriously about taking a job with the Society and intended to travel alone to South Africa, leaving him to look after Nora and the children, so that he could make enough money to send back their fares and thus enable them to follow him. As it turned out Joyce was not offered the position, but even if his application had been successful his health problems would have prevented him from going. According to Ellmann, Joyce was hospitalized in the Ospedale Maggiore for a month in the summer of 1907 and forced to spend the best part of three months at home convalescing. "The new disaster was rheumatic fever, which afflicted him in mid-July, possibly, he suspected, as an aftermath of his carefree nights in Roman and Triestine gutters. He had to be put in the city hospital, and remained there into August. He was not fully recovered until well into September" (*JJ*, 262). Ellmann states that Joyce "told an opthalmologist [*sic*] in Paris that it was an aftermath of a night on the ground after a drinking bout" (*JJ*, 769).

In his diary, Stanislaus goes into quite a lot of detail about his brother's recurring bouts of ill health – his rheumatism and his eye problems – but makes absolutely no mention of Joyce being hospitalized in this period. According to Stanislaus, his brother was treated at home for the duration of his illness by the family doctor, Dr Sinigaglia. These memories are valuable because they correct Ellmann's version of events and cast doubts on a recent suggestion made by Kathleen Ferris that Joyce was actually suffering from a sporadic attack of syphilis. In her controversial book *James Joyce and the Burden of Disease*, she diagnoses *tabes dorsalis* and claims that Joyce's eye problems were a complication resulting from this.[107] Stanislaus, in his highly detailed and sometimes personally compromising diary, makes no mention of Joyce ever having contracted syphilis. In an entry of 4 August 1907, referring to Nora's hospitalization for the birth of Giorgio, he notes that there was a special syphilitic ward in the Ospedale Maggiore before concluding by saying: "It's a wonder how Jim escaped in Dublin where such a universal ignorance of sexual matters reigns." He would hardly have written down such an observation had his brother been suffering from syphilis or its possible complications at this time; and given the intimate nature of their relationship in these years there seems little likelihood that Joyce would have kept such an important fact from him.

Nora's second pregnancy proved more tiring than the first and she suffered often with stomach cramps, which Stanislaus blamed on the bad food being dished up to her by the landlady. She was increasingly moody and sulky and her rows with Joyce were more and more regular. On 28 June, Joyce summoned Dr Sinigaglia, who, after examining her, announced that the baby would be born within three weeks. He also prepared the papers for an eventual admission into hospital, having persuaded the couple to pretend they were married so as to avoid bureaucratic difficulties.

Lucia's birth is another episode that has caused confusion among Joyce's biographers. Ellmann reported it thus: "Some days after Joyce was hospitalized Nora's labor began, and she too went to the hospital. The baby was born on July 26 in the pauper ward, 'almost born on the street,' as she admitted later" (*JJ*, 262). Brenda Maddox's version is similar: "How Nora made her way to the Ospedale Civico di Trieste on July 26 … is not known. Probably Stanislaus escorted her. She told the Francinis later that the baby girl had been born 'almost in the street'."[108] Both these versions rely on Ellmann's 1954 interview with Francini Bruni[109] and strangely ignore Stanislaus's diary, which provides an eyewitness account of what happened. The diary states clearly that Joyce went with Nora to the hospital on 25 July as soon as the midwife said it was time.[110] While Stannie was busy entertaining young Georgie, Joyce helped Nora get settled. Then the two men and the little boy left her in the hospital, went out for dinner and then home to bed confident that the birth would not take place until the following day. The next morning Joyce returned and was a little surprised to be told that Nora had given birth to a baby girl at four in the morning. They decided to call her Lucia, but both he and Nora were slightly disappointed, as they had been hoping for another boy. Nora left hospital on 5 August having been given twenty crowns in charity. On the same day summons to "Sig Joyecs [*sic*] Giacomo, professore di lingua inglese" arrived from the "amministrazione del civico ospitale" asking him to call by immediately to pay Nora's hospital fees or else to produce a "certificato di povertà".[111] Like most such requests, this one was probably ignored.

In mid-August Joyce found better rooms for his expanding family "in the very large old and dirty looking remains of what was once a very fine house indeed in Santa Caterina", partially overlooking Corso Italia.[112] Even though he felt that it was overpriced at thirty crowns a month, Stanislaus also agreed to join them in this flat having accepted Jim's opinion that it would take him a month to find a better room where they would be willing to take children.

Shortly after his return from Rome, to Stannie's astonishment, Joyce had managed to convince Artifoni to rehire him and pay him fifteen crowns for six hours of teaching per week, probably because the director of the Berlitz school did not want to run the risk of having a popular and successful former employee poach some of his more regular and prestigious students. Oblivious to any possible objections on Artifoni's part, Joyce also went back to giving lessons to many of his former private students.

He also resumed his habit of attending the theatres of Trieste, and although he missed the Italian premiere of Franz Lehar's *Die Lustige Witwe* (*The Merry Widow*), which was held in the Teatro Filodrammatico on 27 February 1907, he would certainly have been impressed by the April concert season in the Teatro Comunale Giuseppe Verdi, which was crowned by the appearance of Gustav Mahler, who conducted the prelude to Wagner's *I Maestri Cantori*, Beethoven's Fifth Symphony and his own First Symphony on 4 April. Of the many operatic high points, the most important was the visit of the composer Umberto Giordano to conduct his own opera *Fedora* at the Verdi in the summer of 1907. In July of the same summer Joyce was given free tickets from his friends at *Il Piccolo* to attend a performance of Gaetano Donizetti's *Lucrezia Borgia* as part of the Anfiteatro Minerva's outdoor summer season.[113] In Trieste, Joyce, unlike Mr Browne in "The Dead" (which he was composing at this time), could certainly not complain that they no longer played "the grand old operas" such as *Dinorah* and *Lucrezia Borgia*.

Nora, too, occasionally went to the opera when she had time and money to do so and sometimes she took two-and-a-half-year-old Giorgio along with her to the matinée performances. She also liked to treat him to occasional visits to the cinema and the theatre. In September 1907 Giorgio was taken to see *Carmen* and, to his father's great pride, could already sing the Toreador song as well as pieces from from *La Bohème, Tosca*, and "even a motif from *Siegfried*".[114]

Not long after his return to Trieste, in May 1907, *Chamber Music* "was published by a professional publisher at the publisher's risk. In other words, Joyce had joined the great company of professional authors and joined it at a moment when he most needed the strengthening reassurance of that fact."[115] How much reassurance this actually gave Joyce is debatable, given the struggle Stannie had to convince him to go ahead with publication. Without his younger brother's determination, the project would probably never have got off the ground:

> It was he [Stanislaus] [...] who put the poems of *Chamber Music* into a
> sequence and thought of that title for them. In 1907, just before they were to
> be published, James suddenly decided that their sentiment was false, and went
> to cable the publisher, Elkin Mathews, not to bring them out. Stanislaus
> walked up and down in front of the Trieste post office arguing with him; he
> finally persuaded James to allow the book to appear because it would help him
> publish other books. The contrast of opinion was typical: Stanislaus's judge-
> ment was sound in practical terms, but James was right in that *Chamber Music*
> looks pale beside his other works.[116]

In reality, Stannie shared Joyce's doubts of the merits of the poems. When he
received the proofs from Jim in Rome on 3 March, he noted that his brother
"has no opinion of his verses: he writes of them as if another had written
them", while Stannie himself felt that "their perfection seemed insignificant.
[...] It seemed to me that Jim had not put his shoulder on to them, that the
strength of his mind and his moral courage had not gone into them."[117] As
it turned out, both Stanislaus's and Joyce's reserve was justified; the few
reviews the slim volume received were unenthusiastic, sales were low and the
book did nothing to ease Joyce's always precarious financial situation or to
nudge along the process of bringing *Dubliners* into print.

Illness aside, this was an infernal period for the Trieste branch of the Joyce
clan. In a disgruntled letter he never actually sent to his father, Stanislaus said
they were "in a really poverty-stricken state", and described the summer of
1907 as a hell. Joyce was too sick to teach, so Stanislaus had to teach both his
own and his brother's lessons before going to keep him company in the
evenings, which they often spent together chatting, or with Stanislaus reading aloud light novels or short stories, with the mysteries of Sherlock Holmes
being particularly favoured. When Joyce began to feel a little better in July,
the two brothers would spend long evenings at Barcola or down the pier (the
Molo San Carlo) in front of the Piazza Grande gazing out to sea, commenting on the passing parade or just talking before returning home via a caffè or
bar where they would drink a quarto of wine.

Nora had a difficult time after the birth. She was frequently sick over the
following year and was eventually forced to stop breast-feeding Lucia in mid-
November. Fortunately Giorgio reacted well to the arrival of his little sister,
sometimes climbing onto the bed beside her, kissing her, and telling her in
Italian not to cry.[118] Yet life with two children in the poorly furnished house
was trying. Nora was constantly tired, Joyce's eyes continued to play up and
very often it fell to Stanislaus to keep a regular income coming in. To make

matters worse, relations between the three adults were often marred by rows and mutual recriminations. Stanislaus, in particular, often felt that Nora was not pulling her weight, while she, on the other hand, was becoming increasingly annoyed by his slighting comments about her. She appealed to Joyce for support and nearly always received it, much to Stannie's frustration. It should also be said, however, that there were moments of tenderness between Joyce and Nora, such as when he bought her a chamois handbag for her twenty-fourth birthday or when she went to the trouble of making them all porridge for breakfast or a *zabaione* for dessert. But these were exceptions to the norm. Increasingly Nora was moody and bad-tempered and she made little secret of the fact that she found Jim's drinking and their collective penury harder and harder to accept. She would vent her frustration by refusing to cook or by sitting stubbornly in what Joyce considered to be his armchair. Verbal rows between them were frequent and sometimes violent, and more than once Stanislaus heard Joyce remonstrate with her for "turning his children against him".[119] She would counter-attack by telling him to go out and get drunk, that that was all he was good for, and by threatening either to leave, to write home to tell everyone how incapable he was of providing for his own children, or to go and have Giorgio and Lucia baptized.

Despite the often dreadful atmosphere in their home, despite their shabby appearances and their obvious material poverty, the Joyce brothers somehow managed to give the impression that they came from a moneyed Dublin family, so much so that in April 1907 their employer Almidano Artifoni proposed to sell them the Berlitz school for 1000 lire, because, as Stannie noted "he, too, thinks that Pappie is well off".[120] Artifoni argued that the school's principal business was English lessons, that both Joyce brothers "were so well-known" that they could "pay back the 1000 lire in 3 years and live meanwhile well enough". Stannie, in particular, was highly dubious that things would proceed so smoothly and saw to it that nothing came of the proposal. Artifoni did not give up, however; on 29 June he offered Joyce a loan to enable him to go to Pola where, having taken the time to restore his health, he could reopen the Berlitz school.[121] Once again, the offer was declined.

When Joyce was at home sick in the summer of 1907, Artifoni told him that the school would cover his expenses as long as he was ill, and presumably added the proviso that he would have to repay the money when he was back on his feet. But the autumn brought big changes in the school, which Artifoni decided to lease to two members of the staff – the teachers of French and German, Guye and Scholz – following the Joyce brothers' refusal. When

Joyce discovered that his debt was also being passed on to them, he left the school in a fury and without notice, feeling rather unjustly that Artifoni had betrayed him. Stanislaus, on the other hand, realized that the family could not afford the luxury of another resignation and soldiered on with his lessons, despite his dislike for the new management.

As the autumn progressed, Joyce began to pick up private lessons here and there but he was still lucky to make thirty crowns per week. Occasionally students called into the Berlitz school looking for him, but Stanislaus, who had signed a contract that threatened him with immediate dismissal if he was found to have helped his brother poach students from the school, refused to risk his own stable position by giving his brother's address. Usually they found him anyway.

In this period, the family were still living in the apartment on the first floor of number 1 via Santa Caterina, and they are listed for the first time in *La Guida di Trieste* (1909 edition), a local equivalent of Dublin's *Thom's Directory.* Joyce appears as "Joyce Giov., Prof. Ingl" and then as "Joyce James, Prof. Ingl", and both brothers are also listed under the section for private language teachers. Jim, probably because he had a degree, has the rather superior title of "Professore d'inglese", while Stannie has to make do with his description as a "Maestro d'inglese".

Joyce took advantage of his lack of work by returning to his writing. During his three-month convalescence, according to Ellmann, he "plotted his literary life for the next seven years" (*JJ*, 263). By the end of September 1907 he had managed to finish writing "The Dead", telling Stannie that "he had put more work in one story than any of the Irish put into two or three plays".[122] In addition to so many other possible interpretations, its warm evocation of the post-Christmas period in Dublin can be read as a corrective to the bleak, pessimistic picture of Ireland as a "centre of paralysis" which he had painted in the other stories of *Dubliners* and in his Trieste articles and lectures.

Stannie was hugely impressed by his brother's new story, which he thought "magnificent [...] a story worthy of any of the Russians I have read. [...] The comedy of the supper table is excellent and so is the end. I wonder will any scruffy old professor recognise Jim's ability to write general noise on paper, a kind of comic chorus, and to balance it against solo and silence. In conception, execution and in its effective ending it, in my opinion, is a magnificent story and if it had been a little more compact, probably the best Jim has done."[123] Stannie shared his enthusiasm with his brother in the hope of encouraging him to resume work on his autobiographical novel, and this ploy paid off. As winter set in, Joyce began rewriting *Stephen Hero* completely as *A Portrait of the Artist as a Young Man*, managing to complete the first revised chapter by 29 November despite his anxiety about whether he would be able find anyone willing to publish it. He continued to write fitfully, alternating between periods of intense work and others of despair, caused by what might be termed his "publisher's block". "Why", he asked Stannie in February 1908, "would I bother my head writing for when nobody will publish what I write?"[124] On 3 March he gave his brother the second chapter to read and by April he had brought the third to a successful conclusion. That, however, was as far as he would get for the moment. With the shadow of the still unpublished *Dubliners* hanging over him, he became discouraged about labouring over another work that risked the same end and so abandoned work on it. He did, however, continue to push *Dubliners*, as Laura Pelaschiar has shown: "Through Stanislaus's diary, we know that Joyce had been relentlessly trying to get his book into print with various English publishers. He sent it to Methuen, which agreed to read it in February 1908 but rejected it just two months later. He then tried with Grenings and Sisley, who offered to consider it only if he would 'go shares in the expenses', but Joyce could not afford the forty pounds they required. He also sent it to Arnolds, who rejected it in July 1908, and later in the same month he sent it to Everetts, unfortunately with the same outcome."[125]

In 1908 and 1909, Joyce's relationship with Nora also continued to be problematic, although they still enjoyed an active sex life, as can be seen from the fact that she had a miscarriage in August of 1908 (to her own relief and Joyce's regret) and from their famous "dirty" letters written in 1909. As was the case in most homes at the time, the burden of looking after the young children fell to the mother, and in Nora's case it weighed heavily. In those days, the common practice was to keep young babies at home for several months, and as a result Lucia's first outing did not take place until April 1908. For the most part, Nora was the one who stayed at home to care for her, and indeed just how little Joyce looked after the children can be surmised from a brief postcard he sent to her after his arrival in Dublin with Giorgio in July 1909, in which he told her to write to one of his sisters "giving her directions" about how to take care of Giorgio (*LII*, 230). At the same time, he enjoyed his son's company, often took him out for walks around Trieste and to the sea, and got a kick out of rough-and-tumble playacting with him. In his diary, Stannie notes how his brother "likes to have Georgie climbing on his knees and contrary to the habit of our family, lavishes signs of affection on him".[126] Judging from Stanislaus's many comments in his Trieste diary, Giorgio was growing up to be a confident, lively and intelligent little boy.

Apart from Joyce's occasional earnings (and Stanislaus's more regular contributions), Nora still never quite knew what financial difficulties each new day would bring. Once, in desperation, "she took money from his pocket to pay an overdue bootmaker's bill. Unfortunately this commendable act disturbed the delicate balance of borrowing and living on credit which James and Stanislaus were so adroit at maintaining" (*JJ*, 268). As a result they were left without money, yet instead of economizing and eating at home, they finished by dining miserably at a workmen's *trattoria*. Stanislaus in particular suffered because of the constantly perilous state of their finances and, despite his titan efforts, often lamented the fact that since his arrival in Trieste they always seemed to be in debt. More than Joyce he was mortified at his own shabby appearance, "his battered hat and soiled threadbare suit",[127] which served as a constant reminder to him of the huge social gap that existed between him and his affluent pupils.

When they had a chance, the two brothers went out at night, usually leaving Nora at home to look after the two children. Almost every evening there were lectures organized by the countless clubs and societies in the city on every conceivable topic – sexual hygiene, alcoholism, Botticelli, De Amicis, Marx, Wagner. Joyce went regularly to the theatre and was often able to wangle free tickets from Francini Bruni, who was now working full-time in *Il Piccolo della Sera*. Ellmann comments:

> Much of Joyce's conversation dwelt on drama rather than on fiction. He still planned to write a play, and regarded his novel and stories as mere preparation for it. [...] From other comments of Joyce at the time about the difference between male and female jealousy, it seems possible that he was already meditating on this theme of *Exiles*. If he postponed writing his own play, he followed the plays of others in Trieste with fascination. (*JJ*, 265).

Joyce was enthusiastic about the great Ermete Zacconi's "verismo" style and his generous performances, firstly in Ibsen's *Ghosts*, in which he played Oswald, and then as Vasili Semenetch Kousfkine in Turgenev's *Il Pane Altrui*, which was produced in November 1907 in the Teatro Verdi to great acclaim and to cries from Joyce "after the scene of the old count in misery, '*Di questi artisti nessuno se ne sogna da noi*' – nobody back home has any idea there are artists like these" (*JJ*, 266).

In early February 1908 he went to the Teatro Fenice to see *Hamlet*, which was being produced as part of a programme including *King Lear*, *The Merchant of Venice* and *Tartuffe* and featuring another renowned Italian actor, Gustavo Salvini. Joyce's reservations about the serious dramatic faults in *Hamlet* were confirmed. While he appreciated Salvini's energetic and intelligent performance in the part of Hamlet, he complained that Ophelia's madness took all the force and drama out of the play, which was presented by Salvini in six acts. Joyce left at half past twelve before it had concluded.[128]

Joyce would have found many people in Trieste who shared his interest in Ibsen. Since the first performance of *The Wild Duck* in 1891 and La Duse's starring role in *A Doll's House* and *Ghosts* in 1893, Ibsen had been one the most popular and highly regarded playwrights in the city. He was also a model for several of Trieste's writers: Scipio Slataper wrote his thesis on him, while Svevo's earlier theatrical writings were very much influenced by the Norwegian. On 28 February 1908 Joyce, having bought and read the play the previous day, went to see *Rosmersholm* with La Duse at the Verdi (she also appeared in productions of Goldoni's *La Locandiera* and D'Annunzio's *La Gioconda*). The next day, he told Stanislaus that Ibsen's drama was slovenly in parts and badly constructed, but excused the author on the grounds of old age. He also regretted having been obliged to see a fading star in it, particularly as her character, Rebecca, was not half as important or interesting as Rosmersholm.[129]

The summer of 1908 brought a variety of interesting operatic productions, including *Cavaleria Rusticana*, *I Pagliacci*, *Lucia di Lammermoor*, *Rigoletto*, *L'Elisir D'Amore* and *Il Barbiere di Siviglia* in the outdoor Anfiteatro Minerva. Perhaps of most interest to him was a production of James Philips's operetta *La Geisha* (libretto by Harry Greenbank), which had a character called Miss Molly and from which Joyce later quoted in the "Hades" episode of *Ulysses*.[130] He may have also gone to see Mascagni conduct a production of his own opera *Amica* on 16 June 1908 in the Teatro Politeama Rossetti. The Triestine public "greeted the shining master of Italian art" with delight, paying "reverent homage to this man who is capable of inspiring with his marvellous original genius the admiration of peoples for the renewed forms of Italian composition".[131]

In the autumn of 1908 the Politeama Rossetti presented a short season of opera which included Puccini's *La Bohème*. Joyce rushed out and bought the libretto (written by Giuseppe Giacosa, an Italian he admired in his notes for *Exiles*) and attended the opera on eight occasions in the first two weeks of October 1908. Joyce and Stanislaus also attended Catalani's *La Wally*, and

Stannie was particularly taken with the soprano Ersilde Cervi Caroli in the title role, writing of her "melodious, expressive voice and really good acting" before affirming that the aria "Ebben? N'andrò lontana" was the best ever written. Joyce was not so keen and observed to Stanislaus that "a musician is generally a decade ahead of his audience and that he [Jim] was probably a decade behind half the audience".[132]

Another highlight of the autumn 1908 season was the opera *Nozze Istriane* by Antonio Smareglia (1854–1929), who would later become a neighbour and friend of Joyce's when he lived on via della Barriera Vecchia. By that time the composer was almost blind, and he and his Irish neighbour attended the same eye specialist, Dr Oscar Oblath. Smareglia made interesting company for Joyce, being probably Trieste's only artist of recognized European standing. His operatic works were regularly performed to acclaim in the world's most famous theatres.[133] Joyce himself noted that "Smareglia (who lives beside me) is held by many to be the most original of the living Italian musicians" (*LII*, 294) and that "he was the only Triestine artist about whom the public and critics would talk in the future".[134]

A close friend of Smareglia's was Romeo Bartoli, a member of the teaching staff of the Conservatorio Musicale di Trieste and the resident choirmaster of both the Politeama Rossetti and the Teatro Verdi. He was also director of the city's highly regarded madrigal choir and a renowned expert in old music.[135] So when Joyce enrolled for lessons at the conservatory in the autumn of 1908, he probably knew that in Bartoli he had one of the best teachers that Trieste had to offer. On hearing Joyce singing drills in an early lesson, Bartoli noted with pleasure that his new Irish pupil could reach B natural, continental pitch, with ease. Thus encouraged, Joyce set about putting on weight and went and placed a fifteen-crown deposit on a piano so that he could practise at home. In early 1909 Joyce may have gone to a production in the Verdi of Wagner's *I Maestri Cantori di Norimberga*, and sometime between May and July 1909 he sang in the quintet from the same opera.[136] There were times in this period when he really believed he could make it as a singer, like his compatriot John McCormack, whose international career he followed with interest and a little envy, reflected in the many references in *Finnegans Wake* to "whatyoumacormack" (*FW*, 450.25) and in his comment to Stannie that it must be a terrible thing to have to practise scales for hours every morning and to have to worry constantly about catching a cold.[137]

Stannie was most unimpressed by Joyce's new passion and poured scorn on "the budding tenorino", who had failed "as a poet in Paris, as a journalist in Dublin, as a lover and novelist in Trieste, as a bank clerk in Rome, and again in Trieste as a Sinnfeiner, teacher, and University Professor".[138] Despite his brother's reservations, Joyce continued lessons with Bartoli in 1909 and, when he was in Dublin from October to December of that year, Stanislaus actually took his place with the Italian maestro. From Dublin, Joyce continued to show interest in his music teacher's successes, asking Stanislaus if he had conducted Donizetti's *L'Elisir d'Amore* well. Stanislaus was disappointed when Bartoli was not particularly impressed with his voice, but his older brother encouraged him to continue with the lessons: "I hope you go on with Bartoli. Don't be discouraged by his sleepy manner. He has heard a lot of tenors in his day and that, added to his natural fat, makes him unenthusiastic. I know he will teach you no vices" (*LII*, 262).

Music played a major role in keeping the Joyce household together, and a love of song and a genuine interest in music was one the few things they all had in common and could share. Joyce sang just about everything from Gregorian liturgical chants to tenor arias from Verdi and Puccini, from traditional Irish airs and Moore's Irish melodies to Triestine drinking songs. He often praised Nora's voice and especially liked to hear her sing "My Dark Rosaleen". Sometimes Francini Bruni, his wife Clotilde, who was a trained soprano, and their son Daniele would come to visit, and often these evenings ended with songs.[139] Clotilde liked to sing "La Cavatina" from Bellini's *La Sonnambula* and Joyce accompanied her on the piano. Stanislaus recalled one occasion on which, much to the discomfort of the neighbours, they all sang choruses and hymns, and generally made bedlam.

Joyce's keenness for the theatre endured over this period, and, as ever in Trieste, there were many opportunities for him to develop his interest. On 25 January 1909, a rather washed-up Sarah Bernhardt appeared in *Les Bouffons* by Miguel Zamacois, and was given a tepid, if respectful, reception. Other productions of note included *King Lear* and *Hamlet* and, on 6 February at the Teatro Fenice, Gorky's *Figli del Sole*. In the same month Ibsen's *Hedda Gabler* was presented at the Fenice.[140]

The characters of John the Baptist and Salomé[141] were very much in evidence in the January–March 1909 opera season, which included Berlioz's *The Damnation of Faust*, Catalani's *Loreley* and Wagner's *I Maestri Cantori* and *L'Oro del Reno*. On 11 February the Teatro Verdi mounted a production of Don Giocondo Fino's *Il Battista* conducted by the composer himself. This was followed a month later with another first for Trieste – a production of Strauss's *Salomé* which aroused huge interest and was probably the musical highlight of

1909, being remembered as "a landmark in modernism previously considered utopian and incapable of realization".[142] Each of the newspapers devoted long articles to Strauss's work and to the soprano, Gemma Bellincioni, and practically all reviewed the opera glowingly. *L'Adriatico* reported:

> Strauss's opera, which has always aroused enormous curiosity, from its very first production in Dresden, to the Italian productions in Turin and Milan, to the most recent in Lisbon, and has also enjoyed great success everywhere, attracted a packed and distinguished audience to our best theatre yesterday evening. All of Trieste's artistic notables, all of its music-lovers and connoisseurs and an enormous gaily-coloured crowd of ladies filled every single seat in the stalls and crammed the galleries. The tense, nervous silence in the audience as the play began was not broken until the very end, except for a round of applause for Bellincioni's first entrance. [...] At the end the applause thundered and the success was consecrated with a dozen enthusiastic curtain-calls.
>
> On the whole it was an indisputable success, the like of which no other new production in our theatre has enjoyed this year.[143]

This production provided Joyce with a fresh journalistic opportunity, and he highlighted Wilde's text as the basis for Strauss's *Salomé* in his article "Oscar Wilde: Il Poeta di 'Salomé'", which appeared in *Il Piccolo della Sera* on 24 March to coincide with the opera's première. Joyce's is basically a biographical piece, sketching Wilde's life, his successes and his ultimate fall. It has a lot in common with his earlier articles in *Il Piccolo della Sera*, centred as it is around another fallen and unappreciated Irishman. Joyce portrays Wilde as a victim not of his fellow countrymen's ignorance and betrayal but of English puritanism and injustice.

His renewed interest in Wilde caused him to write to the Milan-based publisher Fratelli Treves Editori, proposing an Italian translation of *The Picture of Dorian Gray*, which he was presumably hoping to do himself. His offer was rebuffed by Fratelli Treves, who wrote on 21 April 1909 saying that they received many proposals to publish translations of "O.W." but that they had never accepted any of them because of "the difficulties in introducing this name and of recommending his works in catalogues and newspapers which had family readerships". It would be even more inopportune to publish the very work in which Wilde laid out "his real aesthetic theories".[144] One can only imagine Joyce's reaction to such a reply.

In spite of this rejection, in the spring of 1909 Joyce brought a translation of Synge's *Riders to the Sea* to a conclusion, "with the assistance of Dr. Nicolò Vidacovitch [*sic*]"[145] and also returned to work on *A Portrait of the Artist as a Young Man*.

Too little importance has been attached to Joyce's relationship with Vidacovich, whom Stanislaus described as "one of the few gentlemen in Trieste".[146] Joyce and he were genuinely close, so much so that even on his
troubled visit to Dublin in 1909 Joyce found time to send him a packet of
Quaker Oats, in one of those small gestures of kindness that were all too rare
in these early years of struggle but became more frequent when he was established in Paris. Vidacovich wrote immediately to thank him; as always, his
note to Joyce was in English:

> I thank you very much for your kind post card. As I opened the packet of
> Quacker [*sic*] oat meal there was no direction in it. I am therefore anxiously
> expecting your return in order to be initiated in the art of preparing porridge.[147]

Vidacovich had already read Yeats and Synge with his teacher of English
before they decided to do their joint translation of *Riders to the Sea*. Earlier,
Joyce had had reservations about this play, which he termed "a tragic poem,
not a drama" by "a tragic poet",[148] but from 1907 on, after the *Playboy* riots
in Dublin, which he followed closely and greatly regretted missing, his attitude to Synge changed. Because of the reception his play received at the
Abbey Theatre in Dublin, his sympathy for the man and his work increased
until at one stage he actually declared Synge's art to be greater than his own.
In particular, he was very taken by the drama's effect on the ear; he "knew
Maurya's final speeches almost by heart – and he repeated them with such a
keen sense of their beauty",[149] and even used to quote the lamentation of
Maurya to his Florentine friend Francini Bruni (who did not know a word
of English) when they were discussing the musicality of language.[150]

Riders to the Sea was Joyce's first real literary translation and his first experience of working creatively on a text with a collaborator. (Later Vidacovich
would attempt to become Joyce's first Italian translator, but the results were
not to Joyce's liking, as he told Yeats in 1916: "Vidacovich also tried his hand
with me on a version of my story *Ivy Day in the Committee Room* for the
Nuova Antologia but the attempt was a dismal failure" [*LI*, 95].) The translation of *Riders to the Sea* was a genuine collaborative effort, with Joyce and
Vidacovich translating separate sections before combining their results and
collectively completing a final version, Vidacovich offering his superior
translating experience and his perfect Italian, Joyce drawing on his familiarity with Synge's Hiberno-English. Together, they produced a text that is
remarkably true to the original, matching Synge's difficult rhythms and
sounds in standard Italian. As Joan Fitzgerald has written: "It is to be

expected that Italian will require a larger number of words and even more so of syllables than English. Other translations, such as Linati's, manage at times to double the number of words used in comparison with the original – Joyce instead on occasion uses less than Synge."[151] In short, Joyce and Vidacovich imitate the flow of Synge's lines without attempting to reproduce the West-of-Ireland English in any possible Italian dialect equivalent. The result is a bare and essential text which is a triumph of simplicity, naturalness and, most of all, rhythm.

> It isn't that I haven't prayed for you, Bartley, to the Almighty God. It isn't that I haven't said prayers in the dark night till you wouldn't know what I'd be saying; but it's a great rest I'll have now, and it's time, surely. It's a great rest I'll have now, and a great sleeping in the long nights after Samhain, if it's only a bit of wet flour we do have to eat, and maybe a fish that would be stinking.[152]

Joyce and Vidacovich translate this as follows:

> Non è certo perché io non abbia pregato Dio onnipotente per te, Bartli. Non perché non sia stata a pregare nella notte nera, a pregare tanto che non sapevo più le parole che dicevo. Ma ora avrò un gran riposo, ed era tempo certamente. Avrò un grande riposo ora ed un gran sonno nelle lunghe notti dopo il giorno dei morti, se anche non ci sarà da mangiare che un boccone di farina bagnata o forse un pesce che sa di marcio.[153]

The Italian translation was finally published in a literary journal called *Solaria* in 1929.[154]

In a letter to Yeats, written during the First World War, Joyce remembered the translation that he and Vidacovich had made and told him of how he had "read it one night to Mrs Sainati, a very original actress, and her husband took away the *copione* to read it again" (*LI*, 95). This event occurred in May 1909 when Alfredo Sainati's Italian Grand Guignol Theatre Company paid a long-awaited visit to Trieste's Teatro Fenice. Joyce presented the illustrious Italian actor-manager and his wife with the translation and, after Sainati had expressed interest in mounting a production, he set about contacting the Synge estate in Dublin. Sainati's company was praised for its talented actors and specialized in producing three or four short plays per evening, normally three popular tragedies followed by a comedy. Judging from the reviews in the local papers, Synge's tragedy would have been a good deal more sophisticated than much of what the company usually produced, and indeed there are reasons to wonder why Joyce chose it for this enterprise. Certainly the critic in *L'Adriatico* was not impressed:

We find ourselves facing a dramatic form which has the same relationship with art as a bloody murderous event in a newspaper has with a novel by Giovanni Verga or Guy de Maupassant. [...] This form of theatre does not allow us time to argue, to reflect, to think. It hits us brutally; it drags us along in a short play which lasts only an hour; and it throws us out, like poor rags, only to bring us back in quickly with another equally violent play or a grotesque farce. Its principal power lies in this speed. Speed, variety, emotional violence; these are the three points upon which this edifice "sui generis" is built.[155]

Had it not been for "the masterly performance of Sainati"[156] there would have been no audience at all.

Partly with the idea of securing the Italian rights for Synge's play, Joyce prepared to depart for Dublin in the summer of 1909. By now he was happy that Nora and the children were well settled in a new flat at number 8 via Scussa, into which they had moved in late March. This transfer had been repeatedly delayed by the landord in via S. Caterina, who had refused to allow them to leave until all the back rent had been paid up there. In order to transfer to the better new "quarter" in via Scussa, Joyce and Stanislaus had also had to raise a substantial deposit of 600 crowns.

In July Joyce set off with Giorgio for Dublin. The principal reason for his trip home was that he hoped to secure a contract with Maunsel and Co. to publish *Dubliners*, but he also wished to take Giorgio to see Nora's parents in Galway and his own father in Dublin, with whom he had re-established relations in late 1908. Years later Stanislaus would recount how it had been decided that he himself should accompany his nephew Giorgio to Ireland; he was all set to travel but "at the last moment my brother wanted to go, as I had always inwardly suspected he would. He was met at the station at Westland Row in Dublin by a family group who asked him 'Where's Stannie?' It's a question I have often asked myself since."[157] Perhaps Stanislaus was not as free to leave Trieste as Joyce was, as he had been appointed acting director of the Berlitz school in the spring of 1909 and his workload was very demanding, but in any case it was Joyce who made the journey back to Dublin for the first time in five years. Little did he know what awaited him.

FOUR

La nostra bella Trieste

It is dangerous to leave one's country, but still more dangerous to go back to it, for then your fellow-countrymen, if they can, will drive a knife through your heart.[1]

Oh how I shall enjoy the journey back! Every station will be bringing me nearer to my soul's peace. O how I shall feel when I see the castle of Miramar among the trees and the long yellow quays of Trieste! Why is it I am destined to look so many times in my life with my eyes of longing on Trieste?[2]

1 *The news from Dublin*

The three years from July 1909 to September 1912 were among the most frustrating of Joyce's life. His efforts to settle down completely in Trieste were dogged by his ongoing problems in Dublin, where he continued to battle to have *Dubliners* published. To this and other ends, he travelled "home" to Dublin three times in three years but gradually came to realize that "home" was now more of a reality in Trieste than in his native city. Each time he was in Ireland, he found himself being drawn inexorably back to his "second country"[3] on the Adriatic, which became "his città immediata, by alley and detour with farecard awailable getrennty years" (*FW*, 228.23–4). The standard biographies devote little space to Joyce's time in Trieste in these years because practically all the published letters of this period were sent from Dublin. As a result, an inordinate amount of attention has been paid to what happened in his native city, while Trieste has been somewhat obscured. The reality is that Joyce spent less than one tenth of this period in Dublin, perhaps four of the forty-one months.

Joyce's first visit to Dublin after his grand departure in 1904 took place in July and August 1909 and initially seemed very promising. He and Giorgio were warmly welcomed by his father and his siblings. Too similar to get along for a protracted period of time, James and John Stanislaus Joyce understood one another well and managed to achieve a reconciliation. In addition, Joyce's father was delighted to see his first grandson. On the publication front, Joyce also appeared to make progress. On 9 August he met Joseph Hone and George Roberts of Maunsel & Co., and within ten days a draft agreement, which offered Joyce favourable terms and the promise that his book would be in print by March 1910, was signed.

However, all of these positive developments were overshadowed by an unexpected event which upset Joyce enormously. Having successfully negotiated his way around old friends and enemies alike, one day he ran into Vincent Cosgrave who informed him that Nora "had gone for walks in the darkness along the river bank with another escort – himself" (*JJ*, 279). Joyce, who probably remembered Nora's angry words to him in yet another of their rows – "Sure Cosgrave told me you were mad" – was appalled[4] (his friend J.F. Byrne later wrote that he "had never seen a human being more shattered"[5]). Suddenly Joyce's rather flippant remark to Stanislaus about a man's jealousy being only "an outraged sense of theatre-ship" must surely have come back to haunt him.[6] He immediately wrote a series of nasty, accusatory letters to Nora and even went so far as to ask her if Georgie was his son: "The first night I slept with you in Zurich was October 11th and he was born July 27th. That is nine months and 16 days. I remember that there was very little blood that night" (*LII*, 232). He wanted to return to Trieste immediately, and might have, had Stanislaus agreed to send him his fare and had his old friend Byrne not talked sense to him and convinced him that the story was a plot hatched by Cosgrave and Gogarty precisely in order to upset him. Stanislaus also weighed in with evidence from Trieste that Nora had rebuffed Cosgrave in 1904, and eventually their collective efforts succeeded in calming him down. But the episode left a lasting mark: later he would draw on it to make betrayal one of the central issues of *Ulysses*, where Cosgrave appears as Lynch, a Judas character who in "Circe" abandons Stephen to the British soldiers and goes off with the prostitute Kitty Ricketts. Joyce also chose his friend Byrne's address, 7 Eccles Street, as the home of Leopold and Molly Bloom.

Upset as Joyce undoubtedly was, he was still capable of getting on with his business in Dublin. Just two days after his confrontation with Cosgrave, he wrote to Arthur Clery thanking him for his 1907 review of *Chamber Music*. He also conducted his negotiations with Maunsel & Co. and sent orders back to Stanislaus in Trieste to organize references from Roberto Prezioso of *Il Piccolo* and Aldo Oberdorfer of the Università Popolare because he had decided to apply for a lectureship in Italian literature at Trinity College. Both Triestines were warm in their praise: Oberdorfer, writing of Joyce's "Ireland, Island of Saints and Sages" lecture, noted that he had received "unanimous plaudit from the public that expressed equal admiration for the depth of the speaker's arguments and for his perfect command of the language".[7]

Joyce also set about mending fences with Nora, buying her an expensive gold necklace and sending her a series of letters in which he begged for forgiveness:

> No man, I believe, can ever be worthy of a woman's love.
> My darling, forgive me. I love you and that is why I was so maddened only to think of you and that common dishonourable wretch.
> Nora darling, I apologise to you humbly. Take me again to your arms. Make me worthy of you.
> I will conquer yet and then you will be at my side. (*LII*, 235)

Nora replied in her own good time on 21 August, two weeks after she had received his first letter of accusation. She did not deny anything nor did she apologize, but with a certain firmness she told him he had been cruel while Stanislaus had been kind to her. At the same time, she also threw him a lifeline by saying that she was missing him and that she had begun to read *Chamber Music*. Joyce replied delightedly:

> Be happy, my simple-hearted Nora, till I come. Tell Stannie to send me a whole lot of money and quickly so that we may meet soon. Do you remember the day I asked you indifferently 'Where will I meet you this evening?' and you said without thinking 'Where will you meet me is it? You'll meet me in bed, I suppose'.
> Magari! magari! (*LII*, 237)

It was to be almost a month before they met again, in bed or anywhere else. In the meantime Joyce was constantly on the lookout for means of financial support, and as Dublin provided little, he continued to look to Trieste to bail him out: firstly Stanislaus, then Artifoni, and finally *Il Piccolo della Sera*, which agreed to accept his article "Bernard Shaw's Battle with the Censor", written to mark the world première of Shaw's play *The Shewing-Up of Blanco Posnet* at the Abbey Theatre, all contributed to keeping him afloat in a city he felt less and less at ease in.

Joyce's disaffection dominates his article for *Il Piccolo della Sera*, in which he claims that Dublin only comes to life on "one gay week every year" – Horse Show week – and otherwise is a "tired and cynical" and "gloomy" place lost in a "senile slumber" (*CW*, 206). He explains that Shaw's play was banned by the Lord Chamberlain in England but, as his writ did not extend to plays produced in Dublin, the Abbey had every right to produce it. Joyce is clearly of the opinion that this decision to prohibit production did honour to the author, who thus joined the distinguished company of the "banned", which included Ibsen, Tolstoy and Wilde. He proceeds then to provide his readers with an erroneous account of the public argument between Shaw and "the public representative of the King" about the banning of the play, failing to point out that it was, in fact, Yeats and Lady Gregory who sprang to Shaw's defence. The row was keenly followed in Dublin, as Joyce, taking another swipe at his native city, points out: "Dubliners, who care nothing for art but love an argument passionately, rubbed their hands with joy" (*CW*, 207).

Whatever the accuracy of his opinion, Joyce was among a huge crowd at the opening of the play, which he clearly did not enjoy in the least:

> It is a sermon. Shaw is a born preacher. His lively and talkative spirit cannot stand to be subjected to the noble and bare style appropriate to modern play-writing. [...] the art is too poor to make it convincing as drama. (*CW*, 208)

Having dispatched this article to Stanislaus in Trieste, Joyce had a visiting card printed which introduced him as a correspondent of *Il Piccolo della Sera*, Trieste. On the strength of this he procured a free train ticket to Galway and travelled there for a successful encounter with Nora's family. From this moment on his enthusiasm for the West (which, like that of many a misinformed middle-class Dubliner, was based on a romanticized vision) increased, just as his disappointment with Dublin grew (by 2 September he was describing Dublin as "a detestable city" [*LII*, 243]).

From Galway, he sent Nora what is probably the first of the so-called "dirty" letters. He was missing her badly, far more than he would probably have ever expected. As soon as he was back in Dublin he began to make arrangements for the journey home to Trieste and decided to take his sister Eva with him, partly to rescue her from the depressing family situation in Dublin, but also to have her give Nora a hand in running the Trieste branch. All this time he kept in regular correspondence with Trieste, sending curt instructions to Stanislaus (for example to "see that *Prezioso* and *Vidacovich* see the allusions to me and to P.d.S" in the *Evening Telegraph*, which had done a piece on himself and his article on Shaw [*LII*, 250]), while bombarding Nora with a variety of missives which ranged from the extravagantly sexual to the lyrical and tender. As his longing for her grew so did his desire to see the city that had become their home:

> *La nostra bella Trieste!* I have often said that angrily but tonight I feel it true. I long to see the lights twinkling along the *riva* as the train passes Miramar. After all, Nora, it is the city which has sheltered us. I came back to it jaded and moneyless after my folly in Rome and now again after this absence. (*LII*, 249)

By now, Trieste and Nora had somehow merged in his mind: Trieste was the city that had offered him and his family a living of sorts and had sheltered them; Nora was the woman who had continued to have faith in him and had stood by him; together they represented home.

With Eva and Giorgio in tow, Joyce arrived back in Trieste on 13 September 1909 and was eagerly welcomed by Nora, but almost shunned by Stanislaus, who was upset at having had to finance the trip to Dublin and worried about how he would pay for the added expense of feeding and clothing Eva. As it was, he had had to pay the rent for Joyce's flat in his absence as well as to pay off some of his brother's creditors, who were threatening to seize the furniture; sometimes he simply did not know where to turn to find the money to feed Nora and little Lucia. Understandably, his irritation grew when he saw Joyce arrive bearing expensive gifts for Nora, while all he had received was a telegram from Milan the previous day which read "Domattina otto Pennilesse" ("Tomorrow morning at eight. Penniless" [*LII*, 252]). On reading the inscription on the pendant Joyce had bought for Nora ("Love is unhappy when love is away"), Stannie commented in a dry fury, "So is love's brother" (*JJ*, 300).

But while Stanislaus had little time to dwell on these issues and was soon back about his routine business of teaching, Joyce felt no such pressure to return to work. He and Nora spent a lot of time together, sorting themselves out after the Dublin débâcle. Later, when back once again in Dublin, Joyce remembered this period with pleasure: "What nice walks we had together this time, had we not Nora? Well, we will again, dear. Coraggio!" (*LII*, 254). On 16 October he took her to see Puccini's *Madame Butterfly*, which was enjoying a highly successful Trieste première, but unfortunately their evening was marred by a row:

> The night we went to *Madame Butterfly* together you treated me most rudely. I simply wanted to hear that beautiful delicate music in your company. I wanted to feel your soul swaying with languor and longing as mine did when she sings the romance of her hope in the second act *Un bel dì*: 'One day, one day, we shall see a spire of smoke rising on the furthest verge of the sea: and then the ship appears'. I am a little disappointed in you. (*LII*, 255–6)

At the root of their quarrel was the fact that Joyce had decided to leave for Dublin again, hot on the heels of a suggestion Eva had unwittingly made when she commented that she "liked one aspect of Trieste, its cinemas, and remarked one morning how odd it was that Dublin, a larger city, had not even one" (*JJ*, 300). Her words would spark the Cinema Volta enterprise.

2 *Cinema pioneer*

In July 1896, a mere six months after the Lumière brothers' first projections at the Salon Indien del Grand Café du Paris, the first of many travelling cinemas opened in Trieste in the Teatro Fenice. Just two years later Joyce's future business partner Antonio Machnich opened his first cinema, the Cinematografo Excelsior, again in the Teatro Fenice; later he would run the Cinematografo Lumière/Excelsior in via Torrente to considerable success.

Joyce's first year in Trieste, 1905, saw the establishment of the city's first permanent cinema, Il Cine Americano in the Piazza della Borsa, an event warmly welcomed in the press.[8] The opening of Il Grande Cinematografo a Colori with *La Bella Addormentata* (Sleeping Beauty) at the Teatro Fenice was another important milestone. Most of the films were French, although there were also some Italian and Triestine ones shown. Pathé's films were favoured and Joyce may well have watched his "Grande corsa automobilistica per la Coppa Gordon Bennett 1905", which was shown in the summer of 1905.[9] The same year also saw the arrival of the first American film in Trieste, Edwin S. Porter's 1903 *Uncle Tom's Cabin*.

In these years, films were made about all sorts of topics: *Dal Socialismo al Nihilismo* (From Socialism to Nihilism), *Aladin, ovvero la lampada merav-*

igliosa (Aladdin, or The Magic Lamp), *Fregoli il Trasformista* (Fregoli the Transformist)[10] and *L'Ebrea* (The Jewess) by Jacques Halévy[11] were just four of hundreds shown between 1906 and 1908. Among the Triestine productions released in 1908 were films of the Carnival celebrations, of Felice Venezian's funeral, and, as an example of the city's fascination with the East, a documentary (in ten parts) on the visit of the Japanese navy to the city in 1907. Although the quality was not always first-class – as Stanislaus rather peevishly noted, having gone to see "The greatest scenes from the history of Trieste", which to his disappointment consisted only of "pictures got from some old history of Trieste, badly reflected on the sheet"[12] – by the end of 1908 the city could boast of seventeen permanent cinemas and was rapidly becoming one of the major film distribution centres for the Austro-Hungarian Empire.

By 1909, the year Eva Joyce arrived in Trieste, there were twenty-one fully functioning cinemas. Another of Joyce's future partners, Giovanni Rebez (originally Janez Rebz), had taken over the Salone Edison, "il più elegante salone di Trieste".[13] Film versions of operas were popular, and among those Joyce may have attended were *Faust* and *Il Flauto Magico* at the Royal Biograph, *Don Giovanni*, accompanied by the accomplished Quartetto Triestino, and Ferruccio Garavaglia's film of *Othello* at the Edison.[14] The cinemas offered very flexible opening hours from mid-morning to late evening.

Perhaps mindful of the lines from the comic operetta *La Geisha* ("By now with the films/a lot of money is being made/They are becoming millionaires/the cinematographers"),[15] Joyce took his idea of opening a cinema in Dublin to his trusted friend Nicolò Vidacovich and together they found a group of business partners: Antonio Machnich, who owned a carpet shop and ran several of the city's cinemas, Giuseppe Caris (owner of the Americano), and Giovanni Rebez (owner of the Edison). Caris kept a textiles shop, while Rebez sold tanned hides; together they were joint owners of a cinema in Bucharest called the Volta.

At their initial meeting, Joyce began by pointing out that Dublin had a population of 500,000 inhabitants but not a single cinema, and before long he managed to convince his future partners to finance his plans to be the first to open one there. A contract was agreed on 16 October and signed by Joyce, Caris, Rebez and Machnich's wife, Caterina.[16] It is a fascinating document which reveals that Joyce must have been an impressive salesman. It also stands as evidence against the notion that he did not know how to handle money, even if he generally found it more convenient to let others worry about such things for him. The contract was drawn up by Vidacovich so that Joyce could not lose:

> Messrs. Iames [*sic*] Joyce, Giuseppe Karis, Giovanni Rebez e Caterina Mach-nich together form a company for the establishment and management of cin-emas in Dublin, Belfast and Cork (Ireland). The latter three will contribute the capital of not less than 20,000 crowns to set up the company, while Mr James Joyce will contribute his knowledge of the places and will work to establish and launch the enterprise, as will be explained below.[17]

The net profits were to be divided among the four partners and Joyce was to receive 10 per cent even though he did not invest a penny, while he was not to be in any way held responsible for possible losses. Joyce never intended that this enterprise would involve his moving back permanently to Dublin, but he had a clause inserted which gave him the sole right to run the opera-tion in August and September, thus finding a clever and convenient way to finance his annual holidays and escape the burning summer heat of Trieste:

> The right to act as administrator of the Dublin cinemas in the months of August and September is expressly reserved to James Joyce, who is also to receive the indicated daily indemnity during this period.

In order to make sure that he would incur no losses when going to Dublin to investigate the possibilities of setting up a cinema, Joyce also ensured that he was covered financially:

> Mr James Joyce is to be provided in advance, from the company's funds, with the costs of travelling second class from Trieste to Dublin and back and he will receive 10 francs per day for the duration of his absence.

On 17 October, Vidacovich wrote telling Joyce that Rebez had left 500 crowns to enable him to travel to Dublin, and asked him to call by to collect the money.[18] Thus financed by his partners, Joyce set off for Dublin the fol-lowing day, to the general disapproval of his family. Stanislaus doubted that the project would be successful, considered the cinema a "sign of American corruption",[19] objected to being left to teach Joyce's lessons as well as his own and resented having to shoulder the financial burden of taking care of Nora, Giorgio, Lucia and Eva. He was also aware that some new creditors who had lent Joyce money to buy furniture for the apartment would come knocking at his door. What really galled him was that Joyce had a generous allowance in Dublin and sent Nora a specially bound copy of *Chamber Music*, yet came up with nothing, except a pound he borrowed from his father, to help keep the house in Trieste. Nora, for her part, was angry at being abandoned once again after such a short time. But Joyce was adamant: this cinema venture was going to be the solution to all their monetary problems.

On the strength of his *Piccolo della Sera* visiting card, Joyce managed to have his second-class ticket upgraded and arrived in Dublin on 21 October after a long but relatively comfortable journey. Within a week he had found a suitable premises for the cinema on Mary Street, and then he had to bide his time until the arrival of his partners on 19 November. Together they travelled to Belfast and Cork to investigate the possibilities for opening cinemas there, but nothing came of these visits. At the end of November they summoned Francesco Novak, a Trieste bicycle-shop owner who had become a partner subsequent to the signing of the original contract, to manage their new Dublin cinema, and he arrived within a couple of days bringing a Triestine projectionist, Guido Lenardon, with him.

In the meantime Joyce busied himself with preparations: he ordered furniture, had the hall decorated and posters and tickets printed, and interviewed and hired staff. Not surprisingly he found the pace hard and struggled to deal with technical and bureaucratic setbacks. He wrote to Nora on 15 December complaining that "the show is not open yet. Every day there are disappointments", and added with customary exaggeration, "Since this work began I have never been in bed before 3 or 3.30" (*LII*, 275). Finally, on Monday 20 December the cinema opened with Pathé's *The Bewitched Castle* and *The First Paris Orphanage,* Caserini's or Pathé's *Beatrice Cenci,* an Italian production called *Devilled Crab,*[20] and *La Pouponnière.* The *Evening Telegraph* commented that "although *The Tragic Story of Beatrice Cenci* was hardly as exhilarating a subject as one would desire on the eve of the festive season [...] the occasion may be described as having been particularly successful".[21] Although the audiences were smaller than they had hoped, Rebez and Machnich left Dublin on 25 December feeling reasonably optimistic. Joyce was pleased with the publicity and wrote to Stanislaus to ask him to try to generate a little more for himself at the expense of his partners in Trieste:

> I send copies of papers. Go at once to Prezioso, show them and get a par: I nostri Triestini in Irlanda or like that. A little allusion to *me* and a little to the enterprise of the proprietors of the Edison and Americano (*without* giving their names) in opening here. (*LII,* 277)

The following week Joyce and Novak presented a new programme: *The Waterfalls of Tanfornan, The Fascination of Snowy Mountain Peaks, Little Jules*

Verne and *The Interrupted Appointment.*[22] On 29 December, Joyce succeeded in getting a permanent licence for the cinema and on 2 January 1910 he set off for Trieste, where he arrived four days later. Perhaps he was a little hasty in departing and abandoning Novak, who was a projectionist and not a publicist and furthermore did not speak English. In spite of this, business initially appears to have gone reasonably well, with Novak being careful to introduce a new programme every Monday and Thursday and to place advertisements regularly in *Sinn Féin* and *The Evening Telegraph.* Among the films sent from Trieste and shown at the Volta were *Sister Angelica, Legend of Lourdes, The Man who would commit suicide, Crocodile Hunting,* and (one Joyce might have done well to watch) *How to pay bills easily!.*[23] *Sinn Féin* published several short articles recommending the new cultural enterprise and confirming that business was going well:

> CINEMATOGRAPH VOLTA
>
> The taste, energy, and accuracy of detail, particularly in the matter of ancient historical costumes and architecture displayed by the management of the Volta have, as the phrase goes, "caught on," and "the man in the street" (with his olive branches and partner from the home) has shown an appreciation of these things that shows him in a new light to many, who thought he only cared for sensationalism or bovine farce and did not understand anything higher. The congested auditorium of the Volta each afternoon and evening should amply dispel this fallacy. The regular mid-week change of programme is a feature which also tends to keep the cosy yet commodious Mary Street Hall well patronised. [...] In our advertising columns the coming week's programme will be found, and those in search of healthy, sane, and educative, informative and pleasant entertainment will be well-advised if they consult it.[24]

Reading reviews like this, Joyce certainly could not have accused his acquaintances in *Sinn Féin* of being anything less than supportive. Just a week later, another favourable article appeared:

> So keen has been the appreciation of "Quo Vadis?" which formed part three of the programme submitted at the Volta, Mary Street, on Monday that the director, Signor Lorenzo Novak, had, in compliance with the unamimous desire of the public, to continue it for the entire week. It is a dramatic pictural presentation of life in the days of the early Christians and one peculiarly suited to the Lenten season.[25]

From Trieste, Joyce continued to stay in close touch with events in Dublin and even offered suggestions about the day-to-day running of the

The Canale Grande, leading to the steps of the Church of Sant'Antonio Taumaturgo

Market stalls in Piazza Ponterosso, where James and Nora had a flat during their first brief stay in Trieste in 1904

Above left: The composer
Antonio Smareglia, Joyce's
neighbour and friend

Above right: Poster for a
Trieste production of Strauss's
Salomé in 1909, which was
the occasion of Joyce's article
"Oscar Wilde: Il Poeta di
'Salomé'"

Left: Il Teatro Verdi, the most
impressive of Trieste's theatres

Above right, Ettore Schmitz with his wife Livia and daughter Letizia; *above left*, a 1912 postcard from Joyce on holiday in Galway to Schmitz in Trieste, and, *below*, Joyce's note on the reverse side addressed to "Hector" Schmitz and signed "Stephen Dedalus"

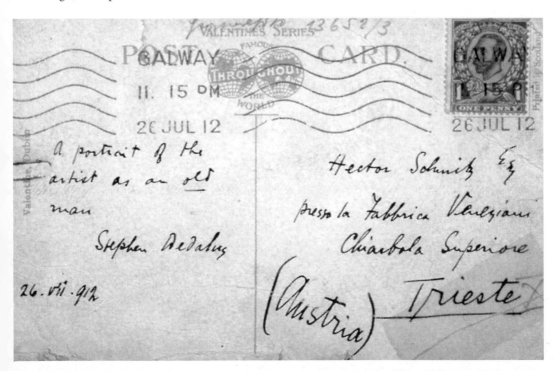

Two of Joyce's most distinguished students: the translator, essayist and irredentist
Nicolò Vidacovich (*left*), and Count Francesco Sordina

Il Caffè Bizantino, one of Joyce's favourite haunts, with his via della Barriera
Vecchia house on right

Il Piccolo della Sera of 16 May 1912, with Joyce's article "L'Ombra di Parnell"

Roberto Prezioso

Left to right: Silvio Benco, Sabatino Lopez, Sem Benelli, Attilio Tamaro, Roberto Prezioso, Arturo Ziffer and Marino de Szombathely

The Schleimer family; Annie is second from left

Giuseppe Cuzzi

Emma Cuzzi

Amalia Popper

Leopoldo Popper

The Jewish cemetery mentioned in *Giacomo Joyce*

Dario De Tuoni

enterprise. In all likelihood he was behind Novak's decision to invite the pupils of the Artane School to attend some matinée shows, a move that generated more good notices for the fledgling cinema:

> On Monday last the boys of Artane School, to the number of 500 with band, availed themselves of the invitation of Signor Novak, who had a special programme arranged, and visited the Mary Street Hall, which for over an hour rang with juvenile laughter and vociferous applause.[26]

Given all the favourable publicity and the apparently full houses, it is hard to understand why Vidacovich wrote telling Joyce, on 18 April 1910, that Mr Caris and the other partners were of the opinion that "the Cin. Volta has turned out a fiasco, and that the concern must be wound up the sooner the better. He said, that if you find a purchaser for 30000. -Kr., he woud [*sic*] give you 10%."[27] Joyce wrote to his father asking him to attempt to interest the English Provincial Theatre Company in the cinema, but John Stanislaus Joyce did not stir himself. Just six months after its opening, on 14 June 1910, Novak sold the Volta to the same Provincial Theatre Company at a loss of over six hundred pounds. Initially Joyce accepted this philosophically enough, still presuming he would be paid 10 per cent of the purchase price. He wrote to Stanislaus: "I want to wind up the affair properly. I leave here before ten as I have a lesson. They have lost money and there is no reason why I should make them lose more so I decided to accept the terms" (*LII*, 286). The following day he discovered that his business partners would give him nothing, although he had calculated that he was due to receive forty pounds – his 10 per cent of the money recouped. His appeals to his Triestine associates fell on deaf ears, and he decided, rather unjustly, that he had been swindled by the very people to whom he had given his good idea.

A number of stylistic techniques in *Ulysses* suggest that despite this debacle, Joyce maintained an ongoing interest in cinema. In "Aeolus", the headings resemble film titles explaining each new picture, while in "Wandering Rocks", itself a series of moving pictures, all sorts of strange "camera angles" are employed to provide a carousel of short clips of Dublin. Joyce may also have found inspiration in the Italian film-makers' attempts to marry classical literature with the new invention of cinema; Liguori's and Caserini's film versions of the *Inferno* and the *Odyssey* would later be paralleled by Joyce's *Ulysses*.

3 *The Trieste branch*

While Joyce was in Dublin, Nora was deeply resentful at having been abandoned again in a precarious situation in Trieste with the responsibility of having to look after the children and take care of Joyce's sister Eva, who spoke practically no Italian and had not settled down well at all. The initial letters between Joyce and Nora reveal quite a lot of tension, before yet another predictable reconciliation. "My soul", he wrote, "is in Trieste. You alone know me and love me. [...] I felt (as I always feel) a stranger in my own country. [...] I felt proud to think that my son – mine and yours, that handsome dear little boy you gave me, Nora – will always be a foreigner in Ireland, a man speaking another language and bred in a different tradition" (*LII*, 255). Having reprimanded her in a letter for being nasty to him, he then promised more presents of tweeds and furs. She replied gratefully on 2 November in a letter addressed to him care of Finn's Hotel, Nassau Street (where she, of course, had been working when they first met):

> dear Mr Joyce how can I thank you for your kindness the box of Gloves which you sent me are lovely and a splendid fit it was a great surprise to get such a nice present I hope you are quite well, and will be very pleased to see you I hope you will write to me and let me know when I am to meet you again at present I am rather busy and cant get out for some time I hope you will excuse me and accept many thanks. (*LII*, 259)

But the truce did not last long. By mid-November she was so desperate about the state of affairs to which he had abandoned her that she threatened to leave him. The problem was that Scholz, the landlord of via Scussa, had demanded his rent for October and November, and since neither she nor Stanislaus had the means to pay, the family were faced with the trauma of yet another move, just before Christmas. Joyce declared himself "in a state of utter despair" (*LII*, 266), scrambled about for money and sent her a grovelling, melodramatic letter:

> I have lost your esteem. I have worn down your love. Leave me then. Take away your children from me to save them from the curse of my presence. Let me sink back again into the mire I came from. Forget me and my empty words. Go back to your own life and let me go alone to my ruin. It is wrong for you to live with a vile beast like me or to allow your children to be touched by my hands.

> Act bravely as you have always done. If you decide to leave me in disgust I will bear it like a man, knowing that I deserve it a thousand times over, and will allow you two thirds of my income. (*LII*, 265)

As it turned out, she was again dissuaded from carrying out her threat and a new process of bonding began in a series of explicitly sexual letters. From an initial desire to "fling you down under me" (*LII*, 269), Joyce passes to images which show her quite clearly in the commanding role, as in these lines written in early December:

> Yet you seem to turn me into a beast. It was you yourself, you naughty shameless girl who first led the way. It was not I who first touched you long ago down at Ringsend. It was you who slid your hand down down inside my trousers [...]. It was your lips too which first uttered an obscene word. [...] Tired of lying under a man one night you tore off your chemise violently and got on top of me to ride me naked. (*SL*, 182).

Even more explicit letters from both Joyce and Nora followed until finally he was to submit completely to her: "The fucking must all be done by you" (*SL*, 190). By now his homecoming was in sight, and she was not only to prepare herself for him in her role as domineering lover, but also as a mother figure. "Try", he wrote, "to shelter me, dearest, from the storms of the world. [...] when I reach Via Scussa I will just creep into bed, kiss you tenderly on the forehead, curl myself up in the blankets and sleep, sleep, sleep" (*SL*, 194). He then listed all the comforts of home with which he hoped to be greeted:

> Get ready. Put some warm-brown-linoleum on the kitchen and hang a pair of red common curtains on the windows at night. Get some kind of a cheap common comfortable armchair for your lazy lover. Do this above all, darling, as I shall not quit that kitchen for a whole week after I arrive, reading, lolling, smoking and watching you get ready the meals and *talking, talking, talking, talking* to you. Oh how supremely happy I shall be! ! God in heaven, I shall be happy there! I figlioli, il fuoco, una buona mangiata, un caffè nero, un Brasil, il Piccolo della Sera, e Nora, Nora mia, Norina, Noretta, Norella, Noruccia ecc ecc ... (*SL*, 191)[28]

Four days later, he was still dreaming about his return: "I would like roast beef[,] rice-soup, capuzzi garbi, mashed potatoes, pudding and black coffee. No, no I would like Stracotto di maccheroni, a mixed salad, stewed prunes, torroni, tea and presnitz. [...] I am so glad I am now in sight of Miramar" (*SL*, 192).

Joyce's return to Trieste depended on Stanislaus finding the price not only of a ticket for him but also for his sister Eileen, whom Joyce had decided to bring out to live with them: "This is such a dreadful house that it is a God's act to rescue Eileen from it" (*LII*, 280). Stanislaus, who had had to deal with Eva's unhappiness in Trieste, was not keen on having another homesick sister on his hands and was annoyed that, once again, he would have to bear all the costs involved in such a move. He was angry that Joyce had gone to Dublin in the first place and also felt that Nora had been mistreated. Although the initial letters between the brothers during Joyce's absence were civil and occasionally warm, from the moment Scholz demanded his rent and served notice on Stanislaus, they became terse and occasionally downright abusive.

On receiving the order to pay the two months' rent, Stanislaus had written in a fury to his brother, but while Joyce had been willing to submit completely to Nora's similar anger, and although he did send about one month's rent, he was too proud and stubborn to yield to Stanislaus's wrath. Instead he argued head-on with him, almost going so far as to make out that the problem was of Stanislaus's making:

> When I left Trieste I handed over to you the following pupils: Popper, Bolaffio, Veneziani (Mrs), Castelbolognese, Sordina to say nothing of Höberth, Bartoli and Latzer. These I presume paid you or some of them in addition to your own pupils. Was nothing out of the money paid to landlord? (*LII*, 262–3)

That Stanislaus probably did not have the time to get around to all of these students, that some of them had probably already paid Joyce himself in advance, and finally that he no longer even lived with the rest of the family, were all factors apparently lost on the elder brother. Finally, as a compromise, they both agreed to pay more or less one month's rent each, and Joyce carefully instructed his brother about how to deal with the landlord, telling him to enlist the help of his solicitor, Giulio Paulina, in order to fend off Scholz and to "prevent an eviction <u>at all</u> costs" (*LII*, 264).

In the end, Stanislaus managed to prevent the eviction, to look after Nora and the family and to pay for Joyce and Eileen's trip back to Trieste. But all this came at a high human cost: relations had been drastically soured between the brothers and were rendered even more difficult by Joyce's decision not to work during the month of January 1910, which Stannie saw as yet another example of his brother taking him and his earnings for granted and assuming that he could always be relied upon to save the day. He knew that no matter how much money he pumped into Joyce's spendthrift household, it would never be enough, and this because Jim and Nora would always continue to grant themselves a standard of living that was far beyond their means. As a result, from now on he decided to contribute only what had already been agreed towards the running of their household and refused to concede any more interim loans or to borrow on Joyce's behalf at the school.

An outraged Joyce reacted as though his brother was betraying him and summoned him at regular intervals to inform him that he had "no money whatsoever" to pay the bills (*LII*, 282). In March Joyce was still attempting to call the recalcitrant Stanislaus to heel:

> On the understanding that you would keep the house I laid out what I got in paying bills. The 25 Cr. you gave Nora will last till Thursday evg. After that what do you expect me to do?
> You owe me:
> 1.60 (balance theatre)
> 2.50 (half of 5 lire sent May)
> 4.10
> I wish you would save me these continual rows as I have already too many worries. [...] Kindly give it up, as I am unwell: and tell me how I am to feed the house. (*LII*, 283)

The dispute came to a head in July when the two had yet another heated row, and Stanislaus, having realized that his brother had, once again, succeeded in turning the entire family against him, walked out telling him that he would never return. He held his nerve for a few days, but was gradually worn down by the collective pressure of the rest of the family. "Even Giorgio, meeting Stanislaus in the street, said to him in Italian, 'We had no dinner today. Keep that in your head.' The pressure upon the young man was very great, but he won support from the Francinis who told him, after hearing the lamentable developments, that they had always felt he was mistreated in the house" (*JJ*, 312).

Joyce, to be fair, had his own share of frustrations, and 1910 was certainly neither an exciting nor a promising year. He was again suffering with his eyes and there was rarely a moment when money was not a problem. Of course his spending habits did not help. In March he bought a piano, spending the equivalent of over three months' rent on the initial deposit, and in that same July in which Stannie almost came to blows with him over his carefree attitude to money, Joyce and Nora coolly went out and put a 30-crown deposit on a Singer sewing machine which would cost them 282 crowns (to be paid off at 12 crowns a month for 21 months). Stanislaus's salary in this period was 50 crowns per week at the Berlitz school.[29]

Even if there were now seven mouths to feed in his ever more numerous family, Joyce did not allow his rather leisurely rhythms to be affected. It was his wont to wake up at around ten. "Sometimes his Polish tailor called, and would sit discoursing on the edge of the bed while Joyce listened and nodded. About eleven he rose, shaved, and sat down at the piano (which he was buying slowly and perilously on the installment plan). As often as not his singing and playing were interrupted by the arrival of a bill collector. Joyce was notified and asked what was to be done" (*JJ*, 308). Things usually finished in the same way: the creditor was received, listened to and skilfully steered into a conversation about music or politics. At the end he was graciously led towards the door without having collected a penny of what he was owed. According to Brenda Maddox, Nora was no better:

> … the familiar shortage of money did not deter Nora any more than Joyce from dressing as well as their credit with tailors and dressmakers would permit. A studio portrait of Eva and Lucia, for example, shows both the three-year-old girl and her aunt sporting enormous hats whose layered ruffles speak of expensive workmanship. It is as if the Joyces needed, in their dress, to proclaim their equality with the snobs whom Joyce had to teach.[30]

Despite their financial problems, a certain optimism still pervaded the Joyce household. As yet there was no reason to doubt that the publication of *Dubliners* would take place before the autumn and that with it sales of *Chamber Music* would also be given a boost. In June, Joyce informed Adolph Mann that he was "engaged in correcting the proofs of a new book, a volume of stories, *Dubliners* which Messrs Maunsel & Co, Dublin, will bring out next month" (*LII*, 287).

Meanwhile there was still much in the intellectual environment of the city to keep Joyce distracted from his still unresolved publishing problems and his perilous financial condition. His regime of late mornings, coupled with afternoons spent teaching his private students, allowed him freedom at night and so he continued to visit the theatre about twice a week, sometimes cancelling private lessons in order to do so. Two years later, he recalled having watched Nora at the opera: "how you sit at the opera with the grey ribbon in your hair, listening to music, and observed by men" (*LII*, 309).

In February 1910 he had an opportunity to renew his acquaintance with the writings of the Italian playwright and novelist Gabriele D'Annunzio, when the Italian première of his *Fedra* was mounted in the Teatro Politeama Rossetti to great acclaim. Joyce also had many occasions to see the plays written by the two exponents of Giovanni Verga's Italian school of *Verismo* whom he most admired, Giuseppe Giacosa and Marco Praga. Productions of Praga's *La Crisi* were staged in the Teatro Verdi in the autumn of 1907 and again in 1911 and 1912, while Giacosa's *Tristi Amori* was produced in the autumn of 1907 and returned, with Ermete Zacconi, in spring 1908 and again in 1911. As Michael Mason has shown, Joyce drew deeply on these plays when composing *Exiles* and *Ulysses*, because he was fascinated by the portrayal of the protagonists' tolerant attitude towards the adultery of their wives.[31] Corinna del Greco Lobner has also commented that Joyce showed "a probing interest in Praga and Giacosa's abilities to shift attention from the dashing male lover to the betrayed husband, who is incapable of handling adultery with a macho display of violence and is willing instead to reach some sort of compromise".[32] Joyce mentions both writers in his notes for *Exiles*:

> Since the publication of the lost pages of *Madame Bovary* the centre of sympathy appears to have been esthetically shifted from the lover or fancyman to the husband or cuckold. This displacement is also rendered more stable by the gradual growth of a collective practical realism due to changed economic conditions in the mass of the people who are called to hear and feel a work of art relating to their lives. This change is utilised in *Exiles* although the union of Richard and Bertha is irregular to the extent that the spiritual revolt of Richard which would be strange and ill-welcomed otherwise can enter into combat with Robert's decrepit prudence with some chance of fighting before the public a drawn battle. Praga in *La Crisi* and Giacosa in *Tristi Amori* have understood and profited by this change but have not used it, as is done here, as a technical shield for the protection of a delicate, strange and highly sensitive conscience.[33]

In December 1913 Joyce had a further opportunity to see a series of plays concerned with marital and extramarital relationships when Emma Gramatica's company came to the Teatro Politeama Rossetti and presented Praga's *La Porta Chiusa* and *La Moglie Ideale*, Pinero's *La Seconda Moglie*, Shaw's *Candida* and *Mrs Warren's Profession*, and finally Giacosa's *Il marito amante della moglie* (The Husband Lover of the Wife), whose themes would soon echo in *Giacomo Joyce*, with its description of a "Belluomo" who "rises from the bed of his wife's lover's wife" (*GJ*, 8).

4 *Among the Futurists and the Vociani*

Around this time in Trieste, a number of what might be termed "angry young men", more or less all of Joyce's generation, began to take part in literary movements essentially based outside the city. There were two basic strands of connection: the first with Filippo Tommaso Marinetti's Futurist movement, the second with the Florence-based *Vociani*.

The artistic and political agenda of Futurism enjoyed a particularly enthusiastic backing in Trieste, where a sizeable group of intellectuals, many of whom Joyce knew, were directly involved. Oddly enough, this most aggressively masculine of literary movements received perhaps its most sustained early support from a group of prominent female journalists and writers, including Delia Benco (perhaps a closer friend of the Joyces than her husband Silvio), Willy Dias, Doria Cambon, and Elda Gianelli, literary contributor to *L'Indipendente* and translator of Marinetti's early French poetry. The leaders of the Futurist enterprise, Marinetti and Aldo Palazzeschi, enjoyed keen personal followings and important friendships in Trieste. Palazzeschi's *I Poemi* was published in 1909 and reviewed by Elda Gianelli (another admirer of Joyce) in *L'Indipendente* on 11 January 1910. The review must have made for uncomfortable reading for the Irish writer, who cannot but have noticed that Palazzeschi was three years his junior and yet had, in addition to *I Poemi*, already published two successful volumes of poetry, *I Cavalli Bianchi* and *Lanterna*, as well as a novel, *Riflessi* (dedicated to Delia Benco).

Marinetti was a regular visitor to Trieste and a contributor to at least two of the city's newspapers, *La Coda del Diavolo* and the short-lived *Lettura Internazionale*. In a letter of 1905, he wrote telling his friend Silvio Benco of his important plans to establish the literary journal *Poesia*, and intimated that Benco's opinions and possible role were important:

> I am working, on a daily basis, to set up a big company, along with four of my capitalist friends, for the foundation of an international publishing house (with capital of half a million) which, under the name of *Poesia*, will embrace the entire Italian intellectual field. For the first time, a big publisher will be seen to freely sustain the human mind in its most audacious efforts. I must ask you to keep all this a secret, because the deal has not yet been concluded and already they are putting dirty spanners in the works, which I of course will break, but which can delay what I want with all my powers to do.[34]

In August 1908, Cesare Mansueti, the editor of the daily *L'Adriatico*, devoted almost half the front page to a review of Marinetti's critical work on D'Annunzio and enthusiastically praised Marinetti's "six years of hard feverish literary work which, with these latest books, have produced seven volumes".[35] Of the first book Mansueti wrote:

> F.T. Marinetti succeeded perfectly in realizing his aim of drawing attention to the defects and the merits of the Pescarese [D'Annunzio] and to the historical and ethical gaps in his exuberant artistic conception. He expressed his doubt that the works of Gabriele D'Annunzio would maintain for posterity that space created for them by the moderns, by comparing him to three gigantic contemporary figures of the third Italy: Giuseppe Verdi, Giosuè Carducci, and the only one still living, Giovanni Pascoli. The contrast is harsh between D'Annunzio and these native Gods of Latin thought who created an era, or better an apotheosis: the first with music destined to challenge eternity, the second with a lyric which influenced the literary education of a whole generation, the third with that poetry which comes directly to the heart like a shower generating feeling and pity.[36]

Marinetti came to Trieste to read his early French poetry at the Società Filarmonica on 9 March 1908,[37] and another highly publicized visit took place in late 1908 when he lectured on D'Annunzio at the Università Popolare. His book on D'Annunzio was reviewed once more and his view that D'Annunzio's work had attracted critical attention not simply for its artistic merit but because of the interest created by the writer's exuberant private life was endorsed.[38] According to Francini Bruni, Joyce was not interested in this aspect of D'Annunzio, but rather in his literary works:

> He loved D'Annunzio's tragedies, *La Nave, La Città Morta, La Phedra*. He said that D'Annunzio had a great genius for the theatre. He loved also *Il Fuoco*, the last work of D'Annunzio, based on Wagner's death, which came out at the beginning of their stay in Trieste. He was not interested in D'Annunzio's life.[39]

In his lecture at the university, Marinetti did not spare D'Annunzio from his criticism but he was careful to get the *Triestini* on his side first. In doing so, he revealed what would later become both a strength and the fatal flaw of Futurism as a literary movement – its openly aggressive political stance:

> A diplomatic incident also took place. At a certain moment Marinetti proclaimed that Italian culture extended from "the tricolour sea of Trieste as far as the lowest point of Sicily" and promised, to the great joy of those present, that "we will have an Italian University at Trieste no matter what the medieval tyrants do".[40]

Marinetti went on to survey all of D'Annunzio's work, focusing in particular on *La Città Morta*, and "received warm applause for his magnificent lecture, which palpitated with all of the vigilant, agile, sonorous, ardent spirit of a Latin artist".[41]

In March 1909 Marinetti launched his manifesto *Trieste: la nostra bella polveriera* (Trieste: Our Beautiful Tinderbox). At this time he was at the peak of his popularity in the city, which he termed one of the three capitals of Futurism along with Milan and Paris. On 12 January 1910 a spectacular Futurist meeting was held (less than a year after the first Futurist meeting was held in Paris in February 1909) in the Politeama Rossetti, before an enormous crowd which welcomed the Futurist poets to Trieste as much for their openly irredentist political stance as for their artistic agenda. It is very likely that Joyce was present, but even if he was not, the event could not but have caught his attention, as the Futurists took the city by storm, bombarding it with advertisements, posters and fliers. Many of Joyce's acquaintances, such as Prezioso and Benco, were in the audience of illustrious local literati, while future students and friends such as the poet Dario De Tuoni and the painter Tullio Silvestri also attended.

In a series of articles entitled "Una Prefazione di Marinetti sui Futuristi a Trieste" (A Preface by Marinetti on the Futurists of Trieste) which were published in *La Coda del Diavola*, Marinetti recounted his visit to the city:

> Finally Trieste! All our friends came to welcome us. One hundred enthusiastic hands being held out to greet us. ... At seven ... at the Teatro Rossetti ... all the population of Trieste is in front of us ... In a box on the right, the gracious, feline and exquisitely spiritual Delia Benco ... with her, Silvio Benco, the great, illustrious writer of *Castello dei Desideri*. In the same box, Willy Dias, the ingenious writer of a hundred unforgettable short novels and the beautiful Signora Ciatto. In another box nearer the stage, the superb, romantic and nocturnal figure of Nella Doria Cambon ... at her side our friend Elda Gianelli, a poetess who recently wrote a book of free verse on the wing of her genius. ... In the stalls *la signorina* Haydée,[42] the well-known writer who does much honour to Trieste with her versatile talent, *il dottor* Prezioso, great patriot, princely journalist, master of ideas and crowds; the editor of *L'Indipendente*, Zampieri, strong proponent of irredentism; *il dottor* Cimadori, the poet Riccardo Pitteri, *il dottor* Spadoni, Carlo Banelli, *l'avvocato* Costellos, president of the Società Filarmonica, the engineer Manzini, the Futurist poet Luigi Crociato, the poet Cesare Rossi and many other notable figures from the city.[43]

The event was made up of readings and proclamations by Marinetti, Palazzeschi, Armando Mazza and Michelangolo Zimolo, and created an enormous stir. *Il Piccolo* of 13 January commented as follows: "The opening was terribly violent; the public had never had such aggressive words thrown at it before." While Marinetti was applauded, Mazza, who read out the Futurist manifesto, was not so lucky:

> When he reached the part about the burning of the libraries, the flooding of the museums full of paintings and statues, about the barbarous joy of the burning of the factories, a murmur began to rise, which shortly became a hostile shout and a loud protest. Part of the audience began to clap their hands, others whistled and made noise, while abuse was thrown from the galleries.[44]

The uproar continued when Palazzeschi read from his "Regola del sole" (Rule of the Sun). After the event, the Futurists left the theatre in a blaze of controversy and adjourned to the Città di Parenzo restaurant, which had been renamed for the event the "Roi Bombance" (King Revelry), after Marinetti's play. There they ate a Futurist dinner beginning with coffee and dessert and finishing with appetizers. The menu, created by a future student of Joyce's, Mario Nordio, wittily recycles many of the Futurists' obsessions and must have proved a stern test for even the most robust of digestive systems:

> Coffee
> Sweet memories frappées
> Fruit of the future
> Marmalade of the glorious dead
> Roast mummies with professors' livers
> Archaeological salad
> Stew of the past with explosive peas in historical sauce
> Fish from the Dead Sea
> Lumps of blood in broth
> Demolition starters
> Vermouth.[45]

Several of Marinetti's more mainstream Triestine admirers, perplexed by his polemical performance, did not go to the dinner. Their scepticism was well captured in the following day's review in *L'Indipendente*:

> The Futurist school certainly did not attract any new admirers last night and there was probably more than one person who, coming out of the theatre, will have said, 'Let's return to the past!'[46]

The irredentist writer and journalist Willy Dias recalled her doubts about the Futurists in her diary in 1910:

My house and the Bencos' house became the general headquarters of Futurism. We spent really enjoyable afternoons together. Armando Mazza, big and fat with his big baritone voice, recited the Futurist programme, and blond Palazzeschi was also there, young and tiny [...]. After having listened to the poetry which we admired or pretended to admire, Delia Benco and I got our revenge by demanding that Marinetti recite something completely un-Futuristic, French poetry. [...] As Marinetti seemed intelligent to me, I reckoned that Futurism was a means like any other for him to make his name, and that he did not really believe in the beauty of an art founded on discordant sounds. [...] With astonishment he tried to convince me to the contrary and he immediately seemed considerably less intelligent.[47]

But even if the old guard began to distance themselves from Marinetti, there were plenty of younger men who were eager to take their place. The following extract from *L'Emancipazione* (a radical irredentist newspaper) provides a typical example of young Trieste's zealous approval of Marinetti and reveals, once again, that much of the enthusiasm was politically rather than artistically motivated:

In Trieste, first among all the Italian cities, the Futurists assailed the public in the vast crowded theatre with the overwhelming violence of their programme's declarations, perhaps because here traditionalism is less deeply rooted and modern ideas meet with less resistance, perhaps also because their visit was a tribute to a city alive with patriotism, ardent in the sometimes bloody struggle of every day.[48]

The writer saw Marinetti's call to burn the libraries as a call to youth to rise up and he praised the action of the Futurists as "a hymn to youth, to force, to the war for rights, to patriotism, to rebellion in work, to the violent gesture".[49] Yet he concluded by saying: "The past cannot be destroyed: the generations do not live only for themselves: humanity is continuity, the sum of all the knowledge fought for and acquired up to the present is ours and the future's. But we must not live in the past, this is the truth to be distilled from the rhetorical exaggerations of Futurism."[50]

This rather Viconian vision has echoes of Joyce's mission in shaking off the dead weight of the past, seizing the present and writing *Ulysses*, which itself is a sum of accumulated knowledge, a grasping of history. Joyce's dismissal of rotting Rome as a place reminiscent of "a man who lives by exhibiting to travellers his grandmother's corpse" resonates with Marinetti's desire to "free the country from the stinking gangrene of its professors, archaeologists, tourist guides and antique dealers"[51] and with the manifesto in which the Futurist painters complained that "for the other peoples, Italy is still a country of the dead, an immense Pompei white with tombs".[52] Like Joyce, who in *Dubliners* wrote of his native city as "a centre of paralysis", Marinetti, in "Uccidiamo il Chiaro di Luna!" (Let's Kill the *Claire de Lune*), urged his followers to destroy "la città di paralisi".[53]

Trieste itself also produced a number of writers whose work reveals all the typical stylistic features of Futurism – the destruction of syntax, the presentation of multiple images simultaneously, the abolition of punctuation, the use of "parole in libertà" (the free placing of words) – as well as its thematic obsessions, the conquest of time and space, the refusal of orthodox sexual morality, the celebration of war, of industrialization, of strength, daring and the love of danger, of feverish insomnia. These Triestine Futurists included Italo Tavolato, Luigi Crociato, known especially for his 1912 volume of poetry *Canta il Selvaggio* (The Wild One Sings), and Teodoro Finzi, who in 1910 under the pseudonym Fedoro Tizzoni published one of Trieste's first books of Futurist poetry, entitled, with characteristic aggression, *Cannonate* (Cannonades). The dedications – to "our irrepressible teacher F.T. Marinetti", to "the weighty muscles of Armando Mazza", to "the strong Adriatic poet Arturo Belotti" – at the beginning of various sections of this book reveal his Futurist affinities. Tizzoni's book received a lot of attention in Trieste although it was reviewed somewhat coolly in *L'Indipendente*:

> Many people ask if the Futurists take what they do seriously or if they do it as a joke. In any case their bold aim to continually remake poetry and art continues to gather strength with the fearless violence of an artillery. Now from the womb of this new and fearful school, a rebel proselyte, following the traditions of Futurism with shrewd obedience (Futurism, quite absurdly, already has traditions!), launches his *Cannonate* right and left, with an enormous show of advertising based on big posters which are stuck up all over the city and leaflets which rain down on the heads of the peace-loving citizens.[54]

The poems in *Cannonate* are simple, rebellious and angry. They celebrate such things as the motor car, physical violence, sporting achievement, rough sex. The direct style is tautly aggressive, masculine, and seeks to exalt the physical prowess of the Italian male in conquering nature and woman. A verse from his "La Corsa: Il Canto del Vittorioso" (The Race: The Song of the Victor) is indicative of the limits of Tizzoni's poetry:

> I, the Italian
> Had triumphed

> Over sixty-nine foreign competitors
> In the hunded metre race.
> The women would want me
> The Virgins would dream about me
> Some pervert would close his/her eyes and possess me
> I thought.
> But I don't want anyone
> I have possessed Victory
> In a Cyclopean embrace.[55]

Another poem, "The Song of the Exploited", which lures the reader into believing the subject is a strong motherless man, in fact celebrates "the purest muscles of iron" of the cranes working in the free port.

Tizzoni's book was just one element of the Futurist presence to which Joyce could not remain immune. In his Triestine library we find two Futurist books – Aldo Palazzeschi's *Il Codice di Perelà* (The Code of Perelà) and Giovanni Boine's *Il Peccato* (The Sin) – and he later owned Marinetti's *La enquete internationale sur le vers libre et manifeste du Futurisme*[56] and in Zürich gave Budgen a loan of "Boccioni's book on Futurism" (probably *Pitture sculture Futuriste – dinamismo plastico*, which had been published by Marinetti's *Poesia* in 1914).[57]

After reading *Ulysses*, Ardengo Soffici, another leading Futurist figure, said that he had "the impression of hearing an echo of some of our things".[58] Just what echoes might Soffici have heard? How might Joyce have been influenced by the Futurists, by a movement that boasted of having no traditions, no masters, no dogma?

The influence of the Futurists on Joyce seems to have been more stylistic than thematic for he would have had little truck with their macho stance.[59] However, one of his poems, "A Memory of the Players in a Mirror at Midnight", uncharacteristically contains much of the violence and harsh abruptness more commonly associated with the Futurists, and Corinna del Greco Lobner has compared it to the Futurist "Paolo Buzzi's preference for shocking metaphors and grotesque effects".[60] Joyce's translator and friend Carlo Linati arranged to have this poem published in Marinetti's *Poesia* in 1920, which suggests that both Joyce and Linati were well aware of the type of work that Marinetti would be willing to publish:

> They mouth love's language. Gnash
> The thirteen teeth
> Your lean jaws grin with. Lash

> Your itch and quailing, nude greed of the flesh.
> Love's breath in you is stale, worded or sung,
> As sour as cat's breath,
> Harsh of tongue.[61]

This is also rather reminiscent of Tizzoni's more overstated (to the point of being ridiculous) "Tigre":

> What if the desire takes her now
> To close her jaws
> And sink her magnificent teeth
> Which have their roots in blood
> Into my neck
> And she will eat my head
> As though it were a meat-ball
> As though it were a small, sweet, meat-ball?[62]

The connection is coincidental, but even the awfulness of a poem like Tizzoni's may not have precluded Joyce from stylistic borrowings. I. Cope Jackson evokes the stylistic elements of Futurism, which parallel some of Joyce's techniques:

> The Futurist poets sought to convey the "simultaneity" of impressions which characterised modern life. The stylistic devices by which they sought to achieve this aim were the abolition of traditional syntax, metre and punctuation and the introduction of mathematical and musical symbols, onomatopoeia and free expressive orthography [...] freely deforming, remodelling the words by cutting or lengthening them [...] enlarging or diminishing the number of vowels and consonants.[63]

It is in *Ulysses*, the structure of which Joyce was beginning to formulate in 1910, that we should look first for evidence of Futurist traits. In "Scylla and Charybdis" he provides the musical symbols for the "Gloria", in "Ithaca" he gives the full musical score of "The Ballad of Little Harry Hughes", while the opening of "Sirens" shares techniques and characteristics with Marinetti's "Parole in Libertà" (Free Words) – compressed, ungrammatical text devoid of linking words. The following is an example provided by Marinetti of this style:

> Advance-guards: 20 metres ant-battalions cavalry-spiders street-fords general-island messengers-grasshoppers sands-revolution howitzer-tribunes clouds-gridirons shotguns-martyrs shrapnels-halos multiplication addition division howitzer-subtraction shell-cancelling drip sink landslide blockade avalanche.[64]

His "translation" of these free words reads as follows:

A distance of twenty metres divided the Italian advance-guard from the Turkish advance-guard. On the immensity of the sands, the battalions stretched out
like interminable rows of ants. A cavalry squadron went forward on the dune
like a long line of spiders. The desert seemed the vast estuary of a river, which
could only be forded with two or three tiny ways. The Italian general climbed
up on a mound, like a island ...⁶⁵

The opening sixty lines of "Sirens", although far more complex and crafted,
and with more sounds and parts of words than entire words, nonetheless
read similarly to Marinetti's "free words" as a type of clipped code, deci-
pherable only through the reading of the rest of the chapter. Many words
have been removed and there is much use of two-word phrases such as "Coin
rang. Clock clacked" (*U*, 11.16). The passage is also rich in onomatopoeia
and free expressive orthography, for example when the sound of Bloom
breaking wind merges with the tram: "Rrrpr. Kraa. Kraandl" (*U*, 11.60).

Although "Penelope" exalts and exemplifies an oral rather than a written
form, and owes a huge debt to Joyce's mother, his sisters and Nora, it is unde-
niable that some of the characteristic stylistic traits of the episode, such as the
partial elimination of traditional syntax and metre, the almost total abolition
of punctuation, and the use of free-spelling and the lengthening of words,
parallel devices adopted by the Futurists to convey simultaneity:

> frseeeeeeeefronnnng train somewhere whistling the strength those engines have
> in them like big giants and the water rolling all over and out of them all sides
> like the end of Loves old sweeeetsonnnng the poor men that have to be out all
> the night from their wives and families in those roasting engines stifling it was
> today Im glad I burned the half of those old Freemans ... (*U*, 18.596–600)

Such techniques are not isolated but crop up again and again in other
episodes of *Ulysses*. A good example of the remodelling of words and of free
expressive orthography, for instance, is to be found in "Lestrygonians",
where advertising, another vital feature of Futurism, is explored:

> A procession of whitesmocked sandwichmen marched slowly towards him
> along the gutter, scarlet sashes across their boards. Bargains. Like that priest
> they are this morning: we have sinned: we have suffered. He read the scarlet
> letters on their five tall white hats: H.E.L.Y.S. Wisdom Hely's. Y lagging
> behind drew a chunk of bread from under his foreboard, crammed it into his
> mouth and munched as he walked. (*U*, 8.123–8)

Later we are told that Bloom "crossed Westmoreland street when apostrophe
S had plodded by" (*U*, 8.155). Here the letters assume a human form, freely

change positions and thus recombine meaning with Futuristic abandon. Joyce cannot but have noted the skill of the Futurists in advertising their own work,[66] but it is somewhat ironic that he turns what for them was an aggressive means of self-promotion into the self-effacing activity practised by the sandwich-board men who advertise everything but themselves, and into the "gentle art of advertising" practised without particular success by Bloom.

The "Aeolus" episode, with its play on spatial and temporal simultaneity – the *Nacheinander* and *Nebeneinander* suggested in "Proteus" – begins with a depiction of a modern means of transport, the electric tram, and a celebration of a certain "busy-ness" that is reminiscent of the Futurists' ideals of dynamism and speed. For these reasons, it can profitably be read in the light of Marinetti's "Distruzione della sintassi. Immaginazione senza fili" (Destruction of Syntax – Wireless Imagination).

Marinetti exalted "a renewal of human sensibility by means of great scientific discoveries" such as "the telegraph, the telephone, the gramophone, the train, the bicycle, the motorcycle, the car, the transatlantic liner, the airship, the aeroplane, the cinematograph, the important newspaper (a synthesis of a day in the world)",[67] and (like the vast majority of the more mainstream modernist writers) believed that these discoveries had significantly affected the human psyche. Joyce at least partially shared this view, and it seems almost redundant to point out that Marinetti's celebration of a newspaper as "a synthesis of a day in the world" could easily be appropriated as a succinct description of the substance of *Ulysses*. "Aeolus" explores a day in the life of a newspaper, the interaction of man with various forms of modern technology (the motor car, the telephone, the telegraph), and it also features the invention which made journalism possible, the printing press, described under the heading "Orthographical". Thus, using onomatopoeia, a favourite device of the Futurists, Joyce gives voice to the *Freeman's Journal* printing press:

> Sllt. The nethermost deck of the first machine jogged forward its flyboard with sllt the first batch of quirefolded papers. Sllt. Almost human the way it sllt to call attention. Doing its level best to speak. That door too sllt creaking, asking to be shut. Everything speaks in its own way. Sllt. (*U*, 7.174–7)

The elimination of vowels in the repeated "sllt" is a common Futurist technique, while the repetition of the word underlines the automated nature of the work being carried out (in this case printing in the opposite direction to the meaning).

Apart from the newspaper life it mirrors and recreates, "Aeolus" offers a series of glimpses of almost mechanical men at work, such as the "grossbooted draymen [who] rolled barrels dullthudding out of Prince's stores and bumped them on the brewery float. On the brewery float bumped dullthudding barrels rolled by grossbooted draymen out of the Prince's stores" (*U*, 7.21–4). Here Dublin is a city full of industry, of Futuristic speed ("SPEEDPILLS VELOCITOUS AEROLITHS" [*U*, 7.1022]), of busy-ness, of clips that run faster than the films Joyce watched in Trieste, an urban reality which is antithetical to the centre of paralysis encountered by the reader in *Dubliners*.

Or so it would seem. Except that by the end of the episode the trams have been brought to a standstill by a power failure and are "becalmed in short circuit" (*U*, 7.1047), the characters who live in the city of *Ulysses* are similarly paralysed, and after lots of windy chat and almost no action, the journalists conclude little more than to agree on where they will go drinking. Leopold Bloom is at his busiest in this episode, but all his activity is in vain, his attempts at getting satisfaction from the editor are repulsed, and he is ultimately shown to be out of sync with the almost fatuous and exclusively male energy to be found in this "omnium gatherum" of newspaper types.

In his 1912 essay on "The Universal Literary Influence of the Renaissance", Joyce listed nearly all the inventions he exhibits in "Aeolus" and revealed his unease with much of the progress that the Futurists were so keen to celebrate. In doing so he not only provided a reply to Marinetti but also a key with which to read *Ulysses*, or at least Bloom:

> The much-trumpeted progress of this century consists largely of a heap of machines the very purpose of which is to gather in haste and fury the scattered elements of utility and knowledge and to redistribute them to each member of the collectivity who is in a position to pay a slight tax. I admit that this social system can boast of great mechanical conquests and great beneficial discoveries. It suffices, to be convinced of it, to make a brief list of what may be seen in the streets of a modern city: the electric tram, telegraph wires, the humble and necessary postman, the newsboys, the large commercial businesses, etc.[68]

Where Marinetti gloried in the new machines presented by progress, Joyce underlines man's alienation in this new world: "But in the midst of this complex and many-sided civilisation the human mind, almost terrified by materialistic vastness, is bewildered, forsakes itself, and withers."[69]

Joyce transfers this unease to *Ulysses*, where he often adopts a style similar to that of the Futurists but turns their message on its head. Apart from the unquestioning celebration of the modern world, what other elements might have put Joyce off? The sense of the "Aeolus" episode is, according to the Linati scheme, "The Mockery of Victory", and therein may lie a clue. Joyce had little truck with the bellicosity of the Futurists. Other aspects of Futurism's message, such as the calls for a new poetry of intuition, the incitement to burn down the libraries and museums, to repudiate reason, can only have alienated him. In 1912 Marinetti described the act of creation almost as if it were automatic writing: "The hand that writes seems to detach itself from the body and reaches out independently far away from the brain."[70] This reliance on intuition and randomness is utterly at odds with what Joyce was doing. His methods of abolishing standard syntax, grammar and spelling were altogether different: the seventeen years spent working on *Finnegans Wake* are testimony enough to the painstaking care he gave to constructing his works, each paragraph, each sentence, each word. Joyce's was an utterly creative enterprise in constructing a new language; Marinetti's linguistic and stylistic destructiveness was a far more facile thing.

A frequent feature of Marinetti's movement was the celebration of powerful men, of Cyclopean figures. This aspect of Futurism was probably what Joyce had in mind when, speaking of "Cyclops", he asked: "Does this episode strike you as Futuristic?"[71] The Citizen can be seen as Joyce's parody of the cult of stubborn, male, nationalistic strength – in many respects a parody as much of Marinetti as of Cuchulainn. The Futurists were in favour of sports in which strength was important, their manifestoes exalted struggles which saw the victor celebrated and the defeated prostrated. In "Cyclops", Joyce subjects these concerns to parody in the recreation of the "Keogh-Bennett" boxing match (*U*, 12.949), in which "the two fought like tigers" and Keogh achieved "a knockout clean and clever" before being "declared victor to the frenzied cheers of the public" (*U*, 12.977–85). Bloom and the Citizen also argue about "the importance of physical culture" (*U*, 12.899–900) and almost come to blows, but for all his brute strength the Citizen is no more effective than Bloom and, far from being acclaimed victor, risks being "lagged for assault and battery" (*U*, 12.899). In fact, despite his humiliation, it is a re-dimensioned Bloom who emerges from the row. Scorned for being one of those "mixed middlings", "a new womanly man", it is precisely these feminine aspects which deepen his personality and elevate it above those of the other characters.

Several of the interpolations in "Cyclops" also draw on stylistic devices similar to those employed by the Futurists. Of particular relevance in this regard is the one in which we read of the "ghastly scene" of Emmet's hanging, which "testified that the artillery of heaven had lent its supernatural pomp to the already gruesome spectacle" (*U*, 12.530–1). This "gruesome spectacle" really took place (albeit in a very different form) and in describing it as he does, Joyce is coming close to the Futurist "fervid passion for real life" that must win over "traditional theatre" which they wanted to "abolish totally".[72] The use of names in this episode is also reminiscent of Futurism. Apart from the vowel-less "L-n-h-n and M-ll-g-n" (*U*, 12.542), the onomatopoeic Italian doyen of the foreign delegation "Commendatore Bacibaci Beninobenone" and his fellow diplomats "Monsieur Pierrepaul Petitépetant, the Granjoker Vladinmire Pokethankertscheff, the Archjoker Leopold Rudolph von Schwanzenbad-Hodenthaler, Countess Marha Virága Kisászony Putrápesti …" (*U*, 12.556–61) sound similar to Marinetti's "artisti onomatopeici" (onomatopoeic artists) "Signorina Tofa (Sprovieri), Sig. Putipù, Sig. Triccabballacche (Radiante), Sig. Scetavaiasse (Despero), Sig. Fischiatore (Sironi)."[73] Later in the argument over "the correct date of the birth of Ireland's patron saint", Joyce describes an intimidating Futuristic display of weapons: "cannonballs, scimitars, boomerangs, blunderbusses, stinkpots, meatchoppers, umbrellas, catapults, knuckledusters, sandbags, lumps of pig iron" (*U*, 12.575–7).

The "Circe" episode, where the chosen organ is the "locomotor apparatus", also reveals a sustained profusion of techniques very close to those of the Futurists and even mentions that one of Bloom's ancestors is "Adrianopoli" (*U*, 15.1861), thus ironically linking peace-loving Bloom with the warmongering, *superuomo* Marinetti, author of *The Battle of Adrianopoli*. One of the hallmarks of Futurist writing was the celebration of feverish insomnia, the freedom of the night, the chaos that might reign among a few noctambulists while the rest of a city slept. The Triestine poet Tizzoni provides a perfect model of this night world in his poem "Nottambulismo",[74] which depicts the city closing down at midnight, the bars, theatres and restaurants emptying, and the workers heading home to bed. At that moment, another city – the city of the strong – comes to life and fills up with groups of young people, criminals, easy women and prostitutes, all of whom are watched over by a helpless, badly paid policeman, an insect they all make fun of. All of these elements are remarkably similar to what we find in the "Circe" episode, where Bloom describes Stephen as "Somnambulist" (*U*, 15.4926).

"Circe", which mirrors Marinetti's aim to "destroy all of our expectations about proportion, time and space",[75] also reveals striking parallels with his ideas written in praise of the variety theatre.[76] The Italian writer exhorted his

followers to "prostitute all of classic art on stage" by "performing for example all the Greek, French, and Italian tragedies, condensed and comically
mixed up, in a single evening".[77] "Circe" too draws on the techniques of variety and certainly mixes up everything we have read up to that point in
Ulysses, drawing the reader into a theatrical world that is closer to what
Marinetti terms "fisicofollia" (physical madness), celebrating the "maximum
anatomic monstrosities", than it is to "psicologia" (psychology), which
"exalts the inner life" and the "boredom of conscience".[78]

While many critics view "Circe" in psychoanalytical terms,[79] Cheryl Herr,
in her *Joyce's Anatomy of Culture*, writes that it is more appropriate and fruit-
ful "to view 'Circe' as a script", which she interprets in terms of the English
pantomime tradition and its use of cross-dressing.[80] It is equally valid to
locate the episode within the Italian, and more specifically the Triestine tradition of variety, with which Joyce had so many years to become familiar.
Trieste offered many examples of what Marinetti had in mind when praising
the variety theatre; and the city's shady night-world entertainment certainly
provided Joyce with material for his Nighttown episode. In "Circe" the
nymph provides a description, complete with the names of Italian performers, that perfectly fits the world of variety as it was in the Adriatic port:

> THE NYMPH
>
> Mortal! You found me in evil company, highkickers, coster picnicmakers,
> pugilists, popular generals, immoral panto boys in fleshtights and the nifty
> shimmy dancers, La Aurora and Karini, musical act, the hit of the century. I was
> hidden in cheap pink paper that smelt of rock oil. I was surrounded by the stale
> smut of clubmen, stories to disturb callow youth, ads for transparencies,
> truedup dice and bustpads, proprietary articles and why wear a truss with testi-
> monial from ruptured gentleman. Useful hints to the married. (*U*, 15.3244–52)

From the turn of the century until the outbreak of the First World War,
variety was an especially popular form of mass entertainment in Trieste. The
streets and bars had long had a wide range of characters who also performed
in a variety of notorious *caffè-chantant*. Many of the sketches were in the Triestine dialect, and such was the success of these small variety shows that big
theatres began to offer their own alternatives. As a result, various singers,
comics and transformists also became popular. Sometimes the shows
assumed a more erotic nature:

> The Caffè-Chantant were looked on as places of perdition by respectable peo-
> ple, even though the shows never went beyond showing a bit of stockinged leg

and everything was reduced to jolly malice. Naturally, after the show, there was, it is true, sinful trading in the booths, but it usually dragged on for so long that the customers ended up drunk under the tables, completely incapable of seeing the propositions through to a conclusion.[81]

It all sounds rather like Stephen Dedalus in Bella Cohen's brothel.

A long article about these cafés was published in *L'Adriatico* in 1908, and the author was clearly quite taken by the strange and fickle audience and the performing stars, Ida Rosa, Mary Fleur and Stella del Nord:

> A beautiful girl with her hair down to her shoulders or puffed up in waves, a rich and elegant outfit which makes her a lively female figure, a short skirt, a *dessou* made of lace, silk stockings, gems or less precious rings in her ears and on her hands, red painted lips which whisper risqué words, the implicit pornography ... how could she not attract the applause of an almost entirely male audience, even if she does not have the sweetest voice? *La Chanteuse* does not seek to be a great singer, she offers herself as she is – a beautiful young thing – and she overcomes her lack of a voice by lifting her skirt in time with the music.[82]

La chanteuse was the main draw at the *caffè-chantant*, but the transformists were also very much in vogue. Perhaps the most famous in Italy was Leopoldo Fregoli, who performed in Trieste's Teatro Politeama Rossetti on 1 May 1912, appearing in the following ten guises in just half an hour: "The newspaper editor, the unemployed Fregoli, the printing-works foreman, the Baron candidate for parliament, the Spanish noblewoman charity-worker, the French impressionist painter, the Italian opera singer, the terrible husband, the weak wife, the tender lover." This ability to transform himself so quickly was admired by Marinetti, who cited him as an example of the "synthesis of speed and transformations".[83] Joyce has Leopold Bloom engaged in a similar number of even more impressive transformations in "Circe", where Bloom is "dutiful son, henpecked husband, masochist, 'lion of the night' ... secret lover of Josie Breen, king of Ireland, and common workman"[84] and also a "charming soubrette with dauby cheeks, mustard hair and large male hands and nose, leering mouth" (*U*, 15.2985–6).

Joyce renewed his interest in Futurism in *Finnegans Wake*. A series of performers appear before "THE CUSTOMERS (Components of the Afterhour Courses at St. Patricius' Academy for Grownup Gentlemen ...)" (*FW*, 221.1–2) in the "Feenichts Playhouse" (*FW*, 219.2) "with Futurist onehorse balletbattle pictures and the Pageant of Past History worked up with animal variations amid everglaning mangrovemazes and beorbtracktors by Messrs Thud and Blunder" (*FW*, 221.18–20). This section ironically recalls many of the crucial elements of Futurism, such as the variety theatre as a place for "Grownup Gentlemen" and the focus on battles and violence.

Comments made by the artist Tullio Silvestri in a letter to Dario De Tuoni reveal the critical interest in Futurism among Trieste's artists, and, more importantly, are inadvertently indicative of Joyce's relationship not only with Futurism, but perhaps with all literary movements:

> A piece of advice, if you'll allow me: "Futurism" is a rusty old tool, better not to talk about it. The new, that is the renewal of the artistic vision, is a very natural phenomenon: it is not with acts of daring that the age-old foundations are shifted; a few solitary figures have received from nature the supreme knowledge which can revitalize the world and the spirits, the task of launching the new flashes; to attempt to force these things is as much an ugly as it is a useless absurdity.[85]

Silvestri's view may not have been far from Joyce's own. Too often these movements provided inspiration for mediocre artists, while solitary geniuses did not need their artistic agendas to be invented for them. Just as Joyce rejected much of the political baggage that was part and parcel of the Irish revival, yet was not above engaging with and borrowing from it, so too was he able to disagree with the substance of Futurism while adopting some of its forms and techniques when they suited his cause.

If Joyce shared stylistic interests with the Futurists, he may well have shared thematic concerns with another group of young intellectuals: the *Vociani*, who were largely based in Florence and took their name from the avant-garde literary journal *La Voce*. Their choice of Florence over Rome was political: Rome symbolized the past, the mediocrity of the present and the possibility of an aggressive, nationalist-imperialist future, while Florence represented a new vision of what it was to be Italian, a place open to other cultures, where new and less dogmatic ideas could be nurtured and developed.

Among the Triestine *Vociani* Joyce may have met were Scipio Slataper and Umberto Saba, with whom he had friends in common,[86] and Angelo Vivante, who shared interests and characteristics with both Bloom and Joyce himself. Born in 1884, Vivante was a journalist of Jewish descent, who started out as an irredentist and was employed by *Il Piccolo* to cover the meetings of the Circolo Socialista only to become so convinced by what he heard there that he converted to socialism and promptly lost his job at the paper. His 1912 *Irredentismo Adriatico* is a brilliant history of Trieste and a cogent analysis of the consequences Trieste would suffer if it left the Austrian Empire. The irredentists never forgave him for it.

The Triestine poet Umberto Saba was also, for a time, associated with the *Vociani* before going on to become one of the major Italian poets of this century. But Scipio Slataper was the *Vociano* par excellence, and his *Lettere triestine*, which he published in *La Voce*, and his *Il mio Carso* (My Karst), became the decisive texts for any understanding of "Triestinità".

Generally speaking, all of these writers were tired of tolerating a situation in which culture was forced to wear the strait-jacket of nationalist politics, and of the polarization of Trieste into a town of us (civilized Italians) and them (barbarous Slavs/brutal Austrians). Unlike the majority of their townsfolk, they did not find it necessary to denigrate their neighbours in order to assert their Italian identity, and their criticism of this form of cultural terrorism was echoed by Joyce in his views of Irish nationalists in his articles in *Il Piccolo della Sera*.

The publication of Slataper's *Il mio Carso* in 1912 was greeted with dismay or, more commonly, simply ignored. *La Coda del Diavolo* termed Slataper's book an "indecent hotchpotch, a hymn to the Slav conquest of Trieste" that could only have been made possible by some Slav benefactor.[87] This, of course, was a cruel simplification of Slataper's message. As a youth, he had dreamt of fighting for Garibaldi and of dying like Oberdan, and he actually died fighting against the Austrians as a volunteer in the Italian army. Like many Triestines, he was of mixed Italian, German and Slav ancestry and in his life and writings he attempted the arduous task of reconciling these three competing identities. He had a profound sense of the city being a place apart and felt himself to be, above all else, a Triestine: "Trieste is my country. I discover more about Trieste everyday. ... It is a point where cultures meet."[88] In *Il mio Carso*, he defined "Triestinità" as an awareness of a real but indefinable difference – real when lived internally, false when expressed. That said, he fundamentally believed Trieste's future rested with Italy and he was not blind to the danger of a Slav penetration. His response to that danger was to provide a means for the Slavs living in and around the city to channel their enthusiasm and intelligence into the very anima of the city. In Slataper's view of things, Trieste was a city without cultural traditions and hence of uncertain identity. If a more secure identity was to be created, it could only be achieved by drawing on the rich cultural mix of people that made up the city's human fabric.

In attempting to create the conscience of his race, Joyce's aim was very similar, so much so that in *Finnegans Wake* he seems to make a link with his Triestine counterpart, whose name in Slovene conveniently means "golden pen": "I titfortotalledup their farinadays for them on my slataper's slate with my chandner's chauk" (*FW*, 542.31–3). In their courageous independence and their refusal to go with the all too well established flow of the city's politics, the *Vociani* were partners in spirit with Joyce's enterprise, and Slataper's writings about Trieste identify exactly what fascinated Joyce about his adopted city.

5 *Business as usual*

With the arrival of autumn 1910 Joyce finally managed to bring about one planned change. In late August, with the inevitable financial assistance from Stanislaus, he took a new apartment on the third floor of number 32 via della Barriera Vecchia, where he would remain along with Nora, Giorgio and Lucia, Eileen and Eva until early September 1912. This was nearer the centre of town than via Scussa and in the middle of a lively residential and shopping area of the city. On the ground floor was a pharmacy called All'Imperatore d'Austria, which was owned and run by Joyce's new landlord, Signor Picciola. Situated almost directly across the road was Alberto Pirona's pretty Art Nouveau Pasticceria Caffè, which would become a regular haunt of Joyce's. Francini Bruni had introduced him to Pirona, who later remembered that from 1910 to 1912 Joyce never missed an opportunity to try Pirona's "select wines" and found inspiration loitering there "and sampling the cakes, which he washed down with *rosolio* (sweet wine)".[89] Just down the street was another of Joyce's preferred bars, the exquisitely ornate Caffè Bizantino.

The presence of Eva and Eileen meant company for Nora, but also put her and Joyce under some pressure to resume the practice of their religion, something which they refused to do. Both sisters were extremely devout, and Eva in particular was troubled by the couple's situation and attempted to convince them to marry, if only for the sake of the children.

It was around this time that the Joyces decided to allow themselves the luxury of hiring a live-in servant, a strange decision given that there were now three women already living in the house. Their new maid was one Maria Kirn, from the countryside near Trieste. Nora was very fond of Kirn, who stayed with them for a little more than a year. Kirn later told the scholar Thomas Staley that she had been happy with the Joyces, who paid well and on time, and that she was also able to supplement her income with the tips she received from Joyce's students, whom she accompanied from the entrance to the house up the stairs to the third-floor flat. She recalled that Ettore Schmitz was among those who visited and he often stayed until late at night talking to Joyce. Their friendship, according to Kirn, was always slightly formal, perhaps because of Schmitz's rather reserved character.[90] She also remembered how Joyce commandeered the kitchen, where he spent most of his day studying and writing at the big table because the light was good there. "Nora would talk a great deal about Ireland. She missed her native land a great deal. [...] Every time she ironed the clothes she would say, 'Oh, you should see how the clothes dry in Ireland, Mary.'"[91]

It was also in the autumn of 1910 that the evening school of the Società degli impiegati civili – La Scuola Commerciale di perfezionamento – appointed Joyce to teach a second English course. (The other course was taught by Phillip Cautley, whom Joyce had already replaced as Svevo's private teacher and whom he would later replace at La Scuola di Commercio "Revoltella"). Joyce's appointment was noted in the society's newspaper, *Il Diritto*, on 19 October 1910. The teaching staff included the prominent socialist deputy Puecher, who taught commercial law, and Joyce's former boss in the Berlitz school, Artifoni, who was the accountancy teacher. It is likely that Artifoni – along with Nicolò Vidacovich, who was a member of the school's board of management – played an instrumental role in getting him the job. Grateful as Joyce may have been for the financial benefits accruing from the position, he is unlikely to have been impressed by the students he encountered at the school, but at least he was obliged to teach only three hours per week. The lessons in the various subjects took place between 7.30 p.m. and 9.30 p.m. daily from October to May, and the students were divided into "*ordinari*" (shopkeepers who were obliged to attend by ministerial order) and "*straordinari*" (employees and shop-assistants). To be accepted into First Year, the students were required to be at least fourteen years old and to have attended La Scuola Popolare. They also had to pass an admittance test in reading, writing and arithmetic. At the end of the 1910–11 academic year, a report summed up the school's activities and included a mention of Joyce:

> On 18 May the academic year 1910–1911 of our Commercial school drew to a close. As the readers know, the school offered three obligatory courses and eight language courses. A second English course was added this year and sig. Ioyce [*sic*] was chosen to give it.[92]

Joyce's position on the staff was renewed in 1911, 1912 and 1913, the year in which the school was forced to close due to a lack of funding. On 23 December 1911 an article in *Il Diritto* noted that of a total of 204 students, thirty-three studied in one or other of the two English courses which were taught by "i professori Filippo Cautley e Mr. James Joyee [*sic*]".

Joyce continued to make the bulk of his living by giving private lessons to an ever-widening circle of students and by doing some translations of commercial letters. In December 1910 he found faith again in his occasional vocation for journalism and contributed an article entitled "La Cometa dell' Home Rule" to *Il Piccolo della Sera*, in which he spares no one in his depiction of the confused situation following the Liberals' partial victory in the Westminster parliamentary elections, one which left them depending on the Irish party for an overall majority.[93] He feels it probable that a Home Rule bill will be presented but is highly dubious about such a bill being passed. He reserves his most venomous comments for the Irish themselves and for their representatives, who now seemed bent on making "common cause with British democracy", a fact that should

> neither surprise nor persuade anyone. For seven centuries she has never been a faithful subject of England. Neither, on the other hand, has she been faithful to herself. She has entered the British domain without forming an integral part of it. She has abandoned her own language almost entirely and accepted the language of the conqueror without being able to assimilate the culture or adapt herself to the mentality of which this language is the vehicle. She has betrayed her heroes, always in the hour of need and always without gaining recompense. She has hounded her spiritual creators into exile only to boast about them. She has served only one master well, the Roman Catholic Church, which, however, is accustomed to pay its faithful in long term drafts. (*CW*, 212–13)

He concludes that "The English will not deliver any more quickly", and will, once again, as the Marquis of Salisbury suggested, "let the Irish stew in their own juice" (*CW*, 213). In other words, the Home Rule comet was destined to fly around for a bit yet before it was brought in to land or, as was more likely, left to burn itself out.

The autumn and winter of 1910 and 1911 offered much that was interesting in the theatre, but before that there was the season of opera in the open air to be enjoyed. Stanislaus had particular reason to remember it as it came immediately after a period in which he had flatly refused to give Joyce and Nora any more money. Eventually he caved in, once more, to their combined pressure and regretted it. Later he remembered this period:

It's enough I think to say that I reached the high water mark of imbecility when I gave them all I had in my pocket to go to the opera in the open air theatre and then went and stood on the roadway outside to see if I could hear the chorus or the tenor's top notes above the rumbling of cars and the noisy play of ragamuffins.[94]

The autumn programme in the Teatro Politeama Rossetti was outstanding and featured the excellent soprano Ersilde Cervi Caroli. It included *Thais, Traviata* ("Signora Cervi Caroli showed off all her artistic treasures, the splendour of her voice, the feeling, the passionate warm phrasing, all her real individuality which was so intellectually strong in this *Traviata*"[95]), *Rigoletto, Madame Butterfly* and a return of Smareglia's *Nozze Istriane* ("Smareglia's music aroused genuine enthusiasm and the opera seemed to be even more complete"[96]). The winter opera season at the Teatro Verdi was equally impressive, with productions of *Vestale, Manon Lescaut,* Mussorgsky's *Boris Godounoff* ("a tremendous turbine of passion"[97]), *La Gioconda,* Wagner's *Il Crepuscolo degli Dei* and Gounod's *Faust.*

On the theatre scene, the autumn of 1910 saw the company of the Teatro Argentina of Rome coming to the Teatro Verdi from 16 to 23 October with an eagerly awaited season of plays by Sem Benelli, another young writer who had been briefly involved with the Futurists and was now enjoying an outstanding period of success. The season included *L'Amore dei tre Re, La Maschera di Bruto, Orione, Andrea del Sarto* and *La Cena delle Beffe.* In December, the great Italian Shakespearian actor Ferruccio Garavaglia brought his Compagnia Italiana to the Rossetti for a successful programme that included Moschino's three-act dramatic poem *Tristano e Isolda* as well as *Hamlet* and *King Lear.*

However stimulating Trieste's cultural programme was, it could not make up for Joyce's failure to get *Dubliners* in print. The year 1910 had passed without the promised publication, and Joyce was becoming increasingly frustrated. In December 1910 Roberts wrote telling him he hoped to publish the book in January 1911 and said he would send on final proofs of "Ivy Day in the Committee Room". January passed and no proofs arrived, and in the spring Joyce was forced to agree to yet more textual changes, but still Roberts procrastinated, his final decision hanging like a dark cloud over the whole Joyce household. Such was Joyce's mounting frustration and bitterness with his inability to see into print the book he knew would launch his literary career that in a fit of temper brought on by a furious row with Nora he seized the manuscript of *A Portrait of the Artist* and stuffed it into the burning stove, declaring that he was giving up writing. But for the presence of mind of the three women present, Nora, Eileen, and Maria Kirn, who managed to retrieve it before much damage was done, part of Joyce's new novel would have been irretrievably lost.

In the summer of 1911 an exasperated Joyce sent a dramatic ultimatum to Maunsel & Co. demanding a final decision on *Dubliners*, but even this had no effect, and so he decided to take the extraordinary step of making his situation public by sending letters to *Sinn Féin* and to the *Northern Whig* of Belfast giving a detailed account of his problems with both Grant Richards and Maunsel and Co. He also sought the opinion of Mr Henry Blackwood Price, the Ulster Protestant assistant manager of the Eastern Telegraph Company in Trieste, whom Joyce and Stanislaus had met in 1906 and with whom they had soon become friends (Joyce would later draw on Price, who repeatedly refused to lend him money, as a model for Mr Deasy in *Ulysses*). Price read the manuscript quickly and expressed his opinion in the following letter:

> My dear Joyce, Excuse me that I did not reply before but was extremely busy. I think your allusion to the late King in "Dubliners" was extremely temperate and moderate *not to say complimentary* so that neither the Royal family or the publishers nor the "man in the moon" have any reason to complain. Whether you will do *yourself* any good by "Dubliners" and all connected with it I still beg to doubt. That you will do more *or less* good to any Irishman of thinking, and rational turn of mind if he reads Dubliners, is I think not so doubtful. I have at last found a box to fit the gas boiler. Did Mrs Joyce find the "travelling knife and fork"?
> Yours to command and very sincerely
> Henry N. Blackwood Price[98]

Bolstered by Price's opinion, Joyce penned an appeal to King George V, but once again all came to nought, as did his subsequent threat to take legal action against Roberts.

In spite of his publishing problems and his many teaching hours, Joyce found time to help Vidacovich work on a translation of Yeats's *The Countess Cathleen*. But as Yeats did not like the early version of his play on which it was based, he refused to grant them rights for publication or performance. Joyce expressed his disappointment to Yeats in a letter written in 1916:

> It is, I think, a great pity that my friend Vidacovich's version was not published. His rendering of many parts (especially of the song *Impetuous heart*) was excellent. (*LI*, 95)

Better results came from Joyce's dabbling in the woollen business, which dated from when he was in Dublin setting up the Volta. A series of letters and invoices from the Dublin Woollen Co. dating from 7 November 1910 to 31 July 1911 reveal that Joyce was actively selling tweeds in Trieste in this period. The speed and success of this business must have made a pleasant contrast to the frustrations involved in his publishing ventures and his endless hours of English lessons. It would even appear that for a time he took to heart the Woollen Company's motto "An ounce of practice is worth a ton of theory."⁹⁹ As can be seen from the invoices, he supplied suits, homespuns and tweeds to several Triestines – including Professor Guido Constantini, Mr C. Bertoli, Mr George Pessi, Mr Egon Bodtkin, Miss Nelly Purkardoger, Mr Carlo Peter, Mr Ruedistrasse, Mr L. Fuchs, Mr Vittorio Venezian, and probably many more. Judging from the correspondence, the company was pleased to do business with Joyce, but predictably problems arose over payments:

> We have gone into matters dealt with in your letters, and write to thank you very much for the interest you have taken in pushing our Irish goods.
>
> As there seems to have been a misunderstanding as to payment, prices, commission etc we will allow whatever you claim as fair, for past order. For future business we would supply you with fresh bunches marked at retail prices and on all cash sales you deduct 10% commission for your trouble. If you wished to allow part of this to your friends – it would be a matter entirely for yourself. If you approve – kindly post us, at our expense, all old bunchs [*sic*] so that we may have fresh sets sent for Autum [*sic*] season.¹⁰⁰

Joyce's commissions helped pay the bills yet the frustrations brought on by his publishing problems were still felt by all the family. Tension between Joyce and Stanislaus, who felt both isolated from and used by the rest of the family, was becoming particularly bitter. In occasional moments of fury, Stanislaus cut off the supply of money he had been pumping into his brother's household and by 1911 he and Jim were scarcely talking, although this did not spare him from Joyce's taunts and tantrums, which now arrived by post, as in the case of this letter sent in January 1911:

> I take the opportunity of letting you know (as you have no doubt heard) that I am about to leave Trieste. [...] I intend to do what Parnell was advised to do on a similar occasion: clear out, the conflict being beneath my dignity, and leave you and the *cattolicissime* to make what you can of the city discovered by my courage (and Nora's) seven years ago, whither you and they came in obedience to my summons, from your ignorant and famine-ridden and treacherous country. My irregularities can easily be made the excuse of your conduct.

A final attempt at regularity will be made by me in the sale of my effects, half of which will be paid in by me to your account in a Trieste bank where it can be drawn on or left to rot according to the dictates of your conscience.

I hope that [...] when I have left the field, you and your sisters will be able, with the meagre means at your disposal, to carry on the tradition I leave behind me in honour of my name and my country. (*LII*, 288)

It seems unlikely that Joyce had serious plans to pack up and leave, or that the letter was anything more than a stratagem to counter his brother's calls for financial rectitude. Joyce's depiction of himself as a martyr to the cause of his writing, his claim of courage for what was chance, his calling to heel of his younger, weaker brother, his association of Stanislaus with Ireland, when Stanislaus, even more than he, had openly rejected that country, were all unfair lines of argument. As always, however, Stanislaus fell back into line. He later gave his side of the story to Ellmann, who took the following notes from their interview:

Joyce would come up to Stannie smiling, cigar sticking out [of the] corner of his mouth, and ask him for money. Stannie would reply, "Not a penny more." Then Joyce would begin talking of his book, of his writing, and Stannie would come through. When he was in distress over *Dubliners* Stannie said to him, "Just don't ask me for any money for a year and I'll be able to pay for the publication of your book myself." But Joyce never stopped asking him.[101]

Stanislaus was not the only one to find Joyce's lifestyle hard to put up with. In July 1911, Eva, the more Catholic of the two "cattolicisissime" sisters, decided she had had enough of this strange foreign city and this peculiar godless household and elected to go home to face an uncertain future in Dublin. Shortly after this, Joyce allowed Maria Kirn to take his other sister Eileen and young Giorgio to her family home in the hills of the Carso above Trieste for a short holiday. Giorgio enjoyed the country air and the rhythms of a more tranquil life so much that he was reluctant to return, and Joyce was obliged to write a letter in Italian reprimanding Kirn for having failed to bring him back as promised and ordering her to do so without delay:

I want you to keep an eye on Georgie particularly at the railroad: and, if he doesn't obey, call a *trooper* at once to put him in his seat.

I have been to the station eight or ten times. So I must ask you not to keep me waiting tomorrow evening. And tell Georgie too that his Daddy feels sad about his not wanting to come home any more. Goodbye and don't fail to come on time. (*LII*, 294)

Kirn duly arrived as instructed with Eileen and Giorgio, who was soon sent to the nearby school on via Parini, where he settled in without particular fuss. Eileen, too, was soon to leave Trieste to take up employment as governess for the Serravallo family in the town of San Daniele del Friuli near Udine. One of her principal tasks there would be to give English lessons to the children, and many of her letters of this period to Stanislaus contain queries on matters of grammar and vocabulary, to which he responded with increasing irritation.

In the years 1911–12 Joyce continued to teach a large number of private lessons and to work in the evening school of the Società degli impiegati civili. But given the frustrations with *Dubliners* and his lack of progress on *A Portrait of the Artist as a Young Man,* he was beginning to feel that he had reached something of a dead end in Trieste. It was fine to have much to talk about in the bars and coffee shops and to have some of Europe's best opera and theatre available on his doorstep, but if he was no nearer to finding a publisher willing to launch his work then he might as well at least find a less stressful means of earning a living.

In the winter of 1911–12 Joyce actively set about finding a job in Italy that would provide a better and more stable income. In November he applied to the Istituto Tecnico in Como, but was told that no position was available and that in any case he would need a teaching diploma in order to be considered should any post arise.[102] Since the same proviso would apply for any teaching job in Italy, Joyce wrote to the Ministry of Education in Rome asking to sit the exam for the teaching diploma which was to be held in Padua.

The Joyces also continued to have housing problems. In February 1912 the landlord in via della Barriera Vecchia, Signor Picciola, served notice on them to leave their flat because of their failure to pay the rent, but Joyce managed to gather enough money to keep him at bay and by the end of May 1912 he was thinking of staying there for another year: "This month I have 300 crowns rent to pay. Possibly we shall be in this flat also next year as the administrator told me he intends to try to bring Picciola and myself to an understanding."[103]

6 *Joyce on English Literature*

In February 1912 Joyce accepted an invitation to deliver two well-paid lectures in Italian at the Università Popolare. He entitled them "Verismo ed idealismo nella letteratura inglese (x De Foe – William Blake)" (Realism and idealism in English literature from Defoe to Blake).[104] They were held in the Civica scuola popolare e cittadina on via Giotto, where Joyce sometimes also gave private lessons. Proof that the lectures took place can be found in the Austro-Hungarian police reports, which note that there were sixty people present at the first lecture on the evening of 9 February 1912 and that the event passed without incident. The report continues: "The lecturer spoke about the English writer Daniele Defoe, born in London in 1660. Of the writer's works, the speaker mentioned especially his most important work: *Robinson Crusoe*. The lecture finished at 9.45 in the evening."[105] The report on the second lecture was even more telegraphic: "About 120 people present. Passed without incident."[106]

The Defoe lecture is evidence of how highly Joyce regarded the English writer, while it also reveals a number of similarities between him and his subject, principally in terms of their common financial and publishing problems. Having placed Defoe in a historical and literary context by discussing his predecessors, who had failed to reveal "the true English soul",[107] Joyce asks "How is the great English nation mirrored in the variegated plays of William Shakespeare, who wrote two hundred years after Chaucer? A boorish peasant; a strolling player; a tatterdemalion, half lunatic half fool; a gravedigger."[108] In his opinion, "Shakespeare's important characters all come from abroad: Othello, a Moorish leader; Shylock, a Venetian Jew; Caesar, a Roman; Hamlet, a prince of Denmark; Macbeth, a Celtic usurper; Juliet and Romeo, residents of Verona",[109] while Defoe's great merit in *Robinson Crusoe* is to have created a character with all the essential traits of the English: "the manly independence, the unconscious cruelty, the persistence, the slow but effective intelligence, the sexual apathy, the practical and well-balanced religiosity, the calculating silence".[110] In so doing, the "father of the English novel", became "the first English author to write without imitating or adapting foreign works, to create without literary models and to infuse into the creatures of his pen a truly national spirit, to devise for himself an artistic form which is perhaps without precedent."[111]

Joyce was evidently pleased with his lecture because shortly after delivering it, on 30 June 1913, he offered it for publication to *Il Marzocco*, the long-established and highly respected Florentine literary journal. He went to considerable trouble to convince the editor by gathering five letters of recommendation, which he enclosed along with his degree certificate.[112] Corinna del Greco Lobner suggests that the editor declined to publish Joyce's lecture because he "may have found Joyce's thinly disguised anti-British sentiments unsuitable for the large number of English subscribers who sustained *Il Marzocco* intellectually and financially".[113]

In the second lecture, Joyce moved on to Blake, whom he also admired. "His spiritual rebellion against the powers of this world was not made of the kind of gunpowder, soluble in water, to which we are more or less accustomed" (*CW*, 215). He also took issue with the notion that Blake was mad: "If we must accuse of madness every great genius who does not believe in the hurried materialism now in vogue with the happy fatuousness of a recent college graduate in the exact sciences, little remains for art and universal philosophy" (*CW*, 220).

On 20 April 1912, after a four-month wait, Joyce was informed in writing by the rector of the University of Padua that he was eligible to sit the exam for the Italian teaching diploma, which would begin just four days later. Joyce readied himself and travelled to Padua to be present for the examination, which began at 8 o'clock on 24 April. His first task was to write a composition in Italian entitled "The Universal Literary Influence of the Renaissance". In his essay Joyce takes issue in a rather polemical way with the thrust of the title by downplaying the influence of the Renaissance when compared with all that had come before it. Thus he pairs off the *Inferno* with *Tristam und Isolde*: the first, the greater work, is "ideational", the second merely "the art of circumstances".[114] However persuasive Joyce's line of argument, the examiner awarded him only 30 out of a possible 50 points. The next day he had to write an essay in English entitled "The Centenary of Charles Dickens". Although keen to put Dickens's achievement in perspective, Joyce finds much that he likes in "the Great Cockney's works" and his essay, especially when dealing with Dickens's relationship with London, is highly suggestive of his own preoccupation with Dublin. He notes that whenever Dickens "went far afield" in his writing, to America or Italy, "his magic seems to have failed him"; and in his appreciation of the English writer's ability to render London life he lists qualities that were also his own and that he would develop and refine to perfection in *Ulysses*. "The life of London", he writes, "is the breath of his nostrils: he felt it as no writer since or before his time has felt it. The colours, the familiar noises, the very odours of the great metropolis unite in his work as in a mighty symphony wherein humour and pathos, life and death, hope and despair, are inextricably interwoven."[115] In a letter to Grant Richards dated 15 October 1905, Joyce expresses a very similar idea, citing "the special odour of corruption which, I hope, floats over my stories (*LII*, 122–3)."

Joyce's examiners were suitably impressed by the essay and awarded him full marks. Not surprisingly, he was also awarded full marks for a dictation in English and for a translation into English of a passage from *Ricordi di mia vita* by Pietro Colletta. With these results under his belt, he returned briefly to Trieste but was back in Padua four days later to take the oral part of the examination, which consisted of translations from English into Italian and Italian into English, questions about English grammar and questions in Italian about English literature. He obtained a total of 421 out of 450 as his final result and was judged to have passed. All he needed now was for the Higher Council of the Ministry of Education in Rome to recognize his Dublin degree.

He had to wait until August 1912 to be told the final outcome. The news was bad: his examination results had been annulled because the Higher Council had not recognized his degree. Joyce decided he was jinxed, telling Stannie: "Of Padua I understand nothing. The sooner you convince yourself that I am pursued by *scalogna* the better" (*LII*, 301). He wrote to the Board of Education in London "to know why a British degree in arts is not recognised as valid for *examination purposes* in Italy", only to be informed that there was no reciprocal arrangement for the recognition of university degrees between the two countries. He also appealed to the Italian Senator Mazzoni, whom he had met in Trieste when Mazzoni had come to lecture at the Università Popolare, and to Carlo Galli, the Italian consul in Trieste. Their efforts on his behalf came to naught.

7 Betrayal

The summer of 1912 is framed by two bitter denunciations of betrayal. The first, written in May for *Il Piccolo della Sera*, and entitled "The Shade of Parnell" (*CW*, 223–8),[116] focuses on the destruction of Joyce's political hero at the hands of his own people; the second, a pamphlet entitled "Gas from a Burner", written on the back of his useless *Dubliners* contract with Maunsel & Co. and later published in Trieste and distributed in Dublin, is Joyce's livid response to the betrayal he himself suffered at the hands of his Dublin publisher and of Dublin in general.

"The Shade of Parnell" sketches the history of the Irish struggle against England. While acknowledging some of the achievements of the key Irish figures in it (such as Gavan Duffy and Davitt) Joyce argues that "these concessions only make more conspicuous the extraordinary personality of a leader who, without forensic gifts or any original political talent, forced the greatest English politicians to carry out his orders; and, like another Moses, led a turbulent and unstable people from the house of shame to the verge of the Promised Land" (*CW*, 225):

> The light of his sovereign bearing, mild and proud, silent and disconsolate, makes Disraeli look like a diplomatic opportunist who dines when he can at rich men's houses, and Gladstone like an imposing major domo who has gone to night school. How lightly Disraeli's wit and Gladstone's culture weigh in the balance today. (*CW*, 226)

Readers of *Il Piccolo*, accustomed to similarly hyperbolic celebrations of men such as Carducci and Venezian and denunciations of their enemies, would have found nothing excessive in Joyce's enthusiasm for Parnell. Despite the inferior qualities of contemporary politicians, Joyce acknowledges that Ireland is now poised for Home Rule (the third Home Rule Bill having been passed on 9 May), but Parnell, he warns, will not be forgotten. "The ghost of the 'uncrowned king' will weigh on the hearts of those who remember him when the new Ireland in the near future enters into the palace 'fimbriis aureis circumamicta varietatibus', but it will not be a vindictive ghost", even though the Irish ignored his plea "not to throw him as a sop to the English wolves howling around them", but "tore him to pieces themselves" (*CW*, 228).

As soon as he had this article behind him, Joyce prepared for the summer ahead with a typical lack of financial caution. When he should have been setting aside money for the lean period ahead he was out spending: he attended the spring opera season and particularly enjoyed a production of *Il Barbiere di Siviglia*; he "bought a 160 crown American desk" and had "the skeleton chairs ... covered in elephant hide" (*LII*, 295); and, finally, he decided to send Nora and Lucia for a visit to Ireland. Of course Nora had not been home since 1904 and perhaps he thought a visit there would do her good after such a long absence, but this was not his only motivation for sending her to Dublin: he wanted her to meet Roberts and to press him about the publication of *Dubliners* before heading to Galway, where he hoped she would be able to wheedle some money out of her uncle Michael Healy.

Meanwhile Joyce himself was left alone in charge of Giorgio and told Signora Schmitz that he was happy to have only men in the house. His serenity, though, did not last long. Perhaps because of the hurt he still felt over the Cosgrave episode, he became deeply worried when he failed to receive a

letter from Nora announcing her arrival in Ireland. Five days after her departure a hurried postcard finally arrived; to this Joyce replied with an angry and
melodramatic letter in which he informed her that he was departing immediately with Giorgio in order to follow her to Ireland:

> Having left me five days without a word of news you scribble your signature
> with a number of others on a postcard. Not one word of the places in Dublin
> where I met you and which have so many memories for us both! Since you left
> I have been in a state of dull anger. I consider the whole affair wrong and
> unjust. I can neither sleep nor think. [...] It is a monstrous thing to say that
> you seem to forget me in five days and to forget the beautiful days of our love.
> I leave Trieste tonight as I am afraid to stay here – afraid of myself. I shall arrive
> in Dublin on Monday. If you have forgotten I have not. I shall go *alone* to meet
> and walk with the image of her whom I remember. (*LII*, 297)

But once again Joyce had underestimated Nora, who, having arrived on
the 8th, had written him a lengthy letter just three days later from Galway
which began: "My darling Jim since I left Trieste I am continually thinking
about you how are you getting on without me or do you miss me at all. I am
dreadfully lonely for you I am quite tired of Ireland already" (*LII*, 296). She
also mentioned that she had gone to see Roberts with his father and later
with "Charley" but that they had made no progress.

Joyce travelled anyway. When passing through London, he was in sufficiently good form to call on Yeats, whom he asked to send a copy of the
revised *Countess Cathleen* to Vidacovich in Trieste. He also visited Joseph
Hone of the London office of Maunsel & Co. and informed him rather dra-
matically: "I have crossed Europe to see you."[117] Hone told Joyce that there
was little he could do for him and advised him to talk to Roberts in Dublin.
Joyce did so as soon as he had arrived there and yet another round of negotiations commenced, as he reported in his letter of 17 July to Stanislaus:

> The new proposals are: either the passage in *Ivy Day* and a passage in *An
> Encounter* are to be deleted, replaced by asterisks and with a note of preface by
> me or the book is to be bought over by me, bound and printed, on my note of
> hand for the cost amount and issue by Simpkin Marshall of London who will
> spread it on commission, the profits being mine. Write and advise me at once
> which way you prefer. Dublin very discouraging. (*LII*, 298)

With these proposals in mind, Joyce travelled to Galway to meet Nora,
who was delighted to see him and quietly pleased that her absence had
inspired such a passionate display of anger. On 14 August she wrote as much

to Eileen: "What must it have been like when you heard Jim was coming. well what have you to say to Jim now after all our little squabbles he could not live without me for a month can you imagine my joy when I received a telegram from London a week after Jim and georgie [*sic*] on their way it seems to me that he can do wonders" (*LII*, 302). Together they toured around Galway and went to the races. Joyce even found the time to write an article entitled "La Città delle Tribù; Ricordi Italiani in un Porto Irlandese" (The City of the Tribes; Italian Echoes in an Irish Port), which was published in *Il Piccolo della Sera* on 11 August 1912. In introducing Nora's native Galway to the Triestines, Joyce gave a potted history of the "Spanish City" but also traced some Italian connections, such as that of Andrea Gerardo, a Florentine merchant who worked there as the government's tax collector in the fourteenth century, and Saint Nicholas of Bari, the guardian of the city. In writing of Galway's importance as a centre of trade, Joyce was touching on a subject which he knew was bound to appeal to his Triestine readership: "Almost all the wine imported into the United Kingdom from Spain, Portugal, the Canary Islands, and Italy passed through this port" (*CW*, 230). He hoped this trading role could be resumed and gave his support to the proposed Galway harbour scheme.[118]

Meanwhile he was a bundle of energy, managing trips by bicycle to Clifden and Oughterard, and by boat to the Aran Islands, about which he decided to write an article for *Il Piccolo della Sera* entitled "The Mirage of the Fisherman of Aran – England's Safety Valve in Case of War", which was published on 5 September,[119] and takes up where the first piece left off. In a mood of gentle appreciation of "Aranmor, the holy island that sleeps like a great shark on the grey waters of the Atlantic ocean, which the Islanders call the Old Sea" (*CW*, 234), Joyce outlines a little history before talking of the commercial possibilities for the port of Galway if the harbour scheme were implemented and the new harbour facilities came to be used as a trade link between the United Kingdom and Canada. Were this to happen, "the old decadent city would rise again. From the new world, wealth and vital energy would run through this new artery of an Ireland drained of blood. Again, after about ten centuries, the mirage which blinded the poor fisherman of Aran, follower and emulator of St. Brendan, appears in the distance, vague and tremulous in the mirror of the ocean" (*CW*, 235).

Teasing his Italian readers a little, Joyce writes that Christopher Columbus was "honoured by posterity because he was the last to discover America", whereas the first to do so had been Saint Brendan, a thousand years earlier;

he then goes on to describe the monastic settlement on Aran and some of its holy men, including Finnian, who became Bishop of Lucca, and concludes on a melancholic note by mourning the loss of this "bygone civilisation", with a rather poetic vision of the mist descending over the island and a Latin flourish designed to impress his Italian readership:

> In the twilight the names of the ports cannot be distinguished, but the line that leaves Galway and ramifies and spreads out recalls the motto placed near the crest of his native city by a mystic and perhaps even prophetic head of a monastery:
>
> *Quasi lilium germinans germinabit*
> *et quasi terebinthus extendans ramos suos* (*CW*, 237)

Behind the trip west was Joyce's desire to come to terms with Nora's past and her people, but also to see and appreciate that part of Ireland which he had mythologized in "The Dead". His was not entirely a mystical journey, however. Joyce was more than willing to cash in on his impressions of the West in his rather hurried and workmanlike newspaper articles, which do not resound with the same ring of intuition and authenticity that characterizes much of his journalism.

In September, Joyce received a barrage of letters from his old friend Henry Blackwood Price, asking him to make public in Ireland an Austrian cure for foot-and-mouth disease that he had discovered. Joyce eventually forwarded a letter from Price to William Field, president of the Irish Cattle Traders Society, and Field was so impressed that he published it in the *Evening Telegraph*. Privately with Stanislaus, Joyce was amused by Price's insistence: "He writes me a letter every day. He has a cure for the foot and mouth disease which is devastating Irish cattle. Styrian oxen suffer from it and are cured but 2000 Irish beasts have been killed. He writes (like you) 'Be energetic. Drop your lethargy. Forget Leinster for Ulster. …'." Joyce concluded his sarcastic epistle by remarking: "I think Price ought to look for a cure for the foot and mouth disease of Anna Blackwood Price" – his wife (*LII*, 300).

Whatever about his scepticism, Joyce was not above writing a sub-editorial himself on the problem for the *Freeman's Journal* of 10 September under the title "Politics and Cattle Disease" (*CW*, 238–41). A competent and convincing piece, it is well informed on the problems afflicting the Irish cattle traders, who were being denied the right to export their healthy livestock to Britain. Joyce blames this embargo on the English protectionists and the Ulster Protestants who have played into their hands.

Price also continued to fight for his "cure" and contributed an article on the subject to *Sinn Féin*. In December 1912 he was still interested in the problem, as his letter to Joyce from Mürzsteg in Austria shows:

> As far as I can understand from the short parliamentary summary the Irish Government under the present Home Rule Bill will have control over the contagious diseases (animals) act so that matter is finished. By the way you never told me what you thought of my article. Though I will be bound it helped "Sinn Fein" to sell, Mr Griffith never offered to pay me anything for it. I wish I was quietly on the permanent staff of his journal. I could write him half a dozen or more caustic articles.[120]

Joyce later parodied Price in the "Nestor" episode of *Ulysses*, using aspects of his character for Mr Deasy and his name for Deasy's cousin. He also remembered mockingly his own advocacy of the Galway Harbour scheme:

> May I trespass on your valuable space. That doctrine of *laissez faire* which so often in our history. Our cattle trade. The way of all our old industries. Liverpool ring which jockeyed the Galway harbour scheme. European conflagration. [...] Foot and mouth disease. Known as Koch's preparation. Serum and virus. Percentage of salted horse. Rinderpest. Emperor's horses at Mürzsteg, lower Austria. Veterinary surgeons. Mr Henry Blackwood Price. (*U*, 2.324–35)

A further extract from Price's letter to Joyce reveals his interest in "the burning question of the day – the threatened European war ...",[121] and his desire to have his cliché-strewn opinions read is rather like Deasy's hope that he will "be printed and read" (*U*, 2.338). Price's letter to Joyce also reveals his meanness, a quality Joyce later transferred to Deasy, who champions the motto "I paid my way" (*U*, 2.251).

> It is very hard to keep up to the times in a Styrian village but I am almost tempted to wish that a European war or something better for humanity would drive me out of Austria and throw me "on the parish" so that I might live as best I could on my pen. There are few men could live as cheaply as I can. I am about the age at which Charles Lever died, and I had more of Trieste than he had, but I have still plenty of go in me, and would give anything for a chance and an excuse to go to Dublin or its neighbourhood.[122]

In late July, when Joyce was still in Dublin, news arrived from Stanislaus that their Triestine landlord, Signor Picciola, had decided to evict them from their apartment in via della Barriera Vecchia and was willing to allow only a couple of days to vacate the premises. As Eileen was alone in the house, having returned from her job in San Daniele to live with her brother and work as governess to Ettore Schmitz's daughter, Letizia, she panicked at the idea of being put out on the street. But it seemed that nothing could be done, as Picciola had already reached an agreement with a new tenant who was waiting to take possession of the property. From Dublin, James tried to reassure both Eileen and Stanislaus, telling them that "the notice to quit was revoked by him 4 times verbally in the presence of witnesses and on that assurance I left Trieste with my family" (*LII*, 298), and claiming that the "new 'tenant'" was a try-on. On 7 August he gave a longer, more belligerent account of his agreement with the landlord and his agent, in which he described Picciola as "a pig" and went on to tell Stanislaus that he would vacate the apartment "for the 24 Feb or 24 November: for the 24 Aug. no"; in the meantime Stannie was instructed to "take possession of the house" until his return (*LII*, 299).

Picciola was not the only Triestine looking for money, as Stanislaus complained. As ever, Joyce was ready with instructions for him: "Don't let my debts trouble you. Tell them I am away and will return in the month of September. They would get the same answer at Economo's door and would salute and go away" (*LII*, 298). Unfortunately Joyce was no Baron Economo (one of the richest men in Trieste) and, to Stanislaus's dismay, was capable of sending little other than instructions. Broke and furious, he wrote telling him to be in Trieste to deal with Picciola himself on eviction day (24 August), but Joyce, who was spending what money he had on the "Dublin branch" of the family, could not afford a trip back. On 17 August he wrote telling Stanislaus to "send to May at once 140 crowns (60 from Piccolo and the rest yourself) so that I can start at a moment's notice" (*LII*, 303); he wrote again on 20 August demanding his fare, and then later the same day changed his mind and told his brother to "place the matter of house at once in the hands of a solicitor" (*LII*, 304). In case Picciola and his agent, two "swindling squinting hell's bitches", should effect an entrance, he sent new strategic instructions: "the little table in my bedroom not the new walnut one", and the desk, were to be carried "carefully and horizontally" into Mrs Borsieri's flat, while his manuscripts and papers were to be entrusted to Mrs Francini (*LII*, 305). These arrangements evidently did not convince Stanislaus, who took matters into his own hands and found Joyce a new flat on the second floor of number 4 via Donato Bramante, which he moved into in mid-September.

Joyce's publishing problems were not so easy to resolve. As August dragged on, Roberts made new demands. On 19 August Joyce, who had returned to Dublin, leaving Nora and the children in Galway, asked his solicitor George Lidwell to write a statement to the effect that the book was not libellous, but he received a far more cautious reply than he had hoped for, in which Lidwell expressed his own objections to "Ivy Day in the Committee Room" and "An Encounter", and gave Joyce the following advice:

> It would be well to remember that although these paragraphs in your book might possibly escape notice that there is at present in existence in this city a Vigilance Committee whose object is to seek out and suppress all the writings of immoral tendencies and I am of opinion that if the attention of the Author-ities be drawn to these paragraphs it is likely they would yield to the pressure of this body and prosecute. Whether a conviction could be obtained is another matter altogether. But I would advise you to take no risks and under the cir-cumstances either delete or entirely alter the paragraphs in question. (*LII*, 306)

Joyce eventually prevailed upon him to write a more positive letter, but even this did not placate Roberts, who demanded that Lidwell write stating that Joyce was prepared to indemnify himself and his firm in the event of prosecution. In desperation, Joyce recounted the story in detail in his letter of 21 August to Nora:

> I said I would sign an agreement to pay him £60 (sixty pounds) the cost of a 1st edition if the book was seized by the Crown. He said that was no use and asked could I get two securities for £1000 (a thousand pounds) each – in all £2000 (two thousand pounds = 50,000 francs) to indemnify the firm for loss over publishing my book. I said that no person admired me so much as that and in any case it could never be proved that the loss (if any) of the firm was due to my book. He said then that he would act on his solicitor's advice and not publish the book. (*LII*, 308)

The same day, "in order to end this interminable discord", Joyce wrote to Roberts agreeing to omit "An Encounter" on four conditions: that a note stating that the book was incomplete be included in the book before the first story; that no further changes be demanded; that he be free to publish "An Encounter" elsewhere; and that the book be published "not later than 6th October 1912" (*LII*, 309–10). But more disappointment arrived from Roberts on 23 August. The book, he wrote, abounded in

> risks of action of libel. [...] That being so, the publication of the book by Maunsel & Co. is out of the question; and I am advised further, that even if the objectionable parts were struck out, there would still remain the risk of some of them being overlooked; and to provide for the risk, should publication be con-templated, they advise that the author must under clause 11 of the Agreement, be bound in two sureties of £500 (five hundred pounds) each to meet possible damages, or, in the alternative, lodge the sum of £1,000 in our bank. (*LII*, 313)

Roberts went on to tell him that according to his solicitors Joyce had broken his contract by submitting a libellous book, and thus caused them a loss which he now demanded Joyce "make a substantial offer towards covering" (*LII*, 313).

Joyce still did not give up: he pawned his watch in order to stay a few more days in Dublin and make one last desperate attempt at convincing Roberts. More inconclusive negotiations ensued, and no matter what changes Joyce offered, Roberts always seemed to have more demands. By the end of August it was clear that Maunsel & Co. were never going to publish *Dubliners*. As a result, Joyce began to think that the only way forward was to publish it himself. On 5 September, Roberts offered to sell 104 copies of *Dubliners* to Joyce for £15 and to have them printed by a fictitious press to be called "Liffey Press" on condition that Joyce say "in the presence of witnesses that he intends bringing the book out in Trieste" rather than Dublin (*LII*, 317). This was something Joyce had already considered doing, as Stanislaus remembered:

> When Jim had the idea of publishing the book in Trieste, he went to all the principal booksellers in Dublin to ask them if they would sell the book for him. They all hesitated when they heard the facts. The manager of one of them told him that a couple of weeks before two young fellows had presented themselves to him and insisted that he should take a certain French novel out of his window. The manager asked them what authority they had for giving such a peremptory order. They refused to say, but told him that if the novel was not withdrawn, he would have his windows broken.
>
> Roberts told Jim that he had no end of trouble with a certain Vigilance Committee and though he was as shifty as they make 'em that fits in with the rest of the story. He mentioned people who were supposed to be on the Committee. I vaguely remember Lady Aberdeen, some priests and priests' creatures [...] who all got in on the good cause. Why should Roberts himself have broken his contract to publish a book that promised to be at least as successful as the others he had published unless he too had yielded to pressure? Falconer, besides his official work for the Crown, did a lot of printing for Catholic Societies.[123]

The same Falconer, the printer, completely derailed the plan to publish the book as a Liffey Press title by refusing to hand the copies over to Roberts. In a letter of 11 September, Joyce's brother Charles narrated the sad conclusion of the saga to Stanislaus:

> Jim then asked what they intended doing with his book and he said they would destroy it. Jim asked him how they would destroy it and he said they would

burn the sheets and break up the type. They cared nothing for the loss of the fifty-seven pounds they had learnt a lesson and would not be so easily fooled again. There was nothing else to do and this is the end of *Dubliners* so far as Dublin in concerned. (*LII*, 319)[124]

Although Joyce managed to obtain at least one complete set of the sheets of *Dubliners*, he knew it was useless to make any further attempts to publish his book in Dublin. He left that very night for London, where, on arrival, he took the time to offer it to the *English Review* and to Mills and Boon.

On his return journey, Joyce exorcised the ghosts of Roberts and Falconer by composing his bitter satire "Gas from a Burner". In it he went back to the by now familiar theme of betrayal with which his summer had begun, writing, in Roberts's voice:

> But I owe a duty to Ireland:
> I hold her honour in my hand,
> This lovely land that always sent
> Her writers and artists to banishment
> And in a spirit of Irish fun
> Betrayed her own leaders, one by one.
> 'Twas Irish humour, wet and dry,
> Flung quicklime into Parnell's eye;
> 'Tis Irish brains that save from doom
> The leaky barge of the Bishop of Rome
> For everyone knows the Pope can't belch
> Without the consent of Billy Walsh. (*CW*, 243)

Joyce would never return to Ireland. From now on exile was his only hope of keeping his creative energies intact. He would allow himself to see only from a distance what he loved and what he despised about his native land, for he knew now what he had long suspected: home was no longer there.

FIVE

Success in the shadow of war

I Return to exile, and "Exiles"

As soon as he was back in what he once called "my poor Trieste" on the "Amaro Adriatico" (*LI*, 71), Joyce had "Gas from a Burner" printed there and immediately sent copies to Charles Joyce for distribution in Dublin. But, as Ellmann narrates it: "Charles hesitated over it, especially since, as he wrote James, 'Pappie kicked up blue hell' when he read it and said, 'He's an out and out ruffian without the spark of a gentleman about him.' John Joyce clung to his conception of himself as a gentleman as to a last fig leaf. But Joyce insisted that Charles deliver the sheets, and at length he did" (*JJ*, 337).

Joyce's more considered rejection of his native city came in *Exiles*, one of the creative projects that were going to occupy him over the following two years. He set his play in Dublin in the "Summer of the year 1912"[1] and, as J.C.C. Mays writes, "It registers his realisation that he did not want to live in Ireland [...] and it explores the nature of the independent life he had chosen in terms of the relationship that was most important to it."[2]

If things went badly for Joyce in Dublin, better news awaited him in Trieste. He was no sooner back than he received an invitation – probably engineered by Vidacovich – to give a series of ten lectures at the most prestigious cultural association in Trieste, the Società di Minerva in via Carducci.[3] Joyce's lectures were so successful that he actually gave a total of twelve, on Monday evenings between 11 November 1912 and 10 February 1913. He makes explicit mention of this in *Giacomo Joyce*:

> I expound Shakespeare to docile Trieste: Hamlet, quoth I, who is most courteous to gentle and simple is rude only to Polonius. Perhaps, an embittered idealist, he can see in the parents of his beloved only grotesque attempts on the part of nature to produce her image . . . . Marked you that? (*GJ*, 10)

Joyce's first talk was prominently reviewed in *Il Piccolo*, which reported that "Prof. James Joyce, whom our intellectual world knows and admires as a thinker, a writer, and a journalist, began his cycle of 10 lectures on Shakespeare's *Hamlet* in the completely packed Minerva hall ... A very warm and insistent round of applause greeted the speaker at the end of his erudite and enjoyable talk."[4] The final lecture was also the subject of a highly favourable *Il Piccolo* review, probably written by Roberto Prezioso:

> Yesterday evening, Dr James Joyce concluded his series of lectures in English on *Hamlet.* The hall was crowded for all of the lectures. It was apparent that the English colony was quite poorly represented and so the assiduous attendance was a tribute firstly to the lecturer but also to his Italian audience who managed to follow his complicated talks.
>
> As Joyce himself mentioned yesterday, he did not wish to make a critical or philosophical appraisal of the play which he was reading and interpreting. His primary task was to explain difficult words. His original and slightly bizarre genius transformed these potentially dry commentaries into charming occasions. The Elizabethan words, fashions and traditions inspired in the able lecturer literary and historical memories which fascinated the audience which was his for many hours.
>
> Yesterday evening, feeling the need to finish the series off with a critical summary, Joyce read (translated into English) Voltaire's attack on *Hamlet* and then Georg Brandes's praise of the same work. We believe that a large section of the audience who were able to follow the lectures will find themselves stimulated – as Joyce hoped – to read some of the great Englishman's other plays in English.
>
> Joyce was thanked by his audience, who gave him a warm and prolonged round of applause yesterday evening. This was surely intended as an invitation to repeat the original and highly successful experiment of holding lectures in English for an Italian audience.[5]

Not long after this review appeared, Prezioso's overzealous interest in Nora provided Joyce with crucial first-hand experience that would enable him to write on the themes of attraction and betrayal, marriage and infidelity and the often ambiguous nature of sexual attraction, which would dominate *Exiles*[6] and play a significant role in *Ulysses*. Of Venetian origin, Prezioso was born in Trieste in 1869. He studied law in Bologna, volunteered for the Italian army and worked for a time both as a solicitor and as a diplomat in the Brazilian consulate in Trieste. Having written a book on the Brazilian economy, he rose to the rank of consul before changing career in 1902 and taking up his position of acting editor of *Il Piccolo* and editor of *Il Piccolo della Sera*, where his cunning and stylish journalism was much admired. He was married with two children.

Joyce had known Prezioso since the early days at the Berlitz school and long after leaving his job there had continued to teach him privately in a group that included Count Francesco Sordina and Baron Ambrogio Ralli. Gradually Joyce and Prezioso became good friends, addressing one another in Italian with the informal "tu" rather than the formal "Lei", something Joyce and Svevo would never do, and a sign that any social gap that existed between them had been overcome.

Prezioso's reputation as a *conquistatore amoroso*, a "*Don Giovanni*", as Francini Bruni described him,[7] is what marks him out among Joyce's companions in Trieste. He was a handsome, dapper man-about-town living at the pinnacle of local society, and Joyce was pleased Nora had such an illustrious admirer. It gave her an edge she had previously lacked in this rather snobbish city, where the women Joyce knew and taught considered her to be "nice" but "poco colta" – not very refined.[8]

Prezioso made a number of afternoon visits to Nora. All proceeded well until the Italian made an explicit declaration to her, saying, "Il sole s'è levato per Lei" – the sun has risen for you (*JJ*, 316). Nora instantly called a halt to his advances and informed Joyce about what had happened. He rapidly sought out the offender and gave him such a virulent public dressing down that Prezioso burst into tears.

Ellmann speculates that these events took place sometime in the gap between Joyce's 22 December 1910 article in *Il Piccolo* and 5 September 1912, "when he published a rather dull piece on British parliamentary betrayal of home rule policy" (*JJ*, 316).[9] A letter written on 26 August and a postcard dated 13 September 1913 from Prezioso to the Joyces place this dating in doubt, since these two documents, which bear absolutely no hint of there having been a problem, include affectionate greetings to "little Ireland" (meaning Nora), and look forward to being back in Trieste: "In a few days we shall see us again!". Prezioso's next surviving letter to Joyce is undated but as it acknowledges receipt of his gift of *Dubliners* it almost certainly was written during the summer of 1914. It is more formal than the previous two, and sends greetings, significantly, "for Mrs Nora". It thus seems likely that Prezioso overstepped the mark with Nora not in 1911 or 1912 but sometime between the September 1913 letter and the summer of 1914. This period can be narrowed down even more if an entry in Joyce's preliminary notes for *Exiles*, which is dated 12 November 1913 and includes Prezioso's name, is taken into account. In the note, Prezioso's name is directly followed by that of Bodkin, the same young Michael Bodkin who fell in love with Nora in Galway and later became the model for Gretta's great lost love in "The Dead":

> N.(B) – 12 Nov. 1913
>   Garter: precious, Prezioso, Bodkin, music, palegreen, bracelet, cream sweets, lily of the valley, convent garden (Galway) sea.[10]

Taken together, these various documents suggest that the Prezioso incident took place sometime between Prezioso's September 1913 letter and Joyce's November 1913 note for *Exiles*.

Whatever about its timing, Prezioso's paying court to Nora, and especially his final pass, left an indelible mark on Joyce, who had Bloom say to Molly "The sun shines for you". He also exploited this episode more thoroughly as material for *Exiles*, where Brigid, the old servant, says to Bertha of Robert Hand, the friend who is trying to seduce her: "Sure he thinks the sun shines out of your face, ma'am."[11]

Prezioso was a model for Robert Hand, and his wife Beatrice Cozzi may well have been among Joyce's sources for Robert's fiancée Beatrice Justice, as Massimo Soranzio has pointed out: "Prezioso was an irredentist journalist with a law degree, married to Beatrice and advocating justice for the Italian subjects of the Austrian Empire, just as Robert Hand is a journalist and a nationalist, engaged to Beatrice and advocating justice for the Irish subjects of the British Empire."[12] There is a parallel between Nora's relationship with Joyce on the one hand and with Prezioso on the other, and Bertha's situation in *Exiles* as it is described by Joyce: "Bertha is fatigued and repelled by the restless curious energy of Richard's mind and her fatigue is soothed by Robert's placid politeness."[13]

Along with Oliver St John Gogarty and Vincent Cosgrave, Prezioso influenced Joyce in his presentation of the two "gay betrayers" in *Ulysses* – Buck

Mulligan and Blazes Boylan. He seems to be alluded to indirectly in the phrase in "Eumaeus" where Bloom, after witnessing with Stephen a row between a group of Italians and discussing the musical qualities of the Italian language, asks him if he wrote poetry in the language. Stephen responds by saying that Italian is as deafening as it is musical and then comments on the row they have just seen, saying that they "were very passionate about ten shillings" before adding in Italian: "Roberto ruba roba sua" (*U*, 16.882–3). The exact meaning of this phrase is not clear, but it probably suggests something like "Roberto robs what is his" or "Roberto robs his stuff (or goods)" and clearly implies the theft of love at the centre of the novel's thematic concerns. If we refer Roberto's robbery of "roba sua" to the threesome – Joyce, Nora, Prezioso – then the "his" could be Joyce's or Prezioso's, precisely the sort of ambiguity Joyce might have been looking for if, as Ellmann suggests, he had been complicit in encouraging Prezioso's advances.

In the context of *Exiles*, the "Roberto ruba roba sua" phrase suggests Robert Hand and the idiomatic Italian phrase "essere di mano lesta" (to be light-fingered/to have a quick hand). In the notes to that play, Joyce writes "Exiles – also because at the end either Robert or Richard must go into exile. Perhaps the new Ireland cannot contain both. Robert will go." By the time Joyce was writing this, Prezioso had moved to Milan and, more importantly for Joyce's purposes, he had abandoned any claim on Nora, "little Ireland". In the first edition of his life of Joyce, Richard Ellmann suggested that the real object of Prezioso's longing was Joyce. Following objections from the Prezioso family, Ellmann was forced to withdraw this claim from the second edition, but Brenda Maddox revealed no such constraint when she stated that Prezioso was bisexual and fascinated by Joyce who "was not ignorant of the psychological vagary called triolism in which a homosexual desire for someone is expressed in sharing, or dreaming of sharing, a partner".[14] Her speculation about Prezioso's supposed homosexuality is based on an interview with the Triestine Joycean Stelio Crise,[15] and on a postcard which Prezioso sent to Teodoro Mayer's son, Aldo, and inscribed "affettuosamente". Maddox errs in translating this word with the rather loaded "lovingly" when it simply means "affectionately" and is standard at the end of friendly letters in Italian. Given Prezioso's long relationship with the Mayer family, to whom he owed his livelihood and position, to sign a letter in such a way hardly carries the implications suggested by Maddox.

It was Joyce's sister Eileen Schaurek who first suggested the homosexuality theory to Ellmann. His interview with her contains the following passage:

"You mean he was a homosexual? Yes. Very attracted to Joyce."[16] While this, like many of Eileen's recollections, should be treated with caution, it is true that Joyce himself left hints to this effect in his notes for *Exiles*, where he wrote of Bertha (the Nora character) and Robert Hand (the Prezioso character): "The bodily possession of Bertha by Robert, repeated often, would certainly bring into almost carnal contact the two men. Do they desire this? To be united, that is carnally through the person and body of Bertha as they cannot, without dissatisfaction and degradation – be united carnally man to man as man to woman?"[17] Again Joyce returns to Prezioso in his 1916 "dream book" in which he interprets Nora's dreams of a cow speaking and making love. He writes: "The cow is warm-bodied, soft-skinned and shining for she expects elements of preciousness (Prezioso?) in her women" (*JJ*, 437).

In a later entry, the Prezioso episode is again suggested:

> Prezioso weeping
> I have passed him in the street
> My book "Dubliners" in his hand (*JJ*, 437)

Joyce's interpretation of this dream returns to the idea of the two men being somehow carnally linked through their loving the same woman. Where Joyce suggests that he himself had used this idea of betrayal to liberate himself in art, he criticizes Prezioso for being unable to use it to liberate himself in life:

> The point with which he tried to wound has been turned against him – by her: the motive from which I liberated myself in art he is unable to liberate himself from in life. Again a suffering and aging wooer. His complaint that I pass him (it is to be read the other way round) is a secret disappointment that for her so far it is impossible to unite the friendship of two men through the gift of herself differently to both for that which seemed possible in the first case is almost impossible in the second case. (*JJ*, 437–8)

Joyce would make much use of such ambivalence in *Exiles* and *Ulysses*.

2 *Giacomo Joyce*

Another site of artistic, sensual, and erotic confusion is *Giacomo Joyce*, Joyce's somewhat obscure Triestine novelette written in this period, sometime between 1911 and 1914. *Giacomo Joyce* is largely in English with a little interwoven Italian, *Triestino* and German, and comprises just sixteen hand-written pages written on both sides of eight large sheets with uneven gaps between the paragraphs or fragments of text. Sometimes the gaps are larger than the fragments themselves. *Giacomo Joyce* is a private manuscript in a way that none of Joyce's other published works is: he never tried and probably never wished to publish it and left it behind him in Trieste with Stanislaus when he departed for Paris. And yet with its heightened awareness of form, its ample use of poetic methods – repetition, alliteration, metaphor – its inter-textual nature, its combining of epiphanies, paraphrases, quotations and descriptions, it has the polished and highly individualized finish, the conscious artistry of a creative work rather than a diary.

Finding suitable terms with which to describe its stylistic and thematic methods remains difficult. *Giacomo Joyce* often seems to function as successfully on a visual as on a verbal plane, a fact which might, for want of a more adequate terminology, profitably lead to it being described as an interior "visualogue" – a jotting down of visions, a rendering of transient images in words – suggestive of the "Proteus" episode of *Ulysses* with its "Ineluctable modality of the visible: at least that if no more, thought through my eyes. Signatures of all things I am here to read" (*U.* 3, 2–3). Many of the signs to be found in the text of *Giacomo Joyce* are biographical in nature and combine to provide at least partial images of Joyce as an artist in transition grappling with new forms of expression; of Joyce's unrequited love for an attractive, young, sophisticated, female student, part-virgin, part-temptress; of the inner turmoil created by this infatuation, by this young woman who was capable of challenging him at every level (as Nora could never do); of a continental Joyce coming to terms with the clash of complex middle-European and Italian identities and cultures that made Trieste a singular place. Furthermore, aside from any of its biographical resonances, *Giacomo Joyce* remains a complex creative work of fiction, which, in the context of its treatment of the dynamics of desire, is a key transitional text in Joyce's canon.

The hybrid Italian-Irish title of this slim volume suggests an alternative vision of what Joyce had become by the time he came to write it: someone who, for all his material difficulties, was comfortably acclimatized to life in Trieste, steeped in Italian culture, literature and language – an Italianized Irishman. The title signals a continental Joyce, happy to wallow in the glow of various Giacomos, including Giacomo Leopardi, one of the few Italian poets Joyce had any time for, and whose phrase "Vanità, vanità! Nella vita umana non c'è che la giovinezza" (Vanity, vanity! In human life there is only youth) resonates surely with Joyce's own turmoil at the passing of his youth

as expressed in the simple words of *Giacomo Joyce*: "Youth has an end".
There was also Giacomo Puccini, a composer whose music he delighted in,
and, of course, Giacomo Casanova, *grande conquistadore di donne*, but also
man of letters, writer, philosopher, and resident in Trieste when waiting in
vain to be allowed to return to Venice.

Richard Ellmann writes that "the Italian form of his name was never used
by Joyce".[18] The written evidence, however, suggests that Joyce (or Zois, as
the Triestines called him[19]) was often referred to as Giacomo: on, for example Nora's hospital bill following Lucia's birth[20], on Lucia's birth certificate,
and in the various entries in the *Guida di Trieste*. There is also proof that he
at least occasionally enjoyed adopting the name Giacomo and that he was
greatly amused at the various Triestine echoes and nuances it carried. He
signed himself "Giacometo" in a letter written in Triestine dialect to Ettore
Schmitz. On 20 February 1924 he mentioned "S. Giacomo in Monte di
pietà" (*LI*, 211–12); here he was referring to the working-class district of Trieste which bore his name and was just up the street from his house in via
Bramante (he changed the name slightly from San Giacomo in Monte, Saint
James on the hill, to the more apt San Giacomo in Monte di pietà, Saint
James in the pawnbrokers, thus drawing attention to his persistent financial
difficulties). He signed himself "Jacomo Del Oio, sudito botanico" in an earlier letter to Francini Bruni (*SL*, 268–9); in this case the "Jacomo" is Giacomo spelt in Triestine dialect, the "sudito botanico" a corruption of
"suddito britannico" (British subject) which Joyce of course was, while the
"Del Oio" carries a second conscious hint of Joyce's money problems in its
echo of a Triestine idiom "Scampar coi bori de l'oio" (to flee from the paying of debts). Finally, in a letter written in the unhappy thirties to Lucia, he
ironically referred to himself as "Giacomo Giocondo" – James joyful (*LIII*,
353).

What was Joyce's view of women at this time? The creative works that
date from the earlier Triestine years show that women held a relatively lowly
place in Joyce's writerly priorities. Most of the female characters in *Dubliners*, with the exception of Gretta Conroy, are seen as misfortunes waiting to
happen to men, while in *A Portrait of the Artist as a Young Man* women characters ranging from the Blessed Virgin to the dreamy Mercedes to Emma,
float in and out of the text almost always as objects of Stephen's desires and
as foils with which the author can develop his hero. Stanislaus's diary suggests that Joyce's private views on women were even more reductive. He
wrote the James "did not regard women as an intellectual or spiritual equal"[21]

and described "the hatred of womankind which is at the foundation of his nature", before noting, on 21 April 1908, that Jim's "dislike for women" had become "almost savage" because "he detests their stupidity, their affectations, their meanness". In another entry Stannie reported that his brother told Francini Bruni that "woman is an aperture. We make no difference between a whore and a wife except that a whore we have for five minutes and a wife for all our life."[22]

What is not present in Stannie's diary but is forcefully so in *Giacomo Joyce* is Joyce's transition from these offensive views of womankind to an acceptance of a fuller and more complex role for women. *Giacomo Joyce* is a rather hesitant step in this direction and reveals all the cultural restraints Joyce had to do battle with in order to overcome his former views. The mystery lady of *Giacomo Joyce*, whom, as Fritz Senn writes, takes in "almost the whole range of the archetypal manifestations of the female"[23], genuinely represents a turning point and would later nourish the more complicated female characters of Molly Bloom and Anna Livia Plurabelle. As Neil Davison put it, Joyce would go on to create Molly "out of the buried remnants of his dark lady (of *Giacomo Joyce*) coupled with the experience of his true intimacy with Nora Barnacle".[24]

What then, we might well ask, was the nature of the mystery lady who could have provoked such turmoil and subsequent growth in Joyce? She did not correspond to any simple stereotype. The young Triestine ladies who took English lessons from Joyce were highly educated and independent and showed a range of qualities not always common in women of their age. They studied music, often attended university (in Vienna, Graz, or Florence); they spoke, in addition to *Triestino*, at least three languages (Italian, German, and English or French), and were usually widely read; they engaged in sporting activities – cycling, horse-riding, skiing, gymnastics – and, at the same time, were highly fashion-conscious, taking their lead from Paris and Vienna, and occasionally even preceding the Austrian capital in adopting trends, such as the wearing of trousers for mountain walks. They were emancipated young ladies, who showed little or no interest in religion, and who were well aware of the sexual and intellectual attraction they could exercise over a young man such as Joyce.

The occasions for Joyce's romantic-sexual commotion were surely his private lessons with these precocious young women. Particularly during his later years in Trieste, Joyce had a large number of middle-class female students, including Emma Cuzzi and Amalia Popper, who, along with Annie

Schleimer (whom he met earlier in his Trieste period), are most commonly identified as the inspirers of *Giacomo Joyce.*

Their experiences with their Irish teacher of English probably had much in common with those of Anna Bonacci, who left the following recollection:

> My father met Joyce in the Caffè Tommaseo and Joyce sometimes translated important letters for him. He was a steamship broker. One day he told Joyce: "My daughter wants to learn English." My father already spoke English and also French, Italian, German, Arabic and Croatian. He learned Arabic when he worked in Egypt where I was born. He brought Joyce home to our house on via Belpoggio but told me beforehand: "I will bring a good Englishman here." I took lessons with Joyce three times a week for about two years. The lessons were varied between reading, writing and speaking. Joyce used a grammar book and an English reader. He told me I must make an effort to speak only in English with him. One day he read a poem to me which he said he was going to publish in an English newspaper.[25]

Pieropaolo Luzzatto Fegiz, the brother of another of Joyce's students, Maria Luzzatto Fegiz, recalled how, in 1912 and 1913, Joyce taught his sister along with two other students, Emma Cuzzi and Olivia Hannappel. "Joyce", he remembered, "liked to have a good time and did not give real lessons but held brilliant discussions, partly in English, partly in the Triestine dialect."[26] Emma Cuzzi later confirmed the undisciplined nature of the lessons:

> I was anything but a diligent student and so James Joyce, who as a teacher was far from traditional or pedantic, was my favourite. Sometimes, to my mother's annoyance, as we waited for him to arrive, I spent entire afternoons playing with the two friends who came to my house for lessons. As this happened repeatedly, my mother felt obliged to say something to him. She was a decent, polite woman and was very embarrassed, but Joyce listened to what she had to say with courteous and respectful ease. [...] Sometimes he had us do dictations, based on whatever was in his mind at that moment, often taking as a prompt some recent event. [...] With regard to English pronunciation I sometimes pronounced words so badly that they seemed like German, a language which I had studied when I was younger, and Joyce corrected me. In order to excuse myself I used to say: "English is a German dialect." He replied to this with a diagram which showed that more than 80% of the English language had Latin roots and the rest was divided up between Greek, Gaelic, Saxon, etc, and very little German.[27]

Roberto Curci makes the case for Emma Cuzzi as the mystery woman who inspired *Giacomo Joyce.*[28] He bases his claim principally on the fact that Emma (unlike Amalia Popper or Annie Schleimer) underwent the appendicitis operation that is mentioned by Joyce in the lines of his Triestine love chronicle: "Operated. The surgeon's knife has probed in her entrails and withdrawn, leaving the raw jagged gash of its passage on her belly" (*GJ*, 11). Emma certainly got along well with Joyce and was one of very few Triestine students to keep in touch with him after his departure from the city.[29] Her father Giuseppe, a successful lawyer, was of Jewish parents and had the "strongly Jewish features and long white whiskers" (*GJ*, 5) described by Joyce. Furthermore, Emma loved horse-riding, which may have suggested "A girl on horseback" (*GJ*, 8). Curci also makes much of the fact that Joyce, in his final draft of *A Portrait of the Artist as a Young Man*, makes "the young girl longed for by the artist, Stephen Dedalus" (in *Stephen Hero* Emma Clery) become "Emma C", still as in Clery, but "also, why not, as in Cuzzi?"[30]

Persuasive as these arguments may be, there are several others that undermine them. Firstly, Emma's Jewish-born father had converted to Catholicism to marry her Catholic mother, which would seem to distance her from Joyce's description of her as a "daughter of Jerusalem" (*GJ*, 10) "rounded by the lathe of intermarriage and ripened in the forcing-house of the seclusion of her race" (*GJ*, 2). In addition, Emma lacked the "pale face", the furs and glasses and sophisticated allure of the girl described by Joyce.

Cuzzi herself seems to have had no idea that Joyce might have fantasized about her. She did recall that Joyce used to give "psychological portraits" of herself and the other two girls in the lessons, but what he said about her leaves little room for believing that he viewed her in anything like the way he viewed the girl in *Giacomo Joyce*. According to Cuzzi's recollection, Joyce said she "was similar to a very tidy and clean place in which everything was in its place and everything had its own boring label".[31] Hardly the stuff of lustful male fantasy, but then Emma would not necessarily have had any idea of the identities and roles which her admirer might have been projecting onto her.

Another possible model for Joyce was his student Anna Maria (Annie) Schleimer, the daughter of a wealthy businessman. She was born in Trieste on 25 July 1881, the daughter of Emilia Baumeister, who had Jewish origins, and Andrea Schleimer, whose prosperous land-owning family originally came from Moswald on the border between Carinzia and Slovenia, and whose company was one of the main food suppliers in Trieste, specializing in citrus fruit and spices from the East. Annie was an excellent pianist and studied at the Trieste Conservatory (hence, perhaps "A long black piano" [*GJ*, 16]), an assiduous reader, and a speaker of several languages. Furthermore she was a highly attractive and stylish girl, who wore the type of eyeglasses evoked in *Giacomo Joyce*, and had a passion for umbrellas. Her parents were on cordial terms with their neighbours in 1905, the Ralli family, which is mentioned in the text of *Giacomo Joyce*: "As I come out of Ralli's house I come upon her suddenly" [*GJ*, 14]).[32] Unlike the other girls she was older than Joyce, by one year. She was first brought to public attention as a possible inspiration behind *Giacomo Joyce* in a lecture given in 1982 by the Triestine Joycean Stelio Crise, who spoke of her having an "affair" with Joyce and of how this was brought to an abrupt conclusion by her father, who was scandalized at the idea of his daughter wanting to marry a mere teacher of English.[33] This version of events has since been confirmed by its original source, Zora Koren Skerk, who boarded in Annie's house for many years in the nineteen-fifties and says she was told of it directly by Annie herself.[34]

Roberto Curci provides the following pithy summary of Mrs Koren Skerk's version of events:

> From Joyce, who was ready to leave Nora for her, Annie got a kiss and a marriage proposal which was knocked on the head by the firm opposition of her elderly father, an able businessman who would never have consented to giving his daughter's hand to a "poor little bit of an English teacher". Annie obeyed him and retreated into the shade, but she continued to like Joyce, even after he left Trieste and became famous: she gathered a collection of his books and jealously hoarded a collection of letters he wrote to her – keeping them bound together with a red band. She died, a severe and proud spinster, in an old folks' home in Gorizia in September 1972 and the evidence of her relationship with Joyce (the books, the letters) was lost.[35]

According to Koren Skerk, "Annie had a copy of *Ulysses* full of notes, which was on show in her apartment on a small table. She also kept the Joyce letters in a bundle, tied with a red ribbon."[36] While there is little reason to doubt her friendship with Joyce and perhaps even a possible infatuation between them, the fact that this occurred as early as 1905 suggests that she cannot have been more than a secondary influence on Joyce as he sketched his Triestine notebook some eight years later.

Letters contained in the Ellmann Collection at the University of Tulsa show that when he was preparing his 1959 biography of Joyce, following signals given by Eileen Joyce, Ottocaro Weiss and Letizia Fonda Savio, Ellmann discarded his original choice of Emma Cuzzi as the mystery lady of *Giacomo Joyce* (which he never disclosed) and decided that Amalia Popper was the real model. Forty years later, even if Ellmann's claim was little more than a best guess, Popper remains the most plausible candidate. She was born in 1891, the eldest daughter of Letizia Luzzatto, a Venetian painter, and Leopoldo Popper, a successful businessman originally from Bohemia.[37] Although her family seems to have been somewhat split between Leopoldo's sensible belief that breaking with Austria would be disastrous for Trieste's economy and his wife's irredentist leanings, they were united in their common Jewish background (being listed, for example, in *Il Corriere Israelitico* of 1907 among the contributors to the "Beneficenza Israelitica"). Amalia Popper alone of the three girls has a clear Jewish identity.

Amalia's early years, like those of many young girls of quality, were charmed and privileged. She was brought up in the spacious family villa at number 16 via Alice and received a first-class education at the Liceo Femminile, the Italian school *par eccelence*, where she stood out as the exceptional student of her year.[38] Her formal education was supplemented by private tutors, and it was in this guise that she first encountered James Joyce in 1907 or 1908. He continued to teach her for at least one year and was most impressed by his young student, who was worthy of the title given in *Giacomo Joyce*, "a lady of letters" (*GJ*, 12).[39] Their lessons came to an end when Amalia, having initially considered enrolling to study at the University of Vienna, finally decided to pursue her studies at the University of Florence. While these facts can be gathered to make a compelling defence of the claim that she is indeed the mystery lady, it should be noted that *Giacomo Joyce* was probably written sometime between 1912 and 1914, a period when Amalia was already away studying in Florence (although she did often visit Trieste), that she never wore the eyeglasses described in the text and that her father Leopoldo was a middle-aged man in these years and not the old man with the "long white whiskers" described in Joyce's text.[40]

When researching his biography of Joyce, Ellmann tried to meet and talk to Amalia, but was constantly blocked by her husband Michele Risolo. After the biographer's public identification of Popper in the second edition of *Giacomo Joyce*, Risolo wrote an article for *Il Corriere della Sera* in which he attempted to prove that his wife could not have been the "Who?" referred to in the text.[41] He also attempted unsuccessfully to convince Ellmann to retract his claim. Ellmann's footnote in the 1982 revised biography reveals that, despite Risolo's objections, he still essentially believed Popper was the model but that he was also open to the possibility of there having been more than one: "Amalia Popper later married Michele Risolo, who denied that she was the model, but with evidence which appeared to support rather than undermine the likelihood. Since the events in it which can be precisely dated occur over several years, it is possible that Signorina Popper lent herself only as part of a composite figure of a Jewish pupil" (*JJ*, 775).[42]

Ninety years after the presumed infatuation this seems the only conclusion that we can possibly accept, even if rumours, always unsubstantiated, are still occasionally heard in Trieste, where locals tell you knowingly that the real mystery lady has yet to be named.

WHAT IS MORE important than a definite identification of the female "culprit" is the depiction of the author's own tussling with his desires and his struggle to invent narrative forms adequate to render his inner turmoil. In its central dynamic of desire and dread, longing and repulsion, *Giacomo Joyce* has much in common with Joyce's better-known fiction. A private notebook, it is autobiographical and confessional in a more immediate way than Joyce's other fiction precisely because, for all its artistic precision, it gives the impression of having been written down "live", in snatches, principally for its composer's delectation, and has less of the irony or distancing with which Joyce treats Stephen in *A Portrait*. The desire felt so deeply by Giacomo in the text is both sexual and aesthetic – a longing to possess the girl and a conscious attempt to complete the perfect picture of her. It is also a power game between the dark lady and her admirer: she is clearly stronger than Giacomo, who is attracted by her gaze, her culture, her style, her education, her physical beauty, her budding sexuality, her frailness, her youth, her manners and by the decadent air he ascribes to her. It is she who fascinates him, causes him to long for her by asserting her sexuality, her sophistication, her social superiority. The social gap between the two is a constant: on one level it is expressed straightforwardly in phrases such as "a young person of quality" and "your ladyship" (*GJ*, 1), but at a deeper level it is to be found in the physical gap which separates them, with Giacomo below gazing up at her window – "I look upward from night and mud" (*GJ*, 6) – or seeing her on the hill – "The lady goes apace, apace, apace . . . . . Pure air on the upland road" (*GJ*, 8). He compensates for his social inferiority by showing off his intellectual superiority, by indulging in his role as her educator, her "maestro inglese", and by his wry irony when she dares express an opinion about *A Portrait of the Artist as a Young Man*. He further undermines her position as a young lady of social standing by referring to her as though she were a little bird "twittering after storm [...] twittering and chirping happily" (*GJ*, 11) or a little hen: "*Parlerò colla mamma* [...] Come! chook, chook! come! The black pullet is frightened: little runs suddenly broken, little timid cries: it is crying for its mamma, the portly hen" (*GJ*, 12).

He resents the power of attraction she holds over him and tries to counter it by fixing her body in silent objectivity, by silencing her in the text, rendering her passive, by exhibiting his intellectual superiority, by presenting her in a series of images at once distorted and stereotypical, reducing her to a series of parts ("pale cheeks", "a moving knee", "long lewdly leering lips", "eyes that dim the breaking East"), and by defining her in terms of how she is dressed ("slim bronze shoes, a leg-stretched web of stocking") – in short, by regarding her with the arbitrary power of a voyeur.

The vision of the mystery body of the dark lady is also presented in stereotypical terms. She is described with images that recall Salomé and convey a coiling, snake-like creature – "a lithe smooth naked body shimmering with silvery scales" – and seen (as Joyce saw so many women) as a being trying to entrap him. She is a threatening figure with "cruel eyes" who exercises a power he fears – "E col suo vedere attosca l'uomo quando lo vede" – and with her look she poisons a man when she sees him (*GJ*, 15).

Giacomo's desire along with his complex strategies to counter the seductive powers of his temptress are the unifying features of the text. The following paragraph, in which he imagines helping the girl put on her gown, describes the gradual descent to the sexual regions – beginning at the neck, then the raised arms, then the shoulders and back, then "the slender buttocks" – and is representative of Joyce's artistic tactics throughout the book:

> She raises her arms in an effort to hook at the nape of her neck a gown of black veiling. She cannot: no, she cannot. She moves backwards towards me mutely. I raise my arms to help her: her arms fall. I hold the websoft edges of her gown and drawing them out to hook them I see through the opening of the black veil her lithe body sheathed in an orange shift. It slips its ribbons of moorings at her shoulders and falls slowly: a lithe smooth naked body shimmering with silvery scales. It slips slowly over the slender buttocks of smooth polished silver and over their furrow, a tarnished silver shadow . . . . Fingers, cold and calm and moving . . . . A touch, a touch. (*GJ*, 7)

Joyce does not allow his mystery lady to speak, but describes her moving mutely, almost one with the gown which both covers and reveals and which in its elegance is in perfect harmony with her sensuous beauty. Using language with the care of a poet, he carefully reinforces the sensual, the sexual, the sculptor's "s" in the repeated plurals – "ribbons, moorings, shoulders, scales, buttocks" – and in the "slips, shoulders, slowly, smooth, silvery scales, slips, slowly, slender smooth, silver shadow". But he also renders his subject passive, and her one effort at movement, her attempt to put on the gown, fails: "she cannot", he repeats twice. Giacomo is the only active agent, he alone can "raise, hold, see", and it is as if she exists only when he calls her to mind, imagines her into being – and the image is as if he is sculpting her with his "Fingers, cold and calm and moving". He is, or rather he wishes to be, the sole controller of the politics of desire in the text. He is the artist/voyeur who sanctions it. As such, this voyeuristic male figure in the Triestine shadows also and very importantly represents Joyce's passage from youthful Stephen to worldly-wise Bloom. Stephen is haunted by self-accusation and his voyeuristic and erotic reveries are always accompanied with or followed by pangs of guilt; Bloom, the European Dubliner, on the other hand, is not burdened by oppressive Catholicism and can glimpse and enjoy freely, for example as he does in "Calypso" when he hurries out of the butchers, allows his eyes to rest on the girl's "vigorous hips" and attempts to "catch up and walk behind her if she went slowly, behind her moving hams. Pleasant to see first thing in the morning" (*U*, 4.148, 172). Giacomo lurks somewhere between the two.

Yet, for all of Giacomo's attempts at controlling and silencing his mystery lady, this figure of extraordinary erotic desire and of equally powerful dread, the text, in its final pages, succeeds in freeing its female protagonist from his lustful and sometimes violent gaze. As Valente puts it: "The poisonous writing of Joyce's antidotal re-reading, which takes some account of her positive otherness, acknowledges, however obscurely, her separate perspective, agency, and value, and in the process, alters the internal design of the work so as to bring out the systematic stifling and gradual emergence of her voice".[43] That Joyce allows her voice to emerge is a fundamental step on the road to the conception of Molly Bloom – the Joycean female voice par excellence. Molly would possess much of the dark lady's Oriental/Mediterranean charm and passion, but it would be a passion she could use as she pleased, which she would express from her own mouth, unlike the mystery lady, who is almost always kept in check and silence. And it would come to pass that that most powerful of words, that "Yes" which timidly opens *Giacomo Joyce*, would eventually transform and multiply itself from the "brief syllable", whispered pianissimo in the initial page of Joyce's lyrical and mysterious novelette, into the allegro andante "yes" which reverberates through the closing bursts of Molly's soliloquy until it finally becomes Molly's and *Ulysses's* last word.

WHATEVER TORMENTS and transformations might have been wrought at this time by his female students, Joyce's more immidiate and pressing concern remained *Dubliners*, which was still unpublished. In the autumn of 1912 he dispatched the manuscript to Elkin Mathews, and on 16 December he wrote asking Yeats if he knew "any publisher in London likely to take my unhappy book?" (*LII*, 322). A sign of just how preoccupied he was by it is to be found in the fact that he dispatched a second letter to Yeats little more than a week later – on Christmas Day 1912 – in which he told him he had sent his "unfortunate book" to Martin Secker and continued: "You would do me a great service if you could intervene in its favour and, I hope, some service also to the literature of our country" (*LII*, 322). In February he wrote again to Mathews asking for a decision on *Dubliners*, offering to have the book printed and corrected in Trieste at his own expense and to take 110 copies himself at trade price. Mathews rejected his offer.

Better news came with regard to the promise of a job at the Scuola Superiore di Commercio "Revoltella". In January 1913 Joyce wrote telling Stanislaus he would apply if a vacancy were to arise:

> If C is sent away I shall of course apply for and try to get his job: but I don't think any move in that direction should be made while C has the position. If they want to dismiss him let them dismiss him and be damned to him and them. Then if they want anybody to teach the sons of bitches broken English I suppose I am good enough for that. I have heard the same talk from Schmitz, Schreiber, and Vidacovich for the last *three* years. Let the board pension him first. I cannot go sneaking behind his back for his job. In any case you can [tell] Veneziani that I am always ready to receive money – *ergo* also ready to take C's job when he's out of it – *not before*. (*LII*, 322)

The unfortunate "C" was the elderly Englishman, Phillip Cautley, whom Joyce had replaced first as Schmitz's private teacher and then at the Scuola Commerciale di perfezionamento. At the end of the 1912–13 academic year the Scuola "Revoltella" retired Cautley on half a year's salary and the way was cleared for Joyce, who was officially appointed in July 1913.[44] In common with most of the other teachers on the staff, he was paid 1,500 crowns per month – a not inconsiderable sum, but still 500 crowns less than the porter earned. He was required to teach six hours per week – three to the First Years and three to the Second – and expected to attend the monthly staff meetings. He gave his lessons regularly in the mornings, starting on 6 October 1913, but his attendance at staff meetings was more occasional.[45]

The course outline drawn up by Joyce's predecessor gives a good idea of the kind of students Joyce faced and the materials he used:

> Texts: Hermann Berger's English grammar, Reading: Texts of English works containing narratives and dialogues concerning business and commercial dealings.
>
> Because almost all of the students have no knowledge of English when they enrol in the school, the course begins, in the first year, with a course in English grammar, which is taught through the Italian language. As soon as the students have reached an adequate level, English begins to be used, normally towards the end of the first year.
>
> In the second year the study of grammar is concluded, an hour a week of commercial correspondence in English is taught, using accountancy texts and English business contracts. In this way the students are offered the opportunity to learn commercial English terms and expressions but also to get a broad knowledge of England's world trade.[46]

A total of 78 students enrolled for the academic year 1913–14. Joyce had 34 students in his First Year course and 21 in his Second Year course. Of the original 78, 26 were from Trieste, 15 from the Istrian coastal towns – referred to as the "Litorale" – 25 from Dalmatia, 3 from other Austrian provinces and 9 from abroad. Forty-seven spoke Italian as their mother tongue, 14 spoke Serbo-Croat, 10 spoke Slovene, 6 spoke German and 3 spoke Greek.

Joyce maintained cordial relations with more than a couple of private students who were also Slavs. One was Alois Skrivanich, a young Croatian man-about-town and "a source of information about the corruptions and distortions of Slovene and Croatian words in the Triestine melting pot".[47] His name appears in *Finnegans Wake* as one of Shem's surnames; he is also one of Shaun's tormentors: "Shem skrivenitch, always cutting my prhose to please his phrase, bogorror: I declare I'll get the jawache" (*FW*, 423.15–17). The "skrivenitch" also suggests many other possible interpretations – the English "scribbling", the Irish "scríobh" (to write), the Triestine "scrivan" (scribe) and the Slovene and Croatian "skriven" (hidden). The "bogorror", which comes from the Hiberno-English "begorrah", also suggests the Slovene word "bog" (God) as used by Joyce in the phrase: "by the wrath of Bog" (*FW*, 76.31). (*Finnegans Wake* contains many other Slovene words and terms that have not yet been systematically identified and catalogued.)

One of Joyce's Slovene pupils was Josip Wilfan, whom he first met while teaching in the Berlitz school. He was "a lawyer and leading political figure among the Trieste Slovenes and after the war one of Trieste's MPs in the Ital-

ian Parliament in Rome".[48] One of the employees in Wilfan's office, Boris
Furlan, a Slovene born in Trieste in 1894, also became a student and friend
of Joyce. Furlan later published studies of Kant, Croce and Massaryk and
went on to become professor of philosophy at the University of Ljubljana.
He recalled his lessons with Joyce very clearly:

> In 1913/14 I started to study English. My teacher was James Joyce, who at that
> time was teaching at the Commercial High School in Trieste. At that time I
> was a great admirer of Schopenhauer and Nietzsche. With Joyce we came soon
> more close than is the use in similar relations. During the lessons he asked me
> sometimes: "Would you have the courage to go to the shop at the corner and
> ask for 5 *centesimi* [the Austrian penny] rocks-drops. He told me, that he was
> so much afraid of storms and lightning, that he used to close the windows, and
> when a storm came, lower the curtain and close the "scuri" [shutters].[49] [...] I
> bought from him a copy of the *Dubliners*, which he published at that time.
> [...] His lessons were – at least what I was concerned – a little bit particular:
> he could ask me to describe a petrol-lamp – of course I was unable to do so,
> with my knowledge of English, and then he started describing it himself for
> about half an hour.[50]

The Joyces were living now in the flat Stanislaus had found for them on
the second floor of a very new house at number 4 via Bramante, overlooking
piazza Vico and in the shadow of the hill of San Giusto. It was here that the
family portraits, which Joyce had had restored in Dublin, were hung in the
spring of 1913 and proudly shown to students and friends alike. The apartment was small and functional "but its hall and the drawing-room provided
a dignified welcome for visitors and students".[51] As he kept his entire library
in his bedroom, there was not a book to be seen in the drawing room where
Joyce gave his lessons; nonetheless, it was rather tight for space as it contained the piano and was almost completely filled with chairs, which were
replicas he had had a local carpenter make from a photograph he had spotted of some Danish ones. According to Letizia Fonda Savio, Joyce used to sit
"on one chair while using four others to rest his arms and long legs".[52]

When living in via Bramante, Joyce saw very little of Stanislaus, who was
finally beginning to create an independent life for himself. As a result Joyce
saw more of his old friend Francini Bruni; together they formed the core of
a small circle of friends who often gathered in Joyce's house, or at a restaurant or bar in town. Francini Bruni recalled that Joyce "received his friends
on one fixed day of the week, perhaps Thursdays", at home.[53] The group
included the artists Argio Orell and Tullio Silvestri as well as Leone Dario

De Tuoni, a young poet, ten years Joyce's junior. De Tuoni was also a student of Joyce's and later recalled his lessons with him:

> Having got to know one another, after a short period of time I began to take lessons with a group of students, among them the young bank clerk who was to be Eileen Joyce's future husband.[54] The other two were friends of mine. Together we were a group that Joyce's brother Stanislaus would have turned up his nose at. The lessons were held in the evenings in Joyce's apartment in via Donato Bramante using the Berlitz method and text. They took place in a rather relaxed atmosphere, which reflected Joyce's understandable aversion to this boring chore which need imposed upon him. However, the fact that he had to give the lessons did not stop him, if the opportunity arose, from making some sarcastic remark which he would underline with a dry laugh. And there were also days when we finished up talking about art and literature. [...] The only ones to benefit from those lessons were the banker from Bohemia who was already flirting with Joyce's sister, and a young philosopher with Polish roots, by profession a sea captain, but also interested in metaphysical problems. [...] René, Ravitz and I were the best of friends, although politically we all had very different views; but the fact that they were active in the irredentist movement did not cause my brain to be fogged up to the point of making me hate all that was not Italian.[55]

Young though he was, De Tuoni was already establishing his literary pedigree; at the age of twenty he published his first volume of poetry, *Preludio*, and he followed it in 1916 with a second collection, *Dall'esilio* (From Exile), which came out in Florence. In August 1912 he gave his first public reading in Trieste:

> He recited some of his poems, in which, among various echoes, an individual note can be heard vibrating. At the age of twenty, one loves, and a twenty-year-old poet naturally dedicates most of his verse to love. But our youthful scholar already feels the suffering of the exile in a foreign land; and the young Triestine student strikes a passionate note when evoking his melancholic pain in the northern mists.[56]

Just a couple of months after this event De Tuoni met one such "exile in a foreign land" – James Joyce – and a rewarding friendship blossomed between them.[57] After lessons they often walked down via San Michele and spent hours discussing literature together. De Tuoni lent Joyce Croce's *Esthetics*, which he eventually returned, and a book about Oskar Kokoschka and Strindberg's *Der Sohn ein Magel*, which he did not.[58] Later De Tuoni's wife recalled: "With regard to the Joyce–De Tuoni friendship, it can be said that theirs was a meeting between poets. [...] They spoke a lot about poetry and often recited to one another."[59] Both writers shared an interest in Paul Verlaine, whom De Tuoni could quote ad infinitum; he was particularly fond of his "O triste, triste était mon âme,"[60] which Joyce later adapted in *Finnegans Wake*, where the "triste" becomes "Trieste": "And Trieste, ah trieste ate I my liver! *Se non é vero son trovatore*" (*FW*, 301.16–17). De Tuoni gave Joyce a copy of his *Preludio* (1909–13), an admirable volume of poetry for such a young writer which revealed how well versed he was in Italian, French, German and English literature and philosophy. In turn, the Triestine poet was one of the select few to whom Joyce gave a copy of *Chamber Music*.

De Tuoni was interested in everything that was new in literature and was in regular contact with writers such as Scipio Slataper, Italo Tavolato, Dino Campana, Emilio Notte, Lucio Venna and Ardengo Soffici. He was a personal friend of Teodor Daubler (whom Joyce had famously encountered in 1903 in Paris), and keenly followed the work of both the *Vociani* and the Futurists. In late 1913 or early 1914 he wrote to Joyce from Mantova asking him to contribute to an avant-garde literary journal called *Procellaria*. The fact that he addresses him as "James" is a sign of the genuine friendship between them:

Dear James!
I need you.
Will you send us some of your poetry or a critical article on contemporary English literature – something avant-garde. I await your reply – our journal welcomes every strong and healthy expression.
Regards
Dario De Tuoni[61]

He enclosed several of his new poems, which Joyce kept, but there is no evidence to suggest that Joyce sent De Tuoni any work to be published in the journal.

Another friend of Joyce's was Argio Orell, the Triestine artist and poet who had studied with Stuck in Monaco and Klimt in Vienna. He partly made his living by crafting fine jewellery and was famous for having made caskets for the King of Italy and for Gabriele D'Annunzio. In Trieste, Orell was primarily sought after as a portrait painter and praised for his ability to draw and for the sobriety of his use of colours.[62]

Joyce was also close to another (lesser) portrait painter, Tullio Silvestri, a self-trained artist who came from a poor background and was even more impecunious than Joyce. When he was down on his luck in 1914 and trying frantically to gather enough money to escape Trieste before the outbreak of war, Joyce generously organized a whip-around for him, raising 100 crowns. He regularly adopted intrepid methods for selling his paintings, such as when he went to Ettore Schmitz with a large package, which aroused the novelist's curiosity. The artist appealed to Schmitz's humanity rather than his artistic interests, telling him that it contained "a coat and shoes" for his daughter. In reality, it was his latest painting, which Schmitz immediately purchased.[63] Silvestri was also something of an itinerant artist, famous for having walked from Trieste to Russia painting portraits and playing his mandolin as he went in order to pay his way. Francini Bruni remembered him as

> a lively, gay man, the perfect Bohemian, always poor, married to a nice wife. Silvestri used to come to see Joyce all the time. He was a Venetian who had lived in Trieste, played the guitar and sang baritone, Joyce would sing with him. Silvestri's style of painting was unique – he charged at the painting with darting strokes – impressionistic, with no preliminary drawing.[64]

In his atelier on via Tor San Lorenzo, Silvestri painted portraits of Nora in 1913 and of Joyce in 1914, both of which were hung in the sitting room of via Bramante. He painted a second portrait of Joyce in 1919. Long after leaving the city, Joyce continued to remember Silvestri and enquired after him to Dario De Tuoni: "And Tullio Silvestri? Where is he and what has become of him? I still have four or five of his paintings in my Paris flat. He was a good painter [una bela macia] and also quite a character, as people used to say."[65]

In these years Giorgio and Lucia (both now bespectacled) attended the local school on via Veronese. They were not particularly successful young students, but they had no shortage of company of their own age and were popular both with the neighbours' children and with their own school friends. In a series of letters to Stelio Crise, written in 1961, Lucia asked if he knew anything about her friends from the old days, mentioning in particular Trevisani, Petech and Tiziani, whom she said were in the "Scuola Comunale" with her.[66] At school, the Joyces picked up the local dialect, as Dario De Tuoni remembered when he wrote of them speaking "both English and the harshest version of Triestine: the dialect of San Giacomo, which was even rougher than that of the old city"[67] – a sure sign that they were fitting in well. Lucia wrote telling Crise how sorry she was that she had forgotten the dialect, which she really used to like.[68]

Still, they suffered from the fact that their father's interest in them was intense but fleeting, as he was almost totally absorbed in his writing and, to a lesser extent, his teaching. Joyce made no secret of the fact that he was already nurturing hopes that Giorgio would pursue a singing career as a tenor, and was pleased to receive a letter dated 28 February 1913 in which Henry Blackwood Price sent his "love to Caruso and Lucia and kind remembrances to Mrs Joyce".[69]

Nora, though she loved her children deeply, was not a particularly attentive mother and the continued presence and support of Eileen, who had a more practical bent than herself, was a huge help in her struggle to rear them. Several students of Joyce's at this time recall that when they were in the apartment for lessons, the children were more or less barricaded in the kitchen where Nora attempted, without particular success, to keep them quiet and amused.

With the security and income offered by his job at the Scuola "Revoltella" and a regular round of private lessons, things should have been easier for his family in these years. Instead, Joyce's income seemed only to accelerate their spending. James and Nora were dreadful housekeepers and had no desire to change. They spent excessively on luxuries, meals out, the theatre and clothes, and Nora continued to throw out the children's clothes and buy new ones at every change of season. They were also fond of buying on credit, and so irate demands for money arrived with almost monotonous regularity, such as the following one, dated 1 July 1913, from the Triestine shipping agent M.B. Katz:

> Dear Signora! Please be so kind as to pay what is due to my company within three days, otherwise I will have no choice but to place the matter in the hands of my lawyers, thus causing your family added expenses and useless boredom.[70]

On 15 October of the same year, the city court wrote to Joyce's employers in the Scuola "Revoltella" telling them that he had not paid a sum of money owed to the Stabilimento Musicale "Giuseppe Verdi", a music shop in Trieste. Joyce had bought music which had cost 62 crowns on 2 May 1913 and had "forgotten" to pay. The court now sought to have the amount deducted on a monthly basis from his salary.

The spendthrift was slightly more attentive when it came to paying for books. A bill dated 23 May 1914 from F.H. Schimpff, one of Trieste's leading booksellers, lists twenty titles bought between October 1913 and May 1914, at a total cost of 222 crowns 90, of which Joyce still owed 50 crowns. Among the books on this list were Oriani's *Gelosia*, Collodi's *Pinocchio*, Ibsen's *Collected Works* (vol. vii) and *Peer Gynt*, Flaubert's *Saint Antoine* and *Premières Oeuvres*, Shaw's *Major Barbara* and *The Devil's Disciple*, Lecky's *History of*

European Morals, Turgenev's *Smoke* and Dostoevsky's *The Idiot*. Three of the books were clearly for teaching purposes: Schlussel's *Engl. Grammatik*, Sauer's *Engl. Grammatik* and Berlitz's *First Book*.

Cinema, theatre and opera continued to be major drains on Joyce's purse. Lucia recalled that she was often taken to the cinema when she was small and that she saw films featuring "Thea Diana Ravenna Almirante Manzini Ivor Novello Tullio Carminati etc".[71] Among the theatrical highlights of 1913 was the world première in March of Sem Benelli's epic drama *La Gorgona*. Joyce was probably in the audience, which included the cream of Triestine society and some of Italy's most august critics, such as Innocenzo Cappa, Domenico Oliva and Giovanni Pozza of *Il Corriere della Sera*, whom Joyce met on this occasion.[72] The year also marked Verdi's centenary. The great composer held a special place in irredentist Trieste's heart,[73] being seen as the ultimate symbol of Italian art, and so his centenary was celebrated accordingly. In February *Rigoletto* and *Nabucco* were performed to the delight of the irredentists, who liked to see a parallel between their own fate and that of the Jews as two peoples deprived of their homelands. Verdi's *Nabucco* symbolized this link for them and afforded them an opportunity to bemoan their own lot as a subject people under Austria while at the same time celebrating one of the triumphs of the Italian *Risorgimento*.[74] Joyce would certainly not have missed this impressive production in Trieste – not least because his friend and former singing teacher Romeo Bartoli prepared the chorus for it:

> The chorus, which in "Nabucco" has the lion's share, trained with love by Maestro Bartoli, gave an excellent performance, particularly in the "Va Pensiero", which was the highlight of the evening. [...] with delirious applause [the audience] demanded an encore of the famous chorus of the Hebrew slaves.[75]

In the autumn the Verdi celebrations continued with a season which included *I Due Foscari*, *La Traviata*, *Il Trovatore*, *Rigoletto*, and *Aida*. On 12 October an enormous statue of the composer was unveiled in Piazza San Giovanni and four separate concerts were organized for the afternoon – in Piazza Barriera Vecchia, Piazza Giuliani, Piazza Goldoni and finally in Piazza Grande, where over 30,000 irredentist protesters sang the banned *Va Pensiero* to the delight of the pro-Italian papers:

> The authorities decided to ban the chorus from "Nabucco", the "Va Pensiero su l'ali ..." but the enormous crowd, with their souls drawn towards thoughts that can only be arrived at with wings, began to sing the harmonious chorus. Starting with single groups of young people the chorus gradually spread until

the whole square was in song and the phrase "O mia Patria sì bella ..." rose to the sky from those thousands and thousands of breasts all in unison and inspired by a deep feeling which united them ...[76]

Apart from Verdi, the spring 1913 opera season at the Teatro Verdi featured the great Italian tenor Tito Schipa and included Mascagni's *Isabeau*, Gounod's *Giulietta e Romeo* and Wagner's *Walkiria*. The autumn–winter seasons brought Wagner's *Tristano e Isotta*, the Trieste première of Puccini's *La Fanciulla del West* (a favourite of Joyce's) and finally Donizetti's *Don Pasquale* and *L'Elisir D'Amore*. But the real highlight came on 20 January 1914 with the Italian première of Wagner's *Parsifal*, which received rave reviews from all the Triestine critics. Joyce, too, was impressed: "The first production of *Parsifal* was in Trieste; Joyce went like everyone else, but Joyce went 3 or 4 times more. It was very long, given in two parts, one started at 4 and the other at 8."[77] He was already well acquainted with Wagner's works before he came to Trieste, but it was in the Adriatic city that he had opportunities to see their complex techniques come alive in the orchestra and on the stage, and to read unusually knowledgeable reviews of them in the local papers.[78] All this could not but have been stimulating for the writer who would later put Wagner's theories about a *Gesamtkunstwerk* – a total artwork – into effect by merging countless literary and musical genres into *Ulysses*.[79]

While all this may have been useful to Joyce for his future literary pursuits, by November 1913 it seemed there was still not a publisher in London or Dublin willing to take on *Dubliners*. For this reason he decided to try one last desperate gambit: to go back to where he had started, to Grant Richards, and ask him once again to reconsider publishing it. To Joyce's surprise, Richards replied with uncharacteristic haste and asked to see the book again. Further good news arrived in an unexpected letter in mid-December 1913 from Ezra Pound. The American writer told Joyce that Yeats had been speaking to him about his writing, that he was involved in a number of "new and impecunious papers" and "two American magazines which pay top rates", and that he would be interested in taking a look at some of Joyce's work with a view to publishing it. Joyce delightedly sent Pound the preface to *Dubliners*, and the American writer was as good as his word. He published it in the *Egoist* on 15 January. Joyce then followed up by sending him a chapter of *A Portrait of the Artist as a Young Man*, which Pound declared to be "damn fine stuff" (*LII*, 327). Encouraged by this praise, Joyce felt his position strengthening and wrote demanding a decision from Grant Richards about *Dubliners*. On 29

January 1914 Richards replied, and to Joyce's enormous relief agreed to publish his book. A contract was signed on 20 March 1914, stating that Grant Richards would initially publish 1,250 copies, that there would be no royalties paid to Joyce on the first 500 copies but he would receive "ten percent of the published price of copies sold" above this number, rising to "fifteen percent after the sale of eight thousand copies". Joyce was to buy the first 120 copies at 2/6 apiece to sell in Trieste. To this end he insisted the book come out in May before his students and friends disappeared for the summer.

Finally, after a struggle that would have killed off many a lesser writer, *Dubliners* appeared on 15 June 1914. It received mixed reviews, and caused little of the scandal that Maunsel & Co. had predicted. Joyce set about selling his copies as quickly as possible. Boris Furlan was just one of the students nabbed by Joyce: "I remember he gave me *Dubliners* on the 'piazza grande' (now Piazza dell'Unità), coming out from a coffee-house, which does not exist any more, I think it was the Caffè Lloyd, and I gave him 5 kronen."[80] Joyce presented the book to a couple of selected friends and students, such as Baron Ralli and Roberto Prezioso, but for the most part he made people pay for it. He asked Grant Richards to send six copies each to himself, Stanislaus, Nicolò Santos (the onion seller), Frantisek Schaurek (Eileen's future husband) and Carlo Bertoli (a student), and when they did not arrive he wrote again on 20 June telling him to "Kindly forward them immediately. These copies are for people who are leaving the city for the summer and must be here at once."[81] On 22 June he sent a cheque for £10 to cover the cost of the remaining eighty copies, which were to be sent to the Libreria Schimpff.

At the same time as *Dubliners* was finally arriving in the bookshops, further good news was reaching Joyce to the effect that the *Egoist* had agreed to publish *A Portrait of the Artist as a Young Man* in fifteen-page instalments. Hans Walter Gabler has established that "the novel attained the shape and structure in which we now possess it during 1912 and 1913",[82] so now in 1914 Joyce had to do little more than check the proofs of his work. In August 1915 he dispatched the last few pages to Pound, who wrote back saying he was tempted to use "inane hyperbole" about the ending (*LII*, 364).

With *Dubliners* and *A Portrait of the Artist as a Young Man* thus well on their way, Joyce was finally able to put the two books of his young manhood behind him. Their composition and his subsequent attempts to publish them had dominated the previous ten years of his life and prevented him from embarking on any further creative projects. Now, in a matter of months, the path had suddenly been cleared for a new literary odyssey that would be called *Ulysses*. A crucial part of that adventure would be lived out in his remaining years in Trieste.

3 *"the society of jewses"*

In 1920 Joyce described *Ulysses* as "the epic of two races (Israel and Ireland)" (*SL*, 270). He might well have called it a tale of two cities, Dublin and Trieste, such was the impact of the Adriatic city on its composition, particularly with regard to Jewish matters. While Joyce of course drew on what he remembered of the Jews of Dublin, he also made extensive use of his knowledge of Trieste's far more prominent and variegated Jewish community.

As early as 1908 Stanislaus, perhaps unwittingly, played a role in alerting Joyce to the affinities between the Irish and the Jews when, after reading Zangwill's *Ghetto Tragedies*, which Joyce had borrowed from one of his students, he noted:

> Zangwill intends to give his idea of the lost race to which he belongs. To [this] lost or outcast race I feel akin.[83]

Joyce later linked the two races in *Ulysses* by showing how both had histories of "dispersal, persecution, survival and revival", and in *Finnegans Wake* he further reinforced the parallel by referring to *Ulysses* as "the farced epistol to the hibruws" (*FW*, 228.33–4).

In *Ulysses*, Joyce treated Jewish issues such as anti-Semitism, Zionism, intermarriage and assimilation as seriously as he treats more overtly Irish themes.[84] By placing an endlessly complex and deeply human Jewish figure at the centre of his novel, he was also engaging in a political act, a challenge to Europe's hostile attitudes towards the Jews.

Joyce's initial source for the Jewish elements in his book was, as ever, Dublin. As a very young writer, and like most middle-class Irish people of his generation, he had demonstrated precious little sensitivity towards the Jews. In 1899 it was his task to describe Michael Munkacsy's 'Ecce Homo' in the Royal Hibernian Academy. Perhaps he was merely describing what he saw, and the stereotype was Munkacsy's, but he did not stint in adopting stereotypical terms to describe what he called a 'well clad Jew', who is:

> a rich man, with that horrible cast of countenance, so common among the sweaters of modern Israël. I mean, the face whose line runs out over the full forehead to the crest of the nose and then recedes in a similar curve back to the

chin, which, in this instance is covered with a wispish, tapering beard. The upper lip is raised out of position, disclosing two long, white teeth, while the whole lower lip is trapped. This is the creature's snarl of malice. (*CW*, 34)

Joyce might not have moved beyond this stereotype if he had stayed in Ireland and if he had not happened upon a city such as Trieste. He seems to suggest as much himself in *Finnegans Wake*, where he writes: "Then he caught the europicolas and went into the society of jewses" (*FW*, 423.35–6). In the "europicolas" there is probably a reference to *Il Piccolo*, but also, taking "picolas" to mean "little", there is a further suggestion of a little Europe – a melting pot where all European races mixed – as well perhaps as Ferrero's *Europa Giovane* (young Europe). The "society of Jewses" is of course a pun on the Society of Jesus. With regard to the Jews of Trieste, "society" may connote high society. In his "Italian notebook", Joyce wrote that "a caste-based aristocracy does not exist in Trieste. Here the aristocrats are simple people who arrived here, who came from nothing ..." The Jews featured prominently among this group.[85] And "society" may also suggest the Italian "*società*", meaning commercial company, for in Trieste Jews were among those at the forefront of practically all the entrepreneurial initiatives which made the city such an important commercial and insurance centre.

Joyce had a wide range of contacts with Jews or lapsed Jews in Trieste, including Moses Dlugacz, Teodoro Mayer, Leopoldo Popper, Oscar Schwarz and Italo Svevo. But to give undue importance to a handful of individuals is to miss the main point that it was Trieste itself which played the key role in informing Joyce's sense of the Jews and of Judaism. The city's Jewish populations, its synagogues, shops and businesses were the very fabric from which he wove Leopold Bloom. The Jewish community – ranging from the wealthy middle-classes working in business and insurance, to the Jews who abandoned their religion in order to dedicate themselves more forcefully and openly to the irredentist cause, to the various Jewish journalists working for *Il Piccolo* and *L'Indipendente*, to the poor Jews arriving from the east and those few from the settled community who promoted the Zionist movement – made a profound impact on Joyce. It is not that the Jewish community in Trieste was unique – indeed it shared many common elements with the communities in Salonicco and Odessa – but it was the only one that Joyce came to know intimately and at first hand before he planned and wrote *Ulysses*.

Joyce was not long in Trieste before he began to show an active interest in the Jews living there, as Stanislaus's diary testifies:

Today until sundown was a Jewish holiday. Jim and I walked through some of the principal streets to see how many shops were shut. It was astonishing: a good third of the principal firms in the city are Jewish. Besides many names I knew to be Jewish, Steiner, Levi, Mendel, I found many I had never suspected before, such as Morpurgo and Bolaffio whom I thought thoroughly Italian. There is a good deal in what I said about children being one of the secrets of Jewish success. One really never knows where Jews are.[86]

Three days earlier, Joyce had gone to a service for the first time in Trieste's Jewish synagogue and was surprised to find so many of his students in the congregation:

He asked had the Jews any theology in the sense that Catholics have one, and was the priesthood with them a caste or a profession. Also he wanted to know whether they had a school of theology in which it was necessary to study, and lamented that none of his pupils ever seemed to know anything about the religions to which they were supposed to belong.[87]

Bloom has an imprecise but proud sense of his own Jewishness, and in this he is a mirror image of many Jews in Trieste, whose lack of knowledge of their own religious identity was telling testimony of the crisis in the Jewish world caused by the ineluctable forces of assimilation and Westernization.

There are many elements in the history of the Jewish community in Trieste that intrigued and influenced Joyce. The first protected Jewish families came to the city in 1236, led by Daniel David "Judeo de Karintia", and worshipped in a number of private synagogues. They worked as moneylenders and were popular with the Triestines because their rates were lower than those of the Florentines, whom they displaced. They were granted access to Trieste because the "Christian laws" – Church teaching based on the canonical doctrine "Pecunia non parit pecuniam" – prevented Christians from lending money for interest.[88] These early Jewish settlers, who were considered as citizens of Trieste, were well treated. In 1490 the Emperor Federico III claimed them as part of the empire, writing of "nostri Ebrei" (our Jews) and decreeing that they must wear a yellow sign so as to be recognized.[89]

Little changed for the Triestine Jews in the sixteenth century, mostly because Trieste itself, given the might of neighbouring Venice, had little opportunity to expand. Occasional outbreaks of anti-Semitism were not tolerated by the city government which, in 1522, issued a proclamation urging people to respect the Jews, pointing out that "even if they are of that race, they are still creatures of God".[90] The Hapsburgs were reasonably tolerant

towards the Jews in Trieste and, in a classic example of their policy of allowing rights to useful Jews, granted them substantial privileges to enable them
to live and do business there in a series of edicts signed by the Emperor Carlo
V and his successors.

The seventeenth century brought problems when a small group of Triestines accused the Jews of spreading the plague and forced them to pay
beyond their means for the construction of a massive fort to protect the city
from Turkish invasion. The city council asked for permission to start its own
lending business in order to put the Jews out of business and in 1675 wrote
to the Emperor Leopold castigating them for greed and asking for permission to expel them from the city. Leopold refused this and other calls for
their expulsion, or at least ghettoization, until finally, after a threatened
pogrom, he decided to grant them new privileges, while at the same time
ordering the construction of a spacious ghetto in the city centre, situated
behind Piazza Grande and Piazza della Borsa, where the statue of Leopold,
which Joyce passed every day, later stood (and still stands). Given Leopold's
sympathetic treatment of the Jews it could well be that Joyce had him in
mind when choosing Bloom's first name. The Triestine ghetto, in fact, was
unusually relaxed and porous compared with ghettos in other Italian cities.

With the eighteenth century came Venice's decline, and thus the way was
opened for Austria's development as a sea power. Trieste and Fiume were
chosen as the two ports from which this expansion would begin and were
declared freeports by Carlo V in 1719. This presented a great opportunity to
the Triestine Jews, who, along with the Greeks, began to form a prosperous
new merchant class, taking advantage of various edicts in their favour signed
by the Empress Maria Theresa. The Jewish community grew from forty in
1700 to over a thousand in 1800, 5.5 per cent of the population of 22,000,
half of all the non-Catholics. Soon the ghetto had become too small, and the
more affluent Jews were thus allowed to live outside. In 1746, a formal Jewish Community was established by statute to cope with growing numbers,
and the first of a series of four public synagogues, or *Scole*, was opened in
1748 (two for the older community who followed the Ashkenazic rite, two
for those who followed the Sephardic).

The Jews continued to be treated with toleration, and a statute issued in
1771 by Maria Theresa confirmed this policy. It was indeed ironic, as Benjamin Braude has pointed out, that Maria Theresa opened the way for the
Jews back into Christendom through Trieste, eight generations after her
ancestor Isabella of Castille (or "Isabelle nag" as she is in "Circe") had ban-

ished them in 1492.[91] Indeed, when Maria Theresa died in 1781, a prominent member of the Triestine Jewish community praised her as as "*eshet hayil*" – a woman of valour – and continued: "If not for her when would I ever have seen ships from the New World land on our shores?"[92] In their praise of Maria Theresa, the Triestine Jews were in a minority among Jews of the Empire, probably because they alone had good reason to remember her well. The Jews in Vienna, on the other hand, were submitted to census every three months and those in Prague were expelled in 1745. In 1777 Maria Theresa said that there was "no worse plague for the state than this nation, because of its deceitfulness, its usury, [for the Jews] bring the state more harm than good".[93] In Trieste, on the other hand, the Jews were singled out for exceptionally favourable treatment, and this simply because they were useful to the city and the empire. One of Bloom's memories of his father in the "Ithaca" episode reads as follows: "Rudolph Bloom (deceased) narrated to his son Leopold Bloom (aged 6) a retrospective arrangement of migrations and settlements in and between Dublin, London, Florence, Milan, Vienna, Budapest, Szombathely with statements of satisfaction (his grandfather having seen Maria Theresia, empress of Austria, queen of Hungary)" (*U*, 17.1906–10). As Maria Theresa is singled out for mention by Bloom, perhaps Joyce was relying here on nostalgic Triestine memories of her, which would not have been plausible among Jews in any other part of the Austro-Hungarian Empire.

In 1785, the ghetto was formally opened as part of the Emperor Joseph II's policy of '*Toleranz*', which sought to bring about the civic integration of the Jews. (This policy was not applied in many other Austrian cities and the Triestine ghetto was the first to be opened in Italy.) German educational reformers like Naftali Herz Wessely and Moses Mendelssohn welcomed the edict, and Mendelssohn even took the trouble to write to the Jews of Trieste expressing his satisfaction. He was an important guiding light for the Triestine Jews, who adopted many of his ideas for easing the position of Jews in the majority society they lived in. He favoured the abandoning of Jewish dress and translated Jewish texts into German to make them accessible to non-Jews. His approach was sharply criticized by most German and Italian rabbis and by Eastern European Jews, but warmly welcomed in Trieste. Following the *Toleranz* edict, Jews were allowed access to universities, and the Trieste community became one of the first to implement Mendelssohn's ideas for modernizing the school system. The Scuola Pia Normale Ebraica, which was founded in 1782, was a unique blend of rabbinical and secular subjects, cited by Mendelssohn as an example to be copied. So when Bloom mentions Mendelssohn by way of urging tolerance in the "Cyclops" episode – it is not clear whether he means Moses Mendelssohn or his grandson the composer Felix Mendelssohn – he may be invoking a name that was particularly dear and important to the Triestine Jews.

The Jewish community, many of whose members occupied pivotal positions in the biggest shipping and insurance companies and headed the leading financial institutions, enjoyed a golden period in the cultural, social and economic development of Trieste in the nineteenth century. From the 1850s on, this élite group began to be joined by many new arrivals from the States of the Church and from central and eastern Europe. In 1891, a large group of Jews fleeing from Corfu arrived and settled in the Adriatic port.[94] In the main, the long-established Austro-German and Italian Jewish population gave the new arrivals a frosty welcome, but could do little to stop the community from growing. The census of 1910 revealed that Trieste had 5,495 Jews, of whom 2,700 spoke Italian as a first language, 564 spoke German, 22 spoke Czech and Polish and 2,209 spoke a language not pertaining to the Empire.

Despite the increase in numbers, by the turn of the century a sense of uncertainty and even fear afflicted Triestine Jews. The ghetto was a thing of the past, but so too was the security it had offered as a custodian of the faith. The community was coming under increasing pressure from within: many members resented concentration of so much power in the hands of a small, secretive élite and felt that they were getting little spiritual return for the high taxes they contributed. In 1901 a petition was signed to this effect:

> The great majority of Jews in Trieste find themselves brought together by our community only through the ancient Jewish tradition, of which they are fond. Their religious sentiments are not being sustained in any way and are destined to weaken, as is unfortunately already tending to happen. The Israelite in Trieste is only offered one opportunity to remember he belongs to the community, that is, when he has to pay his taxes.[95]

An indirect but powerful response to these criticisms came with the announcement made in *Il Corriere Israelitico*[96] of March 1908 that work on a new synagogue was about to begin. On 27 June 1912 this new temple, which followed a style borrowed from fourth-century Syria emphasizing the Oriental aspect of Judaism, was inaugurated as the second largest in Europe and judged "a delightful creation and totally Italian in spirit" by *Il Piccolo*, which gave Jewish affairs prominent coverage.[97] It should have been a crowning glory for Trieste's Jews, but instead was an oversized symbol of the passing glory of a community racked by divisions based on class, race (German against Eastern and Spanish), religion (modernizers against Zionists) and politics (pro-Austrians against pro-Italians). The pro-Austrians were, in the main, the wealthier members of the community who sought to maintain close links with Vienna and political loyalty to the Empire in order to preserve their convenient status quo, while the pro-Italians who had not already abandoned the Jewish community did their utmost to oppose the Empire.

The tensions within the Triestine Jewish community represented, on a small scale, those within European Jewry in general and made a nonsense of the stereotyped views of the Jews as expressed in *Ulysses* by, among others, Deasy and the Citizen. Furthermore, they provided Joyce with concrete evidence to support the theories about Judaism that he was reading at this time in Maurice Fishberg's *The Jews: A Study of Race and Environment*, which he bought while in Trieste, and which reinforced an idea Joyce believed in: that "the alleged purity of the Jewish race is visionary and not substantiated by scientific observation ... there are just as many differences among the Jews as there are among the various races and peoples of the European continent".[98] This belief left the Irish writer free "to create his Jew from a blend of sources and origins, combining Semitic with Gaelic, Jew with Greek".[99]

Differences within the community sometimes had ugly consequences. In Trieste, as in many other European cities, the settled well-off community looked down on the new Eastern European arrivals, whom they saw as a threat to their own privileged position. They openly disapproved of their backward customs, dress and orthodox religious practices, were clearly keen to forget a past that was symbolized by these unwanted newcomers from the east, and sought to embrace, instead, a process of modernization and secularization. In Joyce's time, attendance at the synagogue dropped sharply, while many Jews began to take part in Catholic religious ceremonies and sought to adapt Jewish rites. A great number of them left their religion in order to marry non-Jews (under Austrian law, Christians could not marry Jews) and as a result countless Jewish families became thoroughly assimilated into non-Jewish society. This process was noticeably quicker in Trieste than in other cities. By 1910 a fifth of the Triestine Jewish population had formally renounced Judaism, while in Vienna the figure was only 512 out of a community of more than 175,000. Few of these ex-members converted to another religion although there were some cases, such as that of Ettore Schmitz (and especially among the richer Jews), in which they became

Catholics in order to facilitate a mixed "disparitatis cultus" marriage. This is
the process referred to by Stephen in "Scylla and Charybdis", when he says
that the "Jews ... are of all races the most given to intermarriage" (*U*,
9.783–4) and it is of course the reason for Leopold Bloom's conversion and
baptism "by the reverend Charles Malone C.C., in the church of the Three
Patrons, Rathgar" (*U*, 17.546–7). Although these unions were rigidly
opposed by the leaders of the Jewish community, 95 of the 428 religious marriages involving members of the community between 1900 and 1914 were
mixed. Many more took part in civil marriages with people from other
faiths, a fact the *Corriere Israelitico* pointed to as a sign of "a huge degeneration among the Jews of Trieste".[100]

Another "sign of degeneration" which the community tried to halt was suicide. An all too familiar phenomenon in Trieste, it was particularly comon
among the Jews.[101] At the end of October 1911, Joyce went to the Jewish cemetery to attend the burial of Filippo Meissel's wife, Ada Hirsch, who had committed suicide, and was so moved that he included a vignette in *Giacomo Joyce*:

> Corpses of Jews lie about me rotting in the mould of their holy field. Here is
> the tomb of her people, black stone, silence without hope . . . . . Pimply Meis-
> sel brought me here. He is beyond those trees standing with covered head at
> the grave of his suicide wife, wondering how the woman who slept in his bed
> has come to this end . . . . . The tomb of her people and hers: black stone,
> silence without hope: and all is ready. Do not die! (*GJ*, 6)

Just three months before Meissel's wife's suicide, *Il Corriere Israelitico* had
published an article which condemned suicide as an act that was profoundly
un-Jewish:

> In the same day two suicides took place among the Jews of Trieste: a young
> woman who wanted to join her husband who had died a few days earlier and
> a very young teacher who seeing his mother suffer an apoplectic fit no longer
> wished to live. Two lives cut short therefore by two stories of love which, being
> too great and too absorbing, became tragedies. This is not normal and it is not
> Jewish. The Jew is a creature in whom love of family reaches the highest levels,
> but this move must be felt for life and not for death, for creation, not for
> destruction. The Jew must be strong and must never submit to excessive feel-
> ings, however noble, that come from the heart. [...] The Jew must not let him-
> self be overwhelmed by the maelstroms of desperation but use his life to
> ennoble and sanctify his martyrdom.[102]

Joyce explored these issues in *Ulysses*, where Leopold Bloom is haunted by
the spectre of his father's death by suicide. Significantly, one of the few doc-

uments from his father which Bloom still possesses is the photocard in which Rudolph tries to explain his awful decision. The card is addressed "To My Dear Son Leopold", and it is this very document, and the consequent and painful consideration of his father's taking his own life, that become the crucial elements in Bloom's dealing with the question of his own Jewish identity. Bloom feels remorse as a result of his father's act, and subsequently because of his own failure to respect his Jewish heritage:

> Why did Bloom experience a sentiment of remorse?

> Because in immature impatience he had treated with disrespect certain beliefs and practices.

> As?

> The prohibition of the use of fleshmeat and milk at one meal: the hebdomadary symposium of incoordinately abstract, perfervidly concrete mercantile coexreligionist excompatriots: the circumcision of male infants: the supernatural character of Judaic scripture: the ineffability of the tetragrammaton: the sanctity of the sabbath (*U*, 17.1893–1901).

This remorse colours the manner in which he thinks of himself as a Jew and plays a fundamental role in his acceptance of his identity.

Part of this identity lies of course in his name, Bloom, which his father adopted instead of the more obviously Hungarian Virag. The practice of changing one's name into a more neutral-sounding one in order to blend in better was also common in Trieste. Some of the name changes, such Ettore Schmitz's adoption of Italo Svevo and Umberto Poli's becoming Umberto Saba, were for artistic reasons, and there is perhaps a hint of this in Bloom's becoming Henry Flower in order to engage in an illicit epistolary romance with Martha Clifford.

But *Ulysses* is full of Jewish names, many of which Joyce found in Trieste, a city that has so far only been credited with providing the names Artifoni, Sinico and Dlugacz. Given Bloom's middle-European background, Trieste was the obvious place for Joyce to discover names for his hero and his ancestors. Although no family called "Bloom" existed in Trieste, there were several called "Blum" in Joyce's time. The majority of them were German-speaking businessmen, but certainly the most likely to have been known by Joyce is Luis Blum, who was born in Budapest of Hungarian parents in February 1865.[103] On 17 March 1902 he married Giustina Bianca Gentilomo, the daughter of Luisa Coen and Oscar Gentilomo, a rich Jewish businessman of

Hungarian origin, who was one of the community elders. In 1906, Luis Blum changed his name to Blum-Gentilomo because his father-in-law had no sons and did not want the family name to die out.[104] Gentilomo was also president of Adriatica Società Anonomia di Spedizioni, a large Trieste-based shipping company in which Blum was a partner along with Amalia Popper's father, Leopoldo. It is very likely that Joyce (a regular client of the Adriatica)[105] put the two names together and came up with Leopoldo Blum – a combination that would assume Ulyssean proportions.

If Bloom owes his name to Trieste, his ancestors as described in "Circe" (*U*, 15.1852–69) may also have some Triestine origins. In choosing "Le Hirsch", for instance, Joyce may have had a Triestine in mind, given that there are more than twenty separate entries under the name Hirsch in *La Guida di Trieste*. In *Giacomo Joyce*, he mentions his Jewish friend Meissel attending the funeral of his wife Ada Hirsch following her death by suicide; and Mario Hirsch would also have been a very suitable ancestor for Bloom, as he worked as the "Custode del cimitero israelitico" (custodian of the Jewish cemetery).[106] "Smerdoz" is probably a Joycean invention taken from the Triestine word *smerdon* – meaning "a shit", "a good for nothing", or "a person who thinks he is more important than he really is", while another root may be *smerdoso* ("shitty" or "covered in shit"), from the Italian *merdoso*.[107] When choosing "Weiss" and "Schwarz" Joyce was thinking of Oscar Schwarz, a student whom he inherited from Stanislaus in 1914, and who, when he departed for Zürich, gave him a letter of introduction to Ottocaro Weiss, a Triestine studying political economy there with whom Joyce also became friendly. In choosing the name Szombathely Joyce may have taken the name of the Hungarian market town that was listed in *La Guida di Trieste* or, as I have discussed in Part Three, he may have had Marino de Szombathely in mind. "Savorgnanovich" might be traced to a teaching colleague of Joyce's, Dr Count Franco Savorgnan di Brazzà, who was from a family of Venetian nobles and the director of the Scuola di Commercio "Revoltella" who hired him. In adding the common Slav suffix "ovich" to Savorgnan, Joyce was doing the opposite of what an irredentist with Slav roots would have done. Joyce liked names ending in "ovich"; in *Finnegans Wake* the reader encounters "Gnoccovitch" (159), "Trovatorovich" (341), and the Irish soldier named Buckley who shoots the Russian general and becomes "Blanco Fusilovna Buklovitch" (49).

In addition to providing the root of "Savorgnanovich", Savorgnan was a prominent sociologist and a regular contributor to *Il Piccolo* who wrote, among other things, about the incidence of mixed marriage in Trieste. He was a somewhat controversial figure because of his views on the connections between language and race. Ferdinando Pasini, one of Trieste's more noted Italian scholars, wrote about Savorgnan's theories in *L'Indipendente* of 16 April 1910:

> Some months ago, Savorgnan published a short article which examined the links between language and race. According to the author the two terms do not mean the same thing; a common language does not mean a common race; race is not determined by language. Nowadays the European peoples are not united by race, "because there is already a fusion of various races of mixed origins, a process which we are currently witnessing in the countries to which people emigrate". The process of penetration and integration of races and languages has been going on without interruption for centuries and is the most remarkable and best known characteristic of the social evolution of humanity. Language cannot as a rule be used to judge race; the identity of a language only proves the links between peoples, not the origins of a people; a century and sometimes less is all that is needed to make differences of race, of language, of culture between a ruling people and a subject people disappear so that they become "a people of one nationality and language".

These opinions were not well received in irredentist Trieste, where the Italian language was the badge of Italian nationality, yet they were rather similar to those held by Joyce, who, as early as 1907, had openly mocked the idea of "purity of race".

As the Jews integrated into all aspects of life in Trieste, they stood out for their innovative and open attitudes towards modern ideas and formed a vital component of the intellectual élite of the city; they also played a fundamental role in rendering the city a filter for new writers and ideas from the northern Europe into Italy. Chief among among their favoured writers were the Viennese Jewish intellectuals Sigmund Freud and Otto Von Weininger, two of Europe's most important *fin-de-siècle* thinkers. Joyce first encountered both Freud and von Weininger through several of his well-read Triestine students. Rosa Maria Bosinelli's comments are instructive here: "In Joyce's Trieste, Freud's work and psycho-analytical theory were discussed animatedly. Whilst in Italy Freud's ideas met with considerable opposition, both in their scientific and cultural implications, in Trieste they took root with relative ease, on account of the particular social and political configuration of the city."[108]

As early as 1911 Joyce heard about psychoanalysis from a variety of sources, including Ettore Schmitz, who learned of it in 1908 from his nephew Dr Edoardo Weiss, one of Freud's earliest pupils and the first to introduce the subject into Italy. Paolo Cuzzi, who was Joyce's student from 1911 to 1913, read Freud's *Five Lectures on Psychoanalysis*, and, according to Ellmann, "remembered talking to Joyce about slips of the tongue and their significance. Joyce listened attentively, but remarked that Freud had been anticipated by Vico" (*JJ*, 340).[109] (He said the same thing to Dario De Tuoni.) Despite his scepticism about "the Viennese Tweedledee, Dr Freud" (*SL*, 282), Joyce owned several books connected with psychoanalysis, including Freud's *A Childhood Memory of Leonardo da Vinci*, Ernest Jones's *The Problem of Hamlet and the Oedipus Complex*, and *The Significance of the Father in the Destiny of the Individual* by "a certain Doctor Jung (the Swiss Tweedledum)" (*SL*, 282).

The question of Otto von Weininger's influence on Joyce is more complex. His book *Geschlecht und Charakter* (Sex and Character) was one of Europe's first twentieth-century best sellers. Marilyn Reizbaum has cogently summarized Weininger's views:

> Just as the woman is the negative force in every human being, so too, according to Weininger, is the Jew. The Jew has no redeeming qualities. He believes in nothing and therefore is useless. [...] The Jew is detestable and the detestable part of every human being is the Jewish part. To cement the link between woman and Jew, Weininger proclaimed that Jews were "weiblich" – the clue that they are the embodiment of the negative.[110]

The book was widely acclaimed in Trieste as it had been in Vienna, where, as Jacques Le Rider has shown, there was something of a convergence of anti-Semitism and anti-feminism.[111] Weininger's fame lay not so much in the originality of his ideas, which owed much to contemporary thinking in Vienna and elsewhere ("his polemical restatement of Arthur Schopenhauer's views on women simply extended the category of the feminine to the Jew"[112]), as in the fact that he committed suicide in Vienna at the age of twenty-three in the room where Beethoven had died. It was the only way he could find to escape his Jewishness, which he considered the mark of "the diseased individual".[113]

In 1912 Weininger's work was translated into Italian by Giulio Fenoglio, and a whole new audience came to read it. His success in Italy was "totally exaggerated compared with what he had enjoyed in other European countries" and the "mediating action of Trieste was essential" in bringing this about.[114] Several of Joyce's Triestine contemporaries openly admitted being influenced by Weininger: Scipio Slataper placed him beside Dante and

Shakespeare as one of his biggest influences, while Ettore Schmitz's cousin, Steno Tedeschi, wrote of Weininger as "the antifeminist philosopher *par excellence*. What Schopenhauer, Nietzsche and Strindberg just about intuit and develop vaguely in their works, he is able with his admirable synthetic spirit to elevate into a robust system, raising the question of woman to a level which has never before been reached."[115] Schmitz also read Weininger and approved of his "rejection of Anglo-Saxon empiricism" with "its soulless philosophers", yet made covert and ironic reference to him in his novel *The Confessions of Zeno* (1923).[116] Other contemporary Triestine writers to read his works were Giani Stuparich, Italo Tavalato and Biagio Marin, who was moved by the depiction of suicide which mirrored that of his friend Carlo Michelstaedter, a young Jewish artist and philosopher, earlier the same year (1913). The Jewish poet Umberto Saba was also deeply affected by Weininger's work, as a note in the diary of his friend Aldo Fortuna shows: "Saba just read a huge volume as big as two upright bricks, *Sex and Character* by Weininger: it deals with questions of genius, masculinity, woman, and he wrote it when he was twenty years old just before he committed suicide. Saba has been hugely, decisively affected by it and he more or less said, that if he had read it ten years ago, he too would have arrived at suicide."[117]

But approval was far from unanimous. Among Weininger's critics were members of the official Jewish community, including the important Zionist Rabbi Dante Lattes, who criticized *Sex and Character* harshly in *Il Corriere Israelitico*: "We do not celebrate [this book] which is dear to many young artists and writers, even Jewish ones; it is too immature, too aprioristic and violent, too anti-Semitic and there is too much hatred of women, even of woman. There is a useless and false exasperation and an excessive pessimism. He is a character out of a modern tragedy just like Uriel Acosta and Spinoza before him. How great an influence on his tragedy does our life of exile have?"[118]

Given the lively general interest in Weininger among Triestines, it would have been difficult for Joyce to have remained immune to his ideas and influence. Weininger's ideas are particularly pertinent to the "Circe" episode, where Bloom's subconscious is created. Reizbaum has argued, "The difference between Weininger and Bloom is that Weininger exorcised his fears by theorizing and dying, whereas Bloom exorcises his through imaginative action and by emerging with a sense of who he is, an acceptance of that self, and with a son, symbol of the continuation of life."[119] His triumph is to accept the "other" (the Jew/the female) within himself, which had terrified Weininger into suicide.[120]

Weininger's concept of femininity/woman was the most important element of *Sex and Character*. As Rosenfeld shows, women for Weininger are "amoral, illogical, passive, animalistic, and both soul- and egoless",[121] a description that fits quite easily Joyce's description to Budgen of Molly Bloom as "perfectly sane amoral fertilisable untrustworthy engaging shrewd limited prudent indifferent *Weib*". For Weininger women have an all-sexual identity; "all that the real woman recalls of her life … is her lovers, their proposals, their presents, their compliments".[122] She cannot think logically, makes endless vague associations and is ruled by instinct. These are all traits which can clearly be seen in Molly Bloom,[123] whose climactic moment in the novel is one of sexual union (according to Weininger "the supremest moment in a woman's life"[124]). But where Weininger wrote in these terms to express his contempt for and pity towards woman, Joyce uses them to celebrate her. To quote Poder: "Joyce's powerful mystification of feminine sexuality at the end of *Ulysses*, his stylization of it as a (male) life-affirming, life-inspiring force – as powerful as nature (Molly as flower) – presents a view of the status of feminine identity that is diametrically opposed to that of Weininger."[125]

Weininger was not the only anti-Jewish writer Joyce knew of when setting out to write *Ulysses*. He was also familiar with openly anti-Semitic texts such as Henry Wickham Steed's *The Hapsburg Monarchy* and Richard Wagner's *Judaism and Music*, yet perhaps even more useful to him was the fact that he was living in Trieste. Although historically it was noted for its tolerance, the city was not without its anti-Semites. In 1898 an anti-Jewish demonstration was organized in honour of the anti-Semitic burgomaster of Vienna to chants of "morte agli ebrei" (death to the Jews). Some elements within the Catholic Church were openly anti-Semitic, including the parish priest of San Giusto Don Giusto Buttignoni, in whose church Eileen Joyce and Frantisek Schaurek were married. A number of openly anti-Jewish newspapers, such as *La Coda del Diavolo*, *L'Avvenire*, *L'Amico*, *L'Avanti!* (and its successor *Il Sole*, which openly vowed to defeat "Jewish despotism in order to give back Trieste to the Triestines"[126]), regularly encouraged their readers to boycott the Jews, whom *L'Amico* termed "an effective force for cosmopolitanism and national decomposition"[127] and therefore disloyal to the irredentist aspirations of the city. *Il Piccolo,* by virtue of the fact that Mayer owned it, was accused of being "the organ of the ghetto",[128] of denigrating the Catholic Church and of propagating the Jewish religion.

In Trieste, anti-Semitism was usually politically motivated, and disagreements often degenerated into anti-Jewish attacks. Thus it sometimes hap-

pened that the Slovene nationalists and the Austrians tried to split the irredentist movement by attacking its leaders for being of Jewish extraction. The
whole dynamic of this tactic is similar to what happens in *Ulysses*, where, as
Neil Davison rightly states, "what begins as an argument about Sinn Féin
nationalism ... degenerates into a hatred based on the oldest tensions
between Jew and Christian".[129] A typical instance of this same process took
place in Trieste in 1904, when the Lega Popolare attacked Felice Venezian:

> Your end will be that which every tyrant deserves! Save yourself now while you
> are still in time and emigrate to Palestine, the land of your fathers – in this way
> at least there will be logic behind your vote! As a Jew your country is there, that
> is where your tribe has its roots and not in conquered Trieste. Leave Trieste to
> the Triestines! [...] The great majority of the people want to be freed from the
> yoke of your Jewish-Masonic tyranny.[91]

Especially after 1880 many irredentists, and most notably Venezian in
1885 and Teodoro Mayer in 1902, but also Sansone Venezian (to whom Joyce
sold tweed and taught English), abjured their Jewish religion. They later
became "prudent members" of the Masonry, chiefly because this organization was the nerve centre of the campaign to take Trieste out of Austria.[130]
The role of the converted Jews "in the craft" (*U*, 8.960) was a major factor
in the growing accusations of secrecy against them. Joyce may well have had
these associations in mind when creating Bloom, "that bloody freemason"
(*U*, 12.300) who is accused of secrecy over a bet on a horse and is constantly
being attacked for his links with the Masons.

The historian Tullia Catalan notes that "Venezian, many times branded
a Jew, didn't hesitate to defend himself by reclaiming with pride his Jewish
roots despite the fact that he had abandoned his religion."[131] In a public
response to one such attack, he defended himself as follows:

> Although I have publicly and officially abjured the religion of my parents, I am
> still not offended if someone calls me a Jew, and this because I honour my
> ancestors who were most respectable and worthy of the highest estimation.[132]

Bloom also defends his ancestors and his race when he is attacked for being
a Jew. In the Cyclops episode, he points out that "Mendelssohn was a jew
and Karl Marx and Mercadante and Spinoza" (*U*, 12.1804). The names that
Joyce chooses to put into Bloom's proud and irate defence are at once significant and problematic: Marx abandoned his faith and became an anti-
Semite, Mercadante was, in fact, an Italian Catholic, and Spinoza's views
were so unorthodox that he was excommunicated. Bloom's list, however, as

Neil Davison points out, is fitting, since his "naming of 'non-Jewish Jews' is more a recognition of his own type of 'Jewishness' than a good defense of the citizen's insult".[134] The list of independent-minded Jews that come into Bloom's mind significantly echoes that of Gino Arias at a lecture given at the Circolo Sionista in Trieste in 1906, which was published in the same year. Having spoken of the "immortal thoughts of Moses Maimonide", he mentions "the Jewish genius of Benedetto Spinoza" and compares him to "his more modest and uncertain Italian precursor Giordano Bruno".[135] In the following paragraphs he praises Mendelssohn and Marx before lauding Cromwell as "the great English reformer and politician" and linking him with "Menassé Ben Israel, the famous Rabbi from Amsterdam".[136] Cromwell is mentioned in a similar light in "Oxexn of the Sun" as "a gracious prince" who admitted "this alien" (Bloom) "to civic rights" (*U*, 14.905). History would suggest that Cromwell's intentions and methods were less noble than is indicated in earnest by Arias and rather more ironically in *Ulysses*.

Another all-too-common mode of attacking the Jews in Europe was to accuse them of carrying out rituals involving blood sacrifice. In fifteenth-century Trentino, for example, Jews had been burnt at the stake for allegedly carrying out ritual murders. In Trieste, in 1695, some Jews were falsely accused of having drugged a Christian child in order to extract blood for a Passover ceremony. Towards the end of the nineteenth century the charge of ritual murder again began to be made against the Jews. It commonly reappeared when there was an international crisis and the spectre of the Jew as the enemy within was evoked. This happened in the lead-in to the Triple Alliance in 1882 and again with the Beilis trial in Kiev during the 1913 Balkan crisis. This latter trial was exploited in Trieste by Catholics and Slovenes who attacked the Jewish-led Liberal Nationalists in order to win consensus in the forthcoming elections. Joyce may also have known about an episode which took place in Polna in Bohemia in 1899 when Leopoldo Hulsner (or Hilsner) was accused of ritual murder, tried in Kuttenberg and found guilty of murder, though cleared of any charge of having taken part in any rite. Trieste's *L'Amico* could not conceal its satisfaction:

> We do not wish to go into detail about the question of ritual assassinations. Neither do we wish to discuss whether the sacred books of the Jews, those which came before the old testament (Talmud), actually insisted upon ritual assassinations. We simply wish to make one point. Now it can no longer be sustained that ritual murders were fables [...] in the course of the centuries, in at least thirty cases it has been historically proven that the Jews carried out assassinations pursuing superstitious ends.[137]

Joyce later included the issue of ritual murder in *Ulysses*, where Bloom states: "It's the blood sinking in the earth gives new life. Same idea those Jews they said killed the christian boy" (*U*, 6.771–2). He could also have had these cases in mind when he included the "Ballad of Little Harry Hughes" in "Ithaca".

As a response to the inexorable disintegration of the Jewish way of life in Europe and to rising anti-Semitism, many Jews came to the opinion that their only future lay in the creation of a Jewish state, in other words, in Zionism. Joyce read quite deeply into the subject and owned books such as Herzl's *The Jewish State* and Sacher's *Zionism and the Jewish Future*, as well as various texts containing fictional portraits of Jews, including Sue's *Le Juif Errant* and Sacher-Masoch's *Scene del Ghetto*. As Louis Hyman has pointed out, Joyce made the "Zion-Palestine" motif one of the most persistent of symbols in *Ulysses*,[138] and created a conscious parallel between Bloom's considerations about "the restoration in Chanah David of Zion" (*U*, 17.759) and Stephen's interest in "Irish political autonomy or devolution" (*U*, 17.760).[139]

Trieste was "to the forefront of Italian Zionism",[140] one of the centres of the Zionist movement in Europe and often referred to as the "Shaar Zion" – the port of Zion – because of the number of emigrants who passed through the city en route to Palestine and the USA. The World Zionist Congress, held in Basel in 1897, was reported in the *Corriere Israelitico*, which aligned itself with the resolutions adopted, organized the first conference in the Italian language on the subject and soon became the official Italian Zionist organ. The arrival, at the turn of the century, of the fervent Zionist Dante Lattes as a teacher at the Trieste Jewish school caused a further increase in Zionist activities. In 1904 Lattes formed the Trieste Zionist circle, which supported Herzl's ideas of political Zionism. In the same year Herzl himself lectured in Trieste shortly before his death. These events coincided with an increase in Jewish emigration through Trieste following the failed revolution in Russia.

While in Trieste, Joyce read about the plight of the Jews in Russia during the pogroms of 1890, in *Ahasuerus* by the Dutch writer Hermann Heijermans. But the city itself would also have presented him with many opportunities to hear about these events first-hand from the refugees arriving there, many of whom were given spiritual and material help by local Jews and by the Committee for the Protection of Jewish Emigrants, whose principal aim was to organize temporary lodgings and financial help and to convince the shipping lines to offer reductions on ticket prices.

The number of poor Jewish immigrants arriving in Trieste en route from

Russia and Poland and bound for the USA and Palestine caused a rise in social, economic and political tensions within the Jewish community. Zionists – who were often sympathetic towards socialism and wanted to reform the community by weakening the power of the small group of men in control, whom they considered to be philistine anti-democratic capitalists – were generally accused of unfaithfulness to their country and of giving only lukewarm support to the different national causes, be they Austrian or Italian. The anti-Zionist Jews claimed that the Zionist assertion of a double national identity – the Jewish and that of the country they came from or lived in – was disrupting their assimilation into society, while the majority of settled Jewish community remained hostile to the idea of double nationality, which they felt could only disrupt their quiet and affluent lives in the city.[141] For the most part, therefore, as elsewhere in the West, most Jews in Trieste continued to reject Zionism as an unworkable intellectual idea which threatened their own well-being. The community elders generally shared this belief and resisted any public demonstrations (Zionist or otherwise) that were "authentically Jewish" for fear of upsetting the equilibrium they had achieved. Their reaction to the "groups of young pioneers, full of faith in a future Jewish state and anxious to convince everyone of the value of their mission" was cold and sceptical.[103]

This crucial and often heated debate informed Joyce in the writing of the "Cyclops" episode of *Ulysses*, when he has the Citizen ask Bloom "What is your nation if I may ask?" (*U*, 12.1430) and later includes the following exchange:

> — And after all, says John Wyse, why can't a jew love his country like the next fellow?
> — Why not? says J.J., when he's quite sure which country it is. (*U*, 12.1631–2)

The argument about Zionism revealed the gulf that existed between the assimilated Jews and recent arrivals from the East. Even Herzl distinguished between cultured assimilated Jews and "ugly Jews". This phenomenon of self-hatred, of the anti-Jewish Jew, was also evident in Trieste and was picked up on by Joyce in his notes for *Ulysses*, where he wrote: "the Jew hates the Jew in the Jew".[143]

Joyce had several contacts with supporters of the Zionist cause, as Cecil Roth pointed out:

> Another of Joyce's students who strongly supported Zionism was Ciro Glass, a young aristocratic Italian Zionist leader (who died in tragic circumstances in

1928). He used to tell us that Joyce had taught him English in his home – one steeped in Jewish tradition, unlike that of Ettore Schmitz.[144]

Ciro Glass, born in 1890, the son of Matteo Glass, himself president of the Circolo Sionista in the years before the First World War, was one of Joyce's keys to Zionism. The Circolo Sionista was based in 7 Piazza della Borsa, in the same building as the kosher Ristorante Ebraico, which "was founded to provide traditional Jewish foods for the more orthodox members of the community and in particular for the Jews in transit towards Palestine".[145] The members of the Circolo also met in the Caffè "Stella Polare" – a regular haunt of James and Stanislaus Joyce.

Perhaps even more important than Glass for Joyce was Moses Feuerstein Dlugacz, an ardent Zionist who was born on 12 January 1884 in Galicia, ordained rabbi when he was fifteen, and in 1918 married Ester Rachele Lapajowker, the daughter of a prominent Triestine Zionist. Dlugacz was well known for his efforts to promote the teaching of Hebrew and organized several courses, which were advertised in the *Corriere Israelitico*:

> Hebrew – a circular addressed to friends of the Hebrew language by Sig. M. Dlugacz announced that a meeting had been called for eight o'clock on 22 April to discuss: 1) the organization of the local forces to bring about a revival of the Hebrew language and culture; 2) the creation of a programme of action; 3) the constitution of a nucleus of people who speak Hebrew.[146]

He was Joyce's student from 1912 to 1915, during the period in which he was employed as chief cashier with the Cunard Line in Trieste. He used this position to help organize special prices for the poor Jews travelling on the steamers to the United States. Traditionally they travelled on the Unione Austriaca, the Austro Americana, the Cunard and the Cosulich lines. When the Great War broke out, Dlugacz remained on in the city and traded as a provisions merchant in a small shop on via Torrebianca, which supplied cheese and meat to the Austrian army fighting along the Isonzo river near Trieste.

With Joyce "he shared an enthusiasm for literature, language, music and philosophy,"[147] and he evidently made quite an impression on the Irish writer, whom he may even have taught some Hebrew. Joyce gave Dlugacz a presentation copy of *Dubliners* and later put some Hebrew words and letters into both *Ulysses* and *Finnegans Wake*. Notes from a letter written by Louis Hyman give an interesting insight into the relationship between the two men:

Joyce often visited Dlugacz in his bachelor flat at Viale 20 Settembre which he shared with Emanuele Freud of Vienna, a teacher of German language and literature at the Scuola Tedesca. There they carried on long discussions on literature, philosophy, art, music, religion, etymology, subjects in which they shared a common interest. [...] This may well be the pleasant evening Bloom spent at the home of Citron.[148]

In *Ulysses*, Joyce adopted his name for the "ferret eyed pork butcher" of Upper Dorset Street, the only shopkeeper in the book who is not listed in *Thom's Directory*. Significantly, Dlugacz keeps advertisements in his shop for the model farm at Kinnereth, and Molly mentions him as that "queerlooking man in the porkbutchers" who "is a great rogue" (*U*, 18.911–12).

The Zionism which Dlugacz both proposes and symbolizes in *Ulysses* fascinates Bloom, who on seeing the advertisements for Kinnereth on the Sea of Galilee thinks of Moses Montefiore and his plans to resettle Palestine. Then he reads "Agendath Netaim: planters' company. To purchase waste sandy tracts from Turkish government and plant with eucalyptus trees. Excellent for shade, fuel and construction. Orangegroves and immense melonfields north of Jaffa. You pay eighty marks and they plant a dunam of land for you with olives, oranges, almonds or citrons" (*U*, 4.191–6). "Nothing doing," thinks Bloom. "Still an idea behind it" (*U*, 4.200). Bloom ultimately sends the whole thing up in smoke by burning the leaflet, which creates a "truncated conical crater summit of the diminutive volcano" that emits "a vertical and serpentine fume redolent of aromatic oriental incense" (*U*, 17.1331–2). But not before Dlugacz has reappeared in "Circe" in slightly modified guise: "The image of the lake of Kinnereth with blurred cattle cropping in silver haze is projected on the wall. Moses Dlugacz, ferreteyed albino, in blue dungarees, stands up in the gallery, holding in each hand an orange citron and a pork kidney" (*U*, 14.887–9). Thus, the Triestine Jew and his belief in Zionism become a symbol of the East, which is a leitmotif in Bloom's stream of consciousness.

Dlugacz's teaching of Hebrew was just another example of the importance given to languages in Trieste and in the Jewish community there. *Il Corriere Israelitico* published an article on 30 April 1908 that drew attention to a new book on philology which posited a Hebrew–Gaelic link in which Joyce himself firmly believed:

There was a time in which all the languages were said to derive from Hebrew. Then the opposite was said. Now Dr A.E. Drake has published a book with Kegan Paul in London entitled *Discoveries in Hebrew, Gaelic, Gothic, Anglo-Sas-*

son [*sic*], *Latin, Basque and other Caucausic* [*sic*] *Languages, showing fundamental kinship of the Aryan Tongues and of Basque with the Semitic Tongues*, in which he sets out to prove that there is a "fundamental derivation" between the Aryan languages, and in particular Gaelic and Basque, and the Semitic languages.[149]

Joyce had already alluded to a similar link between Gaelic and the Semitic tongues in his 1907 lecture "Ireland, Island of Saints and Sages", where he suggested that Irish was Oriental in origin and similar to the languages of the Phoenicians. Drawing on the writings of Charles Vallancey, Joyce also pointed to religious similarities.[150] He further developed the links between the "ancient Hebrew and ancient Irish" in "Ithaca", in which Bloom and Stephen write some letters of the two alphabets before Bloom establishes the historical and philological connections between the Irish and the Phoenicians, Greeks and Semites:

> What points of contact existed between these languages and between the peoples who spoke them?
>
> The presence of guttural sounds, diacritic aspirations, epenthetic and servile letters in both languages: their antiquity, both having been taught on the plain of Shinar 242 years after the deluge in the seminary instituted by Fenius Farsaigh, descendant of Noah, progenitor of Israel, and ascendant of Heber and Heremon, progenitors of Ireland ... (*U*, 17.745–51)

These linguistic links point to the other fundamental factor connecting the Irish and the Jews: both peoples have been dispossessed of their homeland and forced into exile, and both still aspire to reclaiming control of the land of their forefathers.

This, of course, is one of the many ironies Joyce wished us to see in "Cyclops": that both the Citizen's and Bloom's racial memories are of dispossession and loss and that they both aspire, through very different means, to the same ends: the restoration of their respective nations. Bloom's desire, though, is much weaker and far less obsessive, and he has more faith in the Irish cause, because he believes that Palestine cannot offer a future to the Jews, that it is no more than "a dead land, grey and old" (*U*, 4.223), while the Citizen, who mourns "our lost tribes" (*U*, 12.1241), vociferously and fanatically believes that "they will come again and with a vengeance" (*U*, 12.1374).

Histories of dispossession, such as those of the Irish and the Jews, almost always lead to an obsession with the past, and this was yet another characteristic which the two peoples had in common and which Joyce himself noted when he wrote: "Jew and Irish remember past".[151] The same, as has been demonstrated in the third chapter, can be said of Trieste and the Triestines, and it is important to remember that it was in this city that Joyce encountered Jews who would have been well aware of all of these correspondences and parallels. From his acquaintance with them, he was able to gather the material necessary to make questions surrounding European Jewry in general, such as exile and dispossession, assimilation, Zionism, anti-Semitism and xenophobia, central to *Ulysses*. In this respect the city, once again, served him well.

4 *In the shadow of war*

By 1914 influences of a more sinister kind were being felt in Trieste as tensions rose between the European nations. By now, the relationship between the Italian majority and an increasingly hostile Austrian minority had almost completely broken down. Furthermore, the Italians barely tolerated the Slavs as guests in what they considered to be their own corner of Austria, while the Slavs gave voice to their right to be there with mounting vehemence. The tensions found their way into the classrooms of the Scuola Superiore di Commercio "Revoltella". In March 1914 *Il Piccolo* reported that there were increasingly frequent rows and scuffles between Italian and Slav students. On 13 March 1914 a first-year Italian student was injured by one of the Slavs, a certain Stefano Sisgoreo, who hit him with a revolver. As a result, Sisgoreo was expelled and lessons of the first course were suspended.[152]

Joyce battled on stoically with his own literary agenda and set about making a book of the articles he had written over the previous years. On 25 March 1914 he sent the socialist publisher Angelo Fortunato Formiggini the nine pieces he had written for *Il Piccolo della Sera*. His proposal was that they should be published in a volume in Italian, and that the title essay should be "Ireland at the Bar". "This year," wrote Joyce, "the Irish problem has reached an acute phase, and indeed, according to the latest news, England, owing to the Home Rule question, is on the brink of civil war. The publication of a volume of Irish essays would be of interest to the Italian public."[153] Joyce concluded the letter with untypical modesty: "I am an Irishman (from Dublin): and though these articles have absolutely no literary value, I believe they set out the problem sincerely and objectively." Although Formiggini does not appear to have replied, there is a sense of finality about Joyce's gesture: he was bringing to an end a cycle of essays entirely written in Italian which dealt extensively with Irish political problems.[154] Perhaps he sensed that the post-Parnell Ireland which he knew so profoundly and wrote so sensitively about, was slowly disappearing now that Home Rule was a real possibility, and that therefore he was no longer qualified as an insider to write articles about the Irish political situation. He delivered no more clear-cut public pronouncements about his native land, wrote no more articles on Ireland and confined *Ulysses*, which he was already working on, to 1904 and the period with which he felt most at home. At the same time he continued to follow the political developments in Ireland closely and, as Enda Duffy and other critics have shown, dealt indirectly with events such as the 1916 rising and the civil war in *Ulysses*, which Duffy goes so far as to read as a "text of Irish independence".[155] In *Finnegans Wake*, Joyce made overt references to recent Irish events, such as the burning of the Custom House during the Anglo-Irish war: "the dynamitization of colleagues, the reduction of all records to ashes, the levelling of all customs by blazes" (*FW*, 189.34–5). David Pierce has written tellingly about the political perspectives of both books:

> Just as *Ulysses* belongs to a period of expectancy that found its now perennially hopeful expression in the one day in June in 1904, in a parallel way *Finnegans Wake* gives voice to the disorder and disillusionment that befell Irish politics in the immediate aftermath of the Anglo-Irish War, when civil war and internecine feuding broke out between the warring brothers Shem and Shaun.[156]

In this period, Joyce had also returned to working on *Exiles*, having abandoned it following the completion of a rough draft of the first act in 1913. Now, in the autumn of 1914, he set about writing the second and third acts returning to measure himself against those issues which were later to form the very heart of *Ulysses*: "Envy, jealousy, abnegation, equanimity" (*U*, 17.2155).

Joyce was also addressing these themes in a series of occasional poems he was writing at the time and which were later among those collected in *Pomes Penyeach*. A total of eight poems, composed between 1912 and 1915 and set in Trieste, register Joyce's coming to terms with the fact that he had passed the age of thirty, with his irreparable rupture with Ireland, with the demands of fatherhood, the frailty of love, his searing jealousy over Nora and his self-indulgent crush on one of his young pupils. Although they depart from actual events in Joyce's life, these compositions melancholically register moods and feelings of lost opportunity, mourning and resignation, rather than strictly identifiable autobiographical facts, and they indirectly reflect the growing gloom hanging over the writer and the increasing desperation felt in Trieste as the continent stumbled towards war.

Lucia and Giorgio are the subjects of two of them – "A Flower given to my Daughter" and "On the Beach at Fontana". The first is a re-elaboration of a brief entry in *Giacomo Joyce*: "A flower given by her to my daughter. Frail gift, frail giver, frail blue-veined child" (*GJ*, 3). The second is also a reworking of earlier material, this time dating back to 1905 and shortly after Giorgio's birth:

> I held him in the sea at the baths at Fontana and felt with humble love the trembling of his frail shoulders: *Asperge(s) me, Domine hyssopo et mundabor: lavibis me et super nivem dealbalor.*
>
> Before he was born I had no fear of fortune.[157]

The Bagni Fontana was situated near the Stazione Meridionale in Trieste. It was a bathing place frequented by locals as it was comfortably close to the city centre. The wind and shingle of the poem, the groaning "crazy pierstakes", are all suggestive of a wild and frightening sea, from which Joyce wishes to protect his son for whom he feels an "ache of love!"

The first poem in the sequence, a little gem called "Watching the Needleboats at San Sabba", was written in 1913 as Joyce watched Stanislaus take part in a sculling race at San Sabba, then a country village overlooking the sea near Trieste, now an industrial suburb. Watching the Italian boats, Joyce is reminded of Galway and its "needleboats", and the melancholic "No more, return no more" refrain suggests his now permanent exile from his native land. The poem is also a forceful expression of Joyce's coming to terms with the passing of time and of his own youth. The final lines are a loose translation of Johnson's aria from Puccini's opera *La Fanciulla del West*,[158] which the scullers are singing. Joyce sent the poem to Stanislaus in September 1913 for his "young friends of the Rowing Club ... for a dinner programme or some such thing – with the rheumatic chamber poet's (or pot's) compliments" (*LII*, 323–4). He subsequently had it published in the *Saturday Review*.

If the "needleboats" of San Sabba are evocative of Galway sculling boats, then "She Weeps over Rahoon" is even more openly Irish and biographical. The speaker of the poem is Nora, who is remembering Michael Bodkin, or perhaps Gretta Conroy remembering her lost love Michael Furey. The echoes from the last lines of "The Dead" are very apparent in the rain which "falls softly, softly falling" in the opening line of the poem. Once again there is a heavily melancholic mood as a young boy is described whose "sad heart has lain/Under the moongrey nettles, the black mould/And muttering rain."[159]

Another poem in the series, "Tutto è Sciolto", takes its title from Elvino's moving lament in Bellini's opera *La Sonnambula*, which was produced in the Teatro Politeama Rossetti in the autumn of 1914, the probable time of the poem's composition. All was lost in many senses: Ireland was no longer home to Joyce, while shortly it would no longer be possible for him to remain in Trieste, because war had just broken out in Europe. More particularly the poem seems to centre on Joyce's distress over Prezioso's courting of Nora, hence the desolate emptiness of the opening stanza: ("A birdless heaven, seadusk, one lone star/Piercing the west,/As thou, fond heart, love's time, so faint, so far,/Rememberest."[160]) A reference to his own temptations to have an affair with a young student ("The clear young eyes' soft look"[161]) – temptations which the poem suggests he did not yield to – appears also to be present.

The final poem, "Nightpiece", lives up to its title by being laden with gloomy images of the night as Joyce contemplates heading into the unknown of a relationship with a girl much like the one he described in *Giacomo Joyce*. Like the previous poem, it was written in that darkest of years, 1915, and it is hard not to see the shadow of war hanging over it, humanity heading "voidward" with a subsequent "waste of souls". The scene is a church, in the same "tawny gloom" of the "vast gargoyled church" which Joyce had described visiting on Good Friday with the "pale and chill" girl in *Giacomo Joyce*.

THE ASSASSINATION of the heir to the Austrian throne, the Archduke Francesco Ferdinando, and his wife Sofia Chotek by a Bosnian student called Gavrilo Princip in Sarajevo on 28 June 1914 dominated the news in Trieste, as it did elsewhere. The bodies returned to Vienna through Trieste in what was destined to be its last important role as an Austrian imperial city.

In reporting the death of the Archduke, *L'Indipendente* of 30 June 1914 immediately gave voice to the fear that war might break out and that Austria might feel persuaded to take up arms against Serbia.[162] This prediction was all too correct. On 26 July 1914, the breakdown of diplomacy between the Austrians and the Serbs was announced, and with it came the suspension of the Austrian constitution in favour of military command. On 28 July war was declared. On 8 August, *L'Indipendente* carried the headline "La Grande Guerra" and reported the involvement of the Germans, French, Russians and British. Things would never be the same again in Trieste or anywhere else.

On 17 September Joyce received word from the Scuola Superiore di Commercio "Revoltella" that he was suspended without pay until further notice. This was a bitter blow because the school had asked the Lieutenancy to approve a renewal of his contract in July. Now the local administration refused to do so until they had official approval from the Ministry of Public Instruction in Vienna. This was slow in coming. On 10 December Joyce wrote a letter to the Lieutenancy, asking for a decision with regard to his position and demanding to have his documents returned:

> To the superior imperial royal Lieutenancy
>   The undersigned, born in Dublin (Ireland) on 2 February and currently professor of English language at the Scuola di Commercio Revoltella, respectfully asks the lieutenancy to give back the documents listed below, which were sent to the Ministry of Public Instruction in Vienna at their request so that that authority could confirm him or otherwise in the above-mentioned position.
>   With kindest regards
>   James Joyce B.A.
>
> Documents
> i) Degree certificate from the Royal University of Ireland (Dublin) – (the original in scroll)
> ii and iii) Press reviews of his literary work – (copies).
> iv and v) Testimonials from the Universita Popolare of Trieste.
> 10 December 1914[163]

On 16 December 1914 the ministry wrote to the offices of the Trieste Lieutenancy requesting more information about Joyce. The chief education inspector, Eugenio Gelcich, examined the request on 8 January 1915 and wrote: "I believe that the renewal of Joyce's contract would be a very good thing, that he is a quiet individual who worries, above all, about making a living."[164] The *Luogotenente* Hohenlohe, who had come to know Joyce as the teacher of his wife (Sua Serenità la principessa Francesca Hohenlohe-Schillingsfürst) and her children, endorsed this view when he added a note on the back of Gelcich's report: "Joyce is known as a quiet young man who is worried only about making a living."[165] Hohenlohe also recommended to the ministry that Joyce be given a permanent job and asked again that his papers be returned to Trieste. Another document signed by Gelcich and the local director of police stated that Joyce had no criminal record, and that during his stay in Trieste from 1904 "his conduct had been unexceptionable both politically and morally".[166]

It was not until 17 February 1915 that the Ministry finally informed Hohenlohe's office that Joyce could begin teaching for the academic year 1914–15, on the grounds that this activity would not have any negative influence on the students. But the Lieutenancy was also instructed to remind the university administration that according to a law of 1850 the employment of a teacher who cannot demonstrate himself to be in possession of Austrian citizenship must be temporary. The letter also included Joyce's documents to allow for the processing of his position.

Almost a month passed before this news was relayed to Joyce. As a result of the delay, and to his great surprise, eighteen of his students rallied on his behalf, organizing a protest against the school administration on 4 March 1915. Finally, on 13 March Joyce received a letter from the school director, Professor Morpurgo, telling him that the Ministry had declared that he could begin teaching and asking him to come on Monday at 10 a.m. to organize his timetable.

In the meantime Joyce had had to survive for over five months without his fixed salary. Fortunately he had been given a part-time job with Gioacchino Veneziani's ship-varnish company in January 1914 and this continued until his departure for Zürich. Presumably with a little prodding from Ettore Schmitz, his son-in-law, Veneziani had agreed to employ Joyce on a part-time basis to write correspondence and help with the books.[167] His salary was just 100 crowns per month, very little compared with the 1500 crowns he was paid by the school, but at least it arrived regularly. At the end of January 1915 he was forced to take out a loan of 600 crowns from Il Consorzio Industriale di Mutui Prestiti. It was underwritten by Vidacovich and guaranteed by Artifoni. The original date for repayment, 30 April 1915, passed and was postponed to 30 July, but predictably, given the onset of war, Joyce was in no position to repay it. (Shortly after Joyce left for Zürich, a bank official went looking for him, and not finding him at home in via Bramante, came to the erroneous conclusion that Joyce had been interned. The original sum of money, along with an additional 138.85 crowns in interest, was eventually paid off in March 1918, probably by Vidacovich.)[168] Joyce genuinely suffered financially during these months and was qualified to tell De Tuoni at the end of December 1914 that "Whoever has the last sack of flour will win the war."[169]

January 1915 brought further bad news when Stanislaus, who had never tried to hide his irredentist sympathies, was arrested and interned in Schloss Kirchberg in Lower Austria.[170] He was destined to remain in Austrian internment camps for the remainder of the war. In his absence, Joyce took on his few remaining private students, essentially those who had not already been called up for military service. Among these were Paul Granichstaedten and Oscar Schwarz, who later remembered his lessons with his Irish teacher:

> I do not know how James spent his time with other pupils: as to myself I can tell you that mostly he declaimed Paul Verlaine in French or read St. Thomas Aquinas in Latin or sang arias by Bellini accompanying himself on the piano which was always open. [...] he treated me more as a friend than as a pupil. I was then 17 years old.[171]

Where Stanislaus had used *Dubliners* as a textbook, Joyce used *Hamlet* and insisted the students learn the monologues by heart. Sometimes he read his more recent poetry to Schwarz. "He explained the symbolic meaning of his poems, but imbued as I then was with Croce, I mustered the audacity to contradict him and tell him that there was nothing of the sort but pure music etc. He took it well and told me (I believe in Italian) "You *do* understand my poems".[172]

For Joyce and the other enemy subjects who were allowed to remain, life became rather restricted. Money was scarce, entertainment more and more limited, and they were subject to a curfew from eight in the evening until six in the morning. How strictly this regulation was enforced is not clear. Schwarz is but one of several students who remembered meeting Joyce in this period in the Ristorante "Antica Bonavia". Another was Mario Nordio, who later recalled the relaxed nature of their lessons: "He continually skipped from one topic to the other, embellishing his words with anecdotes told in his favourite form, that of the fable. I remember how disappointed I was after I had told him a funny story that I thought would make him smile: he listened to me in silence and then mumbled with a sigh: *And Jesus wept.*"[173]

It was just as well that he entertained himself in his lessons because there was little going on in Trieste to keep him amused. In the summer of 1914 most of the theatres stayed closed although an opera season was mounted in the autumn. It was smaller in scale than in previous years and included *La Sonnambula, Rigoletto, Il Barbiere di Siviglia* and *L'Elisir d'Amore*, and all the leadings roles were sung by local artists. Nineteen-fifteen was even bleaker, although the cinemas continued to show new films, and in the early spring the Teatro Politeama Rossetti managed to put on *La Bohème, Werther, Lucia di Lammermoor* and *I Pagliacci*. But by April all the theatres had closed down.

On 12 May, Eileen Joyce married Frantisek Schaurek, the Czech bank

clerk whom she had got to know during his visits to the house in via Bramante for English lessons. The wedding took place in the Cathedral of San
Giusto, just up the hill from Joyce's house. A year earlier, in May 1914, she
had announced her engagement and had written telling her father of her
intentions. He had immediately quizzed Joyce: "I am *most anxious* to know
the *full particulars* concerning Eileen, viz. *who* and *what* this gentleman is? I
am satisfied both you and your brother will look to her future and see that
she does not take any step that may mar her future" (*LII*, 331). Joyce was
Schaurek's best man and turned up for the occasion in a borrowed dress suit
that was several sizes too big for him. Directly after the wedding the couple
set off for Prague, where Schaurek had been called up for military service.
Now the only Joyces left in Trieste were James and his immediate family.

Despite major difficulties, the Scuola "Revoltella" remained open in this
period. On 6 May 1915, along with other teachers and the acting director,
Professor Morpurgo, Joyce signed the official notice announcing that the
exams would be held. But the student body and teaching staff were dwin-
dling. The school received a final death-blow when the Austrian government
issued a decree which conscripted all males under the age of forty-two. As a
result some 30,000 Triestines were called up to serve in the Austrian army.
Although oral exams were held Morpurgo had no choice but to send a letter
to the Lieutenancy on 16 June in which he announced that it was no longer
possible to keep the school open. Most of the students had already left for
the front.

Later in the same month, Joyce, ever the optimist, went to the school
looking for his salary for July. The only people still around were Giovanni
Benedetti, the porter, and Professor Grignaschi, who sent him away empty-
handed. A few days later Benedetti wrote to Morpurgo, who had gone to live
in Vienna, to tell him of Joyce's visit. The following is an English version of
his almost unreadable Italian:

> A few days ago Professor Jojce [*sic*] came looking for a written document from
> the school to confirm that he is a teacher here. Professor Grignaschi gave him
> one, but it is useless because he will have to leave Trieste, indeed he will have
> to travel a long way from Arch to Ravalico in order to get his salary for July.[174]

In other words, Joyce did not have a hope of getting paid. Despite this he
still seemed disinclined to move on to a safer city. But it was becoming hopeless and dangerous to stay on. On 23 May the predictable news arrived that
Italy had entered the war, and Trieste was plunged into chaos. The Lieu-

tenancy of Trieste ordered the closing of the borders and within a couple of hours anti-Italian demonstrations had already broken out at various hot-points around the city. Pro-Austrian mobs roamed the city attacking irre-dentists and key irredentist symbols. The irredentist clubs and gyms were destroyed, their caffès, such as the Caffè San Marco, the Milano, the Fabris and the Stella Polare, were ransacked and vandalized, the statue of Verdi demolished, and the offices of *Il Piccolo* destroyed by arsonists. The rioters were, in the main, added and abetted by the Austrian police.

Despite the tensions and tumult around him, Joyce forged ahead with his work and, extraordinarily, none of his letters contains any reference to the events going on around him in Trieste or in Europe. It is as if he was too absorbed with *Ulysses* to notice. On the highly symbolic date of 16 June 1915, he sent Stanislaus a postcard in German reporting that "the first episode of my new novel *Ulysses* is written. The first part, the Telemachiad, consists of four episodes: the second of fifteen, that is, Ulysses' wanderings: and the third, Ulysses' return home, of three more episodes" (*SL*, 209).

But that, for the moment, was as far as he would get. By now there was little choice left but to leave Trieste. Nearly all his friends and acquaintances were already long gone and his protector, Prince Hohenlohe, had left in Feb-ruary to take up a new position as President of the Supreme Court of the Counts in Vienna.

As an enemy subject, Joyce was tempting fate by remaining. On top of this, his financial situation was hopeless. He later outlined his difficulties in a letter of 30 July 1915 to A. Llewelyn Roberts, Secretary of the Royal Liter-ary Fund:

> At the outbreak of war I was in Trieste where I have lived for the last eleven years. My income there was derived from two sources: i) my position in the Higher School of Commerce ii) private lessons. After the outbreak of war I was confirmed in my position by the Austrian Ministry of Public Instruction, Vienna, from whom I held and hold it. The school however closed in spring, nearly all the professors having been called up as officers of the reserve. My sec-ond source of income in normal times, viz., private lessons, produced very lit-tle in the first months and nothing at all in the next months owing to the critical conditions of the city. In these circumstances I lived with great difficulty and was obliged to recur to the assistance of friends, as stated under. (*LII*, 356)

When he decided to leave, he was helped on his way by his old friend Baron Ralli, who loaned him 300 crowns, and by Gioacchino Veneziani, who gave him a further 250. He and his family were issued passports from the American consulate (which was also looking after British interests in the area) but still needed permission from the Austrian authorities to depart. With the help of Count Sordina and Baron Ralli, he managed to obtain the travel pass, as he later explained to Frank Budgen:

> It was through the intervention of a Greek merchant prince of the great house of Ralli and of a Greek nobleman, Count Francesco de Sordina, the Grand Seigneur of Trieste [...] that I was able to leave Austria in war time on parole.[175]

Sordina went directly on Joyce's behalf to a relative of his, Cavalier Manussi de Montesole, who also had Greek roots and was, more importantly, the director of the Triestine police. Joyce was just one of the many people Sordina assisted before and during the war, as Silvio Benco recalled:

> The only one who, with nobility of character, intervened everyday for some-one or other, and was not afraid of climbing the same fearsome steps ten at a time, to personally act as a barrier against the overflowing persecution, was Count Francesco Sordina, whose social and familial status allowed him access where others would have been turned away.[176]

On 27 June 1915, Joyce and his family reluctantly left the city that had been their home for over ten years. They faced an uncertain future but were pleased to meet one of Joyce's Greek pupils, Mario Megaris, as soon as they boarded the train, and even more reassured to find that the first control officer was another of Joyce's students. They were bound for Zürich, a city that had taken on a role once played by Trieste: to provide refuge to strangers from foreign lands.

Afterword: Tergestis Exul

Joyce's unsuccessful postwar return to Trieste has been well documented by Richard Ellmann, whose task was made easier by the fact that many of the people who knew Joyce in that late period were still alive when he was writing the biography. This brief afterword seeks to show that during the Zürich period Joyce's links with Trieste were lively and regular, and that he never doubted that he would return there after the war. Secondly it suggests that Joyce's inability to settle back there was largely due to the extent to which Trieste had changed during the war and in its immediate aftermath. In 1915 Joyce left behind a cosmopolitan Austrian city; when he returned in 1919 he soon came to realize that the rich and varied elements which had provided him with an invaluable workshop for his writing no longer existed.

During his time in Switzerland, Joyce remained friendly with many Triestines who had also settled there. These included Ottocaro Weiss, one of his closest friends there, and Vela and Olga Pulitzer, who went to him for English tuition. Vela later described the lessons as "a perfect joy" to Richard Ellmann, who noted: "Mrs Pulitzer's family were great friends, for Joyce missed Trieste and he had known these people in Trieste – they therefore spoke much of Trieste and life there."[177] Joyce also spent time with Edoardo Schott, whom he had earlier judged to be his best Triestine student[178] and who was an irredentist and socialist, and as such the black sheep of his upper-middle-class, pro-Austrian family.[179] During the war, he worked as a journalist and spy in Zürich and published his articles – under the pen name of Desico – in the socialist *Il Popolo d'Italia*, which was edited by Mussolini. Schott later wrote of his friendship with Joyce and seemed to imply that Joyce was involved in work similar to his own:

> My [espionage] work was flanked by that of a great writer, one of the greatest in this century, who also considered himself to be a *Triestino* by choice: James Yoyce [*sic*], who was in Zürich with me, a refugee from Trieste where he had passed many years of his youth teaching English and at the same time had begun his major works *Dubliners* and *Ulysses* [...] Trieste has remembered very modestly its adopted son, who is still talked about [...] On our long walks along the lake in Zürich and on the hills that overlook this magnificent city, we talked in pure Triestine mainly about the problems of the war and the future of Trieste.[180]

Joyce's family, as he himself noted in a letter of 24 June 1921 to Harriet Shaw Weaver, believed he "enriched" himself "in Switzerland during the war by espionage work for one or both combatants" (*SL*, 282). Ellmann writes: "The origin of this story was that Joyce courteously served in Zurich as mailing intermediary for his Triestine friend Mario Tripcovich and the latter's fiancée, who were separated by the war" (*JJ*, 510). This is certainly true. Joyce taught Mario and Maria Tripcovich, the children of an important shipbuilder with Dalmatian origins, Count Diodato Tripcovich, for several years before the war and acted as go-between for Mario, who spent the war in Graz, and his Jewish fiancée, Silvia Mordo, who was in Italy.[181] This activity came to the attention of the Austrian police, who commented as follows: "Joyce was previously their English teacher. As far as politics is concerned, there is nothing alarming to report with regard to any of the above-mentioned. While none of them are members of any subversive societies, Joyce was politically suspect although he never expressed his views openly."[182] Joyce probably acted as intermediary for several other Triestines divided by war, who were trying to stay in touch with letters to and from neutral Switzerland rather than from enemy states.

It is most unlikely, however, that he was involved in pro-Italian propaganda while in Zürich, although he was viewed with great suspicion throughout the war by the Austrian secret services, which actually went to the trouble of sending a spy to take English lessons with him in an attempt to extract information. The spy came away convinced Joyce was an ardent anti-British Sinn Féiner. It seems that Joyce had immediately realized what this agent was after and had given him what he wanted to hear.[183]

Stanislaus's war was a lot less pleasant than Joyce's. He was interned in Austria from 1915 to 1918 as a "internierter britischer Staatsangehoriger" – a British subject – firstly in the "Schloss Kirchberg" and then in the "Schloss Grossau bei Raabs".

After the war Stanislaus, Eileen and Frantisek Schaurek settled back in Trieste several months before Joyce. No sooner had Stannie returned than he was faced with his brother's creditors and the necessity of finding new accommodation for Joyce and his family in advance of their return. A world war had disrupted old ways of life, but some things never changed. Yet, as his letter of 25 May 1919 shows, Stannie was no longer willing to do the impossible:

> Some eight years ago I took the quarter for you, moved in and paid the first rent. Now I have paid the last rent for you and moved out. The packing up and moving out of a flat ankle-deep in dust has been a week's dirty work for Frank and Eileen. It has cost me nearly three hundred lire. I have just emerged from four years of hunger and squalor, and am trying to get on my feet again. Do you think you can give me a rest? (*LII*, 443)

Five months later, in mid-October 1919, Joyce finally came back with Nora and the two children. Their first problem was finding a suitable place to live. It was not as easy as they had hoped because Trieste had become expensive and they could not afford a large deposit. As a supposedly temporary solution (which in fact lasted the full nine months of their return) and despite the objections from both Schaurek and Stanislaus, they went to live in the flat in number 2 via della Sanità, which was already home to Stanislaus and to the Schaurek family.[184] In all there were eleven of them: Joyce and Nora, Lucia and Giorgio, Stanislaus, Eileen and Frantisek Schaurek and their two daughters Eleonora and Bozena Berta, Ivanka the cook and Loiska the babysitter.

Relations were rather strained. Eileen's marriage to Schaurek was not working out, as Letizia Fonda Savio recalled, having met Eileen in this period and found her aged and troubled. When she congratulated her on her marriage Eileen said sadly: "When a girl, a woman wishes to be married; when she is married, she wishes to be dead."[185] Schaurek was also cold towards Joyce and resented having to share an apartment with him and his family.

Joyce found that Stanislaus had become even cooler towards him now and was much more independent than he had been before the war. Stanislaus felt aggrieved that his brother had not made more effort to stay in touch and struggled to come to terms with his relegation from a position in which he was Joyce's primary financier, companion and confidant to now being just another supporter. He quickly came to realize that he no longer played a significant role in his brother's creative life, and where he had once tolerated his excesses and his casual attitude towards him, he now took steps to protect himself. Joyce, in turn, complained somewhat peevishly to Budgen in Zürich that Stanislaus "has a devil of a lot to do and likes a gay elegant life in his own set" (*LI*, 134).[186]

Although he never really settled back in Trieste, Joyce was still not anxious to leave it. Yet he was shocked at how much the city had changed. Boris Furlan recalled meeting him after the war:

> I met him by chance in Piazza Caserma [...] he complained that the town was dirty, especially the streets – well, they were to a small extent compared with the former Austrian standard and he used the word "letamaio" (dungheap) but I am positive he was thinking about all the other changes, all the new people pouring in from Italy looking to make money, generally they came poor to Trieste. Many of his former friends had gone, well, it must have looked like "the dead man's return".[187]

He did see some of his old friends and students, people like Francini Bruni, who found Joyce much "more stylized" and whose wife Clotilde said of Joyce "non è più quello" (he's not like he used to be).[188] He also spent time with Ettore and Livia Schmitz, Oscar Schwarz, Silvio Benco, Tullio Silvestri and Argio Orell, but whatever it was that had made Trieste special for him was no longer there. Now that he had chosen not to give private lessons, he missed the conviviality of Zürich life and lacked friends to socialize with. Benco, who had become editor of *Il Piccolo*, remembered him during this period:

Many times during that last year of his life in Trieste, he offered to take me
with him to one of those old inns of Città Vecchia which he loved so much, to
spend the evening chatting, smoking, and drinking – as indeed poets and
philosophers have always enjoyed doing.[189]

Despite his unease in the city, Joyce tried his best to settle down: he went
back to his job teaching in the Istituto di Commercio "Revoltella", which
was in the process of being turned into a university, and in November he
returned to *Ulysses* and began to work on the "Nausicaa" episode. But he
greatly missed having people to talk to about his writing, now that Stanislaus no longer listened with the interest he had once had, and the great
friend he had acquired in Zürich – Frank Budgen – was not interested in
coming to spend time in Trieste. He repeatedly tried to convince him to
come and settle for a while there, promising him the use of Tullio Silvestri's
studio as well as lots of English lessons and telling him that he would "surely
find something to paint in this colourfull [*sic*] place" (*LI*, 138). His entreaties
to Budgen were very similar to those he had sent Stanislaus way back in 1905,
and again he was careful to draw attention to Trieste's attractions: "I hope
you will come for a time anyway. Spring here is very pleasant. Opera continues also after Easter. Sigfrido with one of the greatest Italian tenors Bassi"
(*LI*, 140). But Budgen always refused to come.[190]

Despite finishing "Nausicaa" in February and launching into work on
"Oxen of the Sun", it was clear that even if he was able to continue writing
he no longer felt at home in Trieste:

Without saying anything about this city (*de mortuis nil nisi bonum*) my own
position for the past seven months has been very unpleasant. I live in a flat with
eleven other people and have had great difficulty in securing time and peace
enough to write those two chapters. [...] Since I came here I suppose I have
not exchanged 100 words with anybody. I spend the greater part of my time
sprawled across two beds surrounded by mountains of notes. [...] I could give
lessons here (most people expected it of me) but I will not. I have a position in
that school which the government has now raised to the rank of a university.
My pay is about 3/- an hour for 6 hours a week. This I shall resign as it wastes
my time and my nerves.[191]

He began to invent excuses for departing and even considered travelling to
spend a couple of months in Ireland in order to finish "Circe" and buy
clothes en route in London for his family. He was therefore in the right
frame of mind to allow himself to be convinced by Ezra Pound, who in the

spring began to write encouraging him to move to Paris. By leaving, Joyce was making sure not to repeat the mistake made by his friend, the Triestine composer Antonio Smareglia. In a lecture given on 15 December 1910, Benco had spoken of Smareglia's error, which took place when he was on the crest of a wave of critical success:

> But it happened that Antonio Smareglia, not particularly suited to, nor, because of his physical disposition, very capable of, understanding the ways of the world, committed an error, which the speaker [Benco] defined as tactical. He should have resolutely entered into the German musical world, settled down in Vienna, Munich or Berlin, but instead, drawn by a deep nostalgia, he wanted to return to these Adriatic provinces. An error – added the speaker – because our provinces, without wishing to do them down, given their ambiguous geographical and political position, are not a suitable place from which to make the world feel the presence of a great living artist. For Italian art, this decision was a good one, but for Antonio Smareglia, it was undoubtedly an imprudent act.[192]

Silvio Benco drove home his point in the following day's paper: "Only in a great national centre can a superior artist illuminate the power of his vision. If, on the other hand, he has to send his light from the periphery to the centre, he will be able to do it only with efforts which are a thousand times more tiring."[193]

Joyce avoided falling into the same nostalgia trap, but even after leaving Trieste he would betimes remember the city fondly and refer to himself as a "Tergestis Exul", an exile from Trieste.[194] He could have used the term to describe his final period there, for throughout it he was like an exile returned to a land that did not exist any more. He was not, contrary to what Furlan said, "like a dead man walking in the city", rather the city itself had died on him and he could no longer bear to live in its ghostly reincarnation ("*de mortuis nil nisi bonum*").[195]

Yet he would continue to remember Trieste (his "second country"[196]) and stay in touch with many of the people who had been close to him over the years – Sordina, Ralli, Prezioso, De Tuoni, Francini Bruni, Schmitz, Amalia Popper and Emma Cuzzi. He would also award the dialect of *Triestino* a prominent place in *Finnegans Wake*.

In the meantime, almost as unsure of his fate as he had been in 1904 when he arrived for the first time in Trieste, he left in early July 1920 with Nora and the children, this time bound for Paris. In leaving Trieste, Joyce was moving from a city which history and war had cast out into the periphery and going to one which, for the better part of twenty years, was to be the great literary centre of the world. And yet, even if Trieste's moment of glory had passed, its immortality was safe in the hands of Joyce, for it was there that he had found "the rock of Ithaca, and on the sea, the sail of Ulysses".[197]

Notes

INTRODUCTION

1. Quoted in Stelio Crise, *Epiphanies & Phadographs: Joyce e Trieste* (Milano: All'Insegna del Pesce d'Oro, 1994), 20 and 22.

2. Mario Doria, con la collaborazione di Claudio Noliani, *Grande Dizionario del Dialetto Triestino Storico, Etimologico, Fraseologico* (Trieste: Finanziaria Editoriale Triestina, 1991), 380.

3. Richard Kearney, *Postnationalist Ireland: Politics, Culture, Philosophy* (London: Routledge, 1997), 116.

PART ONE: HEADING EAST

1. From "The Ballad of Finnegan's Wake", quoted in Roland McHugh, *Annotations to Finnegans Wake* (London: Routledge and Kegan Paul, 1980), 4.

2. Herbert Gorman, *James Joyce: A Definitive Biography* (London: The Bodley Head, 1941), 131.

3. The statue had been unveiled a couple of years earlier and was funded by a pro-Austrian committee chaired by Count Francesco Sordina, who would later become one of Joyce's most loyal students. Period photographs show that the Empress Elisabetta was a beautiful woman with hair to her heels, a feature Joyce later attributed to Anna Livia Plurabelle.

4. *Il Piccolo* of 19 and 20 October 1904 contains reports revealing that several English sailors had indeed deserted and been involved in a number of minor scrapes.

5. Stanislaus Joyce, *Triestine Book of Days 1907–1909*, 3 January 1907. Photocopies of this entire unpublished document are kept in the Richard Ellmann Collection at the McFarlin Library at the University of Tulsa.

6. *Ibid.* According to a report in *Il Piccolo* on 10 March 1905, Churchill spent six years in Trieste before being promoted to the post of Consul in Lisbon. The report states: "Mr Churchill spent many years of his career in the Far East where he studied the languages and habits of the people. A perfect gentleman, he was popular for his friendliness and his polite and distinguished demeanour." Surprisingly, given Joyce's notorious contempt for British officialdom, Joyce was on friendly terms with Churchill's successor in Trieste, J. Browning Spence. In a letter dated 18 October 1912, Spence thanked Joyce for his gift of *Chamber Music*: "Altho 'un profano' in such matters I have enjoyed much pleasure in reading the small book: I hope that the success that same has earned from the Press will lead you to higher flights!" He then wished Joyce well with

his series of *Hamlet* lectures. In a friendly four-page letter dated 28 June 1917, Spence, who had since become British Consul General in Tripoli, thanked Joyce for his gift of *A Portrait of the Artist as a Young Man*, praised him for having "struck out a line on your own – out of the ruck of the 'banal' fiction we are now fed with", and asked him for news on their shared acquaintances in Trieste. The two letters are kept at the Cornell Joyce Collection (Scholes nos 1258 and 1259).

7. Artifoni would have agreed with Bloom's opinion, "for an advertisement you must have repetition" (*U*, 12.1147–8).

8. Figures taken from the census of 1900. By 1910 the population had risen to 70,000, a sign that the city was enjoying a period of sustained economic growth.

9. Dante Alighieri, *La Divina Commedia*, Inferno, Canto IX, line 114.

10. *Il Giornaletto di Pola*, 2 January 1905. This was Pola's principal daily paper.

11. Alessandro Francini Bruni, "Joyce Stripped Naked in the Piazza", in Willard Potts, ed., *Portraits of the Artist in Exile: Recollections of James Joyce by Europeans* (Dublin: Wolfhound Press, 1979), 12.

12. Brioni was later chosen by Tito as his exclusive summer home and is now one of the finest natural parks on the Adriatic.

13. In a letter of 9 October 1906 (*LII*, 171), Joyce writes: "I am following with interest the struggle between the various socialist parties here at the Congress. Labriola spoke yesterday, the paper says, with extraordinarily rapid eloquence for two hours and a half. He reminds me somewhat of Griffith." The letter goes on to summarize Labriola's speech.

14. The lectures were reported in the local papers and in Trieste's *Il Lavoratore*, which wrote of the extraordinary success in Pola of Labriola, who had been "continuously interrupted with hurricanes of applause". See *Il Lavoratore* of 17 January 1904.

15. *Il Giornaletto di Pola*, 18 December 1904.

16. *Ibid.*, 6 November 1904.

17. Ivo Vidan, "Joyce and the South Slavs", in Niny Rocco Bergera, ed., *Atti del Third International James Joyce Symposium* (Trieste: Università degli Studi, 1974), 118.

18. Brenda Maddox, *Nora: A Biography of Nora Joyce* (London: Minerva, 1988), 73.

19. Joyce reported this to Stanislaus in a letter of 15 December 1904 (*LII*, 74). It was quite a turnabout given that only a month earlier Joyce had described Moore's "Untilled Field" as "Damned stupid" and complained about his factual errors and punctuation (*LII*, 70–1). Joyce's enthusiasm for Moore was short-lived and by 1906 he was making fun of him in his letters to Stanislaus, who evidently had praised him: "Yerra," wrote Joyce, "what's good in the end of *The Lake*?" (*LII*, 162).

20. Francini Bruni's 1922 lecture, which was published under the title "Joyce Stripped Naked in the Piazza", reveals his jealousy and is a colourful if not always reliable account of Joyce's early years in Pola and Trieste. Through Gorman, Joyce later took the trouble to protest about his former friend's published lecture in a footnote which began, "Alas for the lasting fidelities of friendship!" (Herbert Gorman, *James Joyce*, 264). On the other hand, Joyce did not break totally with Francini Bruni and at least one letter, and a friendly one at that, dated 23 March 1924 and written in Italian by Joyce, survives at the University of Southern Illinois library.

21. Advertisement of 7 September 1904 in *Il Giornaletto di Pola*.

22. Alessandro Francini Bruni, "Joyce Stripped Naked in the Piazza", 14.

23. Advertisement in *Il Giornaletto di Pola*, 6 November 1904.

24. Herbert Gorman, *James Joyce*, 132.

25. Advertisement in *Il Giornaletto di Pola*, 6 November 1904.

26. See Roy Gottfried, "Berlitz Schools Joyce", *James Joyce Quarterly* 16 (Fall 1978/Winter 1979), 223–37, and Hugh Kenner, "Approaches to the Artist as a Young Language Teacher", in H. Regnery, ed., *Viva Vivas!* (Indianapolis: Liberty Press, 1976), 331–53.

27. Alessandro Francini Bruni, "Joyce Stripped Naked in the Piazza", 15.

28. Stelio Crise, *Scritti*, a cura di Elvio Guagnini (Trieste: Edizioni Parnaso, 1995), 79.

29. This document is kept in the Archivio di Stato in Trieste.

30. See Albert J. Solomon, "Charles Lever: A Source for Joyce", *James Joyce Quarterly* 29, no. 4 (Summer 1992), 791–7.

PART TWO: A PORTRAIT OF "TARRY EASTY"

1. Louis Gillet, "The Living Joyce", in Willard Potts, ed., *Portraits of the Artist in Exile*, 192.

2. Giuseppe Bertelli, *Chi siamo e che cosa vogliamo* (Firenze: Edizioni Nerbini, 1902), 57.

3. Herbert Gorman, *James Joyce*, 142.

4. Philippe Soupault, "James Joyce", in Willard Potts, ed., *Portraits of the Artist in Exile*, 110.

5. Robert Musil, *Man Without Qualities*, translated by Eithne Wilkins and Ernest Kaiser (London: Secker & Warburg, 1960), 211.

6. Silvio Rutteri, *Trieste Romantica: Itinerari Sentimentali d'altri Tempi* (Trieste: Edizioni Italo Svevo, 1988), 88.

7. Scipio Slataper, *Il Mio Carso* (Milano: Mondadori, 1995 [1912]), 42.

8. Isabel Burton, *AEI – Arabia Egypt India, A Narrative of Travel* (London and Belfast: Mullan, 1879), 59.

9. Alessandro Francini Bruni, "Joyce Stripped Naked in the Piazza", 15.

10. From the preface to *First Book of English*, quoted by Roy Gottfried in his "Berlitz Schools Joyce", 224.

11. Alessandro Francini Bruni, "Joyce Stripped Naked in the Piazza", 24.

12. Giuseppe Bertelli, *Chi siamo e che cosa vogliamo*, 10.

13. *Ibid.*, 2.

14. Silvio Benco, "James Joyce in Trieste", in Willard Potts, ed., *Portraits of the Artist in Exile*, 50.

15. Brenda Maddox, *Nora*, 82.

16. Isabel Burton, *AEI – Arabia Egypt India, A Narrative of Travel*, 12.

17. Alma Mahler, *Gustav Mahler*, a cura di L. Rognoni, Italian translation by L. Dallapiccola (Milano: Il Saggiatore, 1960), 169.

18. *La Guida di Trieste* lists well over 150 private music teachers working in the city, compared with 45 private language teachers.

19. *Il Piccolo*, 3 July 1905.

20. Mario Doria, *Grande Dizionario del dialetto Triestino Storico, Etimologico, Fraseologico*, 173–4.

21. Brenda Maddox, *Nora*, 83.

22. La Signora Moisè Canarutto was born Eugenia Vivante in Ancona. She and her husband were practising Jews, and their marriage and the births of their children (Aida and Marcade) are registered in the archives of the synagogue in Trieste. He owned a carpet shop in Piazza Scuole Israele.

23. Robert Scholes and Richard M. Kain, eds, *The Workshop of Daedalus: James Joyce and the Raw Materials for A Portrait of the Artist as a Young Man* (Evanston, Ill.: Northwestern University Press, 1965), 99. This volume contains forty of Joyce's "epiphanies", the originals of which are kept at the University of Buffalo and at Cornell University.

24. Heyward Ehrlich, "'Araby' in context: The Splendid Bazaar, Irish Orientalism, and James Clarence Mangan", *James Joyce Quarterly* 35, nos 2 and 3 (Winter and Spring 1998), 309.

25. V.G. Kiernan, *The Lords of Human Kind: Black Man, Yellow Man and White Man in an Age of Empire* (Boston: Little Brown & Co., 1969), 131.

26. Edward Said, *Orientalism* (New York: Random House, 1978), 177.

27. *Ibid.*, 43.

28. R. Brandon Kershner, "*Ulysses* and the Orient", *James Joyce Quarterly* 35, 274.

29. See Raffaella Sgubin, "Between Paris and Vienna: Fashion in Joyce's Trieste", in Renzo S. Crivelli and John McCourt, eds, *Le Donne di Giacomo* (Trieste: Hammerle Editori, 1999), 30.

30. Interestingly in "Circe", as Carol Loeb Shloss points out, "when Zoe begins to fondle

Bloom, all of the red-light district begins to change into a scene of Oriental splendour". See
"Behind the Veil: James Joyce and the Colonial Harem", *James Joyce Quarterly* 35, 333.

31. This advertisement regularly appeared in the city papers. See *L'Adriatico*, 14 April 1909.

32. *Il Sentiero dei Mille Draghi, Viaggio, viandanti, donne e sogno nel mito dell'Estremo Oriente.*
Presentazione: Laura Ruaro Loseri; Catalogo: Luisa Crusvar; Contributi: Roberto Benedetti,
Marcello Manetti (Asolo: Acelum Edizione D'Arte, 1982), xvi–xvii.

33. In an unpublished letter of 11 April 1906 from Stanislaus Joyce to Katsy Murray, Stanislaus mentions "the Cing-alee" – a play that was staged in Trieste in 1906: "'Sherlock Holmes'
has been here and 'the Gheisha' and the 'Cing-alee' are coming for Easter." The letter is kept in
the Fallon Collection at the National University of Ireland.

34. Bryan Cheyette, "'Jewgreek is greekjew': The Disturbing Ambivalence of Joyce's Semitic
Discourse in *Ulysses*", *James Joyce Studies Annual* 3 (Summer 1992), 49.

35. See *Ibid.*, 54, for a discussion of the significance of the "biblically named 'Rehoboth ter-
race'".

36. For a convincing discussion of Molly's Jewishness see chapter 5 of Phillip Herring's *Joyce's
Uncertainty Principle* (Princeton: Princeton University Press, 1987).

37. In Gianni Pinguentini, "Come un francese vedeva Trieste nel 1890", *La Porta Orientale*,
Anno XVI, nos 1–3 (Jan.–March 1946), 47.

38. Stanislaus Joyce, *Triestine Book of Days*, 4 January 1907. In *Ulysses*, Joyce too would create
an "odalisk" called Zoe, who mocks Bloom's advances in the "Circe" episode.

39. Simonetta Chiabrando and Erik Schneider pointed this out to me.

40. A reference such as this can surely be employed to contradict Brandon Kershner's assertion that "in *Ulysses* … the Orientalism is entirely and explicity intertextual". See "*Ulysses* and
the Orient", *James Joyce Quarterly* 35, 293.

41. George Eliot, *Daniel Deronda* (Boston: Aldine Book Publishing, n.d.), 148.

42. R. Brandon Kershner, "*Ulysses* and the Orient", 291.

43. Suzette Henke, *James Joyce and the Politics of Desire* (New York and London: Routledge,
1990), 172.

44. The melon is also present in Stephen's mind in "Proteus" and in the following passage in
"Circe":

> STEPHEN
> Mark me. I dreamt of a watermelon.
> ZOE
> Go abroad and love a foreign lady.
> LYNCH
> Across the world for a wife.
> FLORRY
> Dreams goes by contraries. (*U*, 15.3922–8)

45. Corinna del Greco Lobner, *James Joyce's Italian Connection* (Iowa City: University of Iowa
Press, 1989), 24.

46. Stanislaus Joyce, *The Complete Dublin Diary of Stanislaus Joyce*, ed. George H. Healey
(Dublin: Anna Livia Press, 1994), 50.

47. Stanislaus Joyce, *My Brother's Keeper*, edited with an introduction by Richard Ellmann
(London: Faber and Faber, 1958), 231.

48. Stanislaus Joyce, *Triestine Book of Days*, 16 January 1907.

49. Quoted in Corinna del Greco Lobner, *James Joyce's Italian Connection*, 22. Lobner also
notes that in *Finnegans Wake* Joyce uses this Triestine form "O ciesa mia!" instead of the Italian
"O chiesa mia".

50. B.B. Delimata, daughter of his sister Eileen, remembered this clearly: "He used to go to
the Greek-Orthodox Church because he said he liked the ceremonies better there." See A. Cur-

tayne's interview published in E.H. Mikhail, ed., *James Joyce: Interviews and Recollections* (London: Macmillan, 1990), 64.

51. Alberto Spaini, "Autoritratto Triestino", in *Scrittori Triestini del Novecento* (Trieste, 1968), 953.

52. Angelo Ara and Claudio Magris, *Trieste: Un identità di frontiera* (Torino: Einaudi, 1982), 17.

53. An example of English in *Triestino* is the word "sonababic", coming from "son of a bitch". Another is the Triestine "mato" (fellow), which, as Stanislaus Joyce liked to point out, comes from the English "mate" and not from the Italian "matto".

54. According to *La Guida di Trieste* of 1905, 340, Trieste had a large group of interpreters working in at least twelve foreign languages: "araba, croato, czeca, ebraica, francese, greca, illirica, inglese, polacca, slovena, tedesca, ungarese".

55. L. Premuda, "La formazione intellettuale e scientifica di Constantin von Economo", *Rassegna di Studi Psichiatrici*, no. 6 (1977), 1327.

56. Two examples will suffice to give an idea. On 29 June 1911 they published one of many articles against the Slavs in this style, complaining that the Slavs had the best of everything Italian in Trieste, but stubbornly insisted on their own identity. "Vol narance Palermo, vol lemone de Messina (ki njanka no xe più zakaj tera de moto ha skovà via de Zezilia); vol kastanjeri farlani; vol lampareti kan mantura i baneto de fantarja de Talia; vol skolamento za pissar i lejer pr taljanska lingva." On 19 March 1912 they published an article in Frenchified Friulan complaining about Marinetti and Futurism: "Folk ti trai, ancemò une volte. Dans le coulonne de l'Indipendente il te ecrive formidables articles su la Torre dei morvi e dei cerli analizando les compagines et les propagines de la strutture de quei do usei tres crepados. Et crie et pleure desesperé sur le vandalisme de Guelfos et de Ghibelinos!"

57. Giovanni Bruggeri, "Joyce in carne ed ossa per le strade di Trieste", *Il Piccolo*, 25 October 1967.

58. Philippe Soupault, "James Joyce", in Willard Potts, ed., *Portraits of the Artist in Exile*, 110.

59. Sometimes the use of foreign languages was not so smooth – as in an advertisement for Emilio Hacher's liquor shop which boasted about its fine range of "Irisch Whisky and Schots Whisky" (*Il Piccolo*, 23 December 1905).

60. Rosa Maria Bosinelli has conclusively demonstrated this in her unpublished thesis *Gli Anni Triestini di Joyce* (University of Bologna, 1968).

61. Silvio Benco, "James Joyce in Trieste", 49. In his *James Joyce in Italia* (Verona: Linotipia Veronese di Ghidini e Fiorini, 1963), the Triestine scholar Gianni Pinguentini has traced a number of Triestine sources for the various nursery rhymes in *Ulysses*, such as "Give a thing and take it back/God'll ask you where is that/You'll say you don't know/God'll send you down below" from "Chi dà e po'l ciol/Ga la bizza soto el cuor/Lùnedì in caldiera/Màrtedi soto tera" or "Clap clap hands till Poldy comes home/Cake in his pocket for Leo alone" from the Triestine "Bati bati le manine che vegnerà papà/El porterà bomboni e Toni magnarà" (8 and 71).

62. Mario Doria, *Grande Dizionario del Dialetto Triestino*, 377. "Malora" in this use is a noun meaning "hell" or "the devil" but it was also used as an adjective meaning "damned".

63. In an entry of 27 May 1907 in his *Triestine Book of Days*, Stanislaus Joyce noted the Triestine fascination with language and expressed his regret at not speaking Irish, which would have been a great novelty: "here in Trieste they have respect for anyone who knows some strange outlandish language of which they are ignorant".

64. Don Gifford (with Robert J. Seidman), *"Ulysses" Annotated: Notes for James Joyce's "Ulysses"*, revised edition (Berkeley: University of California Press, 1982), 522.

65. *Ibid.*, 233.

66. Stanislaus Joyce, *Triestine Book of Days*, 15 August 1907. Joyce's interest in words that might be suitable in a Triestine brothel finds a parallel in the notebook kept by Doctor Sturli, a prominent consultant in the Ospedale Civico and a private student of his in 1913. The notebook contained an exercise to practise the pronunciation of the word "whore" and three pages of words "in use at that time for visits to brothels". As soon as he came to know that Sturli was to visit

London, Joyce "said that that (the brothels) would be the most interesting part of the journey". This information and these quotations are contained in a letter written by Bianca de Toma, to whom Sturli left the notebook, dated 20 May 1993. Sturli's notebook was also examined by Stelio Crise, who wrote a detailed description of it entitled "James eats jams" (a pronunciation exercise devised by Joyce to distinguish vowel sounds) and published in his *Scritti*, 64–6.

67. Stanislaus Joyce, *Triestine Book of Days*, 6 April 1907.

68. For further information on this topic see John McCourt and Erik Schneider, "Zois in nighttown", in Renzo S. Crivelli and John McCourt, eds, *Le Donne Di Giacomo*, 66–71.

69. Stanislaus Joyce, *Triestine Book of Days*, 17 April 1908.

70. Roland McHugh, *Annotations to Finnegans Wake* (London: Routledge and Kegan Paul, 1980), 237.

71. Among the families who came during this war were the Rallis, who were driven out of Smirne by the Turks. The Greek War of Independence is alluded to in "Proteus" by Stephen, who recalls Shelley's poetic drama *Hellas* which supported the cause of Greek liberty and hoped to see exiled Greeks return to the native land: "Across the sands of all the world, followed by the sun's flaming sword, to the west, trekking to evening lands" (*U*, 3.391).

72. He later bought six copies of Joyce's *Dubliners*.

73. In 1921 Ralli became the only Triestine subsriber to *Ulysses*, and is mentioned in *Finnegans Wake*, as "Fino Ralli" (*FW*, 447.24). According to a letter from the Joyce collector Croessmann to Ellmann, Joyce inscribed Ralli's copy of *Ulysses* "Al Barone Ambrogio Ralli, in segno di riconoscenza" – "To Baron Ralli with gratitude". Box 7, Ellmann Collection.

74. In a letter to Stanislaus dated 7 August 1912 (*LII*, 298) Joyce gives him instructions from Dublin about dealing with their landlord: "Don't let my debts trouble you. Tell them I am away and will return in the month of September. They would get the same answer at Economo's door and would salute and go away." Economo was probably the richest man in Trieste.

75. *L'Indipendente*, 28 November 1913.

76. In Robert Scholes and Richard M. Kain, eds, *The Workshop of Daedalus*, 104.

77. Two years later, on 17 November 1907, Stanislaus noted similar impressions in his diary following a visit to the Serb Orthodox Church, and this entry may later have been adopted by Joyce for Bloom's impressions of Mass in Westland Row: "I went to the Russian Church to see the Mass there. The singing was good. Their way of giving communion is the funniest I have seen yet. At the end of Mass, the celebrant announces the communion, disappears into the holy of holies, and reappears again with a large dish piled with small rolls of white bread. This is the signal for the congregation and all the little boys in the church to rush towards him and crawl and jostle round him, as in a football scrummage, stretching out their hands towards the dish. He holds the dish above his head and tries to control them, and laughs and talks with the ladies at the eagerness of the younger spry. I suppose he says, 'Can't you be patient, now! There's a lump of Him for everyone if you can take your time.' When the congregation have had their lumps they come away munching and putting on their hats."

78. For a detailed discussion on Joyce's borrowings from the Greek rite in "The Sisters", see Fred K. Lang, *Ulysses and the Irish God* (London and Toronto: Associated University Presses, 1993), 27–44. Lang believes that the relative informality of the Greek rite may have been the source for Fr Flynn's mass in "The Sisters".

79. Umberto Eco, *The Aesthetics of Chaosmos: The Middle Ages of Joyce* (Tulsa: The University of Tulsa Monograph Series, no. 18, 1982), 3.

80. Stanislaus Joyce, *Triestine Book of Days*, 18 September 1907.

81. *Ibid.*, 21 November 1907.

82. Among the studies of this issue, William T. Noon's *Joyce and Aquinas* (New Haven: Yale University Press, 1957) remains a seminal text.

83. Alessandro Francini Bruni, "Joyce Stripped Naked in the Piazza", 41.

84. From an interview carried out in July 1954 by Richard Ellmann. The interview is in Box 5 of the Richard Ellmann Collection.

85. Richard Ellmann's typescript of an unsent and unpublished letter written by Stanislaus Joyce to his father around 1910. The letter is in Box 77 of the Richard Ellmann Collection.

86. Trieste also had several caffès-chantant, ice-cream parlours, Hungarian-style bakeries and Viennese coffee shops.

87. Stanislaus Joyce, *Triestine Book of Days*, 7 June 1907.

88. "Andemo" – *Triestino* for "Let's go to …".

89. Ennio Gerolini, *Sempre alegri e mai passion! Fritolini, petesserie, teatri e cine de la Trieste de una volta* (Trieste: Editoriale Danubio, 1994), 22.

90. Alessandro Francini Bruni, "Joyce Stripped Naked in the Piazza", 31.

91. Brenda Maddox, *Nora*, 95.

92. Quoted in Bernard Wall, "Joyce e Svevo", *La Gazzetta dell'Emilia*, 16 March 1954.

93. Alessandro Francini Bruni, "Joyce Stripped Naked in the Piazza", 32.

94. *Il Piccolo*, 9 May 1905. Francesco Tamagno was an Italian tenor famous for being the first to play the leading role in Verdi's *Othello*. Joyce would later refer to him in *Finnegans Wake* in the phrase "Tamagnum sette-and-forte and his loud boheem toy" (*FW*, 404.26). Gemma Bellincioni was a particular favourite of Verdi and the first Santuzza in *Cavalleria Rusticana*. Joyce saw her singing the leading role in Strauss's *Salomé* in the Teatro Verdi in 1909. Patti was another renowned Italian opera singer.

95. Quoted in Stelio Crise, *Scritti*, 105.

96. A substantial figure compared with Dublin. Joyce noted the contrast in a letter to Stanislaus on 6 November 1906: "The Irish proletariat has yet to be created. A feudal peasantry exists, scraping the soil …" (*LII*, 185).

97. The official organs of the Italian and the Triestine socialist parties respectively.

98. Later from Rome on 6 February 1907, when Joyce's interest in socialism was already fading, he remembered Artifoni's interest in a letter to Stanislaus: "I have given up reading *Avanti* but enclose paragraph for Artifoni" (*LII*, 210).

99. Alessandro Francini Bruni, "Joyce Stripped Naked in the Piazza", 16.

100. Having left the Berlitz school, Almidano Artifoni taught several courses in accountancy at an evening school run by this society and later in 1910 Joyce joined him on the staff.

101. Giuseppe Bertelli, *Chi siamo e che cosa vogliamo*, 18.

102. *Il Piccolo*, 2 May 1905. Writing to Stanislaus from Rome in October 1906 about the Socialist Congress there, Joyce notes that "the two sub-editors of the *Avanti!* resigned. Ferri replaced them by Cicotti, formerly editor of the *Lavoratore* of Trieste and Labriola, who is to be German correspondent of the paper" (*LII*, 183).

103. *L'Indipendente*, 6 May 1905.

104. Folco Testena (Comunardo Braccialarghe), *Il Socialismo Triestino* (Milan, 1910), 11.

105. Susan L. Humphreys, "Ferrero Etc: James Joyce's Debt to Guglielmo Ferrero", *James Joyce Quarterly* 16 (Fall 1978/Winter 1979), 245.

106. Guglielmo Ferrero, *Militarism: A Contribution to the Peace Crusade*, anon. trs. (Boston: L.C. Page & Company, 1903), 82.

107. Giorgio Melchiori, "The Genesis of Ulysses", in Giorgio Melchiori, ed., *Joyce in Rome: The Genesis of Ulysses* (Rome: Bulzoni, 1984), 42.

108. *Ibid.*, 43.

109. *Ibid.*, 42–3.

110. Susan L. Humphreys, "Ferrero Etc: James Joyce's Debt to Guglielmo Ferrero", 246.

111. Robert Spoo, "'Una Piccola Nuvoletta': Ferrero's Young Europe and Joyce's Mature *Dubliners* Stories", *James Joyce Quarterly* 24, no. 4 (Summer 1987), 401–10.

112. *Ibid.*, 402–3.

113. Edward Brandabur, *A Scrupulous Meanness: A Study of Joyce's Early Work* (Urbana: University of Illinois Press, 1971), 96.

114. Giulio Caprin, *Trieste e L'Italia* (Milano: Rava & C. Editori, 1915), 19.

115. Quoted in Folco Testena, *Il Socialismo Triestino*, 20.

116. Isabel Burton had noted this thirty years earlier: "Panslavism is still rampant in Austria, and the clergy puff up the patriotic movement with all their might." Isabel Burton, *AEI – Africa, Egypt, India, A Narrative of Travel*, 51

117. Cesare Battisti quoted in Livia Battisti, "Socialismo Trentino ed Adriatico nell'Impero Absburgico", Conferenza tenuta il 29 Aprile 1971 al Circolo di studi politico-sociali "Che Guevara" di Trieste, 21.

118. Giorgio Pittoni in *Il Lavoratore*, 31 August 1901.

119. Quoted in *L'Indipendente*, 28 April 1905, from a pamphlet entitled *Socialismo, Nazionalismo, Irredentismo nelle provincie adriatiche orientali*.

120. *Ibid.*

121. John Gatt-Rutter, *Italo Svevo: A Double Life* (Oxford: Clarendon Press, 1988), 227.

122. Stanislaus Joyce, *The Complete Dublin Diary of Stanislaus Joyce*, 54.

123. Stanislaus Joyce, *Triestine Book of Days*, 10 May 1907.

124. *Ibid.*, 22 April 1907.

125. There was a remarkable interest in Esperanto in Trieste and in 1910 a *Circolo Esperantistico* was founded and ran courses in the Civica Scuola on via Giotti, a school where Joyce also held lessons. The newspapers also carried regular features on Esperanto.

126. Herbert Gorman, *James Joyce*, p. 188.

127. Ellmann (*JJ*, 199) states incorrectly that his singing teacher was Giuseppe Sinico, who was famous for having composed the city's anthem *L'Inno di San Giusto*. In 1905 Giuseppe Sinico was in such bad health that he had already passed his teaching commitments over to his son. He died two years later.

128. According to Ellmann, Joyce later recalled that in one of his dreams Molly Bloom "had become slighly grey and looked like *La Dusè*" (*JJ*, 549).

129. The next day *L'Indipendente's* critic was enthusiastic about the concert and found space to praise Schott: "All the lovers of music must thank Mr Enrico Schott who, with the disinterest of a patron in love with the beautiful art of sounds, made possible a concert of such rich importance, and is preparing others." Schott was an older brother of Edoardo Schott, Joyce's best Triestine student and later one of his friends in Zürich. The Schott family were important for Joyce and provided him with many links to literary and musical culture in Trieste. Joyce mentions Enrico Schott in a letter of 5 September 1909 to Nora from Dublin (*LII*, 168): "But I will send on a copy of *Chamber Music* from London. Tell Stannie to take it to my binder and have it done exactly like the one for Schott …".

130. According to *Il Piccolo* of 7 December 1905, *Ali-Babà* included scenes entitled *Il bazar di Cassini, La piazza di Bagdad, La grotta dei 40 ladroni, Il mercato di Bagdad, Il Palazzo di Alì*. Perhaps Joyce was influenced by this show in the writing of "Araby". When Joyce has the boy read "the words Café Chantant" which "were written in coloured lamps" this may also be a Triestine reference as there were at least four such cafés in the city.

131. Alessandro Francini Bruni, "Recollections of Joyce", in Willard Potts, ed., *Portraits of the Artist in Exile*, 40.

132. The original document is kept in the Cornell Joyce Collection while a facsimile version is available in M. Groden, ed., *The James Joyce Archive* (New York and London: Garland Publishing, 1979), vol. II, 1–105.

133. See Robert E. Scholes, *The Cornell Joyce Collection: A Catalogue* (Ithaca: Cornell University Press, 1961), 17.

134. Serenella Zanotti's "Per un ritratto dell'artista Italianato: Note sull'Italiano di James Joyce", in *Studi Linguistici Italiani*, vol. XXV (Rome: Salerno Editore, 1999), 16–64, spots a reference to Giovanni Scholz, Joyce's landlord in via Scussa (where he lived in 1909) and to Tolstoy's being "al punto di morte" – on the brink of death ; the Russian writer died on 8 November 1910.

135. This was in fact a children's edition of *Tresor* edited by Luigi Carver. See Serenella Zanotti, op. cit., 34.

136. Francini Bruni left the school shortly after Joyce and took up a position as a proofreader and occasional journalist in *Il Piccolo.*

PART THREE: WAS IST EINE NATION?
1. Title of essay set for the final-year students in the state school of Trieste in 1913. Evidently the issue of nationhood was a very live one in Trieste at this time. Quoted in Anna Millo, *L'Elite del potere a Trieste: Una biografia collettiva 1891–1938* (Milano: Franco Angeli, 1989), 187.

2. "Orco Dio" is a strong Italian/Triestine curse roughly translating as "Pig God".

3. Franco Onorati, "Bank Clerk in Rome", in Giorgio Melchiori, ed., *Joyce in Rome: The Genesis of Ulysses,* 31.

4. Herbert Gorman, *James Joyce,* 188.

5. John Francis Byrne's prophecy was that Joyce would become a drunkard.

6. Stanislaus Joyce, *Triestine Book of Days,* 7 March 1907.

7. *Ibid.,* 7–31 March 1907.

8. *Ibid.*

9. *Ibid.,* 7 March 1907.

10. This information is contained in Stanislaus Joyce, *Triestine Book of Days.* In a document sent from the Ospitale Civico of Trieste, dated 5 August 1907, Joyce's address is given as via Nuova, 45 (Cornell Joyce Collection, Scholes no. 1414). Although Ellmann had access to these documents he makes no mention of the Joyces ever having lived at this address. He simply says "They had stayed only a few days with Francini in 1907, then took some adjoining rooms, rather than a flat, a 1 via Santa Catarina, where Stanislaus, to save money, joined them" (*JJ,* 267).

11. This was complicated further by the fact that Joyce regularly, and not always successfully, tried to borrow money from Svevo. In 1932, having read a draft of Stanislaus's preface to *As a Man Grows Older,* a translation of Svevo's *Senilità,* Joyce wrote to his brother: "I wish it were a little clearer than it is that Schmitz was very careful of his money." And in a postscript to the same letter, he added: "Also my relations with S were quite formal. I never crossed the soglia except as a paid teacher" (*LIII,* 241).

12. Livia Veneziani Svevo, *Memoir of Italo Svevo,* trs. Isabel Quigly (London: Libris, 1989), 6.

13. Elio Schmitz, *Lettere a Svevo e Diario di Elio Schmitz* (Milano: dall'Oglio, 1973), 254; and Livia Veneziani Svevo, *Memoir of Italo Svevo,* 9.

14. Stanislaus Joyce, *The Complete Dublin Diary of Stanislaus Joyce,* 50.

15. Elio Schmitz, *Lettere a Svevo e Diario di Elio Schmitz,* 7.

16. Livia Veneziani Svevo, *Memoir of Italo Svevo,* 16.

17. Silvio Benco, "Prefazione" to *La Coscienza di Zeno* (Milan: dall'Oglio, 1962), 12.

18. John Gatt-Rutter, *Italo Svevo: A Double Life* (Oxford: Clarendon Press, 1988), 230.

19. Quoted in Ettore Mo, "Quando Svevo e Joyce litigavano", *Corriere della Sera,* 21 November 1987.

20. John Gatt-Rutter, *Italo Svevo,* 231.

21. Brian Moloney, *Italo Svevo narratore Lezioni triestine* (Gorizia: Libreria Editrice Goriziana, 1998), 24.

22. Stanislaus Joyce, *The Meeting of Svevo and Joyce* (Udine: Del Bianco, 1965), 18.

23. John Gatt-Rutter, *Italo Svevo,* 234. Gatt-Rutter also points out that Svevo remarked of Bloom for his lecture: "A practical man. In the funeral carriage he considers advising the town council to arrange for corpses to be transported by tram: Practical. Non-stop to the cemetery entrance in special coffins. As they do in Milan, he says. The elder Dedalus ridicules the idea: Pullman, restaurant car? But Bloom likes it. He is the practical fantast."

24. Antonio Fonda Savio, "Ettore Schmitz (in arte Italo Svevo) nella vita di ogni giorno", published version of a lecture held at the Italian-American Cultural Association in Trieste on 8 January 1966.

25. Quoted in Livia Veneziani Svevo, *Memoir of Italo Svevo*, 7.

26. Joyce alluded to this in a letter to Stanislaus dated 29 March 1932, when he wrote "his wife became longsighted when she met Nora in the street" (*LIII*, 241).

27. The original letter is in Italian. Joyce remained in regular contact with the Schmitzes after leaving Trieste and was deeply shocked to hear of Ettore's death in a car accident in 1928. He wrote a warm letter of sympathy to Livia, recalling an "old friend for whom I had always affection and esteem" (*LI*, 270).

28. The columnist Vespertino in *L'Emancipazione*, 5 December 1908.

29. Stanislaus Joyce, *Triestine Book of Days*, 9–31 March 1907.

30. Quoted in Stanislaus Joyce, *Triestine Book of Days*, 11 August 1907.

31. Isabel Burton, *The Life of Sir Richard Burton* (London and Belfast: Mullan, 1891), 306–7.

32. Isabel Burton, *AEI – Arabia Egypt India, A Narrative of Travel*, 44–6.

33. Teodoro Mayer was born in Trieste on 17 February 1860. His parents were Ladislao Mayer and Zanobia Ascoli. His mother was a cousin of the famous glottologist GraziaDio Ascoli. After Trieste rejoined Italy he was made a senator. Because of the racial laws he had to cede *Il Piccolo* to Rino Alessi in 1938. He died in Rome in 1942.

34. This happens, for instance, in the "Cyclops" episode where we read of Bloom "selling bazaar tickets or what do you call it royal Hungarian privileged lottery. True as you're there. O, commend me to an israelite! Royal and privileged Hungarian robbery" (*U*, 12.776–80). In the third version of the same episode Bloom is hailed in Hungarian: "A large and appreciative gathering of friends and acquaintances from the metropolis and greater Dublin assembled in their thousands to bid farewell to Nagyasàs uram Lipòti Virag" (*U*, 12.1814–16). A few lines later Bloom is applauded as follows: "The departing guest was the recipient of a hearty ovation, many of those who were present being visibly moved when the select orchestra of Irish pipes struck up the well-known strains of *Come Back to Erin*, followed immediately by *Rakóczsy's March*" (*U*, 12.1825–9).

35. Virag's second cousin, Stephen Virag, is also cited in *Ulysses* and he too comes from Hungary, this time from Szekesfejervar, a town which is also listed in *La Guida di Trieste* on the same page as the market town of Szombathely. Bloom's mother also has a Hungarian root: "Ellen Higgins, second daughter of Julius Higgins (born Karoly)" (*U*, 17.536–7).

36. Bruno Coceani, "Ricordo di Marino de Szombathely", *La Porta Orientale*, Anno VIII, N.S., no. 1–2, 1972.

37. Herbert Gorman, *James Joyce*, p. 143; Mary Colum, *Life and the Dream* (New York, 1947).

38. Angelo Vivante, *L'Irredentismo Adriatico*, 62.

39. F.K. Stanzel, "All Europe Contributed to the Making of Bloom: New Light on Leopold Bloom's Ancestors", *James Joyce Quarterly* 32, nos 3 and 4 (Spring and Summer 1995), 619–30.

40. Quoted by Attilio Tamaro in Mario Alberti et al., *Italy's Great War and Her National Aspirations* (Milan: Alfieri & Lacroix, 1917).

41. F.K. Stanzel, "All Europe Contributed to the Making of Bloom", 626.

42. A member of the *consiglio direttivo* of the Liberal Nationalist party, Tamaro was an intransigent irredentist, a leader in the battles for an Italian-language university in Trieste as well as a journalist who worked for both *Il Piccolo* and *L'Indipendente*.

43. Information on the Università Popolare is contained in "Relazione sul Primo decennio d'attività della Università Popolare Triestina, 1900–1910", Editrice L'Università Popolare Triestina. The university organized concerts and big lectures, often on Sundays, and weekly lessons on particular themes. The public lectures were very well attended. In 1905–6, there were 17 lectures attended by a total of 14,986 students, an average of 893. In 1906–7, 14 lectures were attended by 9,564 people, an average of 683. In 1907–8, 23 lectures were attended by a total of 21,360 students, an average of 928. In 1907–8 Joyce's was one of 136 lessons attended by 9,070 students, an average of 66 students per lesson.

44. See Giorgio Negrelli, "In Tema di Irredentismo e di Nazionalismo", in Roberto Pertici, ed., *Intellettuali di Frontiera: Triestini a Firenze 1900–1950* (Milano: Olschki Editore, 1985), 291.

45. Claudio Magris, "Tavola Rotonda", in Roberto Pertici, ed., *Intellettuali di Frontiera: Triestini a Firenze 1900–1950*, 402.

46. Quoted in Seamus Deane, "Joyce and Nationalism", in Colin MacCabe, ed., *James Joyce: New Perspectives* (London: Harvester, 1982), 170.

47. Frank Budgen, *James Joyce and the Making of Ulysses* (Oxford: Oxford University Press, 1972), 359. Jim also told Stannie that he considered "every hour spent in the study of Irish an hour wasted" (Stanislaus Joyce, *Triestine Book of Days*, 10 May 1907).

48. Attilio Tamaro in Mario Alberti et al., *Italy's Great War and Her National Aspirations*, 37.

49. Giulio Caprin, *Trieste e L'Italia* (Milano: Rava & C. Editori, 1915).

50. *Ibid.*, 11.

51. Attilio Tamaro, *L'Adriatico – Golfo d'Italia* (Milano: Fratelli Treves Editori, 1915), 135.

52. *Ibid.*, 144.

53. Emer Nolan, *James Joyce and Nationalism* (London and New York: Routledge, 1995), 129.

54. Attilio Tamaro, *L'Adriatico – Golfo d'Italia*, 148–51.

55. Attilio Tamaro in Mario Alberti et al., *Italy's Great War and Her National Aspirations*, 107.

56. *Ibid.*, 109–10.

57. Statute of the Società Triestina, Austria (Trieste, 1893), 3.

58. Attilio Tamaro, *Storia di Trieste*, vol. II (Trieste: Lint, 1976), 465.

59. *Ibid.*, 40.

60. *Ibid.*, 448.

61. *Ibid.*, 449.

62. *Ibid.*, 463.

63. *L'Adriatico*, 28 January 1909.

64. *Ibid.*, 10 August 1908.

65. John Gatt-Rutter, *Italo Svevo: A Double Life*, 219.

66. Vidacovich served as President of the Biblioteca Popolare Communale and was also on the board of the Biblioteca Civica. He was Consigliere Communale in 1913. He was also a member of the "Commisione Ordinatice" of the Università Popolare, 1900–1910.

67. *Il Palvese*, 12 May 1907.

68. *Ibid.*, 7 March 1907.

69. Stanislaus Joyce, *Triestine Book of Days*, 8 March 1907.

70. Attributed to Joyce by Alessandro Francini Bruni in his "Joyce Stripped Naked in the Piazza", 29.

71. *Il Palvese*, 14 April 1907. Vidacovich's review is almost prophetic for future readers of Joyce, not only because Joyce would later draw heavily on Georg Brandes's *William Shakespeare* for the "Scylla and Charybdis" episode of *Ulysses*, but because it actually suggests a way of reading Joyce's own work: "No detail of a poet's life is without importance for us: in the ethnic and familial origins we look for the early signs of his human and poetical nature; his education and childhood environment help explain his character to us; the personal affairs are reflected in the poetic output and the poetry reverberates in their lives [...] Even when he does not speak in the first person, the poet always reveals something of himself." Vidacovich's comments about Brandes also prefigure Stephen's belief about *Hamlet*: that Shakespeare was essentially writing about his own life. In a letter to Stanislaus in 1906, Joyce noted with interest that "Brandes is a Jew", and this fact also intrigued Vidacovich, who wrote: "Everyone knows that Giorgio Morris Cohen Brandes was born into a Jewish family, and it is easy to link certain characteristics of his spirit, such as his almost religious enthusiasm for the cause of freedom, and his practical sense which he showed when inspiring and leading the great movement which renewed the intellectual life of the North after 1870, to these origins."

72. The middle-class Italian culture was catered for by the Società filarmonica-drammatica, while the Slovenes founded their own Narodni Dom in 1904 and the Austrians had their Schiller-Verein. Reading was encouraged among the lower classes and made available through

the libraries. The irredentists ran the Società per la lettura popolare and the Biblioteche popolari circolante, the Slovenes had the Slovanska Citalnika and the Trzasko podporno in bralno drustvo, the Germans the Deutsches Haus.

73. The Slav Trzaski Sokol and German Turnverein Eintracht and the Società triestina Austria performed similiar functions for the Slovene and Austrian populations.

74. Letter of 1 May 1913 from Sansone Venezian. The letter is kept in the James Joyce Collection at Cornell University (Scholes no. 1292).

75. Stanislaus Joyce, *My Brother's Keeper*, 191

76. *Il Piccolo della Sera*, 17 April 1907.

77. *Ibid.*, 11 May 1907.

78. *Ibid.*

79. *Ibid.*, 28 May 1907.

80. This letter is in the possession of Mrs Teresita Zajotti and is dated 9 June 1929.

81. This edition is signed F. Venezian – suggesting that the leader of Trieste's irredentist movement was familiar with Ireland's literature and that Joyce may have even given him English lessons.

82. The article was entitled "Il Fenianismo. L'Ultimo Feniano", and appeared on 22 March 1907.

83. Silvio Benco, "James Joyce in Trieste", in Willard Potts, ed., *Portraits of the Artist in Exile*, 52.

84. Stanislaus Joyce, *Triestine Book of Days*, 9–31 April 1907. Unfortunately Stanislaus does not explain the nature of these changes.

85. *Ibid.*, 14 May 1907.

86. Giorgio Melchiori, "The Genesis of *Ulysses*", in *Joyce in Rome*, 46.

87. Joseph Valente, *James Joyce and the Problem of Justice*, 46.

88. *Il Piccolo della Sera*, 6 August 1907.

89. This is a three-page document containing notes for these articles and for his lecture, kept in the Cornell Joyce Collection (Scholes no. 43). Scholes dates it circa 1907–12 but there are so many parallels between the notes contained in it and the 1907 articles that it can confidently be dated in 1907.

90. Stelio Crise, *Scritti*, 51.

91. Gianni Pinguentini, *James Joyce in Italia*, 235.

92. Dominic Manganiello, *Joyce's Politics* (London: Routledge and Kegan Paul, 1980), 139.

93. Stanislaus Joyce, *Triestine Book of Days*, 2 April 1907. Joyce justified his publishing in England on the grounds that if his book (*Chamber Music*) came out in Dublin it would not sell more than thirty copies, whereas "The English was the biggest reading public in the world".

94. Stanislaus Joyce, *Triestine Book of Days*, 16 May 1907.

95. *Ibid.*, 24 April 1907.

96. Emer Nolan, *James Joyce and Nationalism*, 99

97. Stanislaus Joyce, *Triestine Book of Days*, 2 May 1907.

98. All of these documents are kept at the Cornell Joyce Collection (Scholes nos 1406 and 1407). They date from 7 November 1910 to 31 July 1911.

99. Letter of 5 September 1912 from Charles Joyce to Stanislaus Joyce (*LII*, 316).

100. "Ireland, Island of Saints and Sages", in *Critical Writings*, 153–74.

101. "Relazione sul Primo decennio d'attività della Università Popolare Triestina, 1900–1910."

102. Stanislaus Joyce, *Triestine Book of Days*, 27 April 1907.

103. Joyce would have been well aware of the parallel here with Trieste, where a foreign-sounding name like Szombathely or Vidacovich or Schmitz was of little use in helping one to identify the national allegiance of a person. The three mentioned, respectively of Hungarian, Slav and German origins, were all irredentists of varying shades.

104. Stanislaus Joyce, *Triestine Book of Days*, 20 April 1907.

105. L.H. Platt, "Joyce and the Anglo-Irish Revival: The Triestine Lectures", *James Joyce Quarterly* 29 (Winter 1992), 262–4.

106. Stanislaus Joyce, *Triestine Book of Days*, 18 April 1907.

107. Kathleen Ferris, *James Joyce and the Burden of Disease* (Oklahoma: University of Oklahoma Press, 1995), 5–6.

108. Brenda Maddox, *Nora*, 112.

109. The typescript of this interview is kept in the Ellmann Collection at the University of Tulsa. Francini Bruni makes several assertions here that contradict his own versions of events given in his earlier essay, "Joyce Stripped Naked in the Piazza". Perhaps, some fifty years after the events he describes took place, his memory was no longer as reliable as it once was.

110. Stanislaus Joyce, *Triestine Book of Days*, 25 July 1907.

111. This document is kept in the Cornell Joyce Collection (Scholes no. 1414).

112. Stanislaus Joyce, *Triestine Book of Days*, 16 August 1907.

113. *Ibid.*, 6 July 1907.

114. *Ibid.*, 25 September 1907.

115. Herbert Gorman, *James Joyce*, 193.

116. Richard Ellmann, preface to Stanislaus Joyce, *My Brother's Keeper*, xvii.

117. Stanislaus Joyce, *Triestine Book of Days*, 3 March 1907.

118. *Ibid.*, 26 August 1907.

119. *Ibid.*, 2 January 1908.

120. *Ibid.*, 16 April 1907.

121. *Ibid.*, 29 June 1907.

122. *Ibid.*, 7 September 1907.

123. *Ibid.*, 20 September 1907.

124. *Ibid.*, 5 February 1908.

125. Laura Pelaschiar, "Of brother, diaries, and umbrellas: News from Stanislaus Joyce", *Joyce Studies in Italy* 5, ed. Franca Ruggieri (Rome: Bulzoni Editore, 1998), 221.

126. Stanislaus Joyce, *Triestine Book of Days*, 1 June 1908.

127. *Ibid.*, 31 May 1908.

128. Stanislaus Joyce, *Triestine Book of Days*, 10 February 1908. *Hamlet* was also produced as part of the 1909 *Stagione di Prosa Autunno* in the Teatro Verdi, which also included Sudermann's *La Fine de Sodoma* and *Pietra*, Hauptmann's *Il Vetturale Henschel* and Sem Benelli's *La Cena delle Beffe*.

129. *Ibid.*, 28 February 1908.

130. *And they call me the jewel of Asia,*
   Of Asia,
   The geisha (*U*, 6.355–7).

131. *Il Gazzettino*, 19 June 1908.

132. Stanislaus Joyce, *Triestine Book of Days*, 11 October 1908.

133. Born in Pola in 1854, Smareglia studied in Gorizia, Vienna, Graz and then Milan, where his first pieces were performed at the conservatory and later at the Paris Exposition. In 1879 his first opera *Preziosa* was performed at the Teatro "Dal Verme" in Milan and was soon followed by other successful operas, including *Bianca di Cernia*. He returned to live in Trieste in the early 1880s, and in 1889 his *Il Vassallo di Szigeth* opened at the Imperial Theatre in Vienna and was hailed by Brahms. In 1895 his most famous work, *Nozze Istriane*, premiered in the Teatro Verdi in Trieste and was later put on in Venice, where it was warmly applauded by Puccini. In 1897 his opera *La Falena* (libretto by Silvio Benco) was produced and earned Verdi's praise. In 1903 *Oceana*, conducted by Toscanini, was enthusiastically received in La Scala in Milan by a huge audience that included Gabriele D'Annunzio.

134. Aurelia Gruber Benco, "Between Joyce and Benco", *James Joyce Quarterly*, Spring 1972, 331.

135. *Il Piccolo* of 13 February 1936 remembered Bartoli fondly on his death: "This magnificent man of music was born on 1 January 1875 … Romeo was very precocious in his musical abilities: at four years of age, without a teacher, he played the piano; at eight he was brought to the opera, and, as soon as he got back home, he began to play by ear all the music he had heard. But he was given no formal musical training and he remained an autodidact … he went to uni-

versity to study mathematics and during his holidays he conducted a small orchestra of friends. His family suffered financial ruin and he was forced to abandon university and thus began a long precarious bohemian existence. His bills were famous and so was the serene indifference which allowed him to live without any money; equally famous was his musical temperament, his superb musical taste. At that time he met *il Maestro Smareglia*, who quickly spotted the young man's genius. Bartoli thus became his inseparable companion for several years, and he learned composition and singing teaching from him. Soon, Bartoli was invited to work as choir-master in our theatres; in 1899 he was conductor for the opera season in the Politeama Rossetti, in which Flotow's *L'Ombra* and other works were performed." The writer goes on to praise his work in the Verdi, as the creator of the madrigal choir and as a teacher: "One of his most precious apostles was Attilio Tamaro, who was then secretary of the Università Popolare. Under its auspices, triumphal evenings of sixteenth- and seventeenth-century Italian madrigal music were held between 1910 and 1912."

136. No record of this concert exists. In a letter of 19 July 1909 to G. Molyneux Palmer, the Irish composer who in 1909 set to music some of the poems of *Chamber Music*, Joyce wrote that he thought the opera was "pretentious stuff" (*LI*, 67). George Borach, on the other hand, said that Joyce referred to it as "My favourite Wagnerian opera". See Georges Borach, "Conversations with Joyce", in Willard Potts, ed., *Portraits of the Artist in Exile*, 72.

137. Stanislaus Joyce, *Triestine Book of Days*, 23 October 1908.

138. *Ibid.*, 12 October 1908.

139. *Ibid.*, 14 October 1908. Mrs Francini Bruni was "a spoiled prima donna" with a diploma from the conservatory of Milan, who had sung twenty-eight times in opera, been offered an engagement worth seven thousand crowns in Spain, but had been forbidden by her father from pursuing a career which he considered morally dangerous.

140. It was first performed in Trieste in January 1905 with La Duse in the title role and came back again in December 1913. This latter production, which took place in the Politeama Rossetti, may have been attended by Joyce and may have contributed to his decision to mention Hedda Gabler in *Giacomo Joyce*.

141. This temptress figure was very much in vogue in contemporary Triestine art and would make its way into the matrix of allusions connected to the mysterious young lady in *Giacomo Joyce*.

142. Guido Hermet, "La Vita Musicale a Trieste (1801–1944), con speciale riferimento alla musica vocale", *Archeografo Triestino*, 1947, 228.

143. *L'Adriatico*, 25 March 1909.

144. The original letter, in Italian, is kept in the Cornell Joyce Collection (Scholes no. 1286).

145. Herbert Gorman, *James Joyce*, 196. Joyce later corrected Gorman's text, adding: "Italian translations were made in collaboration with Dr. Nicolò Vidacovich of Trieste." See Hugh Witemeyer, "'He gave the Name': Herbert Gorman's Rectifications of *James Joyce: His First Forty Years*", *James Joyce Quarterly* 32, nos 3 and 4 (Spring and Summer 1995), 527.

146. Quoted in Stelio Crise's commentary in Bruno Chersicla, *E' Tornato Joyce, iconografia triestina per Zois* (Milano: Nuova Rivista Europea, 1982, unpaginated).

147. The original of this letter, dated 21 August 1909, is kept in the Cornell Joyce Collection (Scholes no. 1294). Stanislaus Joyce's *Triestine Book of Days*, 9 January 1908, reveals that "Jim seems better today: no talk of rheumatism, and an appetite. He has discovered some place where they sell oatmeal – real live oatmeal – and Nora made porridge for him and herself this morning."

148. James Joyce, "Programme Notes for the English Players" (*CW*, 250).

149. Stanislaus Joyce, *My Brother's Keeper*, 215.

150. *Ibid.*

151. Joan Fitzgerald, "James Joyce's translation of *Riders to the Sea*", *Joyce Studies in Italy* 2, ed. Carla de Petris, 154.

152. J.M. Synge, *The Playboy of the Western World* and *Riders to the Sea* (London: Unwin Books, 1971), 83.

153. James Joyce and Nicolò Vidacovich, *La Cavalcata al Mare*, in *Poesie e Prose*, a cura di Franca Ruggieri (Milano: Arnoldo Mondadori, 1992), 670.

154. As Dario Calimani has discovered, Joyce's "The Boarding House" was also published in Italian in *Il Popolo di Trieste* 1929 under the title "Petali d'Arancio" (see Dario Calimani, "'The Boarding House': An Italian Variant?", *James Joyce Quarterly* 32, no. 2 [Winter 1995], 209–26.) Calimani rules out Amalia Popper as translator, but does not consider Vidacovich, who could well have worked on this short story. (Letter of 14 September 1916 to W.B. Yeats [*LI*, 95].)

155. "La Fortuna del Grand Guignol", *L'Adriatico*, 6 April 1909.

156. *L'Adriatico*, 20 May 1909.

157. Stanislaus Joyce, *My Brother's Keeper*, 52.

PART FOUR: LA NOSTRA BELLA TRIESTE

1. Joyce as quoted in Italo Svevo, *James Joyce* (Norfolk, Conn.: New Directions, 1950).

2. James Joyce to Nora Barnacle, 22 December 1909 (*SL*, 193).

3. In a partially unpublished interview with Richard Ellman in July 1954, Francini Bruni claimed that Joyce "used to say, 'Trieste is my second country'". He also stated that Joyce said "his personality had been formed at Trieste". Ellmann's notes are to be found in Box 5 of the Richard Ellmann Collection at the University of Tulsa.

4. Stanislaus Joyce, *Triestine Book of Days*, 6 February 1908.

5. J.F. Byrne, *Silent Years* (New York: Farrar, Straus and Young, 1953), 156.

6. Stanislaus Joyce, *Triestine Book of Days*, 17 April 1907.

7. Quoted in Corinna del Greco Lobner, "A Giornalista Triestino: James Joyce's Letter to *Il Marzocco*", *Joyce Studies Annual*, 1993, 189.

8. *Il Piccolo*, 27 August 1905.

9. Dublin was the setting for the 1903 Gordon Bennett International Automobile Racing Cup and the backdrop for Joyce's short story "After the Race", which he published in *The Irish Homestead* on 17 December 1904. In *Ulysses* Joyce makes many allusions to the Gordon Bennett Cup of 1904, beginning in "Hades" when Martin Cunningham mentions it: "That will be a great race tomorrow in Germany. The Gordon Bennett" (*U*, 6.369–70).

10. Leopoldo Fregoli was an important transformist who performed several times in Trieste and is a plausible model for Leopold Bloom in "Circe". Further information on Fregoli is to be found in the section on Futurism below.

11. This was a German production originally entitled *Die Judin* made by the Deutsche Bioscop in 1908.

12. Stanislaus Joyce, *Triestine Book of Days*, 1 November 1908.

13. *Il Piccolo*, 4 April 1909.

14. *Ibid.*, 15 August 1910.

15. This operetta was produced in the Anfiteatro Minerva in the summer of 1908. Stanislaus saw another production of it in April 1906. The main female character was called Miss Molly.

16. Contrary to Ellman's statement that "all five partners" signed the agreement, there is no mention in it of the fifth, Francesco Novak, who appears to have entered the company later.

17. The original copy of the contract is in the possession of Signora Teresita Zajotti, Trieste. All quotations from it are taken from this source.

18. This letter of 17 October 1909 from Vidacovich to Joyce is kept in the Cornell Joyce Collection (Scholes no. 1295).

19. Stanislaus Joyce, *Triestine Book of Days*, 20 July 1908.

20. Bloom mentions "Devilled Crab" in "Laestrygonians" (*U*, 8.762).

21. *Evening Telegraph*, 21 December 1909.

22. These titles are quoted in Peter Costello's *James Joyce: The Years of Growth*, 291.

23. These titles are listed in *Sinn Féin* and in *The Evening Telegraph* from January to April 1910.

24. *Sinn Féin*, 12 February 1910.

25. *Ibid.*, 19 February 1910.

26. *Ibid.*, 26 February 1910.

27. This letter of 18 April 1910 from Vidacovich to Joyce is kept in the Cornell Joyce Collection (Scholes no. 1295).

28. The last sentence of the letter can be translated as: "The children, the fire, a nice meal, an espresso, a Brasil [a type of cigar] ..."

29. The invoice from the Campagnia Singer Società Anonima in Macchine da cucire, dated 15 July 1910, is kept in the Cornell Joyce Collection (Scholes no. 1416).

30. Brenda Maddox, *Nora*, 150–1.

31. Michael Mason, "Why is Leopold Bloom a Cuckold?", *English Literary History* XLIV, 1977, 171–88.

32. Corinna del Greco Lobner, *James Joyce's Italian Connection*, 11.

33. *Poems* and *Exiles*, 344.

34. The letter is kept in the Fondo Benco of the Biblioteca Civica di Trieste.

35. *L'Adriatico*, 13 August 1908.

36. *Ibid.*

37. Before this he wrote to the Triestine writer Elda Gianelli, asking her to organize "through the intellectual salons, a favourable reception for him and a well-disposed audience". Quoted in Roberto Curci and Gabriella Ziani, *Bianco, Rosa e Verde: Scrittrici a Trieste fra '800 e '900* (Trieste: Lint, 1993), 265.

38. *L'Adriatico*, 3 December 1908. The front-page article was entitled "Marinetti" and was written by Faust.

39. Francini Bruni in a partially unpublished interview with Richard Ellmann carried out in July 1954. Ellmann's notes are to be found in Box 5 of the Richard Ellmann Collection.

40. Curci and Ziani, *Bianco, Rosa e Verde*, 107.

41. *Ibid.*

42. Signorina Haydée was the pseudonym of Vita Finzi, a popular local writer of romantic novels or "romanzi rosa". Joyce seems to allude to her in *Finnegans Wake* when he writes "in rosescenery haydyng" (*FW*, 359.33–4).

43. *La Coda del Diavolo*, 24 and 26 March 1910.

44. *Il Piccolo*, 13 January 1910.

45. Quoted in Guido Botteri and Vito Levi, *Il Politeama Rossetti 1878–1978: Un secolo di vita triestina nelle cronache del Teatro* (Trieste: Editoriale Libraria, 1978), 215.

46. *L'Indipendente*, 13 January 1910.

47. Willy Dias, *Viaggio nel tempo* (Bologna: Capelli, 1958), 101.

48. *L'Emancipazione*, 15 January 1910.

49. *Ibid.*

50. *Ibid.*

51. F.T. Marinetti, "Manifesto del Futurismo", *Opere di F.T. Marinetti*, vol. II (Verona, 1968), 11.

52. *L'Indipendente*, 4 March 1910.

53. "Uccidiamo il Chiaro di Luna", in F.T. Marinetti, *Teoria e Invenzione Futurista*, a cura di Luciano De Maria (Milano: Mondadori, 1983), 17.

54. *L'Indipendente*, 3 August 1910.

55. "La Corsa", in Fedoro Tizzoni, *Cannonate* (Trieste: G. Caprin, 1910), 27.

56. Richard Ellmann, *The Consciousness of Joyce* (New York: Oxford University Press, 1977), 118.

57. Frank Budgen, *James Joyce and the Making of Ulysses* (Oxford: Oxford University Press, 1972), 193–4.

58. Quoted in Gianni Pinguentini, *James Joyce in Italia*, 176.

59. See Suzette A. Henke, *James Joyce and the Politics of Desire*, 2.

60. Corinna del Greco Lobner, *James Joyce's Italian Connection*, 93.

61. Written in 1917 and later published in *Pomes Penyeach*.

62. Fedoro Tizzoni, *Cannonate*, 44–5.

63. I. Cope Jackson, *Joyce's Cities: Archaeologies of the Soul* (Baltimore and London: The Johns Hopkins University Press, 1981), 104.

64. Marinetti's text is quoted in Bruno Basile and Paolo Pullega, eds, *Letterature Stile Società: testi e profili di cultura europea XX secolo* (Bologna: Zanichelli, 1977), 249.

65. *Ibid.*

66. Jo Anna Isaak portrays Marinetti as "the greatest adman" of commodity capitalism in *The Ruin of Representation in Modernist Art and Texts* (Ann Arbor: University of Michigan Research Press, 1986), 55.

67. This excerpt from Marinetti's "'Distruzione della sintassi. Immaginazione senza fili': Il Futurismo come ideologia totale" (1913) is quoted in Bruno Basile and Paolo Pullega, eds, *Letterature Stile Società: testi e profili di cultura europea XX secolo*, 251.

68. Quoted in Louis Berrone, ed., *James Joyce in Padua* (New York: Random House, 1977), 19.

69. *Ibid.*

70. Judy Rawson, "Italian Futurism", in *Modernism 1890–1930*, ed. Malcolm Bradbury and James Mc Farlane (Harmondsworth: Penguin, 1976), 244.

71. Frank Budgen, *James Joyce and the Making of Ulysses*, 153.

72. Marinetti, Settimelli, Corra, "Il teatro Futurista sintetico (Atecnico-dinamico-simultaneo-autonomo-alogico-irreale)" in F.T. Marinetti, *Teoria e Invenzione Futurista*, a cura di Luciano De Maria (Milano: Mondadori, 1983), 120.

73. *Ibid.*, 127.

74. "Nottambulismo", in Fedoro Tizzoni, *Cannonate*, 49–54.

75. Marinetti, "Il Teatro di Varietà", 86–8.

76. Nora liked to read the *Daily Mail* when she lived in Trieste and so it is very possible that Joyce saw Marinetti's long article on the variety theatre, which was published in that newspaper on 21 November 1913.

77. I. Cope Jackson, *Joyce's Cities*, 104.

78. Marinetti, "Il Teatro di Varietà", 89.

79. See, for example, Mark Shechner, *Joyce and Nighttown* (Berkeley: University of California Press, 1974).

80. Cheryl Herr, *Joyce's Anatomy of Culture* (Urbana: University of Illinois Press, 1986), 146.

81. Sergio Mattioni, *Trieste variété* (Trieste: Fachin, 1990), 36.

82. *L'Adriatico*, 4 November 1908.

83. Marinetti, "Il Teatro di Varietà", 85: "sintesi di velocità + trasformazioni (esempio: Fregoli)".

84. Cheryl Herr, *Joyce's Anatomy of Culture*, 160.

85. From a letter written by Tullio Silvestri to Dario De Tuoni and sent shortly after the First World War. The address on the letter is Androna del Pozzo 4, which was where Silvestri painted Joyce's portrait in 1919.

86. Joyce's best student, Edoardo Schott, had been a classmate of Scipio Slataper. Schott was a member of the radical irredentist party La Democrazia Sociale Irredenta, founded in 1909 as a breakaway group from the offical socialist party, which was seen as being too pro-Austrian. It was linked with the Mazzini-inspired Democrazia Sociale Italiana. Another of Joyce's students, Dario De Tuoni, noted in his diary having gone to see Slataper several times in 1913. The diary is in the possession of the De Tuoni family.

87. *La Coda del Diavolo*, 6 July 1912.

88. Quoted in Biagio Marin, "Scipio Slataper e l'anima di Trieste", *Rivista Trieste*, Jan.–Feb. 1956, no. 11.

89. Dr Mario Pirona, the eldest son of Alberto, now living in Turin, provided this information in an interview with Renzo Crivelli which is published in Crivelli's *Triestine Itineraries*, 122.

90. Quoted in Thomas Staley, "Joyce and Svevo", text of a RAI/TV programme made by the

international "Guglielmo Marconi" University in collaboration with *The Voice of America* on 24 February 1965.

91. Quoted in Thomas Staley, "James Joyce in Trieste", *The Georgia Review*, vol. xvi, no. 4 (Winter 1962), 447 and 449.

92. *Il Diritto*, 24 August 1911.

93. "La Cometa dell'Home Rule," in *Il Piccolo della Sera*, 22 December 1910.

94. Richard Ellmann's typescript of an unsent and unpublished letter written by Stanislaus Joyce to his father around 1910. The letter is in Box 77 of the Richard Ellmann Collection.

95. *L'Indipendente*, 16 October 1910.

96. *Ibid.*, 7 November 1910.

97. *Ibid.*, 7 January 1911.

98. Unpublished letter of 25 August 1911 from Henry Blackwood Price to Joyce. The original is held in the James Joyce Collection at Cornell (Scholes no. 1085).

99. This motto was printed on the company's letterhead.

100. Unpublished letter of 28 July 1911 from V.J. Roche of the Dublin Woollen Co. to James Joyce. The original is held in the James Joyce Collection at Cornell (Scholes no. 1089).

101. Contained in typed notes entitled "Stanislaus Joyce London, August 1, 1954" in Box 55 of the Richard Ellmann Collection.

102. The manuscript of the letter from the Instituto in Como is in the James Joyce Collection at Cornell (Scholes no. 882).

103. Letter of 30 May 1912 to Eileen Joyce in *LII*, 295.

104. Published as "Daniel Defoe", edited from Italian manuscripts and translated by Joseph Prescott (Buffalo: State University of New York at Buffalo, 1964).

105. From documents kept in the Trieste State Archive.

106. *Ibid.*

107. "Daniel Defoe", 6.

108. *Ibid.*

109. *Ibid*, 7.

110. This is taken from an incomplete typed fragment of Joyce's talk on Defoe, entitled "Lecture on Defoe" (the title is handwritten by Stanislaus) and kept in the James Joyce Collection at Cornell (Scholes no. 44), 1.

111. "Daniel Defoe", 7.

112. The president of the Università del Popolo, Dr Benussi, the secretary, Dr Oberdorfer, the secretary of the Commissione dell'Università Popolare, Attilio Tamaro, as well as Prezioso and Francini Bruni wrote the letters of recommendation.

113. Corinna del Greco Lobner, "A *Giornalista Triestino*: James Joyce's Letter to *Il Marzocco*", *Joyce Studies Annual*, 1993, 187. See also Caterina Del Vivo, "Joyce, *Il Marzocco*, Daniel Defoe", *Il Viesseux* 12, Sept.–Dec. 1991, 44–5.

114. "The Universal Literary Influence of the Renaissance", in Louis Berrone, ed., *James Joyce in Padua*, 22.

115. "The Centenary of Charles Dickens", in Louis Berrone, ed., *James Joyce in Padua*, 34.

116. "L'Ombra di Parnell", *Il Piccolo della Sera*, 16 May 1912.

117. Joseph Hone, "A Recollection of James Joyce", *Envoy*, vol. v (April 1951), 45.

118. Joyce later mentioned this scheme in the "Eumaeus" episode of *Ulysses*: "What he wanted to ascertain was why that ship ran bang against the only rock in Galway bay when the Galway harbour scheme was mooted by a Mr Worthington or some name like that" (*U*, 16.964–6).

119. The original Italian title was "Il Miraggio del Pescatore di Aran. La Valvola del l'Inghilterra in Caso di Guerra."

120. Unpublished letter of 2 December 1912 from Price to Joyce. The letter is kept in the Joyce Collection at Cornell (Scholes no. 1088).

121. *Ibid.*

122. *Ibid.*

123. Letter of 2 March 1955 from Stanislaus Joyce to Constantine Curran. The letter is in the Curran Collection at University College Dublin.

124. Joyce included a version of these events in *Finnegans Wake* as follows: "when Robber and Mumsell, the pulpic dictators, on the nudgment of their legal advisors, Messrs Codex and Podex, and under his own benefiction of their pastor Father Flammeus Falconer, boycotted him of all mutton-suet candles and romeruled stationery for any purpose, he winged away on a wild-goup's chase across the kathartic ocean and made synthetic ink and sensitive paper for his own end out of his wit's waste" (*FW*, 185.1–8).

PART FIVE: SUCCESS IN THE SHADOW OF WAR

1. *Poems* and *Exiles*, 114.

2. *Ibid.*, 340.

3. Among the other speakers on the 1912–13 programme were Senator Guido Mazzoni on Pascoli and the young intellectual Marino de Szombathely on his fellow Triestine, the poet Umberto Saba.

4. *Il Piccolo*, 12 November 1912.

5. *Il Piccolo*, 11 February 1913.

6. Nora Joyce told Maria Jolas that "*Exiles* was a mixture of two cases, one in Dublin, one in Trieste". The Trieste incident she was referring to was presumably the Prezioso one although Jolas also notes that Nora "was violent against Stanislaus, perhaps because he had made advances". These assertions are contained in the typed notes Richard Ellmann took during his interview with Mrs Jolas on 22 July 1953 and are kept in the Richard Ellmann Collection.

7. In a partially unpublished interview Francini Bruni gave Richard Ellmann in July 1954. Ellmann's notes are to be found in Box 5 of the Richard Ellmann Collection.

8. Quoted in typed notes of an interview carried out by Richard Ellmann with Signora Vela Pulitzer in Trieste, July 1954. The notes are kept in Box 181 of the Richard Ellmann Collection.

9. Ellmann bases his dating of this event on the fact that for a period Joyce had no article in *Il Piccolo della Sera*. The interval was not quite so long as Ellmann states. Joyce's first article after 1910 was published in *Il Piccolo della Sera* on 16 May 1912.

10. *Poems* and *Exiles*, 346.

11. *Poems* and *Exiles*, 231.

12. Massimo Soranzio, "The Expatriate and Ex-Patriot: Joyce's Friend Roberto Prezioso", *Prospero*, no. 6, 135.

13. *Poems* and *Exiles*, 173.

14. Brenda Maddox, *Nora*, 156

15. Although she footnotes the date of the interview, Maddox does not actually report what Crise said.

16. Quoted in typed notes of an interview carried out by Richard Ellmann with Eileen Schaurek in Trieste, June 1953. The notes are kept in Box 185 of the Richard Ellmann Collection.

17. *Poems* and *Exiles*, 351.

18. *Giacomo Joyce*, Introduction, XI.

19. See his letter of 30 December 1921 in *LIII*, 56.

20. On 5 August 1907, a summons to "Sig Joyecs [*sic*] Giacomo, professore di lingua inglese" arrived from the "amministrazione del civico ospitale" asking him to call by immediately to pay Nora's hospital fees or else to produce a "certificato di povertà". This document is kept at the Cornell Joyce Collection (Scholes no. 1414).

21. Stanislaus Joyce, *Triestine Book of Days*, 19 April 1907.

22. *Ibid.*, 6 April 1907.

23. Fritz Senn, "Some Further Notes on *Giacomo Joyce*", *James Joyce Quarterly* 5 (1968), 233.

24. Neil Davison, *James Joyce, Ulysses, and the Construction of Jewish Identity*, 52.

25. From an interview I carried out with ninety-eight-year-old Mrs Bonacci in Trieste on 30 October 1996. She was Joyce's student from 1912 to 1914.

26. Pierpaolo Luzzatto Fegiz, *Lettere da Zabodaski – Ricordi di un Borghese Mitteleuropeo 1900–1984* (Trieste: Lint, 1984), 51.

27. From a letter from Emma Cuzzi Brocchi to Richard Ellmann kept in Box 5 of the Richard Ellmann Collection. Emma's brother Paolo was also a student of Joyce's.

28. Roberto Curci, *Tutto è sciolto: L'amore triestino di Giacomo Joyce* (Trieste: Lint, 1996).

29. Joyce wrote to Emma from Zürich on 7 December 1915 thanking her for a gift of "the two prints of the bas-relief which I had been looking for, as you know, for a good while. I shall have the un-retouched one framed in an oval frame which I shall then have stained in sky-blue and grey (Silvestri style) to create the illusion of the 'great bridge of the sky' around the image of the artificer. Besides, I am superstitious. Who knows if the coming into my house of this man will not bring me good news? If this should happen may your kind thought be doubly praised. Best regards to you and your family."

30. Roberto Curci, "Emma, almost a (serial) novel", in Renzo Crivelli and John McCourt, eds, *Le Donne di Giacomo*, 59.

31. From a letter from Emma Cuzzi Brocchi to Richard Ellmann kept in Box 5 of the Richard Ellmann Collection.

32. The Schleimers moved from here in mid-1906 to number 10 corsia Stadion.

33. See Stelio Crise, "Il Triestino James Joyce", in *Il ritorno di Joyce* (Trieste, 1982), 94–5.

34. I interviewed Mrs Zora Koren Skerk in 1995 and she confirmed this version of events.

35. Roberto Curci, "Chi? Quella 'fiamma' triestina", *Il Piccolo*, 13 January 1991, 4. Peter Hartshorn, in *James Joyce and Trieste*, 92, notes however that an obituary of Stanislaus Joyce was found among her papers.

36. From my 1995 interview with Mrs Koren Skerk.

37. His curriculum vitae is summarized in a report sent to the Italian prime minister just after the war, which lauded him as someone who could work to reopen trade links with Czechoslovakia. Part of the report, from the Italian embassy in Czechoslovakia, reads as follows: "Leopoldo Popper was born in Horgdiowitz, not far from Pilsen, in 1862. He speaks perfect Boemo, German, and also Italian which he writes well. … From an economic or material point of view in the past he was convinced that the breaking with Austria would be ruinous for Trieste, but now, given that this has happened and as his financial and familial interests are indissolubly based in Trieste, it would appear certain that he, anything but a protester, actively wants to see the re-launching of Triestine traffic in the light of the new situation." This document is kept in the Italian Central State Archive in Rome in the section "Presidenza del Consiglio dei Ministri", Gabinetto: Guerra Europea, file 196, sheet number 19.26.27.

38. Her school reports are kept along with those of her classmates at the Trieste State Archive.

39. Long after Joyce had gone on to greater things in Zürich and Paris, Amalia maintained her interest in his writings and translated a number of the short stories that make up *Dubliners*, sending some of her translations to Paris for the author's approval. She published her translations of "A Little Cloud" ("Una Nuvoletta") in *Il Piccolo della Sera* in October 1929, "The Dead" and "Eveline" in *Il Popolo di Trieste* in 1931. She later published a collected volume of five stories from *Dubliners* entitled *Araby* in 1935, which included the first short biography of Joyce in Italian.

40. The middle-aged Leopoldo was much more likely to have been a prototype for Leopold Bloom. Helen Barolini, in her article attacking Ellmann's identification of Popper, correctly states that Ellmann was wrong in his claim that Amalia Popper lived "on the via San Michele" because the Villa Popper was actually located at the corner of via Alice and via Bellosguardo. To quote Barolini: "Ellmann let himself be influenced by the fantasy of *Giacomo Joyce* itself which he first saw when it was in Stanislaus's possession; all the elements he saw written there – the via San Michele address, the description of the student's father as an old white-whiskered man, the account of the girl's operation, her having read *Portrait*, etc. – he simply transferred to the son of Amalia Popper." This quote from Barolini is taken from a typed version of her article entitled "The heroine of Giacomo Joyce: A Literary Puzzle", which is kept in Box 180 of the Richard

Ellmann Collection. This quote comes on page 10 of the article, which was published as "The Curious Case of Amalia Popper", *New York Review of Books*, 20 November 1969.

41. Ellmann had identified Popper in the 1959 first edition, but evidently Risolo was not aware of this and hence made no objections. I spoke to two of Popper's nieces, Antonietta and Livetta, both of whom are rather pleased by the idea that Amalia might have had a relationship with Joyce. The same is true for Annie Schleimer's family. Emma Cuzzi has no surviving family.

42. Ellmann's view that Amalia Popper is the inspiration behind *Giacomo Joyce* has been almost universally accepted by Joyceans. The most important recent proponent of this theory has been Vicky Mahaffey in her article "Fascism and Silence: The Coded History of Amalia Popper", in *James Joyce Quarterly* 32, nos 3 and 4 (Spring and Summer 1995), 501–22. The central claim of Mahaffey's article – that Amalia was caught between Joyce and her husband, Michele Risolo, two men who were diametrically opposed, one a great writer at home with words, the other a fascist who was terrified by them – is both fascinating and credible, but does little to demonstrate that she is the "who" in question.

43. Joseph Valente, *James Joyce and the Problem of Justice: Negotiating Sexual and Colonial Difference* (Cambridge: Cambridge University Press, 1995), 70.

44. According to the *Annuario* della Scuola Superiore di Commercio "Revoltella", Anno XXXV, 1913–14 (Trieste: Giovanni Balestra, 1914), 88: "At the sitting of 2 July 1913, Mr James Joyce B.A. was appointed to teach English language and English commercial correspondence."

45. Whenever he did attend staff meetings, he was always careful to follow his signature on the minutes with his academic qualification "B.A.".

46. In the *Annuario* della Scuola Superiore di Commercio "Revoltella", Anno XXXV, 1913–14.

47. Ivo Vidan, "Joyce and the South Slavs", in Niny Rocco Bergera, ed., *Atti del Third International James Joyce Symposium*, 121.

48. *Ibid.*

49. "Scuri" is a Triestine word for shutters.

50. From a letter of 22 November 1953 from Furlan to Richard Ellmann, which is kept in Box 46 of the Richard Ellmann Collection.

51. Dario De Tuoni, *Ricordi di Joyce a Trieste* (Milano: All'insegna del Pesce d'Oro, 1966), 12.

52. Letizia Fonda Savio, "James Joyce: Two Reminiscences", in E.H. Mikhail, ed., *James Joyce: Interviews and Recollections*, 64.

53. From notes of Ellmann's interview of July 1954 with Francini Bruni kept in Box 5 of the Richard Ellmann Collection.

54. De Tuoni is referring to Frantisek Schaurek, who married Eileen just before the war.

55. Dario De Tuoni, *Ricordi di Joyce a Trieste*, 33.

56. *L'Emancipazione*, 16 August 1912.

57. Joyce seems later to have alluded to De Tuoni in *Finnegans Wake*: "he began Tuonisonian but worked his passage up as far as the we-all-hang-together Animadovites" (*FW*, 8.23–4).

58. From notes of Ellmann's interview of July 1954 with Dario De Tuoni kept in Box 5 of the Richard Ellmann Collection.

59. Frida and Silvia De Tuoni, "Memorie Joyciane", in Niny Rocco Bergera, ed., *Atti del Third International James Joyce Symposium*, 335.

60. From notes of Ellmann's interview of July 1954 with Dario De Tuoni.

61. The original Italian version of this letter is kept in the Cornell Joyce Collection (Scholes no. 480).

62. Joyce may have had him in mind when using the Slovenian "Orel" (eagle) in the phrase "Orel Orel the King of the Orlbrdsz" (*FW*, 105.11).

63. Ellmann was told this story by Livia Schmitz in 1954.

64. In Richard Ellmann's partially unpublished interview with Francini Bruni in July 1954, to be found in Box 5 of the Richard Ellmann Collection.

65. Letter of 20 February 1940 from James Joyce to Dario De Tuoni (*LIII*, 466).

66. Photocopies of the original letters are contained in Rosa Maria Bosinelli's unpublished dissertation, *Gli Anni Triestini di James Joyce*. The section from the letter, dated 10 June 1961, reads as follows in Italian: "Mi piacerebbe avere notizie dei Trevisani o dei Tiziani o della Petech che era alla Scuola Comunale con me. Maria Tripcovich anche." Lucia's illness is clearly evident in the letters, which mix confused comments about the present with lucid recollections of her past in Trieste, all in excellent Italian.

67. Dario De Tuoni, *Ricordi di Joyce a Trieste*, 12.

68. Photocopies of the original letter dated 20 June 1961 are contained in Rosa Maria Bosinelli, *Gli Anni Triestini di James Joyce*.

69. Letter of 28 February 1913 from Henry Blackwood Price to Joyce. The letter is held in the Cornell Joyce Collection (Scholes no. 1089).

70. The note came into the possession of Dario De Tuoni, long after Joyce had accidentally left it in one of the books he used during English lessons.

71. A photocopy of the original letter dated 20 June 1961 is contained in Rosa Maria Bosinelli, *Gli Anni Triestini di James Joyce*.

72. "On this occasion Giovanni Pozza came from Milan to Trieste, and met Joyce. He stayed an extra day to talk with Joyce." In Richard Ellmann's partially unpublished interview with Francini Bruni in July 1954, to be found in Box 5 of the Richard Ellmann Collection.

73. He had visited the city several times and in 1850 the world première of his opera *Stiffelio*, part of which he had written in Trieste, was held in the city's Teatro Grande, which later became the Teatro Verdi.

74. To prepare the public for this production of *Nabucco*, *Il Piccolo* published a series of articles to introduce it: "The Nabucco or Nabucodonosor of the opera is not the one-dimensional Asian tyrant described by history. The biblical legends insist that the God of the Jews punished Nabucodonosor for the crime of having destroyed the Jewish kingdom by having him eat grass like a poor cow for seven years. But history shows that he in fact ruled his vast Assyrian Kingdom for 43 years and was probably without remorse for the conquest of Israel, for the massacres of the Jews, for the blinding of King Sedcia and for having reduced the Jews to slavery" (*Il Piccolo*, 28 January 1913). With great irony Joyce would later name "Ichabudonosor" (*U*, 15.1862) as one of Bloom's ancestors. According to Gifford's *Annotations*, this name at least partly derives from "Nebuchadnezzar, king of Babylon", who "besieged and reduced Jerusalem and carried the Israelites captive into Babylon (*Ulysses Annotated*, 482). Taking the Italian spelling "Nabucodonosor", which is so much closer to Joyce's spelling, this link seems even more likely. Joyce also explicitly mentions Nabucdonosor in *Finnegans Wake*: "Nomad may roam with Nabuch but let naaman laught at Jordan! For we, we have taken our sheet upon her stones where we have hanged our hearts in her trees; and we list, as he bibs us, by the waters of babalong" (*FW*, 103.9–12).

75. *Il Piccolo*, 29 January 1913.

76. *L'Indipendente*, 13 October 1913. Part of the reason for the scale of the Verdi celebrations was that just two months earlier, in August 1913, the Governor, Prince Hohenlohe, partly in response to the Liberal-National victory in the local elections, had issued four highly controversial decrees, one of which ordered the dismissal of all foreigners employed by the city administration. He was attempting to force out as many as possible of the "regnicoli" – native Italians – who had come to live and work in Trieste. They could keep their jobs only by becoming Austrian citizens. These measures caused outrage both in Trieste and in Italy and attracted so much attention that they turned out to be a godsend for the irredentists, whose case was suddenly being debated in newspapers throughout Europe, including *The Times* of London.

77. In Richard Ellmann's partially unpublished interview with Francini Bruni in July 1954, to be found in Box 5 of the Richard Ellmann Collection.

78. See G. De Ferra, "Musica in casa", in *Quassù Trieste*, a cura di L. Mazzi (Bologna, 1968), 188.

79. Wagner's leitmotif technique was also fundamental for Joyce, as Klaus Reichert has pointed out: "As he went on to *Ulysses* the Wagnerian technique taught him how to present the

multi-layered facets of his characters. He learned from Wagner how a simultaneous presentation of character – at once focusing on both conscious and preconscious or unconscious layers – was to be achieved on the various planes of language." Klaus Reichert, "The European background of Joyce's Writing", in Derek Attridge, ed., *The Cambridge Companion to James Joyce* (Cambridge: Cambridge University Press, 1990), 55–82.

80. Letter of 24 January 1954 to Richard Ellmann. The letter is in Box 46 of the Richard Ellmann Collection.

81. Unpublished letter of 20 June 1914 from Joyce to Grant Richards. The original is kept in the Houghton Library at Harvard University.

82. Hans Walter Gabler, "The Seven Lost Years of *A Portrait of the Artist as a Young Man*", in *Approaches to Joyce's "Portrait": Ten Essays*, ed. Thomas F. Staley and Bernard Benstock (Pittsburgh: University of Pittsburgh Press, 1976), 53.

83. Stanislaus Joyce, *Triestine Book of Days*, 4 March 1908. Further proof that Joyce had at least some familiarity with Zangwill's writings is to be found in a document kept in the Cornell Joyce Collection (Scholes no. 43) entitled "Notes on Ireland", which contains a list of contemporary novelists including Zangwill, whom he places between James and Moore.

84. Joyce does not always deal directly with these issues. He treats the issue of assimilation with a great sense of comedy by using the kidney to symbolize it. Many Triestine Jews, like Bloom, were so assimilated that they would have tucked into kidneys for breakfast without giving it a second thought, but few would have come to see this inner organ, as Joyce has Bloom see it in "Circe", as a symbol of the potential harmony of assimilation in the "new Bloomusalem".

85. Quoted in Serenella Zanotti, op. cit., p. 58.

86. Stanislaus Joyce, *Triestine Book of Days*, 18 September 1907.

87. *Ibid.*, 15 September 1908. The mere fact that Joyce attended the Jewish synagogue in Trieste contradicts Mario Stock's claim as reported in Marilyn Reizbaum's *James Joyce's Judaic Other*, 25, that "Joyce had no immediate contact with the established Jewish community in Trieste". Stock also claims to have frequented the Joyce home during the Trieste years, but as he was not born until 1906 his recollections must surely be considered second-hand and unreliable.

88. Stephen Dedalus shows his awareness of this role of the Jews in "Scylla and Charybdis": "Jews, whom christians tax with avarice, are of all races the most given to intermarriage. Accusations are made in anger. The christian laws which built up the hoards of the jews (for whom, as for the lollards, storm was shelter) bound their affections too with hoops of steel" (*U*, 9.783–6).

89. This was in line with the order of the Lateran Council of 1215 and is an example of what is referred to as "the proscription of their national costumes in penal laws and jewish dress acts" in "Ithaca" (*U*, 17.758–9).

90. Quoted in Mario Stock, *Nel Segno di Geremia: Storia della Comunita' Israelitica di Trieste dal 1200* (Udine: Istituto per L'Enciclopedia del Friuli-Venezia Giulia, 1979), 18.

91. Braude's comment is quoted in Giovanni Paolin, "Considerazioni sugli Ebrei Triestini", in G. Todeschini and P.C. Ioly Zorattini, *Il Mondo Ebraico*, 223.

92. Mario Stock, *Nel Segno di Geremia*.

93. Benjamin Braude, "The Jews of Trieste and the Levant Trade in the Eighteenth Century", in *Il Mondo Ebraico*, 347.

94. One thousand Jews arrived from Corfu in 1891 and against the wishes of the settled community most of them decided to stay. Several prominent members of the community wrote to the chief rabbi saying that their presence compromised the commercial interests of the community. They also wrote to the police asking them to expel them.

95. Tullia Catalan, *La Comunità Ebraica di Trieste: Politica, Società, Cultura, 1848–1918*, unpublished doctoral thesis for the University of Urbino, 1994, 93. Joyce taught the children of at least three of the signatories: Brunner, Mordo and Castelbolognese.

96. The principal Jewish newspaper in Italy along with *Il Vessilo Israelitico, Il Corriere Israelitico* (1861–1915) was published weekly in Trieste and included news on Jewish events throughout Italy, the Austro-Hungarian Empire, and Europe.

97. *Il Piccolo*, 28 June 1912. For a detailed description of the synagogue see Ira Nadel, *Joyce and the Jews*, 199.

98. Maurice Fishburg, *The Jews: A Study of Race and Environment* (London: Walter Scott Publishing, 1911), 474.

99. Ira Nadel, *Joyce and the Jews*, 228.

100. *Il Corriere Israelitico*, 15 October 1909.

101. Svevo made suicide a central event of his novel *Senilità*.

102. *Il Corriere Israelitico*, 21 July 1911.

103. Luis Blum was born of Giacomo Specht and Luisa Beer on 28 February 1865 in Budapest. Budapest had a regular fair of Saint Leopold on 15 November in Buda. There was also a fair in Nagy Karoly, and both were advertised annually in the *Guida di Trieste* along with Szombathely fair.

104. See the register of names in the synagogue of Trieste. The entry on Blum-Gentilomo is dated 28/10/06.

105. Joyce mentioned this company in a letter of ?8 September 1920 to Alessandro Francini Bruni which he wrote from Zürich in Triestine, referring to "un zerto sior Driatiko" – a certain Mr Driatiko – who had temporarily mislaid some of his papers being shipped from Trieste to Zürich (*LII*, 269).

106. *Guida di Trieste* (1907 edition), 141.

107. Mario Doria, *Grande Dizionario del Dialetto Triestino Storico*, 643. The example cited in the dictionary to explain "smerdon" might suit Bloom particularly as he is seen by the narrator of the "Cyclops" episode: "Ma vara 'sto smerdon de mula che voria 'ver l'ultima parola!" – Look at that shit of a young fellow who wants to have the last word!

108. Rosa Maria Bosinelli, "The Importance of Trieste in Joyce's Work, with Reference to His Knowledge of Psycho-Analysis", 177.

109. Rosa Maria Bosinelli, who interviewed Cuzzi, notes that when she pressed him on this conversation he could not remember it having taken place. *Gli Anni Triestini di James Joyce*, 214.

110. Marilyn Reizbaum, "The Jewish Connection, Cont'd", in *The Seventh of Joyce*, ed. Bernard Benstock (Bloomington: Indiana University Press, 1982), 231.

111. Jacques Le Rider, *Modernity and Crises of Identity: Culture and Society in Fin-de-Siècle Vienna*, trs. Rosemary Morris (New York: Continuum Publishing Group, 1993).

112. Sander L. Gilman, *Freud, Race and Gender*, 79.

113. *Ibid.*, 83.

114. Alberto Cavaglion, "Otto Weininger tra Trieste e Firenze", in Roberto Pertici, ed., *Intellettuali di Frontiera: Triestina a Firenze 1900–1950*, 664 and 666.

115. Steno Tedeschi, "Un filosofo antifemminista", *L'Indipendente*, 28 March 1905.

116. Alberto Cavaglion, "Otto Weininger tra Trieste e Firenze", 673–4.

117. Entry of 4 December 1912, quoted in Umberto Saba, *Tutte le Poesie*, a cura di Arrigo Stara, Introduzione di Mario Lavagetto (Milano: Mondadori, 1994), lxxviii.

118. "Quelques Juifs", *Il Corriere Israelitico*, 31 March 1914. Lattes would also have objected to Weininger because he had converted to Christianity and was openly hostile to Zionism, which he felt contradicted Judaism: "The conception of Judaism involves a world-wide distribution of the Jews. Citizenship is an un-Jewish thing, and there has never been and never will be a Jewish state." Quoted in Ira Nadel, *Joyce and the Jews*, 69, from Weininger's *Sex and Character*.

119. Marilyn Reizbaum, "The Jewish Connection, Cont'd", 232.

120. See Natania Rosenfeld, "James Joyce's Womanly Wandering Jew", in *Jews and Gender: Responses to Otto Weininger*, 223.

121. *Ibid.*, 215.

122. Otto Weininger, *Sex and Character* (London: William Heinemann, 1906), 124.

123. As Elfriede Poder puts it in her "Molly is Sexuality: The Weiningerian Definition of Woman in Joyce's *Ulysses*", in *Jews and Gender, Responses to Otto Weininger*, 230: "Molly's pre-

vailing traits even suggest that Weininger's concept of woman was something like a blueprint for the construction of the most fully delineated female character in *Ulysses*. This, however, is not to deny that it is Joyce's language … [that] makes Molly so alive."

124. Otto Weininger, *Sex and Character*, 296.

125. Elfriede Poder, "Molly is Sexuality: The Weiningerian Definition of Woman in Joyce's *Ulysses*", 234.

126. Quoted in Ellen Ginzburg Migliorino, "Antisemitismo", in G. Todeschini and P.C. Ioly Zorattini, eds, *Il Mondo Ebraico*, 437.

127. *L'Amico*, 17 June 1901.

128. Perhaps Joyce had this fact in mind when he provided another Irish–Jewish link in *Finnegans Wake*, where he writes of the bilingual Shem, who has just "caught the europicolas" and gone "into the society of Jewses" wanting to write for the "*Ikish Tames*" – which suggests *The Irish Times* and The Jewish Times, in this case *Il Piccolo*. "One temp when he foiled to be killed, the freak wanted to put his bilingual head intentionally through the *Ikish Tames*" (*FW*, 424.1–3).

129. Neil R. Davison, *James Joyce, Ulysses, and the Construction of Jewish Identity*, 148.

130. In the Archivio Felice Venezian, Documenti Trieste TS 8241/14.

131. The link between irredentism and Masonry was well known in Joyce's Trieste. Scipio Slataper wrote an article attacking the "monarchic … anti-clericalism of the irredentist Masonry" entitled "Irredentismo massonico", which was published in *L'Amico* of 25 December 1910. For further information on this subject see Silvio Gratton, *Trieste Segreta*, con un introduzione di Manlio Cecovini (Trieste: Edizioni Italo Svevo, 1987); and Anna Millo, *L'Elite del Potere a Trieste: Una biografia collettiva 1891–1938* (Milan: Franco Angeli, 1989), 109–13. Venezian kept in close contact with Ernesto Nathan, future mayor of Rome and Grand Master of the Masons in Italy, writing to him as follows in 1898: "You are the only, and I mean the only person in whom I have complete faith. … There is however – thanks to you – a centre in which I place many hopes: it is the Masonry. I believe that, if we really wish it to be so, it can along with its liberal programme seriously seek to rebuild a little love of country" (quoted in A. Levi, *Ricordi della vita e dei tempi di Ernesto Nathan* (Firenze, 1945), 157.

132. Tullia Catalan, "Società e sionismo a Trieste fra XIV e XX secolo", in *Il Mondo Ebraico*, 468.

133. Tullia Catalan, *La Comunità Ebraica di Trieste*, 244.

134. Neil R. Davison, *James Joyce, Ulysses, and the Construction of Jewish Identity*, 219.

135. Gino Arias, *Il Sionismo e le Aspirazioni della Società Moderna* (Trieste: Edit. Il Circolo Sionistico, 1906), 8–9.

136. *Ibid.*, 10.

137. *L'Amico*, 24 September 1899.

138. Louis Hyman, *The Jews of Ireland*, 187.

139. Joyce had good reasons for making this link, reasons which he found in Chaim Weizmann's introduction to Harry Sacher's *Zionism and the Jewish Future*: "Palestine will be the country in which Jews are to be found, just as Ireland is the country in which Irishmen are to be found, though there are more Irishmen outside of Ireland than in it." Another link between the Irish and the Jews is to be found in N. Gaster, "Judaism – A National Religion", which asserts that "the Jews are a nation just like the Irish". In Harry Sacher, ed., *Zionism and the Jewish Future* (Westport, Conn.: Hyperion Press, 1976), 10.

140. Anna Millo, *L'Elite del Potere a Trieste*, 333.

141. See Tullia Catalan, *La Comunità Ebraica di Trieste. Il Corriere Israelitico* endorsed the Zionist outlook in articles such as "Are the Jews a Nation?", published on 31 January 1908.

142. Tullia Catalan, "L'emigrazione ebraica in Palestina attraverso il porto di Trieste (1908–1938)", *Qualestoria*, nos 2–3 (Aug.–Dec. 1991), 59.

143. Phillip F. Herring, ed., *Joyce's Ulysses Notesheets in the British Museum* (Charlottesville: University of Virginia Press, 1972), 119.11.

144. Cecil Roth, "James Joyce in Trieste", *Times Literary Supplement*, 7 August 1948, 443.

145. Alfieri Seri, Pietro Covre and Livio Grassi, *Le Insegne dell'ospitalità: due secoli di esercizi pubblici a Trieste* (Trieste: Lint, 1988), 44.

146. *Il Corriere Israelitico*, 30 April 1914. "The language of the fathers was generally known in a partial and fragmentary way by many Triestine Jews, and they often used it without understanding its meaning in ritual. Among the poorer Jews, it was polluted by the local Triestine dialect. And so a type of 'Hebrew–Triestine' was created", according to Tullia Catalan, *La Comunità Ebraica di Trieste*, 56.

147. Ira Nadel, *Joyce and the Jews*, 70

148. Letter of Hyman to Richard Ellmann in 1966, kept in Box 53 of the Richard Ellmann Collection.

149. *Il Corriere Israelitico*, 30 April 1908.

150. Carol Loeb Shloss, "Joyce in the Context of Irish Orientalism", *James Joyce Quarterly* 35, 268.

151. Phillip F. Herring, ed., *Joyce's Ulysses Notesheets in the British Museum*, 82.

152. *Ibid.*, 89. A staff meeting of 4 April 1914 decided on these measures and Joyce, who was absent, later added his approval. The Italian word "revoltella" means revolver, and this incident gave Joyce, in his letter to Stanislaus written in July 1920, all the more reason to refer to the Scuola, or University as it became after the war, as "the revolver university" (*LIII*, 10). In reality the school was named after the Triestine magnate Baron Pasquale Revoltella.

153. Throughout March, the Triestine newspapers carried extensive reports on this problem and reported that the King did not want to allow Home Rule for fear of civil war. The full text of the letter is quoted by Giorgio Melchiori in his "The Language of Politics and the Politics of Language" in *The James Joyce Broadsheet*, vol. 1, no. 1, February 1981.

154. As Melchiori points out, typewritten copies of all the articles, along with full or partial English translations, are kept in the Joyce Collection at Cornell. These translations are superior to those in the *Critical Writings* and were probably carried out, at least partially, by Stanislaus before his internment with a view to having them published for an English-speaking audience. The project was abandoned with the onset of the war. (See Giorgio Melchiori, "Joyce's Feast of Languages: Seven Essays and Ten Notes", *Joyce Studies in Italy* 4, ed. Franca Ruggieri (Rome: Bulzoni Editore, 1995), 113–14.

155. Enda Duffy, *The Subaltern Ulysses* (Minneapolis and London: University of Minnesota Press, 1994), 18. See also chapter four of Emer Nolan's *James Joyce and Nationalism*, which links the "Circe" episode in *Ulysses* to the Easter Rising.

156. David Pierce, "The Politics of *Finnegans Wake*", *Textual Practice*, vol. 2, no. 3 (1988), 369.

157. *The Workshop of Daedalus*, 98–9.

158. This opera was given its première in Trieste in December 1913.

159. *Poems* and *Exiles*, 45.

160. *Ibid.*, 46.

161. *Ibid.*

162. *L'Indipendente* of 30 June 1914.

163. In the course of researching this book I unearthed this unpublished letter kept in the Italian State Archive in Trieste. The original Italian reads as follows:

Via Donato Bramante 4, II
Trieste

All'Eccelsa i.r. Luogotenenza
Trieste

L'infrascritto, nato a Dublino (Irlanda), oddì 2 febbraio 1882 già professore di lingua inglese presso la Scuola di Commercio Revoltella, rivolge rispettosa istanza a codesta eccelsa luogotenenza onde gli siano restituiti i documenti in calce inviati a suo tempo al ministero della pubblica istruzione a Vinenna dietro invito di detto ministero pendente la riconferma o meno da parte dell'autorità scolastica del carico di cui sopra

Con ossequi
James Joyce B.A.
Documenti
i) Laurea della regia universita d'Irlanda (Dublino) – (l'originale in pergamena)
ii e iii) Criticiche della stampa sulle sue opere letterarie – (copie).
iv e v) Attestati dell'universita popolare di Trieste.
li 10 Dicembre 1914.

164. This document is held in the Italian State Archive in Trieste.

165. *Ibid.*

166. *Ibid.*

167. On 4 January 1914 Veneziani sent Joyce written confirmation that he had been taken on and that his payment would be 100 crowns per month. This letter is in the Cornell Joyce Collection (Scholes no. 1293).

168. Stelio Crise, "La Cambiale di James Joyce – Suddito Inglese Internato", *Il Piccolo*, 26 May 1971.

169. De Tuoni remembered this in an interview with Ellmann carried out in July 1954. The notes from the interview are kept in Box 11 of the Richard Ellmann Collection.

170. Oscar Schwarz described Stanislaus as "irrepressibly anti-German" in a letter dated 16 August 1955 to Richard Ellmann. The letter is kept in Box 185 of the Richard Ellmann Collection.

171. *Ibid.*

172. *Ibid.*

173. Mario Nordio, "Gli anni triestini di James Joyce", *Il Gazzettino*, 15 April 1960.

174. The letter is kept in the Archivio dell' Università di Trieste in the "Scuola Revoltella" file for the year 1915.

175. Frank Budgen, *James Joyce and the Making of Ulysses*, 175.

176. Silvio Benco, *Gli ultimi anni della dominazione austriaca a Trieste* (Milano: Casa Editrice Risorgimento), 1919.

177. From an interview with Signora Vela Pulitzer carried out by Richard Ellmann in Trieste in July 1954. The text of the interview is kept in Box 181 of the Richard Ellmann Collection.

178. For evidence of this see, for example, Michele Risolo, "Mia moglie e Joyce", *Il Corriere della Sera*, 27 February 1969.

179. Joyce may allude to this Schott and this episode in *Finnegans Wake* where he writes: "Or (soddenly) Schott, furtivfired by the riots. No flies. Agreest?" (*FW*, 514.27–8).

180. Desico (Edoardo Schott), *Diario ed Aventure (1914–1922) di un triestino del primo Novecento: pubblicista, corrispondente di guerra, politico, delegato al Congresso della Pace a parigi – Versailles 1919* (Udine: Editrice grillo, 1979), 26–7. One of Joyce's dreams links Schott with spying and sees Joyce himself as a provider of "useful" information:

Dublin. Dame Street. A Scotch soldier dressed in a Chinese mandarin robe walks in front of me. I know that he is going to the theatre. I follow him murmuring: 'Liebmann, Schott.' An official on a bicycle comes by, stops, and confronts me. He asks me pointblank: 'Which play?' I murmur: 'Le Champ de Bruyère.' He asks: 'Where is it?' I begin to understand that he is a Castle spy. I try to think of the name of a theatre. Impossible to say 'Kaufleuten' because it is a German word. I answer finally: 'Les Droits du Roi.' He asks again: 'But who are these Liebmann and Schott you were just talking about?' I reply: 'I? Not on your life!' He then opens his coat, shows me a badge, and tells me to follow him to the commissariat because I have spoken in German. To mollify him and allay his suspicions, I ask him if he knows the Adriatic. No. Then I tell him that Liebmann is at present physician to the Queen of Italy, and that Schott belongs to a Milanese Jewish family, the Weil-Schotts of Milan. They are both Italian patriots, and of course great friends of mine. He is impressed. I hastily tell him the history of Austrian families. Their names are so deceptive! Tallavicini, an Austrian ambassador, Vescovo, a Slav leader, Berger, Oberdank, Italian patriots. ... (*JJ*, 548)

181. Judging from a letter of 25 May 1919 it seems that Tripcovich paid Joyce's rent in the via Bramante flat until the war's end but then refused to continue doing so: "I have received from your landlord's agent an intimation to pay the last quarter's rent of your flat and clear it out within a week. He says that Tripcovich declines all further responsibilities for it. I have no time to run after Tripcovich" (*LII*, 442).

182. Trieste State Archive, Imperial regia direzione di Polizia, envelope 395, 1916, K.K. Polizei-Directions-Prasidium, Graz 9 May 1916.

183. I was told this story by Professor Franz Stanzel of the University of Graz, who is currently researching Joyce's relationship with the Austro-Hungarian empire. He has found documents containing the spy's reports in the Austrian State Archive in Vienna and will shortly publish the results of his research.

184. Eileen Schaurek, in an interview with Richard Ellmann carried out in June 1953 and kept in the Richard Ellmann Collection, recalled Nora thanking her with the words "Thanks, Eileen. We didn't have a penny left."

185. In an interview with Rosa Maria Bosinelli, in her unpublished dissertation, *Gli Anni Triestini di James Joyce*, 107. When Eileen was returning from holidays in Dublin in 1926, Schaurek committed suicide after it was discovered that he had been embezzling funds. Joyce described the event in a letter to Harriet Shaw Weaver: "my brother-in-law in Trieste blew his brains out while my sister was on her way from Ireland to Trieste. He was dead when she was here and neither she nor my wife [...] knew about it. [...] He lived, unconscious, for 26 hours after rolling his eyes from side to side" (*SL*, 320). The task of breaking the news to Eileen, when she reached Trieste, fell to Stanislaus. Both he and Joyce contributed thereafter to the support of Eileen and her children.

186. Richard Ellmann notes that Stannie wrote to Joyce shortly after the latter's departure for Paris as follows: "I am sorry that for reasons best known to myself [...] which have no kind of relation to uncertain domestic conditions [...] I was not in a very sociable mood during your stay here." This letter is kept in a file titled "miscellaneous" in the Richard Ellmann Collection.

187. Letter of 24 January 1954 from Boris Furlan to Richard Ellmann. The letter is kept in Box 46 of the Richard Ellmann Collection.

188. In an interview with Richard Ellmann carried out in July 1954. The interview notes are kept in Box 5 of the Richard Ellmann Collection.

189. Silvio Benco, "James Joyce in Trieste", in Willard Potts, ed., *Portraits of the Artist in Exile*, 58.

190. Joyce had met Budgen, a convivial, self-educated English artist, in 1918, and they had become close friends. To a large extent Budgen assumed the role that had been Stannie's; he genuinely got to know Joyce well, became a vital source of help and encouragement to him and was a more indulgent and practised drinking partner than Joyce's brother had ever been.

191. Letter of 31? May 1920 to Ezra Pound in Forrest Read, ed., *Pound/Joyce: The Letters of Ezra Pound to James Joyce* (London: Faber and Faber, 1967), 167–8.

192. *Il Piccolo*, 16 December 1910.

193. *L'Indipendente*, 16 December 1910.

194. Letter of 29 August 1920 to Stanislaus Joyce (*SL*, 268).

195. Letter of 31? May 1920 to Ezra Pound in Forrest Read, ed., *Pound/Joyce*, 168.

196. He used to say, "Trieste is my second country", according to Francini Bruni in an interview with Richard Ellmann carried out in July 1954.

197. Louis Gillet, "The Living Joyce", in Willard Potts, ed., *Portraits of the Artist in Exile*, 192.

Bibliography

Alberti, Mario, General Carlo Corsi, Armando Hodnig, Tomaso Sillani, Attilio Tamaro, and Ettore Tolomei, with an introductory chapter by Nelson Gay. *Italy's Great War and Her National Aspirations.* Milan: Alfieri & Lacroix, 1917.

Alessi, Rino. *Trieste viva: Fatti – Uomini – Pensieri.* Roma: Gherardo Casini, 1954.

Altichieri, Gilberto. "*Giacomo Joyce*: un romanzo triestino." *Il Gazzettino*, 12 March 1968.

—. "James Joyce voce di Trieste." *Il Gazzettino,* 8 February 1968.

Anderson, Chester G. *James Joyce and his World.* London: Thames & Hudson, 1968.

Angiolettti, G.B. "Joyce o i dinamitardi delle lettere." In *I Grandi Ospiti.* Firenze: Vallecchi Editore, 1960, 185–9.

Annuario della Scuola Superiore di Commercio "Revoltella", Anno XXXIV e XXXV. Trieste: Giovanni Balestra, 1914.

Anonimo. *Diario triestino 1815–1915: cent'anni di lotta italiano.* Milano: Rava, 1915.

Anzelotti, Fulvio. *Il segreto di Svevo.* Pordenone: Studio Tesi, 1985.

Apih, Elio. *La Società Triestina negli anni di Svevo.* Palermo: Palumbo, 1976.

—. *Il Socialismo italiano in Austria.* Udine: Saggi, 1991.

—. *Trieste* (con un saggio sull'economia di Giulio Sapelli e un profilo letterario di Elvio Guagnini). Bari e Roma: Laterza, 1988.

Ara, Angelo. "Gli ebrei a Trieste, 1850–1918." *La Rivista Storica Italiana*, no. 1, 1990.

Ara, Angelo and Claudio Magris. *Trieste: Un identità di frontiera.* Torino: Einaudi, 1982.

Arias, Gino. *Il Sionismo e le aspirazioni della società moderna.* Trieste: Edit. Il Circolo Sionistico, 1906.

Attridge, Derek, ed. *The Cambridge Companion to James Joyce.* Cambridge: Cambridge University Press, 1990.

Avon, Francesca. "Per fortuna c'era Stannie." *Il Piccolo*, 2 February 1982.

Barison, Cesare. *Trieste, Città Musicalissima.* Trieste: Lint, 1976.

Barolini, Helen. "The Curious Case of Amalia Popper." *New York Review of Books*, 20 November 1969.

Basile, Bruno and Paolo Pullega, eds. *Letterature Stile Società: testi e profili di cultura europea XX secolo.* Bologna: Zanichelli, 1977.

Battisti, Livia. "Socialismo Trentino ed Adriatico nell'Impero Absburgico." Conferenza tenuta il 29 Aprile 1971 al Circolo di studi politico-sociali "Che Guevara" di Trieste.

Beja, Morris. *James Joyce: A Literary Life.* Dublin: Gill and Macmillan, 1992.

Beja, Morris, and Shari Benstock, eds. *Coping with Joyce: Essays from the Copenhagen Symposium.* Columbus: Ohio State University Press, 1989.

Benco, Aurelia Gruber. "Between Joyce and Benco." *James Joyce Quarterly,* Spring 1972. .

—, ed. *Umana, Joyce Special Issue.* Trieste, 1971.

Benco, Silvio. *Gli ultimi anni della dominazione austriaca a Trieste.* Milano: Casa Editrice Risorgimento, 1919.

—. *Il Piccolo di Trieste. Mezzo secolo di giornalismo.* Milano: Fratelli Treves, 1931.

—. "James Joyce in Trieste." In Willard Potts, ed., *Portraits of the Artist in Exile: Recollections of James Joyce by Europeans,* 47–58.

—. "L'Ulisse di James Joyce." *Pegaso,* vol. 1, January 1929. Firenze: Felice le monnier.

—. "Ricordi di Joyce." *Pegaso,* vol. II, August 1930, 150–65.

—. "Un illustre scrittore inglese a Trieste." *Umana,* Trieste, 6 luglio 1918, 1–3.

Benstock, Bernard. "Paname-Turricum and Tarry Easty: James Joyce's *Città Immediata.*" In Jacquet Claude and Jean-Michel Rabaté, eds. *James Joyce 3: Joyce et l'Italie.* Special Issue of *La Revue des Lettres Modernes.* Paris: Lettres Modernes, 1994, 29–37.

—, ed. *The Augmented Ninth: Proceedings to the Ninth International Joyce Symposium.* Frankfurt, 1984.

Berlam, Arduino. "La colonia greca di Trieste ed i suoi addentellati con la guerra d'indipendenza ellenica (1821–1830)." *Archeografo Triestino,* IV, vol. 10–11, 1944, 369–404.

Bertelli, Giuseppe. *Chi siamo e che cosa vogliamo.* Firenze: Edizioni Nerbini, 1902.

Bettiza, Enzo. *Il Fantasma di Trieste.* Milano: Longanesi & Co., 1958.

Bianchi, Claudio. *Trieste: la città di Ulisse.* Trieste: Civici Musei di storia ed arte di Trieste, 1991.

Bianchi, G., et al., ed. *Scrittori triestini del novecento.* Trieste: Edizioni Lint, 1968.

Bishop, John. *Joyce's Book of the Dark.* Madison: University of Wisconsin Press, 1987.

Blum, Cinzia Sartini. *The Other Modernism: F.T. Marinetti's Futurist Fiction of Power.* Berkeley: University of California Press, 1996.

Borach, Georges. "Conversations with Joyce." In Willard Potts, ed., *Portraits of the Artist in Exile: Recollections of James Joyce by Europeans,* 69–72.

Boralevi, Lea Campos. "Un triestino a Firenze: Dario De Tuoni (1892–1966)." In Roberto Pertici, ed., *Intellettuali di Frontiera: Triestini a Firenze 1900–1950,* 511–22.

Bosinelli, Rosa Maria, *Gli Anni Triestini di James Joyce.* Unpublished thesis submitted to the University of Bologna, 1968.

—. "The Importance of Trieste in Joyce's Work, with Reference to His Knowledge of Psycho-Analysis." *James Joyce Quarterly,* vol. 7. no. 3 (Spring 1970), 177–9.

—, et al., eds. *The Languages of Joyce: Selected Papers from the 11th International James Joyce Symposium.* Venice, 12–18 June 1988. Philadelphia/Amsterdam: John Benjamins Publishing Company, 1992.

Botteri, Guido. *Trieste 1868–1918: Storia e cronaca di mezzo secolo attraverso i giornali.* Trieste: Lint, 1968.

— and Vito Levi. *Il Politeama Rossetti 1878–1978: Un secolo di via triestina nelle cronache del Teatro.* Trieste: Editoriale Libraria, 1978.

Bradley, Bruce, SJ. *James Joyce's School Days.* Dublin: Gill and Macmillan, 1982.

Brancati, Vitaliano. "Ricordi di professor Joyce." *Nuova Stampa Sera,* 30–31 August 1948.

Brandabur, Edward. *A Scrupulous Meanness: A Study of Joyce's Early Work.* Urbana: University of Illinois Press, 1971.

Braude, Benjamin. "The Jews of Trieste and the Levant Trade in the Eighteenth Century." In G. Todeschini and P.C. Ioly Zorattini, eds, *Il Mondo Ebraico,* 327–51.

Bremini, I. *Il Politeama Rossetti di Trieste dalla sua inaugurazione ai giorni nostri – cenni storici e statistici.* Trieste, 1957 (unpublished manuscript kept in Trieste's Museo "Schmidl").

Bruggeri, Giovanni. "Joyce in carne ed ossa per le strade di Trieste." *Il Piccolo*, 25 October 1967.

Budgen, Frank. *James Joyce and the Making of Ulysses and Other Writings*. Oxford: Oxford University Press, 1972.

Budigna, L. "Documenti dell'amicizia; storia di un carteggio inedito: Joyce–Svevo." *Il Momento*, Roma, 26 October 1951.

Burton, Isabel. *AEI – Arabia Egypt India, A Narrative of Travel*. London and Belfast: Mullan, 1879.

—. *The Life of Sir Richard Burton*. London and Belfast: Mullan, 1891.

Bushrui, Suheil, and Bernard Benstock, eds. *James Joyce: An International Perspective*. Irish Literary Studies 10. Gerrards Cross: Colin Smythe, 1982.

Byrne, J.F. *Silent Years*. New York: Farrar, Straus and Young, 1953.

Calimani, Dario. *Riders to the Sea: i problemi di una traduzione letteraria*. Venezia: Libreria Editrice Cafoscarina, 1982.

—. "'The Boarding House': An Italian Variant?" *James Joyce Quarterly* 32, no. 2 (Winter 1995), 209–26.

Camerino, G.A. *Italo Svevo e la crisi della Mitteleuropa*. Milano: Istituto di Propaganda Libraria, 1996.

Caprin, Giulio. *Trieste e L'Italia*. Milano: Rava & C. Editori, 1915.

Carey, Joseph. *A Ghost in Trieste*. Chicago and London: The University of Chicago Press, 1993.

Catalan, Tullia. "L'emigrazione ebraica in Palestina attraverso il porto di Trieste (1908–1938)." *Qualestoria*, no. 2–3 (August–December 1991).

—. *La Comunità Ebraica di Trieste: Politica, Società, Cultura, 1848–1918*. Unpublished doctoral thesis for the University of Urbino, 1994. (To be published by Lint, Trieste in 2000.)

—. "Società e sionismo a Trieste fra XIV e XX secolo." In G. Todeschin and P.C. Ioly Zorattini, eds, *Il Mondo Ebraico*, 459–90.

Catsiyannis, Timotheos, Bishop of Militoupolis. *The Greek Community of London*. London: Nikos Smyrnis, 1992.

Cavaglion, Alberto. *Otto Weininger in Italia*. Roma: Carucci, 1982.

—. "Otto Weininger tra Trieste e Firenze." In Roberto Pertici, ed., *Intellettuali di Frontiera: Triestina a Firenze 1900–1950*, 661–74.

Cesari, Giulio. *Sessant'anni di vita italiana: Memorie della Società Operaia Triestina*. Trieste: Editrice la Società Operaia Triestina, 1929.

—. "Una famiglia Triestina di musicisti. I Sinico." *Rivista mensile della città di Trieste*, V, no. 4, 1932, 187–97.

Cheng, Vincent. *Joyce, Race, and Empire*. Cambridge: Cambridge University Press, 1995.

Chersicla, Bruno. *E' Tornato Joyce, iconografia triestina per Zois*. Con una prefazione di Giancarlo Vigorelli e un commentario di Stelio Crise. Milano: Nuova Rivista Europea, 1982.

Cheyette, Bryan. "'Jewgreek is greekjew': the Disturbing Ambivalence of Joyce's Semitic Discourse in *Ulysses*." *James Joyce Studies Annual*, vol. 3 (Summer 1992), 32–56.

Cianci, Giovanni. *La Fortuna di Joyce in Italia*. Bari: Adriatica Editrice, 1974.

Coceani, Bruno. "Ricordo di Marino de Szombathely." *La Porta Orientale*, Anno VIII, N.S., no. 1–2, 1972.

Colum, Mary. *Life and the Dream*. New York, 1947.

Comitato per l'Anno Joyciano. *Il ritorno di Joyce – Atti delle giornate celebrative a Trieste*. Trieste: Università degli studi di Trieste, 1982.

Corsini, Gianfranco. "La Politica di Joyce." In *Scritti Italiani*, a cura di Gianfranco Corsini e Giorgio Melchiori, con la collaborazione di Louis Berron, Nino Frank e Jacqueline Risset. Milano: Arnaldo Mondadori Editore, 1979.

Costello, Peter. *James Joyce: The Years of Growth, 1882–1915*. London: Kyle Cathie Limited, 1992.

Crise, Stelio. "Absender: James Joyce." *Letteratura*, January–February 1961, 81–6.

—. "Joyce, un cittadino della docile Trieste." *Il Piccolo*, 13 January 1961.

—. "Su una strada chimata Alice: Il paese delle meraviglie di Joyce." *Il Piccolo*, 10 December 1968.

—. "Ahab, Pizdrool, Quark." *James Joyce Quarterly* 7 (Fall 1969), 65–9.

—. "La Cambiale di James Joyce – Suddito Inglese Internato." *Il Piccolo*, 26 May 1971.

—. "James eats Jams." *Umana*, May–September, 1971, anno XX, 5–8.

—. "Joyce, Trieste e una libreria." *Il Piccolo*, 26 February 1971.

—. "Il Professor Zois? No, solo Jacomo." *Il Piccolo*, 2 February 1982.

—. "Tra bettole e amori giuliani Joyce matura il caso *Ulisse*." *Il Piccolo*, 7 February 1982.

—. *And Trieste, Ah Trieste*. Milano: All'Insegna del Pesce d'Oro, 1971.

—. "Joyce e Trieste – In margine ad una mostra." Roma: Accademie e Biblioteche d'Italia, XXIX, no. 5, 1961, 2–16.

—. *Scritti*, a cura di Elvio Guagnini. Trieste: Edizioni Parnaso, 1995.

—. *Epiphanies & Phadographs: Joyce & Trieste*. Milano: All'insegna del Pesce d'Oro, 1994.

Crivelli, Renzo S. *James Joyce: Itinerari Triestini/Triestine Itineraries*, trs. John McCourt. Trieste: MGS Press Editrice, 1996.

—."Annie, the first inspiration behind *Giacomo Joyce*." In Renzo Crivelli and John McCourt, eds, *Le Donne di Giacomo*, 49–54.

— and John McCourt, eds. *Joyce in Svevo's Garden*. Trieste: MGS Press Editrice, 1995.

— and John McCourt, eds. *Le Donne di Giacomo: Il mondo femminile nella Trieste di James Joyce/The female world in James Joyce's Trieste*. Trieste: Hammerle Editori, 1999.

Crusvar, Luisa (a cura di). *Il Sentiero dei Mille Draghi, Viaggio, viandanti, donne e sogno nel mito dell'Estremo Oriente*. Presentazione: Laura Ruaro Loseri; Contributi: Roberto Benedetti, Marcello Manetti. Asolo: Acelum Edizione D'Arte, 1982.

Culleton, Claire A. *Names and Naming in Joyce*. Madison: University of Wisconsin Press, 1994.

Curci, Roberto. "Chi? Quella 'fiamma' triestina." *Il Piccolo*, 13 January 1991.

—. *Tutto è sciolto. L'amore triestino di Giacomo Joyce*. Trieste: Lint, 1996.

—. "Emma, almost a (serial) novel." In Renzo Crivelli and John McCourt, eds, *Le Donne di Giacomo*, 55–9.

Curci, Roberto and Gabriella Ziani. *Bianco, Rosa e Verde: Scrittrici a Trieste fra '800 e '900*. Trieste: Lint, 1993.

Curran, C.P. *James Joyce Remembered*. London: Oxford University Press, 1968.

Davison, Neil R. *James Joyce, Ulysses, and the Construction of Jewish Identity*. Cambridge: Cambridge University Press, 1996.

Deane, Seamus. "Joyce and Nationalism." In Colin MacCabe, ed., *James Joyce: New Perspectives*. London: Harvester, 1982, 168–83.

De Ferra, G. "Musica in casa." In *Quassù Trieste*, a cura di L. Mazzi. Bologna: 1968, 179–203.

De Petris, Carla, ed. *Joyce Studies in Italy 2*. Roma: Bulzoni, 1988.

De Smecchia, Giuseppe Rismondo. "James and Stanislaus Joyce a Trieste." Typescript of unpublished lecture given at the Associazione Italo–britannico on 20 March 1996.

De Tuoni, Dario. *Preludio* (1909–1013). Città di Castello: Casa Editrice S. Lapi, 1913.

—. *Ricordi di Joyce a Trieste*. Milano: All'insegna del Pesce d'Oro, 1966.

—. *Tergeste. Scene e Figure di Vita Triestina*. Trieste: Caprin, 1926.

—. "James Joyce nella vecchia Trieste." *La Fiera Letteraria*, 26 February 1961.

—. "L'Ultima casa di Joyce a Trieste." *La Fiera Letteraria*, 30 April 1961.

—. "James Joyce a Trieste." *La Fiera Letteraria*, 28 May 1961.

—. "Recenti pubblicazioni su James Joyce." Unpublished essay in the possession of Mrs Frida De Tuoni.

—. "Reminiscenze personali su James Joyce." Unpublished essay in the possession of Mrs Frida De Tuoni.

De Tuoni, Frida and Silvia. "Memorie Joyciane". In Niny Rocco Bergera, ed., *Atti del Third International James Joyce Symposium*. Trieste: Università degli Studi, 1974.

Del Vivo, Caterina. "Joyce, Il Marzocco, Daniel Defoe." *Il Viesseux* 12, September–December 1991, 44–5.

Delimata, Bozena Berta. "Reminiscences of a Joyce Niece." *James Joyce Quarterly* 19 (Fall 1981), 45–67.

Dias, Willy. *Viaggio nel tempo*. Bologna: Capelli, 1958.

Di Margutti, Baron Alberto. "Le Avventure di un console inglese a Trieste. Sir Richard Burton, le sue bizzarie e il suo viaggio all Mecca." *Il Piccolo della Sera*, 12 October 1923.

Doria, Mario, con la collaborazione di Claudio Noliani, *Grande Dizionario del Dialetto Triestino Storico, Etimologico, Fraseologico*. Trieste: Finanziaria Editoriale Triestina, 1991.

Duffy, Enda. *The Subaltern Ulysses*. Minneapolis and London: University of Minnesota Press, 1994.

Duiz, Roberto, and Renato Sarti. *La vita xe un Bidòn: Storia di Angelo Cecchelin Comico Triestino*. Milano: Baldini & Castoldi, 1995.

Eco, Umberto. *The Aesthetics of Chaosmos: The Middle Ages of Joyce*. Tulsa: The University of Tulsa Monograph Series, no. 18, 1982.

Ehrlich, Heyward. "'Araby' in context: The Splendid Bazaar, Irish Orientalism, and James Clarence Mangan." *James Joyce Quarterly* 35, nos. 2 and 3 (Winter and Spring 1998), 309–32.

Ellmann, Richard. *James Joyce*. London: Oxford University Press, 1982 (revised edition).

—. *Ulysses on the Liffey*. London: Faber and Faber, 1972.

—. *The Consciousness of Joyce*. London: Oxford University Press, 1977.

Fabris, Vittorio. *Storia di storie di Casini Triestini (ovverso "Nel regno delle oche')*. Trieste: Edizioni Italo Svevo, 1996.

Fairhall, James. *James Joyce and the Question of History*. Cambridge: Cambridge University Press, 1993.

Fasolato, Patrizia. *Tullio Silvestri*. Trieste: Lint, 1991.

Ferrero, Guglielmo. *L'Europa giovane*. Milano: Treves, 1898.

—. *Militarism: A Contribution to the Peace Crusade*, anon. trs. Boston: L.C. Page & Company, 1903.

Ferris, Kathleen. *James Joyce and the Burden of Disease*. Oklahoma: University of Oklahoma Press, 1995.

Fishburg, Maurice. *The Jews: A Study of Race and Environment*. London: Walter Scott Publishing, 1911.

Fitzgerald, Joan. "James Joyce's translation of *Riders to the Sea*." *Joyce Studies in Italy* 2, ed. Carla de Petris. Rome: Bulzoni Editore, 1988, 149–60.

Fonda Savio, Antonio. "Ettore Schmitz (in arte Italo Svevo) nella vita di ogni giorno." Published version of a lecture held at the Italian-American Cultural Association in Trieste on 8 January 1966.

Fonda Savio, Letizia. "James Joyce: Two Reminiscences". In E.H. Mikhail, ed., *James Joyce: Interviews and Recollections*.

Francini Bruni, Alessandro. "Ricordi personali su James Joyce." *Nuova Antologia*, LXXXII (September 1947), 71–9.

—. "Recollections of Joyce." In Willard Potts, ed., *Portraits of the Artist in Exile: Recollections of James Joyce by Europeans*, 39–46.

—. "Joyce Stripped Naked in the Piazza." In Willard Potts, ed., *Portraits of the Artist in Exile: Recollections of James Joyce by Europeans*, 7–38.

Fuchs, René. *Termini erotici e sessuali del dialetto Triestino*. Trieste: Edizioni Luglio, 1999.

Furbank, P.N. *Italo Svevo: The Man and the Writer*. Berkeley, Calif.: University of California Press, 1966.

Gabler, Hans Walter. "The Seven Lost Years of *A Portrait of the Artist as a Young Man*." In Thomas F. Staley and Bernard Benstock, eds, *Approaches to Joyce's 'Portrait': Ten Essays*. Pittsburgh, Penn.: University of Pittsburgh Press, 1976.

Galli, Lina. "Livia Veneziani Svevo and James Joyce." *James Joyce Quarterly*, Spring 1972.

—. "Svevo and Irredentism." *Modern Fiction Studies*, Spring 1972.

Gatt-Rutter, John. *Italo Svevo: A Double Life*. Oxford: Clarendon Press, 1988.

Gerolini, Ennio. *Sempre alegri e mai passion! Fritolini, petesserie, teatri e cine de la Trieste de una volta*. Trieste: Editoriale Danubio, 1994.

Ghidetti, Enrico. *Italo Svevo – La coscienza di un borghese triestino*. Roma: Editori Riuniti, 1980.

Gifford, Don (with Robert J. Seidman). *Ulysses Annotated: Notes for James Joyce's Ulysses*, revised edition. Berkeley, Calif.: University of California Press, 1982.

Gillespie, Michael Patrick. *Inverted Volumes Improperly Arranged: James Joyce and his Trieste Library*. Ann Arbor, Michigan: UMI Research Press, 1980.

—. *James Joyce's Trieste Library: A Catalogue of Material at the Harry Ransom Humanities Research Center*. Austin: Harry Ransom Humanities Research Center, 1986.

Gillet, Louis. "The Living Joyce." In Willard Potts, ed., *Portraits of the Artist in Exile: Recollections of James Joyce by Europeans*, 170–204.

Gilman, Sander L. *Freud, Race and Gender*. Princeton: Princeton University Press, 1993.

Giovannangeli, Jean-Louis. "Geographie, Politique et Histoire: Joyce et L'Europa Giovane de Guglielmo Ferrero." In Claude Jacquet and Jean-Michel Rabaté, eds, *James Joyce 3: Joyce et l'Italie*. Special Issue of *La Revue des Lettres Modernes*. Paris: Lettres Modernes, 1994, 39–54.

Goldman, Arnold. "Stanislaus, James and the politics of family." In Niny Rocco Bergera ed., *Atti del Third International James Joyce Symposium*. Trieste: Università degli Studi, 1974, 60–75.

Gorman, Herbert. *James Joyce: A Definitive Biography*. London: The Bodley Head, 1941.

Gottfried, Roy. "Berlitz Schools Joyce." *James Joyce Quarterly* 16 (Fall 1978/Winter 1979), 223–37.

Gratton, Silvio. *Trieste Segreta*, con un introduzione di Manlio Cecovini. Trieste: Edizioni Italo Svevo, 1987.

Groden, Michael, et al., eds. *The James Joyce Archive*. New York and London: Garland Publishing, 1979, vol. II.

Guido, Augusto. "Gli anni triestini di Joyce." *Umana*, May /September 1971.

Hartshorn, Peter. *James Joyce and Trieste*. Westport: Greenwood Press, 1997.

Henke, Suzette A. *James Joyce and the Politics of Desire*. New York and London: Routledge, 1990.

Hermet, Guido. "La Vita Musicale a Trieste (1801–1944), con speciale riferimento alla musica vocale." *Archeografo Triestino*, IV, vol. XII–XIII, 1947, 220–32.

Herr, Cheryl. *Joyce's Anatomy of Culture*. Urbana: University of Illinois Press, 1986.

Herring, Phillip F. *Joyce's Uncertainty Principle*. Princeton: Princeton University Press, 1987.

—. "Richard Ellmann's James Joyce." In Jeffrey Meyers, ed., *The Biographer's Art: New Essays*. London: Macmillan, 1989, 106–27.

Hone, Joseph. "A Recollection of James Joyce." *Envoy*, vol. V, April 1951.

Humphreys, Susan L. "Ferrero Etc: James Joyce's Debt to Guglielmo Ferrero." *James Joyce Quarterly* 16 (Fall 1978/Winter 1979), 239–51.

Hutchins, Patricia. *James Joyce's World*. London: Methuen, 1957.

—. "Due aspetti di Joyce nel cinema." *Cinema Nuovo, Rassegna bimestrale di cultura*. Anno IX, January –February 1960.

Hyams, Barbara and Nancy A. Harrowitz. 'A critical introduction to the history of Weininger Reception." In Barbara Hyams and Nancy A. Harrowitz, eds, *Jews and Gender: Responses to Otto Weininger*, 3–20.

—, eds. *Jews and Gender: Responses to Otto Weininger*. Philadelphia: Temple University Press: 1995.

Hyman, Louis, *The Jews of Ireland from Earliest Times to the Year 1910*. Shannon: Irish University Press, 1972.

Isaak, Jo Anna. *The Ruin of Representation in Modernist Art and Texts*. Ann Arbor: University of Michigan Research Press, 1986.

Jackson, I. Cope. *Joyce's Cities: Archaeologies of the Soul*. Baltimore and London: The Johns Hopkins University Press, 1981.

Jackson, John Wyse, with Peter Costello. *John Stanislaus Joyce: The Voluminous Life and Genius of James Joyce's Father*. London: Fourth Estate, 1998.

Jacquet, Claude, and Jean-Michel Rabaté, eds. *James Joyce 3: Joyce et l'Italie*. Special Issue of *La Revue des Lettres Modernes*. Paris: Lettres Modernes, 1994.

Joly, Ralph Robert. "Chauvinist Brew and Leopold Bloom: The Weininger Legacy." *James Joyce Quarterly* 19, no. 2 (Winter 1982), 194–8.

Joyce, James. *Araby*. Traduzione e biografia essenziale di Amalia Popper. Nota di Stelio Crise. Firenze: Ibiskos di Empoli, 1991.

—. *The Critical Writings of James Joyce*. Edited by Ellsworth Mason and Richard Ellmann. Ithaca, New York: Cornell University Press, 1989.

—. "Daniel Defoe." *Buffalo Studies* 1 (December 1964), 1–27. Translated and edited from Italian manuscripts by Joseph Prescott.

—. *Dubliners*. With an introduction and notes by Terence Brown. London: Penguin Books, 1992.

—. *Finnegans Wake*. London: Faber and Faber, 1989.

—. *Giacomo Joyce*. With an introduction and notes by Richard Ellmann. London: Faber and Faber, 1984.

—. *James Joyce in Padua*. Edited, translated and introduced by Louis Berrone. New York: Random House, 1977.

—. *Letters of James Joyce*. Three volumes. Vol. I edited by Stuart Gilbert (1957); vols II and III edited by Richard Ellmann. New York: Viking Press, 1966.

—. *Joyce's Ulysses Notesheets in the British Museum*. Edited by Phillip F. Herring. Charlottesville: University of Virginia Press, 1972.

—. *Poems* and *Exiles*. Edited by J.C.C. Mays. London: Faber and Faber, 1992.

—. *Poesie e Prose*. A cura di Franca Ruggieri. Milano: Arnoldo Mondadori, 1992.

—. *A Portrait of the Artist as a Young Man*. Corrected by Chester Anderson and edited by Richard Ellmann. London: Paladin, 1987.

—. *Scritti Italiani*. A cura di Gianfranco Corsini e Giorgio Melchiori, con la collaborazione di Louis Berrone, Nino Frank e Jacqueline Risset. Milano: Arnaldo Mondadori, 1979.

—. *Selected Letters of James Joyce*. Edited by Richard Ellmann. London: Faber and Faber, 1975.

—. *Stephen Hero*. Edited with an introduction by Stuart Gilbert. London: Faber and Faber, 1966.

—. *Ulysses*. The Corrected Text, edited by Hans Walter Gabler et al. New York: Random House, 1984.

—. *The Workshop of Daedalus: James Joyce and the raw materials for A Portrait of the Artist as a Young Man*. Edited by Robert Scholes and Richard M. Kain. Evanston Ill.: Northwestern University Press, 1965.

Joyce, Stanislaus. *The Complete Dublin Diary of Stanislaus Joyce*. Edited by George H. Healey. Dublin: Anna Livia Press, 1994.

—. "James Joyce e Italo Svevo." *Il Popolo di Trieste*, 24 January 1933.

—. *The Meeting of Svevo and Joyce*. Udine: Del Bianco, 1965.

—. *My Brother's Keeper*. Edited with an introduction by Richard Ellmann. Preface by T.S. Eliot. London: Faber and Faber, 1958.

—. "Ricordi di James Joyce." *Letteratura*, no. 3, 1941, 25–35.

Kearney, Richard. *Postnationalist Ireland: Politics, Culture, Philosophy*. London: Routledge, 1997.

Kelly, Joseph. "Stanislaus Joyce, Ellsworth Mason, and Richard Ellmann: The Making of James Joyce." *Joyce Studies Annual*, 1992, 98–140.

Kenner, Hugh. *Dublin's Joyce*. London: Chatto and Windus, 1955.

—. "Approaches to the Artist as a Young Language Teacher." In H. Regnery, ed., *Viva Vivas!*. Indianapolis: Liberty Press, 1976, 331–53.

Kershner, R. Brandon. *Joyce, Bakhtin and Popular Literature: Chronicles of Disorder*. Chapel Hill: University of North Carolina Press, 1989.

—. "ReOrienting Joyce." In *James Joyce Quarterly* 35, nos 2 and 3 (Winter and Spring 1998), 259–63.

—. "*Ulysses* and the Orient." In *James Joyce Quarterly* 35, nos 2 and 3 (Winter and Spring 1998), 273–96.

— and Carol Shloss, eds. "ReOrienting Joyce", *James Joyce Quarterly, Special Double Issue*, vol. 35, nos 2 and 3 (Winter and Spring 1998).

Kiberd, Declan. *Inventing Ireland.* London: Jonathan Cape, 1996.

—. "Bloom the Liberator." *Times Literary Supplement,* 3 January 1992, 3–6.

Kiernan, V.G. *The Lords of Human Kind: Black Man, Yellow Man and White Man in an Age of Empire.* Boston: Little Brown & Co., 1969.

Knowles, Sebastian D.G., ed. *Bronze by Gold: The Bronze of Music.* New York: Garland Publishing, 1999.

Kosanovic, Dejan. *1896–1918 Trieste al Cinema.* Gemona: La Cineteca del Friuli, 1995.

Lang, Fred K. *Ulysses and the Irish God.* London and Toronto: Associated University Presses, 1993.

Lattes, Dante A. *Il Sionismo* (2 vols). Milano: Paolo Cremonese Editore, 1928.

Le Rider, Jacques. *Modernity and Crises of Identity: Culture and Society in Fin-de-Siècle Vienna,* trs. Rosemary Morris. New York: Continuum Publishing Group, 1993.

—. *Mitteleuropa: Storia di un mito.* Bologna: Il Mulino, 1995.

—. "'The Otto Weininger Case' Revisited." In Barbara Hyams and Nancy A. Harrowitz, eds, *Jews and Gender: Responses to Otto Weininger,* 21–33.

Levi, A. *Ricordi della vita e dei tempi di Ernesto Nathan.* Firenze, 1945.

Levin, Harry. "Letter Svevo–Joyce: carteggio inedito." *Inventario,* Milano, anno II, no.1, Spring 1949, 106–38.

Lobner, Corinna del Greco. *James Joyce's Italian Connection.* Iowa City: University of Iowa Press, 1989.

—. "A Giornalista Triestino: James Joyce's Letter to *Il Marzocco.*" *Joyce Studies Annual,* 1993, 184–91.

Lund, Steven. *James Joyce: Letters, Manuscripts, and Photographs at Southern Illinois University.* Troy, New York: Whitson Press, 1983.

Luzzatto Fegiz, Pierpaolo. *Lettere da Zabodaski – Ricordi di un Borghese Mitteleuropeo 1900–1984.* Trieste: Lint, 1984.

MacCabe, Colin. *James Joyce and the Revolution of the Word.* London: Macmillan, 1978.

McCourt, John. "Eternal Counterparts: Stanislaus and James Joyce." In Renzo S. Crivelli and John McCourt, eds, *Joyce in Svevo's Garden,* 61–73.

—. "Tarry Easty – Joyce's Oriental Workshop." *Joyce Studies in Italy* 5, ed. Franca Ruggieri. Rome: Bulzoni Editore, 1998, 23–58.

—. "Amalia Popper: 'The ghost in the mirror'." In Renzo S. Crivelli and John McCourt, eds, *Le Donne di Giacomo,* 60–5.

— and Erik Schneider, "Zois in nighttown." In Renzo S. Crivelli and John McCourt, eds, *Le Donne di Giacomo,* 66–71.

McGinley, Bernard. *Joyce's Lives: Uses and Abuses of the Biografiend.* London: University of North London Press, 1996.

McHugh, Roland. *Annotations to Finnegans Wake.* London: Routledge and Kegan Paul, 1980.

Maddox, Brenda. *Nora: A Biography of Nora Joyce.* London: Minerva, 1988.

Mahaffey, Vicky. "Fascism and Silence: The Coded History of Amalia Popper." In *James Joyce Quarterly* 32, nos 3 and 4 (Spring and Summer 1995), 501–22.

Magris, Claudio. "I triestini e la mediazione tra le culture." In Roberto Pertici, ed., *Intellettuali di Frontiera: Triestini a Firenze 1900–1950,* 31–8.

—. "Tavola Rotonda." In Roberto Pertici, ed., *Intellettuali di Frontiera: Triestini a Firenze 1900–1950,* 401–4.

Mahler, Alma. *Gustav Mahler,* a cura di L. Rognoni, Italian trs. L. Dallapiccola. Milano: Il Saggiatore, 1960.

Maier, Bruno. "Triestinità di un grande scrittore irlandese: James Joyce." *Il Ragguaglio Librario, Nuova Serie, Rassegna mensile bibliografico-culturale,* anno 51, November 1984.

Manganiello, Dominic. *Joyce's Politics.* London: Routledge and Kegan Paul, 1980.

—. "The Politics of the Unpolitical in Joyce's Fictions." *James Joyce Quarterly* 29, Winter 1992, 241–57.

Marengo Vaglio, Carla. "Trieste as a linguistic melting pot." In Claude Jacquet and Jean-Michel Rabaté, eds, *James Joyce 3: Joyce et l'Italie.* Special Issue of *La Revue des Lettres Modernes.* Paris: Lettres Modernes, 1994, 55–74.

—. "Yeats' The Countess Cathleen: Vidacovich and Joyce's translation." *Joyce Studies in Italy* 2, ed. Carla de Petris. Rome: Bulzoni Editore, 1988, 197–212.

—. "*Giacomo Joyce* or the *Vita Nuova.*" *Joyce Studies in Italy* 5 ed. Franca Ruggieri. Rome: Bulzoni Editore, 1998, 91–106.

Marin, Biagio. "Scipio Slataper e l'anima di Trieste", Estratto dalla rivista *Trieste*, January–February 1956, no.11, unpaginated.

Marinetti, F.T. *Opere di F.T. Marinetti.* ed. Luciano De Maria. Verona, 1968, vol. II.

—. *Teoria e Invenzione Futurista*, a cura di Luciano De Maria, Milano: Mondadori, 1983.

Martin, Augustine, ed. *James Joyce: The Artist and the Labyrinth.* London: Ryan Publishing, 1990.

Martin, Timothy. *Joyce and Wagner: A Study of Influence.* Cambridge: Cambridge University Press, 1991.

Mason, Michael. "Why is Leopold Bloom a Cuckold?" *English Literary History* XLIV, 1977, 171–88.

Mattioni, Sergio. *Trieste variété.* Trieste: Fachin, 1990.

Mays, J.C.C. Review of Michael Patrick Gillespie's *James Joyce's Trieste Library: A Catalogue of Materials at the Harry Ransom Humanities Research Center.* *Review of English Studies,* n.s. 39, November 1988, 589–90.

Melchiori, Giorgio. "Joyce's Feast of Languages: Seven Essays and Ten Notes", *Joyce Studies in Italy* 4, ed. Franca Ruggieri. Rome: Bulzoni Editore, 1995.

—, ed. *Joyce in Rome: The Genesis of Ulysses.* Rome: Bulzoni, 1984.

—. "Leopold Bloom: What's in a Name?". In Carla de Petris, ed., *Joyce Studies in Italy* 3, 1990, 22–30.

Miglia, Guido. "James Joyce a Pola." In *Bozzetti Istriani.* Trieste: Associazione delle comunità istriaine, 1968, 115–19.

—. "Il Mito di Brioni." In *Le nostre radici.* Triestc: Edizioni comunità istrianc, 1969, 74–7.

Migliorino, Ellen Ginzburg. "Antisemitismo." In G. Todeschini and P.C. Ioly Zorattini, eds, *Il Mondo Ebraico,* 433–57.

Mikhail, E.H., ed. *James Joyce: Interviews and Recollections.* Foreword by Frank Delaney. London: Macmillan, 1990.

Millo, Anna. *L'Elite del potere a Trieste: Una biografia collettiva 1891–1938.* Milano: Franco Angeli, 1989.

—. "Elites politiche ed elites economiche ebraiche a Trieste alla fine del XIX secolo." In G. Todeschini, and P.C. Ioly Zorattini, eds, *Il Mondo Ebraico,* 381–403.

Mo, Ettore. "Quando Svevo e Joyce litigavano." *Corriere della Sera,* 21 November 1987.

Moloney, Brian. *Italo Svevo narratore Lezioni triestine.* Gorizia: Libreria Editrice Goriziana, 1998.

Monti, Silvana. *I Giornali Triestini dal 1863 al 1902: Società e cultura di Trieste attraverso 576 quotidiani e periodici.* Trieste: Lint, 1976.

Musil, Robert. *Man Without Qualities*, trs. Eithne Wilkins and Ernest Kaiser. London: Secker & Warburg, 1960.

Nadel, Ira B. *Joyce and the Jews: Culture and Texts.* Iowa City: University of Iowa Press, 1989.

—. "The Incomplete Joyce." *Joyce Studies Annual,* 1991, 86–100.

Negrelli, Giorgio. "In Tema di Irredentismo e di Nazionalismo." In Roberto Pertici, ed., *Intellettuali di Frontiera: Triestini a Firenze 1900–1950,* 251–92.

Nolan, Emer. *James Joyce and Nationalism.* London and New York: Routledge, 1995.

Noon, William T. *Joyce and Aquinas.* New Haven: Yale University Press, 1957.

Nordio, Mario. "Gli anni triestini di James Joyce." *Il Gazzettino,* 15 April 1960.

—. "James Joyce pioniere del cinema in Irlanda." *La Porta Orientale*, N.S., VIV, nos 3–4, March–April 1971.

—. "Quel mio maestro d'inglese." *Il Piccolo*, 2 February 1982.

Onorati, Franco. "Bank Clerk in Rome." In Giorgio Melchiori, ed., *Joyce in Rome: The Genesis of Ulysses*. Rome: Bulzoni, 1984.

Pagnini, Cesare. *I giornali di Trieste dalle origini al 1959*. Milano: Centro Studi, 1959.

Paolin, Giovanni. "Considerazioni sugli Ebrei Triestini." In G. Todeschini and P.C. Ioly Zorattini, eds, *Il Mondo Ebraico*, 215–59.

Pelaschiar, Laura. "Of brother, diaries, and umbrellas: News from Stanislaus Joyce." *Joyce Studies in Italy* 5, ed. Franca Ruggieri. Rome: Bulzoni Editore, 1998, 213–24.

Pertici, Roberto, ed. *Intellettuali di Frontiera: Triestini a Firenze 1900–1950*. 2 vols. Milano: Leo S. Olschki Editore, 1985.

Pierce, David. "The Politics of *Finnegans Wake*." In *Critical Essays on James Joyce's "Finnegans Wake"*, 243–57; also in *Textual Practice*, vol. 2, no. 3 (1988).

Pinguentini, Gianni. "Come un francese vedeva Trieste nel 1890." *La Porta Orientale*, Anno XVI, nos 1–3, January–March 1946.

—. *James Joyce in Italia*. Verona: Linotipia Veronese di Ghidini e Fiorini, 1963.

—. "James Joyce a Trieste nella casa di via Bramante." *La Porta Orientale*, April 1970.

Platt, L.H. "Joyce and the Anglo-Irish Revival: The Triestine Lectures." *James Joyce Quarterly* 29, Winter 1992, 262–4.

—. *Joyce and the Anglo-Irish: A Study of Joyce and the Literary Revival*. Amsterdam: Editions Rodopi B.V., 1998.

Poder, Elfriede. "Molly is Sexuality: The Weiningerian Definition of Woman in Joyce's *Ulysses*." In Barbara Hyams and Nancy A. Harrowitz, eds, *Jews and Gender: Responses to Otto Weininger*.

Poliaghi, Nora Franca. "James Joyce: An Occasion of Remembrance." *James Joyce Quarterly* 9, Spring 1972, 326–7.

—. "Il loggione di Joyce al Verdi di Trieste." *La Gazzetta di Parma*, 1 January 1969.

—. "La beffa del destino di James Joyce." *La Porta Orientale*, N.S., VIV, nos 3–4, March–April 1971.

Potts, Willard, ed. *Portraits of the Artist in Exile: Recollections of James Joyce by Europeans*. Dublin: Wolfhound Press, 1979.

—. "Joyce's notes on the Gorman biography." *Carbondale*, vol. 4, Spring 1981, 83–99.

Powell, Nicolas. *Travellers to Trieste*. London: Faber and Faber, 1977.

Power, Henriette Lazaridis. "Incorporating *Giacomo Joyce*." *James Joyce Quarterly* 28, Spring 1991, 623–30.

Rabaté, Jean-Michel. "La Seconde Patrie de L'Exile: Joyce a Trieste." *Critique Special Issue: Les Mysteres de Trieste*, August–September 1983, 691–716.

Radole, Giuseppe. *Ricerche sulla vita musicale a Trieste 1750–1850*. Trieste: Ediz Italo Svevo, 1988.

Rawson, Judy. "Italian Futurism." In Malcolm Bradbury and James Mc Farlane, eds, *Modernism 1890–1930*. Harmondsworth: Penguin, 1976, 243–58.

Read, Forrest, ed. *Pound/Joyce: The Letters of Ezra Pound to James Joyce*. London: Faber and Faber, 1967.

Reichert, Klaus. "The European background of Joyce's Writing." In Derek Attridge, ed., *The Cambridge Companion to James Joyce*. Cambridge: Cambridge University Press, 1990, 55–82.

Reizbaum, Marilyn. "The Jewish Connection, Cont'd." In Bernard Benstock, ed., *The Seventh of Joyce*. Bloomington, Ind.: Indiana University Press, 1982, 229–37.

—. *James Joyce's Judaic Other*. Palo Alto: Stanford University Press, 1999.

—. "Weininger and the Bloom of Jewish Self-Hatred in Joyce's Ulysses." In Barbara Hyams and Nancy A. Harrowitz, eds, *Jews and Gender: Responses to Otto Weininger*, 207–13.

Relazione sul Primo decennio d'attività della Università Popolare Triestina. 1900–1910. Editrice L'Università Popolare Triestina, 1910.

Risolo, Michele. "Lettere al direttore: Casanova senza qualità." *L'Espresso*, 24 November 1968, 3.

—. "Mia moglie e Joyce." *Il Corriere della Sera*, 27 February 1969.

Rocco-Bergera, Niny. *Itinerario Joyciano e Sveviano a Trieste*. Trieste: Azienda Autonoma Soggiorno e Turismo, 1971.

—, ed. *Atti del Third International James Joyce Symposium*. Trieste: Università degli Studi, 1974.

Rosenfeld, Natania. "James Joyce's Womanly Wandering Jew." In Nancy A. Harrowitz and Barbara Hyams, eds, *Jews and Gender: Responses to Otto Weininger*, 215–26.

Roth, Cecil. "James Joyce in Trieste." *Times Literary Supplement*, 7 August 1948, 443.

Ruggieri, Franca, ed. *Joyce Studies in Italy* 5. Rome: Bulzoni Editore, 1998.

Rutteri, Silvio. *Trieste Romantica: Itinerari Sentimentali d'altri Tempi*. Trieste: Edizioni Italo Svevo, 1988.

Saba, Umberto. *Tutte le Poesie*, a cura di Arrigo Stara, introduzione di Mario Lavagetto. Milano: Mondadori, 1994.

Sabatti, Pierluigi. "Così cocolo, gioviale." *Il Piccolo*, 2 February 1982.

Sacher, Harry, ed. *Zionism and the Jewish Future*. Westport, Conn.: Hyperion Press, 1976.

Said, Edward. *Orientalism*. New York: Random House, 1978.

—. *Culture and Imperialism*. London: Chatto & Windus, 1993.

Sapelli, Giulio. *Trieste Italiana: Mito e Destino Economico*. Milano: Franco Angeli, 1990.

Schachter, Elisabeth. "The Enigma of Svevo's Jewishness: Trieste and the Jewish Cultural Tradition." *Italian Studies*, L, 1995, 24–47.

Schenoni, Luigi. "The Formiggini Letter." *James Joyce Quarterly* 21, no. 1, Fall 1983, 80–4.

Schiffrer, C. "L'irredentismo massonico di Felice Venezian." In *Trieste: Rivista politica giuliana* (1968), 82, 15–18,

Schmitz, Elio. *Lettere a Svevo e Diario di Elio Schmitz*. Milano: dall'Oglio, 1973.

Scholes, Robert E. *The Cornell Joyce Collection: A Catalogue*. Ithaca, New York: Cornell University Press, 1961.

— and Richard M. Kain, eds. *The Workshop of Daedalus: James Joyce and the Raw Materials for A Portrait of the Artist as a Young Man* (Evanston, Ill.: Northwestern University Press, 1965).

Schott, Edoardo (Desico). *Diario ed Aventure (1914 – 1922) di un triestino del primo Novecento: pubblicista, corrispondente di guerra, politico, delegato al Congresso della Pace a parigi – Versailles 1919*. Udine: Editrice grillo, 1979.

Schwarz, O.D. "Alla 'recerche' della vecchia Trieste di Joyce." *Il Globo*, 25 January 1974.

—. "Profumo del vicino Oriente nelle strade di Trieste." *Il Globo*, 11 May 1974.

—. "Aria di Vienna tra gli ebrei di Trieste." *Il Globo*, 5 June 1974.

Seri, Alfieri, Pietro Covre, Livio Grassi. *Le Insegne dell'ospitalità: due secoli di esercizi pubblici a Trieste*. Trieste: Lint, 1988.

Senn, Fritz. *Inductive Scrutinies: Focus on Joyce*. Edited by Christine O'Neill. Dublin: Lilliput Press, 1995.

Sgubin, Raffaella. "Between Paris and Vienna: Fashion in Joyce's Trieste", Renzo S. Crivelli and John McCourt, eds, in *Le Donne di Giacomo*.

Shechner, Mark. *Joyce and Nighttown*. Berkeley: University of California Press, 1974.

Shloss, Carol Loeb. "Joyce in the Context of Irish Orientalism." *James Joyce Quarterly* 35, nos 2 and 3 (Winter and Spring 1998), 264–72.

Slataper, Scipio. *Il Mio Carso*. Milano: Mondadori, 1995.

—. *Scritti politici*, a cura di G. Stuparich. Milano: Mondadori, 1954.

Solomon, Albert J. "Charles Lever: A Source for Joyce", *James Joyce Quarterly*, vol. 29, no. 4 (Summer 1992), 791–7.

Soranzio, Massimo. "The Expatriate and Ex-Patriot: Joyce's Friend Roberto Prezioso." *Prospero*, VI, 1999, 133–45.

Soupault, Philippe. "James Joyce." In Willard Potts, ed., *Portraits of the Artist in Exile: Recollections of James Joyce by Europeans*, 108–18.

Spaini, Alberto. "Autoritratto Triestino." In *Scrittori Triestini del Novecento*. Trieste, 1968.

Spoo, Robert. "'Una Piccola Nuvoletta': Ferrero's Young Europe and Joyce's Mature *Dubliners* Stories." *James Joyce Quarterly* 24, no. 4, Summer 1987, 401–10.

—. *James Joyce and the Language of History: Dedalus's Nighmare.* Oxford: Oxford University Press, 1994.

Staley, Thomas F. "James Joyce in Trieste." *The Georgia Review*, vol. xvi, Winter 1962, no. 4, 446–9.

—. "The Search for Leopold Bloom: James Joyce and Italo Svevo." *James Joyce Quarterly* 1, Summer 1964, 59–63.

—. "Joyce and Svevo." Text of an RAI/TV programme made by the international "Guglielmo Marconi" University in collaboration with the Voice of America on 24 February 1965.

—. "'The Italian Swabian': An English Assessment of Italo Svevo." *James Joyce Quarterly* 3, Summer 1966, 290–3.

—. "Composition of Place: Joyce and Trieste." *Modern British Literature* 5, 1980, 3–9.

—, ed. *James Joyce Quarterly – Joyce and Trieste Issue*, vol. 9, no. 3, Spring 1972.

Staley, Thomas F., and Bernard Benstock, eds. *Approaches to Joyce's "Portrait": Ten Essays.* Pittsburgh: University of Pittsburgh Press, 1976.

Stanzel, F.K. "All Europe Contributed to the Making of Bloom: New Light on Leopold Bloom's Ancestors." *James Joyce Quarterly* 32, nos 3 and 4, Spring and Summer 1995, 619–30.

Stefani, Giuseppe. *La lirica Italiana e l'irredentismo: Da Goffredo Mameli a Gabriele D'Annunzio.* Bologna: Capelli, 1959.

Stock, Mario. *Nel Segno di Geremia: Storia della Comunita' Israelitica di Trieste dal 1200.* Udine: Istituto per L'Enciclopedia del Friuli-Venezia Giulia, 1979.

Stuparich, Giani. *Trieste nei miei ricordi.* Milano: Garzanti, 1948.

Svevo, Italo. *As a Man Grows Older.* Trs. Beryl De Zoete, introduction by Stanislaus Joyce. Westport, Conn: Greenwood Press, 1977.

—. *A Life.* Translated by Archibald Calquhoun. London: Martin Secker, 1963.

—. *La Coscienza di Zeno*, with "Prefazione" by Silvio Benco. Milano: Dall'Oglio, 1962.

—. *James Joyce.* Norfolk, Conn.: New Directions, 1950.

—. *Scritti su Joyce.* Edited by Giancarlo Mazzacurati. Parma: Pratiche, 1986.

—. "James Joyce in Trieste." In E. H. Mikhail, ed., *James Joyce: Interviews and Recollections*, 45–7.

—. *Faccio Meglio di restare nell'ombra – Carteggio inedito con Ferrieri e conferenza su Joyce.* A cura di Giovanni Palmieri. Milano e Lecce: Editori di Comunicazione, 1995.

Svevo, Livia Veneziani. *Memoir of Italo Svevo*, trs. Isabel Quigly. London: Libris, 1989.

—. *Vita di Mio Marito.* Milano: Dall'Oglio, 1976.

Synge, J.M. *The Playboy of the Western World and Riders to the Sea.* London: Unwin Books, 1971.

—. *La Cavalcata al Mare* in *Poesie e Prose.* Trs. James Joyce and Nicolò Vidacovich, a cura di Franca Ruggieri. Milano: Arnoldo Mondadori, 1992.

Tamaro, Attilio. *L'Adriatico – Golfo d'Italia: L'italianità di Trieste.* Milano: Fratelli Treves Editori, 1915.

—. *Storia di Trieste* con saggio introduttivo di G. Cervani, 2 vols. Trieste: Lint, 1976.

Tedeschi, Steno. "Un filosofo antifemminista." *L'Indipendente*, 28 March 1905.

Testena, Folco (Comunardo Braccialarghe). *Il Socialismo Triestino*, Milano, 1910.

Thornton, Weldon. *Allusions in "Ulysses".* Chapel Hill: University of North Carolina Press, 1982.

—. *The Antimoderism of Joyce's Portrait of the Artist as a Young Man.* Syracuse, New York: Syracuse University Press, 1994.

Tizzoni, Fedoro. *Cannonate.* Trieste: G. Caprin, 1910.

Todeschini, G., and P.C. Ioly Zorattini, eds. *Il mondo ebraico: Gli ebrei tra Italia nord-orientale e Impero Asburgico dal Medioevo all'Età contemporanea.* Pordenone: Studio Tesi, 1991.

Valente, Joseph. *James Joyce and the Problem of Justice: Negotiating Sexual and Colonial Difference.* Cambridge: Cambridge University Press, 1995.

Vetta Federica. *L'Arpa di Davide – ricerche sulla presenza ebraica nell'attività musicale triestina tra ottocento e novecento.* Unpublished thesis completed at the University of Trieste, 1989.

Vidan, Ivo. "Joyce and the South Slavs." In Niny Rocco Bergera, ed., *Atti del Third International James Joyce Symposium.* Trieste: Università degli Studi, 1974, 116–33.

Vivante, Angelo. *L'Irredentismo Adriatico*. Trieste: Edizioni Italo Svevo, 1984.

Voghera, Giorgio. *Gli anni della psicanalisi*. Pordenone: Edizioni Studio Tesi, 1980.

Wall, Bernard. "Joyce e Svevo." *La Gazzetta dell'Emilia*, 16 March 1954.

Weininger, Otto. *Geschlecht und Charakter* (*Sex and Character*). Authorised translation from sixth German edition. London: William Heinemann, 1906.

Witemeyer, Hugh. "'He gave the Name': Herbert Gorman's Rectifications of *James Joyce: His First Forty Years*." *James Joyce Quarterly* 32, nos 3 and 4, Spring and Summer 1995.

Zanotti, Serenella. "Per un ritratto dell'artista Italianato: Note sull'Italiano di James Joyce." *Studi Linguistici Italiani*, vol. XXV (Roma: Salerno Editore, 1999), 16–64.

Ziani, Gabriella. "Letizia Svevo: Vi racconto il vero Joyce." *Tuttolibri*, Anno XIX, n. 612, Inserto redazionale della *Stampa*, 30 luglio 1988.

Zingrone, Frank. "Joyce and D'Annunzio: The Marriage of Fire and Water." *James Joyce Quarterly* 16, Fall 1978/Winter 1979, 253–9.

NEWSPAPERS 1904–1920

L'Adriatico
L'Amico
La Coda del Diavolo
Il Corriere Israelitico (1904–1913)
Il Diritto
L'Emancipazione (1907–1913)
Il Gazzettino
Il Giornaletto di Pola
L'Indipendente
Lettura Internazionale (1907–1908)
Il Lavoratore
Nèa Imèra (1904–1912)
Il Palvese (1907–1908)
Il Piccolo
Il Piccolo della Sera

ARCHIVES

Archive of the Jewish synagogue, Trieste
Archivio di stato di Trieste
Archivio Saranz, Trieste
Archivio dell'Università degli studi di Trieste
Biblioteca Civica di Trieste
Civico museo teatrale "Carlo Schmidl", Trieste
The Carl A. Kroch Library, Cornell University
The McFarlin Library, University of Tulsa
The Morris Library, University of Southern Illinois
The National Library of Ireland
The University College Dublin Library
Special Collections, University College Dublin
Zürich James Joyce Foundation

Index